SQL Performance
Tuning

SQL Performance Tuning

Peter Gulutzan and Trudy Pelzer

◆▼ Addison-Wesley

Boston • San Francisco • New York • Toronto • Montreal
London • Munich • Paris • Madrid
Capetown • Sydney • Tokyo • Singapore • Mexico City

Many of the designations used by manufacturers and sellers to distinguish their products are claimed as trademarks. Where those designations appear in this book, and Addison-Wesley, Inc. was aware of a trademark claim, the designations have been printed with initial capital letters or in all capitals.

The authors and publisher have taken care in the preparation of this book, but make no expressed or implied warranty of any kind and assume no responsibility for errors or omissions. No liability is assumed for incidental or consequential damages in connection with or arising out of the use of the information or programs contained herein.

The publisher offers discounts on this book when ordered in quantity for bulk purchases and special sales. For more information, please contact:

> U.S. Corporate and Government Sales
> (800) 382-3419
> corpsales@pearsontechgroup.com

For sales outside of the U.S., please contact:

> International Sales
> (317) 581-3793
> international@pearsontechgroup.com

Visit A-W on the Web: www.awprofessional.com

Library of Congress Cataloging-in-Publication Data

Gulutzan, Peter.
  SQL performance tuning / Peter Gulutzan and Trudy Pelzer.
     p. m.
  Includes bibliographical references and index.
  ISBN 0-201-79169-2 (alk. paper)
  1. SQL (Computer program language) 2. Relational databases. I. Pelzer, Trudy. II. Title.

  QA76.73.S67 G853 2003
  005.75'6—dc21

                                                      2002074418

ISBN 0-201-79169-2
Text printed on recycled paper
1 2 3 4 5 6 7 8 9 10—CRS—0605040302
First printing, September 2002

Contents

CHAPTER 10   Constraints   257

Preface

A poorly performing database application can cost each user time and have an impact on other applications running on the same computer or the same network.

The purpose of this book is to help you improve the performance of your SQL database. It is not an introduction to SQL syntax, not a tuning manual for a specific SQL implementation, and not a guide to design or data modelling. Instead, we've written it for users and programmers who want to improve SQL performance, no matter what brand of SQL they use. In this book, you'll find tuning tips for common situations, such as, "How to change a query so it will go faster," "What an index does," and "Shifting work from the server to the client."

Rather than exploiting the unique features of a single DBMS, we're going to give you ideas that are good for all of the major SQL DBMSs. Client/server programmers and consultants need to appreciate what can happen when the DBMS changes, or—the most challenging situation—the DBMS is unknown. So we tested all the ideas in this book on eight well-known DBMSs.

A good DBMS already contains a good optimizer. Yet you have picked up a book that promises to help you do your own tuning. That means that either you don't know something . . . or you do know something.

- You don't know that your DBMS is good.
- You know that even good tools work better in skilled hands.

You Don't Know that Your DBMS Is Good . . .

That could be true if you're a student or new on the job. That could be true especially if you're writing queries or programs that should work on more than one DBMS. You're most likely to encounter one of the following RDBMSs with the largest market shares (based on new license sales figures for the year 2001)[1]:

Oracle	39.8%
IBM	30.7% (prior to acquisition of Informix)
Microsoft	14.4%
Sybase	3.3%
Informix	3.3%

You might also run into DBMSs that are popular for Web work (like MySQL), for work with Borland products (like InterBase), for desktops (like Access), for mobile and Java interfacing (like Cloudscape), or for embedded systems (like Solid), or a host of small fry, like mSQL and gadfly. This book tries to be useful for the common denominator in all products. To use automotive analogies, it's not a "mechanic's guide to tuning the 1999 Cadillac" book, it's a "driver's guide to optimizing performance of modern cars" book—even if you have a manual transmission.

You Know that Even Good Tools Work Better in Skilled Hands . . .

Everybody has heard of sluggish SQL queries, or even whole systems, that a heroic someone improved with small effort. Usually the improvement is small too, so we will avoid extravagant promises. But we will make you the following guarantees.

- You will be able to follow our arguments without deep thinking or hard work. All we assume is that you have basic knowledge of programming and standard SQL syntax. In fact, you can read this book on a plane or at the beach.

- All of our observations have been confirmed by tests on real DBMSs within the last several months.

---

1. Data from Gartner Dataquest (May 2002).

- We know that "optimizing" is very different from "over-clocking," and we only discuss safe, rational, relational techniques.

One accusation that could be leveled, and to which we plead guilty, is that some of our material is ad hoc advice instead of general principles. Of course! There are only a few general principles in DBMS optimization.

- First, do no harm. (Actually that's from Hippocrates' ancient manual on medical treatments. It applies to anybody fixing what ain't really broke.)
- Get more memory, add indexes, re-cable the network. (If you can influence the environment like that, then do so.)
- Design right in the first place.
- Understand the query.

Instead of general principals, we will be looking at what can be done with what's likely to be at hand. If we descend sometimes to mere tips and warnings about traps, that's because we've seen over the years that examples of real situations can help people realize what the general rules are. As has often been observed, tips should be based on principles.

The DBMSs that we looked at while preparing this book include IBM DB2, Informix, Ingres II, InterBase, Microsoft SQL Server, MySQL, Oracle, and Sybase (MS Windows NT versions). Each was installed and tested using the default switches recommended in the vendors' instructions. To avoid favoring any vendor's idiosyncrasies, all SQL examples in this book are written in ANSI/ISO Standard SQL:1999. Host-language examples are written in C plus ODBC, or Java plus JDBC.

Your DBMS is your pal. We won't counsel you to subvert it, be paranoid about it, or insult it by assuming it's stupid. Rather, as you would with a pal, you should try to get to know it better, and help it to help you.

Acknowledgments

Several people took the time to look at draft manuscripts of this book, and we would like to pass on our grateful acknowledgments to them, without suggesting that they share any responsibility for our book's flaws or views.

To Judy Bowman, author of *Practical SQL: The Sequel,* for insights about Sybase and an eye for jarring phrases.

To Keith Hare, member of the ANSI SQL standards committee, for identifying several technical mistakes.

To Dan Hotka and Chuck Kosin, for their helpful and encouraging comments.

To Craig Mullins, author of *DB2 Developer's Guide,* for explaining as only he can what IBM DB2 really does.

To Alexander Tarasul, who gave us the viewpoint of a veteran who has consulted for many database projects.

To Mika Wendelius, Oracle whiz, for taking the time and patience to show us in person some surprises that only a true Oracle expert can know.

And to Martti Laiho, Senior Lecturer in Data Management at Helsinki Business Polytechnic, not only for his long hours doing multiple reviews, but for giving us a chance to test our ideas in front of a live audience.

Facilis Descensus Averni[1]

When we decided to write this book, we chose the topic "Tuning Client/Server SQL Programs" because we had a specific plan. Each word in the topic narrows the focus. Let's look at the main words.

Tuning means enhancing speed. It's possible to make a distinction between tuning and optimizing—tuning is what you do to a database (e.g., change cache size, repartition, rebuild indexes) while optimizing is what you do to a program (e.g., adjust queries, take advantage of existing resources, rewrite application code). But we do not make such a fine distinction in this book. As for *speed*, the word can mean two things: **response time** (the time a statement takes to execute) and **throughput** (the number of operations the DBMS can do in a time unit). Our concern here is mostly with throughput.

SQL is a language that is supported by a **Database Management System (DBMS)** implementation. We decided to use a generic term so you'll know that we're not talking about a particular brand—this book is about what's in common for all major brands. There really is a standard core that they all share, so we can be specific in our recommendations without having to be specialists. Where there are many differences between DBMSs, you'll see charts outlining

---

1. Literally, "the descent into Hell is easy" . . . it's getting back out again that's hard! From Virgil.

the differences. Where there are few differences, you'll see a discussion of what's normal and (if necessary) a sidebar about the exceptional case.

Programs are things you write in a language such as SQL, C, or Java. So don't expect to see long discussions about how to choose equipment, what flags to set when you install, or which tools you'll need to monitor the users. Those tasks properly belong to the **Database Administrator (DBA).** We know that much of this book will interest DBAs; we know that many readers are both DBAs and programmers. That's great. We only want to make it clear that, in this book, we are addressing the people who write applications.

This Subject Is Important

"In our experience (confirmed by many industry experts) 80% of performance gains on SQL Server come from making improvements in SQL code, not from devising crafty configuration adjustments or tweaking the operating system."

—Kevin Kline et al., *Transact-SQL Programming,* O'Reilly & Associates

"Experience shows that 80 to 90 per cent of all tuning is done at the application level, not at the database level."

—Thomas Kyte, *Expert One on One: Oracle,* Wrox Press

No matter which DBMS you use, you can enhance its performance by doing the right thing. Enhancing performance is a broad field. It includes:

- Coding SQL statements without doing things that everyone knows are counter-productive

- Understanding the physical structure of a typical database

- Solving real problems rather than imaginary ones

Let's take a trivial example. Suppose you have this SQL statement:

```
SELECT column1 FROM Table1
  WHERE column1 = 77
```

For this kind of statement, we believe the essential question is—Should there be an index on `column1`? So we've devoted a whole chapter to the subject of indexes—what they look like, what variations exist, how indexes affect data changes, and so on. In another chapter, we address the question of how to use EXPLAIN (or its equivalent) to find out whether your particular DBMS actually uses an index for a particular SELECT. That illustrates our priority—we think that the first priority is the concept: indexes. Certainly, though, we must also care about the method: diagnostic tools. We hope that, with the concepts firmly planted in your mind, you will quickly arrive at the right point. We don't recommend that you implement any idea in this book without testing it first— but without ideas, you'll flounder randomly between plans without knowing if your final choice really is the best one.

We think an idea is sound if performance improves by 5% or more on most DBMSs. That may appear to be a modest goal, but consider. First, we always test to ensure that the idea doesn't *harm* performance on some other DBMS—we believe an idea is only good when it applies universally. Second, we think that even a small number like 5% matters when an operation occurs many times for many rows. Third, we are asking you to read only once, because once you have the information, it's a tiny effort to reuse it for years. Fourth, the improvement often will be many times more than 5%. Fifth, effects may be small, but they're also cumulative.

We also hope that you find the topic, well, interesting. If it's any incentive at all, let us assure you that many database practitioners, and all the good ones, are fascinated by these two questions—How does it work? How ought it to work?

The Big Eight

"In theory there is no difference between theory
and practice. But, in practice, there is."
                    —Jan L.A. van de Snepscheut

You don't have to specialize to find useful ideas in this book. Over and over again, we have found that basic matters that are true for DBMS #1 are also true for DBMS #2, DBMS #3, and so on, across the board. For example, we can say that "DBMSs store data in fixed-size pages and the size is a power of two." But isn't that a bold generalization? Let's be honest. We have not checked this statement on every DBMS that exists, we know it's not a law of nature, and in fact we know of at least two DBMSs for which the statement is false. But, in this book, when we make a claim for "all DBMSs" or just "DBMSs" we're not being vague or general—we mean, very specifically, eight particular DBMSs that we have actually tested and for which we guarantee that the statement is true at time of writing. We call these DBMSs "the Big Eight"—not a standard term, but a convenient way to direct your memory to this introductory explanation.

We chose the Big Eight according to the following criteria:

- The DBMS must be an SQL client/server DBMS. DBMSs of other types were excluded.
- The DBMS must have at least a 1% share of the market in North America and Europe according to published and verifiable surveys, or it must be widely known because it's open source.
- The DBMS must support **Java Database Connectivity (JDBC)** and **Open Database Connectivity (ODBC)**.

We want to emphasize that no DBMS got on our list due to its quality. We chose each of the Big Eight based only on the probability that you'll encounter it or something very much like it. Because the Big Eight have a combined market share of over 85%, with the open source DBMSs having been downloaded hundreds of thousands of times from Internet sites, we're confident that you'll be dealing with one of the Big Eight at least 90% of the time. Table 1–1 shows which DBMSs were tested for this book.

When researching the material for this book, we installed the latest versions of each DBMS available for the MS WindowsNT platform at the time of writing. Each DBMS was installed and tested using the default systems recommended in the vendors' instructions, except as indicated in the following section, "Installation Parameters." In some cases, we used evaluation copies or personal editions; in no case did we test with extra-cost or little-used options—our policy was to ignore nondefault installation options, settings, and switches.

Table 1–1   *The Big Eight*

Short Name	Product Name & Version	Remarks
IBM	IBM DB2 Universal Database 7.2	
Informix	IBM Informix Dynamic Server 9.3	Now owned by IBM
Ingres	Ingres II 2.5	Owned by Computer Associates International
InterBase	InterBase 6.0	Open source version. Owned by Borland Software Corporation
Microsoft	Microsoft SQL Server 2000	
MySQL	MySQL 3.23	Open source. Owned by MySQL AB
Oracle	Oracle 9i	
Sybase	Sybase ASE 12.5	

We have avoided endorsing or denouncing any vendor, because our object is to help you improve your SQL, given the hand you've been dealt.

There are test results throughout this book; however, there are no absolute performance figures or inter-DBMS comparisons. There are two reasons for this. One is obvious: such figures wouldn't fit the purpose of the book. The other is interesting: three of the Big Eight—Informix, Microsoft, and Oracle—have end-user license agreements that specifically prohibit publication of benchmarks.

Installation Parameters

As indicated earlier, in order to minimize our use of extra-cost or little-used options and to level the playing field between DBMSs as much as possible, we installed the Big Eight using the default systems recommended in the vendors' instructions except in the following cases:

- For the sake of consistency, we wanted to run all our tests using the same character set—the Windows 1252 code page—for every DBMS if at all possible. We chose this code page because we were testing on a Windows NT system and wanted to utilize international character set possibilities.

- We wanted to test the differences between dictionary and binary sorts for every DBMS if at all possible.

For IBM, these criteria meant that the IBM database was created with the default "IBM-1252" character set and default "Local Alphabet" dictionary sort order. We used CHAR columns to test dictionary sorts and CHAR FOR BIT DATA columns to test binary sorts. IBM doesn't provide SQL Standard-compliant CHARACTER SET or COLLATE options.

For Informix, these criteria meant that Informix was installed with the default "EN_US 8859-1" for client and server locales, and nondefault "EN_GB.8859-1" db_locale, which provides a dictionary sort order for NCHAR columns. We used NCHAR columns to test dictionary sorts and CHAR columns to test binary sorts. Informix doesn't provide SQL Standard-compliant CHARACTER SET or COLLATE options.

For Ingres, these criteria meant that the Ingres database was created with the default "WIN1252" character set and the nondefault "lmulti" dictionary sort order. We used CHAR columns to test dictionary sorts and BYTE columns to test binary sorts. Ingres doesn't provide SQL Standard-compliant CHARACTER SET or COLLATE options.

For InterBase, these criteria meant that the InterBase database was created with DEFAULT CHARACTER SET WIN1252. We used NCHAR columns with COLLATE EN_US to test dictionary sorts and NCHAR columns with no COLLATE clause to test binary sorts. We also used NCHAR columns with (a) COLLATE DA_DA to test Danish/Norwegian sorts, (b) COLLATE DE_DE to test German sorts, (c) COLLATE IS_IS to test Icelandic sorts, (d) COLLATE EN_UK to test Irish sorts, (e) COLLATE ES_ES to test Spanish sorts, and (f) COLLATE FI_FI and COLLATE SV_SV to test Swedish/Finnish sorts.

For Microsoft, these criteria meant that SQL Server was installed with the default "1252/ISO" Character Set and the default "Dictionary Order, case insensitive" Sort Order for CHAR columns, and a nondefault "Binary" Unicode Collation. We used CHAR columns with no COLLATE clause to test dictionary sorts and CHAR columns with COLLATE SQL_Latin1_General_BIN to test binary sorts. We also used CHAR columns with (a) COLLATE SQL_Danish to test Danish/Norwegian sorts, (b) COLLATE German_PhoneBook to test German phone book sorts, (c) COLLATE SQL_Icelandic to test Icelandic sorts, (d) COLLATE Mexican_Trad_Spanish and COLLATE Modern_Spanish to test Spanish sorts, and (e) COLLATE SQL_SwedishStd to test Swedish/Finnish sorts. (Note: Where applicable, PREF was always indicated, the code page was 1252, case sensitivity was CI, and accent sensitivity was AS.)

For MySQL, these criteria meant that MySQL was installed with the default "Latin1" (aka iso_1) character set. We used CHAR columns to test dictionary sorts and CHAR BINARY columns to test binary sorts. MySQL doesn't provide SQL Standard-compliant CHARACTER SET or COLLATE options.

For Oracle, these criteria meant that Oracle was installed with the default "WIN1252" character set. We used CHAR columns with NLS_SORT=XWEST_EUROPEAN to test dictionary sorts and CHAR columns with NLS_SORT=BINARY to test binary sorts. We also used CHAR columns with (a) NLS_SORT=DANISH and NLS_SORT=NORWEGIAN to test Danish/Norwegian sorts, (b) NLS_SORT=XGERMAN to test German dictionary sorts, (c) NLS_SORT=GERMAN_DIN to test German phone book sorts, (d) NLS_SORT=ICELANDIC to test Icelandic sorts, (e) NLS_SORT=XWEST_EUROPEAN to test Irish sorts, (f) NLS_SORT=XSPANISH to test Spanish Traditional sorts, (g) NLS_SORT=SPANISH to test Spanish Modern sorts, and (h) NLS_SORT=FINNISH to test Swedish/Finnish sorts.

For Sybase, these criteria meant that Sybase was installed with the non-default "Character Set = iso_1" and nondefault "Sort Order = Dictionary." We used CHAR columns to test dictionary sorts and BINARY columns to test binary sorts. Sybase doesn't provide SQL Standard-compliant CHARACTER SET or COLLATE options.

Test Results

Throughout this book, you'll see sets of SQL statements that show a test we ran against the Big Eight. The second statement in each example includes a note at the bottom that states: *GAIN:x/8*. That's an important number. The gain shows how many of the Big Eight run faster when an SQL statement is optimized by implementing the syntax shown in the second example. We recorded a gain for a DBMS if performance improved by 5% or greater. Mileage varies with different data and different machines, of course. We're only reporting what our tests showed.

"GAIN: 0/8" means "you'd be wasting your time if you rearranged this particular SQL statement into optimum order because the DBMS does this for you." "GAIN: 4/8," on the other hand, means that half of the Big Eight performed better when the suggested syntax was used, while the other half executed both statements equally well. Even if the gain is only 1/8 (meaning only one of the Big Eight improved on the second statement), you'll be better off using our suggested syntax because this means you'll improve performance some of the time without ever harming performance the rest of the time. That is, none of our suggestions will cause a performance decline on any of the Big Eight— with one exception.

The exception is that, in a few cases, one DBMS showed aberrant behavior and declined in performance on the second statement, while all the rest showed impressive gains. In such cases, we felt the possible improvement was worthy of mention anyway. Each exception notes the DBMS with which you should *not* use our improved syntax.

All tests were run on a single CPU Windows NT machine, with no other jobs running at the same time. The main test program was written in C and used ODBC calls to communicate with the DBMSs. A second test program used JDBC to test the DBMSs' response to specific calls. Unless otherwise indicated, each performance test was run three times for 10,000 rows of randomly inserted data, with the relevant column(s) indexed as well as without indexes. The gain for each DBMS was then calculated as the average of the three test runs.

We want to emphasize that our gain figures do *not* show absolute performance benchmark results. That is, a "GAIN: 4/8" note does not mean that any or all DBMSs ran 50% faster. It merely means that 50% of the DBMSs ran faster, and the rest showed no change.

Portability

As a bit of a bonus, because we had access to all these DBMSs, we will also be able to give you some information about portability.

We regard portability as a matter of great importance. In the first place, this book is about client/server applications. We anticipate that you will want to write code that works regardless of DBMS. In fact, we anticipate that you may not even know for which DBMS you are coding!

To avoid depending on any vendor's idiosyncrasies, all SQL examples and descriptions of SQL syntax in this book are written in standard SQL—that is, ANSI/ISO SQL:1999—whenever possible. When standard SQL omits a feature but it's common to all DBMSs—for example, the CREATE INDEX statement— our examples use syntax that will run on most platforms. Where nonstandard and uncommon syntax exists or had to be tested, we have identified it as such. Look for our "Portability" notes; they indicate where syntax other than standard SQL might be required.

To aid you, we've also added comparison charts that highlight differences between the SQL Standard and the Big Eight. In these tables, you'll sometimes see "N/S" in the ANSI SQL row. This means that the SQL Standard considers the feature to be implementation-defined; that is, there is no Standard-specified requirement. Instead, the decision on how to implement the feature is made by the DBMS vendor.

Optimizing SQL for all dialects is different from tuning for a single package. But the coverage in this book is strictly the universal stuff.

Terminology and Expectations

We expect that you're a programmer coding for (or about to begin coding for) an SQL DBMS. Because of this, we won't be explaining basic SQL syntax or programming techniques. Our assumption is that you already know basic SQL syntax, how to program with an SQL **Application Programming Interface (API)** such as ODBC or JDBC, how to write stored procedures, are familiar with how indexes operate, and so on. We also expect that you're familiar with SQL terms as used in introductory SQL texts. For example, suppose we illustrate a SELECT statement like this:

```
SELECT <select list>
  WHERE <search conditions>
  FROM <Table list>
  GROUP BY <grouping columns>
    HAVING <conditions>
  ORDER BY <sorting columns>
```

We assume you've already seen terms like "select list" and "search condition" and "grouping column," and we won't repeat their well-known definitions. At most, we'll just provide a brief refresher for common SQL syntax and concepts.

Some further terms are not so well known, but are important for understanding this book. We will define such terms the first time we use them. If you miss such a definition, you can look it up in the glossary in Appendix B.

Conventions

We use a particular style in our examples. SQL keywords are always in uppercase (e.g., SELECT). Table and other major SQL object names are initial capitalized (e.g., Table1, Index1); column names are in lowercase (e.g., column1). When it is necessary to use more than one line, each line will begin with a clause-leader keyword.

We deliberately avoid "real-world" names like Employees or cust_id because we believe that meaningful names would distract from the universality of the example. Sometimes, though, when illustrating a particular characteristic, we will use a name that hints at the item's nature. For example:

```
SELECT column1, column2
  FROM Table1
  WHERE indexed_column = <literal>
```

This book doesn't contain many SQL syntax diagrams, but here's a very brief refresher on the common variant of **Backus-Naur Form (BNF)** notation that we've used:

- < >

  Angle brackets surround the names of syntactic elements. Replace the names with real data.

- [ ]

  Square brackets surround optional syntax. You may either use or omit such syntax.

- { }

  Braces surround mandatory syntax groups. You must include one of the options for the group in your SQL statement.

- |

  The vertical bar separates syntactic elements. You may use only one of the options in your SQL statement.

Generalities

> "Beware of entrance to a quarrel; but being in,
> Bear't that th'opposed may beware of thee."
> —William Shakespeare, *Hamlet*

We can start off with some general tips.

SQL is a procedural language. Despite the confusion and outright lies about this point, it is a fact that an SQL statement's clauses are processed in a fixed order. And despite the set orientation of SQL, the DBMS must often operate on an SQL result set one row at a time. That is, if you're executing this statement:

```
UPDATE Table1
   SET column1 = 5
   WHERE column2 > 400
```

SQL's set orientation means the DBMS will determine that, for example, six rows meet the condition that requires them to be updated. After that, though, the DBMS must actually change all six of the rows—one row at a time.

The relational model is inherently efficient. Dr. Codd's rules and the subsequent work on **normalization** are based on the proven truism that mathematical foundations lead to solid structures. (Normalization is the process of designing a database so that its tables follow the rules specified by relational theory.)

Always assume you will do a **query** at least 100 times. That will make you ask yourself whether you want to use a procedure, a view, a trigger, or some other object and might also make you ask—If this is so common, has someone already written something like it?

And now, let's get started.

2

Simple Searches

In this chapter, we'll talk about syntax-based optimizing and simple search conditions.

A **syntax** is a choice of words and their arrangement in the SQL statement. To optimize based on syntax, assume that nonsyntactic factors (e.g., indexes, table sizes, storage) are irrelevant or unknown. This is the lowest level of optimizing—it's usually predictable, and some of it can be done on the client.

There's no point in attempting to optimize most SQL syntax because only certain SQL statements have options that lend themselves to optimization. The particular syntax that offers many optimization possibilities is the SQL **search condition**. Here are three examples of search conditions:

```
... WHERE title LIKE 'The %' OR title LIKE 'A %'
... WHERE name <> 'Smith'
... WHERE number = 5
```

Although the slowest search conditions are those that contain joins and subqueries, this chapter deals only with single-table searches. (We'll talk about joins and subqueries later.) Also, although search conditions can appear in HAVING, IF, or ON clauses, we'll talk only about search conditions in WHERE clauses. So the chapter title—"Simple Searches"—is an understatement. Don't worry—the complex queries will come later.

General Tuning

In this part of the chapter, we'll look at some general ideas you should keep in mind when writing simple search conditions.

Code for Points

The best search conditions are those that work on few rows with easy-to-do comparisons. Table 2-1 and Table 2-2 show typical lists (derived from vendors' manuals) of types of search conditions, in order from best to worst. Each search condition component has a "point count"—the better the component, the higher the score. You can see from the allotted points shown in Tables 2-1 and 2-2 that the best search condition is something like:

```
... WHERE smallint_column = 12345
```

Table 2-1 *Search Condition Point Counts for Operators*

Operator	Points
=	10
>	5
>=	5
<	5
<=	5
LIKE	3
<>	0

Table 2-2 *Search Condition Point Counts for Operands*

Operand	Points
Literal alone	10
Column alone	5
Parameter alone	5
Multioperand expression	3
Exact numeric data type	2
Other numeric data type	1
Temporal data type	1
Character data type	0
NULL	0

This example gets a total of 27 points, calculated as follows:

- Five points for the column (`smallint_column`) alone on the left
- Two points for the exact numeric (`smallint_column`) operand data type
- Ten points for the equals operator
- Ten points for the literal (`12345`) alone on the right

Here's another example:

```
... WHERE char_column >= varchar_column || 'x'
```

The point count for this type of search condition is much lower—only 13:

- Five points for the column (`char_column`) alone on the left
- Zero points for the CHAR (`char_column`) operand data type
- Five points for the greater than or equal to operator
- Three points for the multioperand expression (`varchar_column || 'x'`) on the right
- Zero points for the VARCHAR (`varchar_column`) operand data type

The precise point count for a search condition varies from vendor to vendor, so it's pointless to memorize anything other than the order and the concept for this optimization technique. So just remember:

> The condition that takes the least time—usually because it involves fewer rows or easier comparisons—gets the most points.

Armed with this concept, you can decide whether to change the order of expressions, or to substitute one expression for another that does the same work. Even though a modern cost-based DBMS optimizer has many more rules that require information outside the SQL statement itself, all DBMSs still fall back on the point count when no other information is available. The possibility is always there that you will use an item of information that the optimizer doesn't. (For more information about cost-based optimizers, see Chapter 17 "Cost-Based Optimizers.")

Another way you can optimize a search condition is by putting multiple expressions in the correct order. The expressions in this WHERE clause are already in optimal order:

```
SELECT * FROM Table1
  WHERE column1 = 5
    AND column2 = 77.3
    AND column3 = 'Smith'
    AND column4 < 117
    AND column4 > column5
GAIN: 0/8
```

The note at the bottom of this example says there is a GAIN: 0/8. That's an important number, and we're going to say "GAIN: x/8" in many of our examples, so let's clarify. As explained in Chapter 1, the gain shows how many of the Big Eight run faster when the search condition is optimized. Mileage varies with different data and different machines, of course. We're only reporting what our tests showed.

So "GAIN: 0/8" means "you'd be wasting your time if you rearranged this particular WHERE clause into optimum order because the DBMS does this for you." All DBMS makers know the basics of point counting, so the rearrangement is automatic. This means that, in ordinary cases, you will gain nothing by doing your own syntax-based optimization. However, there are many exceptions to the rule. For the rest of this chapter, we'll look at cases where the gain is both significant and predictable.

Constant Propagation

> "All men are mortal. Socrates is a man.
> Therefore, Socrates is mortal."
> —Attributed to Aristotle

Formally, the Law of Transitivity states that:

```
IF
(A <comparison operator> B) IS TRUE AND (B <comparison operator> C) IS TRUE
THEN
(A <comparison operator> C) IS TRUE AND NOT (A <comparison operator> C) IS FALSE
```

(Comparison operator is any one of: = or > or >= or < or <= but not one of: <> or LIKE.)

The Law of Transitivity leads to the simple observation that we can substitute C for B without changing the meaning of an expression. When such a substitution involves substituting a constant value, the process is called **constant propagation.**[1]

The next two expressions mean the same thing, but the second expression has a better point count because it substitutes a literal (5) for a column name (column1):

```
Expression #1
... WHERE column1 < column2
      AND column2 = column3
      AND column1 = 5

Expression #2
... WHERE 5 < column2
      AND column2 = column3
      AND column1 = 5
GAIN: 2/8
```

Expression #2 is called a **transform** of Expression #1. (Writing a transform means rewriting an SQL statement to produce the same result but with different syntax. When two SQL statements have different syntax, but will predictably and regularly produce the same outputs, they are known as transforms of one another.) Most good DBMSs do this sort of thing automatically. But some DBMSs won't try transforms when the expression contains multiple parentheses and NOTs. For example, this SELECT statement can be slow:

```
SELECT * FROM Table1
  WHERE column1 = 5 AND
    NOT (column3 = 7 OR column1 = column2)
```

---

1. The Law of Transitivity, like many arithmetic rules, uses two-valued logic. That's unsafe if NULLs are involved, so it's a lucky thing that SQL never returns true when any operand is NULL. And—betcha didn't know—the SQL Standard definition of a literal is "a constant that is not NULL." So constant propagation is a misleading term—it would be better to call it "literal propagation."

Applying the transforms ourselves, we came up with this statement:

```
SELECT * FROM Table1
  WHERE column1 = 5
    AND column3 <> 7
    AND column2 <> 5
GAIN: 5/8
```

The transformed statement is faster more than half of the time. In other words, sometimes it pays to do your own transforms.

Sometimes constant propagation won't work with floats, because it's possible to be both "greater than" and "equal to" at the same time when approximate numeric comparisons happen. When it does work, though, expect a GAIN: 5/8. And sometimes, constant propagation won't work for CHAR expressions. But when it does, expect a GAIN: 4/8.

Exercise time: The MySQL online documentation has this example:

```
... WHERE a < b AND b = c AND a = 5
```

transforms to:

```
... WHERE b > 5 AND b = c AND a = 5
```

The quiz question here is—Did the MySQL folks make a mistake?[2]

In the real world, you'll find many semiconstant operands, as program parameters or functions. Examples are the niladic functions like CURRENT_ DATE (a **niladic function** is a function that has no arguments). Because using a constant value always accelerates accesses, try a transform to speed up these cases. Here's an example: Query #1 transforms to Query #2:

```
Query #1:
SELECT * FROM  Table1
  WHERE date_column = CURRENT_DATE
    AND amount * 5 > 100.00
```

---

2. Answer to the quiz question: No. The MySQL people were correct.

```
Query #2:
SELECT * FROM Table1
  WHERE date_column = DATE '2002-01-01'
    AND amount * 5 > 100.00
GAIN: 5/8
```

If you're thinking of transforming this type of expression, keep in mind that (because of the DATE constant), you'd have to change the query every day. That's only practical when an application program is generating the queries on the server.

Dead Code Elimination

> "Branches with no leaves should be cut off."
> —*Ortho Guide To Pruning Bushes and Shrubs*

In some old SQL programs, you'll encounter literals on both sides of the comparison operator, as in this example:

```
SELECT * FROM Table1
  WHERE 0 = 1
    AND column1 = 'I hope we never execute this'
```

In the days before C-style /* comments */ were legal in an SQL statement, this was a way to add an inline comment string. Because the expression 0 = 1 is always false, this query will always return zero rows, and therefore DBMSs can skip the whole WHERE clause. But some of them don't. We tested this by removing the WHERE clause and got a gain:

```
SELECT * FROM Table1
GAIN: 5/8
```

It is, of course, obvious that these two queries aren't equivalent—the point is merely that it should take less time to retrieve zero rows due to an always-false condition than it should to do a full table scan—provided the DBMS doesn't evaluate the always-false condition. This example shows that DBMSs don't always throw out always-false conditions and all their dependents in the PREPARE stage. But they're pretty reliable at throwing out always-true conditions. So you can use always-true conditions for an SQL equivalent of conditional compilation. For example, if you worry that a DBMS won't give high precision for division results, add a separate condition that comes into play only when necessary—as in this example:

```
... WHERE (77 / 10 = 7.7 AND column1 / 10 = 7.7)
      OR (77 / 10 = 7 AND column1 * 10 = 77)
GAIN: 5/8
```

Because of the unreliability aspect, though, it is usually a bad idea to put in redundant code. Suppose that a column, `indexed_column`, is an indexed NOT NULL column. You could transform this SQL statement:

```
SELECT * FROM Table1
```

to this statement:

```
SELECT * FROM Table1
  WHERE indexed_column > 0
```

This is a way of forcing the DBMS to look up via the index. Alas, it works only with a few DBMSs. In general, then, don't add redundant conditions to WHERE clauses.

Ensure You Use the Right DBMS

There are several ways to ensure that a specific DBMS (and no other) executes an expression. Here are three examples, all of which use nonstandard SQL extensions:

```
Example 1:
... WHERE :variable = 'Oracle'
      AND /* Oracle-specific code here */

Example 2:
SELECT /* ! HIGH_PRIORITY */ ...
    /* all DBMSs except MySQL ignore this */

Example 3:
... WHERE <escape-sequence> AND /* ODBC code */
```

While we're on the subject, Oracle allows you to add a comment that indicates what index you want to use. It looks like this:

```
SELECT /*+ INDEX(Widgets Widget_index) */
       column1, column2, column3
    FROM Widgets
    WHERE column1 <> 7;
GAIN: only 1/8 because it's Oracle-specific
```

Oracle-specific optimizations are bad ideas if they tie you to Oracle. In this case, the hint is in a comment, so other DBMSs will ignore it. That's good—it's more portable than putting hints outside comments as Microsoft and Sybase do. So it's okay—until other DBMSs start to put executable data inside comments too. Some are already starting to do so. So right now hints are okay, but eventually they will lead to conflict and chaos.

Constant Folding

> "Go north one mile, west one mile, west one more mile, then
> south one mile, and you will be at your starting point."
> —The South Pole Riddle

Anyone who has used C will know that the expression x=1+1-1-1 is folded to x=0 at compile time. So it may surprise you that many SQL DBMSs do not fold these five obvious-looking transform candidates:

```
... WHERE column1 + 0
```

```
... WHERE 5 + 0.0
```

```
... WHERE column1 IN (1, 3, 3)
```

```
... CAST(1 AS INTEGER)
```

```
... WHERE 'a' || 'b'
```

If you find expressions like these in old code though, our tip is—Leave them alone. They are there for historical reasons, such as forcing the DBMS to ignore indexes, changing the result data type, allowing for the difference between SMALLINT and INTEGER, or evading a limit on line size. Sorry—but the obvious-looking cases are precisely the cases where you should stop and wonder whether the original programmer had some reason for the weird syntax choice. We read a Java optimization article once that sums it up nicely: "Rule #1: Understand the code." Nevertheless, we do recommend that you transform this search condition:

```
... WHERE a - 3 = 5
```

to:

```
... WHERE a = 8          /* a - 3 = 5 */
GAIN: 6/8
```

Although it's useless in simple cases, constant folding can lead to constant propagation and is therefore A Good Thing.

Case-Insensitive Searches

Microsoft's Access Jet considers the strings 'SMITH' and 'Smith' to be equal, so Access is called a **case-insensitive** DBMS. Oracle, on the other hand, is usually **case sensitive** (the engine would say 'SMITH' and 'Smith' are unequal strings). Sybase allows you to decide about case sensitivity when you install, and a true SQL Standard DBMS will allow you to switch case sensitivity at runtime. We've seen many programmers try to ensure case insensitivity by using the fold function UPPER, as in:

```
... WHERE UPPER(column1) = 'SMITH'
```

That can be a mistake if you're dealing with strings that contain anything other than strictly Latin letters. With some DBMSs, when you translate certain French or German strings to uppercase, you lose information. For example, the function:

```
... UPPER('résumé')
```

returns RESUME—that is, the accent marks are lost, changing the meaning of the word from "curriculum vitae" to "begin again." Because information isn't lost going the other way, it's better to use the LOWER function, like this:

```
... WHERE LOWER(column1) = 'résumé'
```

An even better way is to eliminate the fold function entirely if that's possible, because—we appeal to authority here—both the Microsoft and Oracle manuals say: "Avoid functions on columns." We're sure they mean "avoid functions on columns when there's another way to get the result needed"—for example, to ensure case insensitivity, the best method is to use a case-insensitive collation rather than a fold function.

A slightly faster search assumes that the data is clean and asks for the only reasonable combinations, like this:

```
... WHERE column1 = 'SMITH'
      OR column1 = 'Smith'
GAIN: 8/8
```

which is still slow. Our tip here is—Take advantage of dead code elimination so that the 'Smith' search happens only when the DBMS is case sensitive. Here's how:

```
... WHERE column1 = 'SMITH'
     OR ('SMITH' <> 'Smith' AND column1 = 'Smith')
GAIN: 3/8
```

Sargability

> "CHUFFED. adj. [1] Pleased. [2] Displeased."
> —*The Concise Oxford Dictionary*

The ideal SQL search condition has the general form:

```
<column> <comparison operator> <literal>
```

In the early days, IBM researchers named these kinds of search conditions "sargable predicates" because SARG is a contraction for Search ARGument. In later days, Microsoft and Sybase redefined "sargable" to mean "can be looked up via the index." Alas—when the same word has two very different meanings, it's not much use as a word any more! So we titled this section "Sargability" just for fun. But although the word is dead, the idea lives on in this rule:

> The left side of a search condition should be a simple column name; the right side should be an easy-to-look-up value.

To enforce this rule, all DBMSs will transpose the expression:

```
5 = column1
```

to:

```
column1 = 5
```

When there's arithmetic involved, though, only some DBMSs will transpose. For example, we tested this transform:

```
... WHERE column1 - 3 = -column2
```

transforms to:

```
... WHERE column1 = -column2 + 3
GAIN: 4/8
```

The gain shows that doing the transform ourselves helped considerably.

On a 32-bit computer, arithmetic is fastest if all operands are INTEGERs (because INTEGERs are 32-bit signed numbers) rather than SMALLINTs, DECIMALs, or FLOATs. Thus this condition:

```
... WHERE decimal_column * float_column
```

is slower than:

```
... WHERE integer_column * integer_column
GAIN: 5/8
```

You might expect "GAIN: 8/8" with the last example, but some DBMSs (Oracle is an example) don't distinguish between 16-bit and 32-bit numbers or store them in binary form. (Recall that dBASE stores numbers in ASCII. When a DBMS stores numbers in ASCII, truncation will always beat division by ten. So store using the base that you might divide by.)

The Bottom Line: General Tuning

The left side of a search condition should be a simple column name; the right side should be an easy-to-look-up value.

Each component of a search condition has a point count. The higher the points, the faster the component. The condition that takes the least time gets the most points.

Put multiple expressions in the correct order.

Use the Law of Transitivity and the concept of constant propagation to substitute a literal for a column name or column expression whenever you can do so without changing the meaning of an expression.

Some DBMSs won't fold most obvious-looking (to a C programmer) expressions. Don't use this principle as the reason to always transform such expressions when you find them in old code though—usually they're there for historical reasons. Remember Rule #1: Understand the code before changing it.

If the code involves an obvious math expression, do evaluate it and transform the condition to the evaluated result. Constant folding can lead to constant propagation and is therefore A Good Thing.

Avoid functions on columns.

If you can't avoid functions, don't use UPPER to ensure case insensitivity. Use LOWER instead.

Specific Tuning

To this point, we've talked about general tuning of search conditions. Now we'll look at how you can improve your code using specific SQL operators.

AND

When everything else is equal, DBMSs will evaluate a series of ANDed expressions from left to right (except Oracle, which evaluates from right to left when the cost-based optimizer is operating). No rule says they must—that's just what they do. You can take advantage of this behavior by putting the least likely expression first or—if both expressions are equally likely—putting the least complex expression first. Then, if the first expression is `false`, the DBMS won't bother to evaluate the second expression. So, for example (unless you're using Oracle), you should transform:

```
... WHERE column1 = 'A' AND column2 = 'B'
```

to:

```
... WHERE column2 = 'B' AND column1 = 'A'
GAIN: 6/7 assuming column2 = 'B' is less likely
```

WARNING   Oracle with the rule-based optimizer shows a gain, but don't do this for Oracle running the cost-based optimizer. The gain shown is for only seven DBMSs.

The gain shown represents an extreme case with this example. In our sample database `column2 = 'B'` is always `false`, `column1 = 'A'` is always `true`, and there are no indexes. With other scenarios the gain is less and can be 0/8. It's never less than zero though, so reordering ANDed expressions is a highly recommended optimization. Rule-based optimizers will transpose two expressions if they have different point counts.

OR

When you're writing expressions with OR, put the most likely expression at the left. That's the exact reverse of the advice for AND, because an OR causes further tests if the first expression is `false`, while AND causes further tests if the first expression is `true`. So, do transform Expression #1 to Expression #2:

```
Expression #1:
... WHERE column2 = 'B' OR column1 = 'A'

Expression #2:
... WHERE column1 = 'A' OR column2 = 'B'
GAIN: 4/7 assuming column1 = 'A' is most likely
```

> **WARNING**   Oracle with the rule-based optimizer shows no change, but don't do this for Oracle running the cost-based optimizer. The gain shown is for only seven DBMSs.

Microsoft specifically recommends this transform. Once again, Oracle users should ignore this advice because Oracle evaluates from right to left when the cost-based optimizer is operating.

ORs are also faster if all columns are the same, because that reduces the number of columns and indexes that the DBMS has to read. Therefore, in a long series of ORs, expressions for the same column should be together. For example, you should transform Expression #1 to Expression #2:

```
Expression #1:
... WHERE column1 = 1
      OR column2 = 3
      OR column1 = 2

Expression #2:
... WHERE column1 = 1
      OR column1 = 2
      OR column2 = 3
GAIN: 1/8
```

AND Plus OR

The Distributive Law states that:

```
A AND (B OR C)
is the same thing as
(A AND B) OR (A AND C)
```

Suppose you have the table shown in Table 2–3, on which you must execute a query where the ANDs come first:

```
SELECT * FROM Table1
  WHERE (column1 = 1 AND column2 = 'A')
    OR (column1 = 1 AND column2 = 'B')
```

Table 2-3 *Table for an AND Plus OR Query*

Row#	column1	column2
1	3	A
2	2	B
3	1	C

When the DBMS does index lookups in the order of the query, it might follow these steps:

- Index lookup: column1=1. Result set = {row 3}

- Index lookup: column2='A'. Result set = {row 1}

- AND to merge the result sets. Result set = {}

- Index lookup: column1=1. Result set = {row 3}

- Index lookup: column2='A'. Result set = {row 1}

- AND to merge the result sets. Result set = {}

- OR to merge the result sets. Result set = {}

Now let's transpose the query using the Distributive Law, in reverse:

```
SELECT * FROM Table1
  WHERE column1 = 1
    AND (column2 = 'A' OR column2 = 'B')
GAIN: 2/8
```

Doing lookups in the new order, the DBMS might follow these steps:

- Index lookup: column2='A'. Result set = {row 1}

- Index lookup: column2='B'. Result set = {row 2}

- OR to merge the result sets. Result set = {row 1, 2}

- Index lookup: column1=1. Result set = {row 3}

- AND to merge the result sets. Result set = {}

This test gave us a gain for only two of the Big Eight. The other DBMSs tend to apply the Distributive Law themselves, so that they will always be working with the same, canonical query. Nevertheless, the evidence shows that, for simple search conditions, you're better off with this construct:

```
A AND (B OR C)
```

than with this one:

```
(A AND B) OR (A AND C)
```

When you're joining, however, it's a different matter; see Chapter 5, "Joins."

NOT

Transform a NOT expression to something more readable. A simple condition can be transformed by reversing the comparison operator, for example:

```
... WHERE NOT (column1 > 5)
```

transforms to:

```
... WHERE column1 <= 5
```

A more complex condition requires more caution, but you can apply DeMorgan's Theorem, which states:

```
NOT (A AND B) = (NOT A) OR (NOT B)
```

and

```
NOT (A OR B) = (NOT A) AND (NOT B)
```

Thus, for example, this search condition:

```
... WHERE NOT (column1 > 5 OR column2 = 7)
```

transforms to:

```
... WHERE column1 <= 5
    AND column2 <> 7
```

If, after transforming, you end up with a not equals operator, expect slowness. After all, in any evenly distributed set of values, when there are more than two rows, the unequal values always outnumber the equal values. Because of this, some DBMSs won't use an index for not equals comparisons. But they will use an index for greater than and for less than—so you can transform this type of condition:

```
... WHERE NOT (bloodtype = 'O')
```

to:

```
... WHERE bloodtype < 'O'
      OR bloodtype > 'O'
GAIN: 3/8
```

The gain for this example is 3/8 if almost everyone has blood type O, as in the original North American population. But it's the other way around if most people have a different blood type—so do this transform only if you know how values are distributed and if a change to the distribution is unlikely. (If the DBMS keeps statistics, it knows this and will override you.)

IN

Many people think that there is no difference between these two conditions because they both return the same result set:

```
Condition #1:
... WHERE column1 = 5
      OR column1 = 6

Condition #2:
... WHERE column1 IN (5, 6)
GAIN: 2/8
```

Those people are 0.01% wrong. With two of the Big Eight, IN is faster than OR. So transform OR to IN when you can. All the other DBMSs will just translate IN back to OR, so you won't lose anything.

When an IN operator has a dense series of integers, it's better to ask "what is out" rather than "what is in." Thus, this condition:

```
... WHERE column1 IN (1, 3, 4, 5)
```

should be transformed to:

```
... WHERE column1 BETWEEN 1 AND 5
      AND column1 <> 2
GAIN: 7/8
```

Similar gains can happen when a series can be represented by an arithmetic expression.

LIKE

Most DBMSs will use an index for a LIKE pattern if it starts with a real character but will avoid an index for a LIKE pattern that starts with a wildcard (either % or _). The only DBMSs that never use indexes for LIKE are Pick and mSQL (on TEXT fields). For example, if the search condition is:

```
... WHERE column1 LIKE 'C_F%'
```

DBMSs will resolve it by finding all index keys that start with C and then filtering those that contain F in the third position. In other words, you don't need to transform this search condition:

```
... WHERE column1 LIKE 'C_F%'
```

to this one:

```
... WHERE column1 >= 'C'
      AND column1 < 'D'
      AND column1 LIKE 'C_F%'
GAIN: -5/8
```

(In fact, with IBM, Informix, Microsoft, Oracle, and Sybase, the transformed expression is actually slower!)

If you want to speed up LIKE with a parameter (LIKE ?) and you know the pattern starts with a character, do the transform yourself. Here's how:

```
... WHERE column1 LIKE ?
```

transforms to:

```
... WHERE column1 > SUBSTRING(? FROM 1 FOR 1)
      AND column1 LIKE ?
GAIN: 4/8
```

Another tempting transform of LIKE with a parameter is to use the equals operator instead of LIKE if the parameter does not contain a wildcard. Surprisingly, this can actually help—for example, you can transform this condition:

```
... WHERE column1 LIKE 'ABC'
```

into:

```
... WHERE column1 = 'ABC'
GAIN: 5/8
```

The trap here is that `LIKE 'A'` and `= 'A'` are not precisely the same conditions. In standard SQL, a LIKE comparison takes trailing spaces into account, while an equals comparison ignores trailing spaces. Furthermore, LIKE and equals don't necessarily use the same collations by default. So don't do the transform on VAR-CHAR columns, and be sure to force the same collation if necessary.

If a column is only two or three characters long, you might be tempted to use SUBSTRING instead of LIKE, but—because functions on columns are bad—LIKE will always beat multiple SUBSTRINGs. That is, you should transform Expression #1 to Expression #2:

```
Expression #1:
... WHERE SUBSTRING(column1 FROM 1 FOR 1) = 'F'
      OR SUBSTRING(column1 FROM 2 FOR 1) = 'F'
      OR SUBSTRING(column1 FROM 3 FOR 1) = 'F'

Expression #2:
...WHERE column1 LIKE '%F%'
GAIN: 5/6
```

Portability   Neither Ingres nor InterBase support SUBSTRING; the gain shown is for only six DBMSs. IBM and Oracle call the SUBSTRING function SUBSTR. Informix puts the substring parameters inside square brackets.

In the near future, some types of LIKE search will become obsolete because full-text indexes will become more common.

SIMILAR

If two expressions you're joining with OR are on columns defined as CHAR or VARCHAR, a new SQL:1999 operator might be faster than OR—the SIMILAR operator. If you haven't heard of SIMILAR yet, and you're not familiar with the grep utility in Unix, here's a short summary.

The basic SIMILAR syntax is:

```
... <string> SIMILAR TO <'pattern'>
```

For SIMILAR, `string` is usually either the name of a column or a column expression. You can put these wildcards inside the pattern:

- % or _ means the same as the wildcards used with LIKE.
- * or + means "the preceding repeats indefinitely"—zero to infinity times in the first case, one to infinity in the second.
- [A-F] means any character between A and F.
- [AEK] means either A or E or K.
- [^AEK] means anything other than A or E or K.
- [:ALPHA:] means anything that is a simple Latin letter. Other options for this enumeration include [:UPPER:] (for uppercase letters only), [:LOWER:] (for lowercase letters only), [:DIGIT:] (for any digit from 0 to 9), and [:ALNUM:] (for any Latin letter or digit).
- | and || mean the logical OR of two expressions, and concatenation, respectively.

Thus, for example, this search condition:

```
... WHERE column1 SIMILAR TO '[A-F][AEK]_'
```

will be `true` for both these strings:

```
DEN
FAB
```

and will be `false` for these strings:

```
GIB
AKRON
```

Because SIMILAR allows OR logic in the pattern, you sometimes won't need OR. For example, you could transform Expression #1 to Expression #2:

```
Expression #1:
... WHERE column1 = 'A'
      OR column1 = 'B'
      OR column1 = 'K'

Expression #2:
... WHERE column1 SIMILAR TO '[ABK]'
GAIN: 1/1
```

Portability   Informix uses MATCHES instead of SIMILAR and supports different pattern wildcards for this operator; the gain shown is for only one DBMS. Both Microsoft and Sybase support some of the SIMILAR pattern wildcards with LIKE, but they often return the wrong result. No other DBMS supports SIMILAR in any fashion.

Only Informix provides support for a SIMILAR-type operator. Until it's commonly supported, add a conditional statement to your code after using SIMILAR, such as:

```
IF (the DBMS returns a syntax error)
   THEN (try the old way with OR)
```

UNION

In SQL, a union of two tables is the set of distinct data values that is found in either table—that is, UNION returns nonduplicate rows from two or more queries. This can be a great way to merge data. But is it the best way? To test this, we ran two different SELECT statements, Query #1 and Query #2:

```
Query #1
SELECT * FROM Table1
  WHERE column1 = 5
UNION
SELECT * FROM Table1
  WHERE column2 = 5

Query #2
SELECT DISTINCT * FROM Table1
  WHERE column1 = 5
     OR column2 = 5
GAIN: 7/7
```

Portability   MySQL doesn't support UNION. The gain shown is for only seven DBMSs.

In our tests, neither `column1` nor `column2` were indexed. Note that Query #1 is longer, uses a relatively rare SQL construct, and—with some SQL packages, at least—is illegal as part of a CREATE VIEW statement. If Query #2 always ran faster, as it does in this example, we could recommend that Query #1 always be transformed to Query #2. However, in one case doing so might actually result in slower execution with some DBMSs. To see why, we need to consider two optimizer flaws.

The first flaw is that many optimizers optimize only within a single WHERE clause in a single SELECT statement. So the two SELECTs in Query #1 are really both performed. First the optimizer finds all the rows where the condition `column1 = 5` is `true`, then it finds all the rows where `column2 = 5` in a separate pass—that is, it scans the table twice! (A **table scan** is a search of an entire table, row by row.) Therefore, if `column1` is not indexed, Query #1 should take precisely twice as long to perform as Query #2.

If `column1` is indexed, the double search still occurs, but an uncommon optimizer flaw, seen in some DBMSs, more than makes up for this. When these optimizers see that a search condition contains OR, they refuse to use indexes at all; so in this instance, and only in this instance, UNION outperforms OR. This is a narrow enough set of circumstances that our advice still is to use OR rather than UNION when the columns in question are not indexed.

EXCEPT

Any A AND NOT B expression can be transformed with EXCEPT. Here's an example—Query #1 transforms to Query #2:

```
Query #1:
SELECT * FROM Table1
  WHERE column1 = 7 AND
    NOT column2 = 8

Query #2:
SELECT * FROM Table1
   WHERE column1 = 7
EXCEPT
SELECT * FROM Table1
   WHERE column2 = 8
GAIN: -2/3
```

Portability Informix, Ingres, InterBase, Microsoft, and MySQL don't support EXCEPT. The gain shown is for only three DBMSs. Oracle and Sybase call EXCEPT the MINUS operator.

The negative gain shows that doing the transform is a bad idea! Coupled with the fact that support for EXCEPT is rare, our advice is—Use AND NOT; avoid EXCEPT.

INTERSECT

Although there are many ways to transform ANDed expressions using INTERSECT, we found none that resulted in any gain. Because many DBMSs won't support INTERSECT anyway, we won't provide details.

Portability Informix, Ingres, InterBase, Microsoft, MySQL, and Sybase don't support INTERSECT.

CASE

Suppose a search condition has more than one reference to a slow routine:

```
... WHERE slow_function(column1) = 3
      OR slow_function(column1) = 5
```

To avoid executing `slow_function` twice, transform the condition with CASE:

```
... WHERE 1 =
       CASE slow_function(column1)
          WHEN 3 THEN 1
          WHEN 5 THEN 1
       END
GAIN: 4/7
```

Portability   InterBase doesn't support CASE. The gain shown is for only seven DBMSs.

It's useful to bury a search condition in a CASE expression if the result is a reduction in the number of references.

CASE expressions are also useful for final filtering in the **select list**. (The select list is everything between the keyword SELECT and the keyword FROM in a SELECT statement.)

Portability   IBM and Informix process the select list at fetch time—that is, at the time you fetch the rows in the result set. The rest of the Big Eight process the select list when you execute the SELECT—that is, at the time the DBMS evaluates the SELECT to determine the rows that belong in the result set.

The Bottom Line: Specific Tuning

When everything else is equal, DBMSs will evaluate a series of ANDed expressions from left to right (except Oracle, which evaluates from right to left). Take advantage of this behavior by putting the least likely expression first. If two expressions are equally likely, put the least complex expression first.

Put the most likely expression first in a series of ORed expressions—unless you're using Oracle.

Put the same columns together in a series of ORed expressions.

Apply the Distributive Law to write simple search conditions with the form A AND (B OR C) rather than (A AND B) OR (A AND C).

Transform a NOT expression to something more readable. For a simple condition, reverse the comparison operator. For a more complex condition, apply DeMorgan's Theorem.

When you know the distribution of a set of values, you can speed things up by transforming not equals searches to greater than and less than searches.

Transform a series of ORed expressions on the same column to IN.

When IN has a dense series of integers, ask "what is out" rather than "what is in."

Most DBMSs will use an index for a LIKE pattern that starts with a real character but will avoid an index for a pattern that starts with a wildcard. Don't transform LIKE conditions to comparisons with >=, <, and so on unless the LIKE pattern is a parameter, for example, LIKE ?.

Speed up LIKE ?, where the parameter does not contain a wildcard, by substituting the equals operator for LIKE as long as trailing spaces and different collations aren't a factor.

LIKE will always beat multiple SUBSTRINGs, so don't transform.

Transform UNION to OR.

Put a search condition in a CASE expression if the result is a reduction in the number of references.

Use CASE expressions for final filtering in the select list.

Style Notes

When you execute several SQL statements sequentially, it's important to use a consistent style. For example, instead of running these two SQL statements:

```
SELECT column1*4 FROM Table1 WHERE COLUMN1 = COLUMN2 + 7
select Column1 * 4 FROM Table1  WHERE column1=(column2 + 7)
```

run these two statements:

```
SELECT column1 * 4 FROM Table1 WHERE column1 = column2 + 7
SELECT column1 * 4 FROM Table1 WHERE column1 = column2 + 7
GAIN: 2/8
```

"But there's no difference!" you may exclaim. Well, semantically all four SELECTs are the same. The trick, though, is that some DBMSs store parsed results from previous queries and will reuse them if the queries are precisely the same—including spaces and capitalization. So a firm, consistent style will not only make SQL statements easier to read—it just might make them run faster!

We're not going to give you a style guide here because that's not the purpose of this book. But we will observe that the transform in the example used some common and easy-to-remember rules:

- Keywords uppercase but column names lowercase.
- Table names initial capitalized.
- Single spaces around each word and around each arithmetic operator.

Parting Shots

Suppose you have a column of prices, defined as DECIMAL(7,2) and you need to answer the question—What prices are even dollars?

To mislead you, here are two quotes from the Microsoft SQL Server 2000 online documentation:

- Quote #1: "Avoid data conversion functions."
- Quote #2: "If the same column is on both sides of the comparison operator, the expression is not sargable."

Now, here are three search conditions that answer the question:

```
Search condition #1
... WHERE MOD(decimal_column, 1) = 0

Search condition #2
... WHERE CAST(decimal_column AS CHAR(7)) LIKE '%.00%'

Search condition #3
... WHERE decimal_column = CAST(decimal_column AS INTEGER)
```

Which expression is best? There is an answer if you've read this chapter so far.

- Search condition #1 is the worst. Although there is no CAST, it depends on an implicit DECIMAL-to-INTEGER data conversion (because modulus operations work on integers). There is also an implicit divide operation.
- Search condition #2 is in the middle. Some DBMSs store DECIMAL values as character strings, so the data conversion isn't hard. Nevertheless, LIKE is slow when the pattern starts with a wildcard.

- Search condition #3 is the best (GAIN: 7/7). It breaks the rules stated in both Quote #1 and Quote #2, but we said those quotes were misleading (Microsoft uses an unusual definition of "sargable"). If you compare all three conditions using the point counts shown in Tables 2–1 and 2–2 at the beginning of this chapter, you'll find that condition #3 scores highest because it uses the equals operator and has the fewest expressions. Also, it's closest to the sargable ideal because it starts with:

```
<column> <comparison operator>
```

Portability   MySQL doesn't support CAST. The gain shown is for only seven DBMSs.

In other words, there's nothing more to say. If you answered "Search condition #3" to the question, you know how syntax-based optimizations work.

3

ORDER BY

The ORDER BY clause causes sorts. Sorts take time. In this chapter, we'll look at how much time, and what you can do about it.

Some of this chapter is also relevant to other situations that cause sorts. It is a simple matter to see that DBMSs may choose to sort a list when they need to discover duplicates, so GROUP BY, DISTINCT, CREATE [UNIQUE] INDEX, and UNION might use the same algorithms that are used by ORDER BY. Less commonly, DBMSs may choose to sort any two lists and merge them when they need to perform either inner or outer joins. In all those cases, though, the sorting is a side effect, so we'll focus on ORDER BY—with the admonishment that what we're saying may be applicable more broadly.

General Sort Considerations

Sorting has been a subject of research for decades, and it is not difficult to find a reasonable recipe nowadays. What we expect, at a minimum, is that each of the Big Eight act this way:

- If physical records are large and ORDER BY columns are small, DBMSs will start by extracting the essential information, loading it into memory, then performing a "tag sort" which compares only the extracted snippets. This procedure makes it unnecessary to reread a whole physical record every time a comparison is performed. The DBMS may have to do large dynamic-memory allocations during the process.

- DBMSs will use one of the better algorithms, such as tournament sort. These algorithms often have a counter-intuitive flaw: If all the rows are already in order or nearly in order, it won't help much because the speed depends very little on the order of the input data, and very much on other factors.

All right, so what *does* affect sort speed? Here's the answer, in order of importance:

- Number of rows selected
- Number of columns in the ORDER BY clause
- Length of the columns in the ORDER BY clause

Figures 3–1, 3–2, and 3–3 show the effect, on sort speed, of increasing each of these variables.

Testing ORDER BY speed

To test a single factor X, it's necessary to keep all other factors equal while re-running SQL statements with different values of X. We tried. First we created a table containing CHAR columns. We populated the table using a randomizer that generated equal amounts of the letters A through G, with the result that some columns contained duplicate values or at least began with the same letters. Filler columns were added as needed to ensure that total row length was the same in all tests. Then we ran these three tests:

Test #1, result shown in Figure 3–1
Number of rows: Varying from 1,000 to 10,000
Number of columns: Fixed at one
Column length: Fixed at CHAR(10)
SQL statements: Fixed at one:

```
SELECT * FROM Table1 ORDER BY column1
```

Test #2, result shown in Figure 3–2

Number of rows: Fixed at 1,000
Number of columns: Varying from one to ten
Column length: Fixed at CHAR(10)
SQL statements: Varying from one to ten:

```
SELECT * FROM Table1 ORDER BY column1
SELECT * FROM Table1 ORDER BY column1, column2
SELECT * FROM Table1 ORDER BY column1, column2, column3
```

etc.

Test #3, result shown in Figure 3–3

Number of rows: Fixed at 1,000
Number of columns: Fixed at one
Column length: Varying from CHAR(1) to CHAR(10)
SQL statements: Fixed at one:

```
SELECT * FROM Table1 ORDER BY column1
```

The timing numbers shown in Figures 3–1, 3–2, and 3–3 are the result and are averages for the Big Eight. Tests were run on a single-processor machine using whatever memory the DBMS chose for its default configuration.

It's no surprise that an increase in the row count has a **geometric** effect—if you increase the number of rows by a factor of ten, the job takes about twenty times as long to complete. We had hoped for a better result. That's achievable by adding more processors and more memory, because DBMSs can sort groups of tags in parallel threads and will thresh less if all tags are in memory.

Surprisingly, an increase in the column count has a more drastic effect than an increase in the column length. Remember, total number of bytes was the same in both cases, so the effect is more than illusion. The likely explanation is that our DBMSs are using multipass algorithms, comparing only one column at a time.

The bottom line: Take drastic action to reduce row count—for example, by selecting only parts of a table at a time. Take severe action to reduce column count—for example, by concatenating two columns instead of specifying them separately. Take moderate action to reduce column length—for example, by using the SUBSTRING function. It's also slightly helpful if values are presorted and unique on the first few characters, but Christmas comes only one day a year.

We make several more statements about what happens with a sort in the following sections.

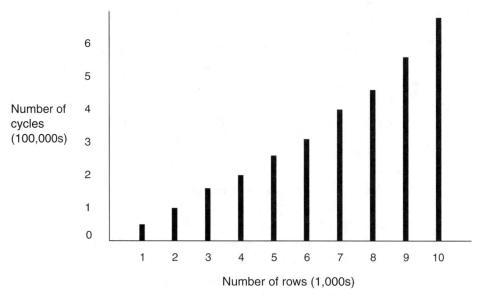

Figure 3–1   *Effect on sort speed of increasing row count; Test #1*

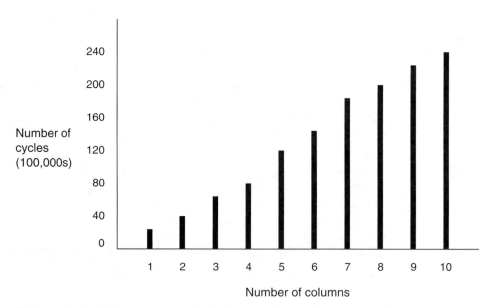

Figure 3–2   *Effect on sort speed of increasing column count; Test #2*

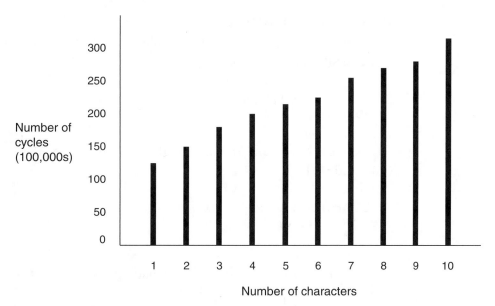

Figure 3–3 *Effect on sort speed of increasing column length; Test #3*

Partial duplicates slow sorts

Suppose you have a table with a CHAR column. Populate the column with data in which the first five characters are duplicates. Now SELECT:

```
SELECT column1 FROM Table1
  ORDER BY column1
```

Delete all rows and repopulate, this time with random data. SELECT again:

```
SELECT column1 FROM Table1
  ORDER BY column1
GAIN: 5/8
```

Skipping the duplicated characters made the sort faster for five DBMSs.

Presorting speeds sorts

Go back to your table with a CHAR column. Populate the column with random data and SELECT:

```
SELECT column1 FROM Table1
  ORDER BY column1
```

Delete all rows and repopulate, this time with data that's in alphabetic order and SELECT:

```
SELECT column1 FROM Table1
  ORDER BY column1
GAIN: 4/8
```

Having the rows already in order made the sort faster for half of the Big Eight.

It's the defined length that matters

Remember that a variable-length column has a defined length and an actual length. For example, a VARCHAR(30) column may contain ABC, in which case its defined length is 30 characters and its actual length is three characters. For sorting, it's the 30-character definition that matters! We tested this by varying the defined length of a VARCHAR column, while keeping the actual data length the same. The result was that Scenario #1 is slower than Scenario #2 even when the contents are the same in both cases:

```
Scenario #1:
CREATE TABLE Table1 (
   column1 VARCHAR(100))

SELECT column1 FROM Table1
  ORDER BY column1

Scenario #2:
CREATE TABLE Table2 (
   column1 VARCHAR(10))

SELECT column1 FROM Table2
  ORDER BY column1
GAIN: 6/8
```

> **Moral**   Defining VARCHAR columns with "room to grow" degrades sorts. The gain might seem surprising, but it's consistent with the way that most sort algorithms work: They allot a fixed memory buffer in advance, and the size of the buffer depends on the maximum anticipated key size.

INTEGERs beat SMALLINTs

On Windows machines, where an INTEGER requires 32 bits and a SMALLINT requires 16 bits, the tendency may be to think that SMALLINT sorting is faster than sorting INTEGER columns. But comparisons of integers are usually faster because 32 bits is your computer's word size and DBMSs are able to take advantage of the fact. So Scenario #1 is slower than Scenario #2:

```
Scenario #1:
CREATE TABLE Table1 (
   column1 SMALLINT)

SELECT column1 FROM Table1
  ORDER BY column1

Scenario #2:
CREATE TABLE Table2 (
   column1 INTEGER)

SELECT column1 FROM Table2
   ORDER BY column1
GAIN: 5/8
```

INTEGERs beat CHARs

We sorted a CHAR(4) column, then we sorted an INTEGER column, both with random data. The INTEGER sort was often faster, because a character string cannot be compared four bytes at a time—but this is done for an integer. Thus Scenario #1 is slower than Scenario #2:

```
Scenario #1:
CREATE TABLE Table1 (
   column1 CHAR(4))

SELECT column1 FROM Table1
  ORDER BY column1
```

```
Scenario #2:
CREATE TABLE Table2 (
   column1 INTEGER)

SELECT column1 FROM Table2
   ORDER BY column1
GAIN: 4/8
```

Sets beat multisets

Technically, a multiset differs from a set because it contains duplicates. Testing against two tables with the same number of rows, but with significant numbers of duplicates in the first table, we found, once again, that sorting is faster when there are no duplicates.

Conclusion

The fastest sort is an ascending sort of an integer with unique values, presorted.

The ORDER BY Clause

A simplified description of the SELECT ... ORDER BY syntax looks like this:

```
SELECT <column list>                       /* the select list */
   FROM <Table list>
   ORDER BY <column expression> [ASC | DESC] [,...]
```

This syntax has a new wrinkle. In SQL-92, you had to ORDER BY <column name>, and the column named had to be in the select list. In SQL:1999, you're allowed to ORDER BY <column expression>. For example, to sort numbers in backwards order, you've now got these two choices:

```
With New SQL:1999 Wrinkle:
SELECT numeric_column
   FROM Table1
   ORDER BY numeric_column * -1

Without New Wrinkle:
SELECT numeric_column, numeric_column * -1 AS num
   FROM Table1
   ORDER BY num
```

Two incidental remarks about this example:

- In theory, an SQL:1999 DBMS silently adds `numeric_column * -1` to the select list just before sorting and takes it out just after sorting.
- The result of `ORDER BY numeric_column * -1` can differ slightly from the result of `ORDER BY numeric_column DESC`. The difference, as usual, is caused by the presence of NULLs.

Table 3-1 shows the SQL Standard requirements and the level of support the Big Eight have for ORDER BY.

Notes on Table 3-1:

- Max Columns column

  Shows how many columns may be listed in the ORDER BY clause.

  :: For Sybase, our tests showed it was possible to sort up to 31 columns. This differs from Sybase's response to JDBC's `getMaxColumnsInOrder-By` call, which returns 16.

- Max Bytes column

  Shows the maximum allowed length, in bytes, of an ORDER BY clause.

  This column shows a significant number. If `column1` is defined as CHAR(500) and Max Bytes shows a value of "500" then ORDER BY

Table 3–1   *ANSI/DBMS ORDER BY Support*

	Max Columns	Max Bytes	NULLs Sort	Sort LOBs	ORDER BY Expression	COLLATE Clause
ANSI SQL	N/S	N/S	Low or High	No	Yes	Yes
IBM	500	253	High	No	Yes	No
Informix	>=1000	>=1000	Low	No	No	No
Ingres	300	>=1000	High	No	Yes	No
InterBase	254	254	At End	Yes	No	Yes
Microsoft	>=1000	>=1000	Low	No	Yes	Yes
MySQL	>=1000	>=1000	Low	Yes	Yes	No
Oracle	254	>=1000	High	No	Yes	Yes
Sybase	31	>=1000	Low	No	Yes	No

`column1, column2` is ineffective because `column2` doesn't get into the tag.

- NULLs Sort column

  Shows where the DBMS places NULLs in a sorted list. This column is "Low" if NULLs are considered less than all other values, "High" if NULLs are considered greater than all other values, and "At End" if the DBMS places NULLs at the end of a sorted list both when you `ORDER BY...ASC` and when you `ORDER BY...DESC`.

  :: For InterBase, our tests showed that NULLs sort At End. This differs from InterBase's response to (a) JDBC's `NullsAreSortedAtEnd` call, which returns `false` and (b) JDBC's `NullsAreSortedHigh` call, which returns `true`.

  :: For MySQL and Sybase, our tests showed that NULLs sort Low. In the first case, this differs from MySQL's response to (a) JDBC's `NullsAreSortedLow` call, which returns `false` and (b) JDBC's `NullsAreSortedAtStart` call, which returns `true`. In the second case, this differs from Sybase's response to (a) JDBC's `NullsAreSortedLow` call, which returns `false` and (b) JDBC's `NullsAreSortedHigh` call, which returns `true`.

  :: For Oracle, our tests showed that NULLs sort High. This differs from Oracle's response to (a) JDBC's `NullsAreSortedLow` call, which returns `true` and (b) JDBC's `NullsAreSortedHigh` call, which returns `false`.

- Sort LOBs column

  This column is "Yes" if the DBMS allows large object data (i.e., BLOB, CLOB, NCLOB, or the nonstandard SQL extensions TEXT, IMAGE, BINARY, GRAPHIC, etc.) to be sorted.

- ORDER BY Expression column

  Shows whether the DBMS allows ORDER BY to contain columns or expressions that are not in the select list. This column is "Yes" if the DBMS supports SQL:1999-style statements like either of these two:

  ```
  SELECT column1 FROM Table1 ORDER BY column2
  SELECT column1 FROM Table1 ORDER BY <function>(column1)
  ```

- COLLATE Clause column

  This column is "Yes" if the DBMS supports SQL Standard-style COLLATE clauses, or Oracle-style NLSSORT() function calls, or a CAST to a different character set with a different collation in ORDER BY, like this:

```
SELECT column1, column2 FROM Table1
  ORDER BY column1 COLLATE SQL_Latin1_General
```

For many DBMSs, NULLs sort Low—that is, NULLs are considered to be less than the smallest non-NULL value. For IBM, Ingres, and Oracle, NULLs sort High—that is, NULLs are considered to be greater than the largest non-NULL value. For InterBase and PostgreSQL, NULLs sort At the End—whether you're sorting in ascending or in descending order. That means the set of values {-1, +1, NULL} sorts four different ways depending on DBMS and depending on your sort order:

- {NULL, -1, +1}

  /* result after ORDER BY column1 for many DBMSs, including Informix, Microsoft, MySQL, and Sybase */

- {-1, +1, NULL}

  /* result after ORDER BY column1 for IBM, Ingres, InterBase, Oracle, PostgreSQL */

- {+1, -1, NULL}

  /* result after ORDER BY column1 DESC for Informix, InterBase, Microsoft, MySQL, PostgreSQL, and Sybase */

- {NULL, +1, -1}

  /* result after ORDER BY column1 DESC for IBM, Ingres, Oracle */

The result is that ORDER BY column1 * -1 and ORDER BY column1 DESC return different results (with NULL in a different spot) unless you use InterBase or PostgreSQL.

The use of expressions in ORDER BY is not 100% portable, but some useful expressions can help speed or clarity:

- ORDER BY LOWER(column1)

  Useful if case-insensitive sorting is unavailable.

- ORDER BY SUBSTRING(column1 FROM 1 FOR 6)

  Rough sorts are faster because tags are small.

- ORDER BY CAST(column1 AS CHAR...)

  Useful if column1's data type is not sortable.

Such functions would be unacceptable if the DBMS called them multiple times. However, the DBMS evaluates the sort-key value only once per input row, at the time it forms the tags. To make sure of this, we tested ORDER BY with a user-defined function that simply counted how many times the function was called. Six of the Big Eight called the function only once per row (GAIN: 6/6).

| **Portability** | Informix and InterBase don't allow expressions in ORDER BY. The gain shown is for only six DBMSs. |

To Sort or Not to Sort

"Do not use ORDER BY if the query has a DISTINCT or GROUP BY on the same set of terms, because they have the side effect of ordering rows."
—Kevin Kline et al., *Transact-SQL Programming,* O'Reilly & Associates

Sometimes there is a temptation to follow such advice and skip ORDER BY if it's certain that the rows are in order anyway. Our tests showed this about such assumptions:

- `SELECT column1 FROM Table1`

  is returned in order by `column1` if `Table1` is clustered and `column1` is the cluster key (see Chapter 9, "Indexes") or is otherwise preordered.

- `SELECT column1 FROM Table1 WHERE column1 > -32768`

  is returned in order by `column1` if `column1` is indexed (in ASC order) and the DBMS makes use of the index.

- `SELECT DISTINCT column1 FROM Table1`

  is returned in order by `column1` if `column1` is not unique.

If you add `ORDER BY column1` in any of these three cases, the SELECT is always slower (AVERAGE GAIN: 5/8 without ORDER BY). This suggests that DBMSs will not remove unnecessary ORDER BY clauses automatically. However, our tests also showed that the effect is unpredictable with more complex statements that contain any of the following: joins, unions, multiple columns in the select list, long columns, columns indexed with a descending index, or columns requiring secondary sorts (we'll talk about secondary sorts later in this chapter). Finally, we failed to find that any such side effect was documented in any vendor manual. So we urge caution.

The Bottom Line: General Sorts

The three variables that affect sort speed are, in order of importance:

- The number of rows you select
- The number of columns you put in the ORDER BY clause
- The defined length of the columns you put in the ORDER BY clause

An increase in the row count has a geometric effect on sort speed. If you multiply the number of rows by ten, the job takes twenty times as long. Take drastic action to reduce the number of rows you sort.

Take severe action to reduce the number of sorted columns.
Take moderate action to reduce the length of sorted columns.
The fastest sort is an ascending sort of a presorted integer with unique values.
Partial duplicates slow sorts.
Presorting speeds sorts.
It's the defined length that matters.

Some DBMSs sort NULL high. Some DBMSs sort NULL low. Some DBMSs sort NULL at the end of a list. Since there's no standard way of sorting NULL; don't write code that depends on the DBMS putting all the NULLs in a specific place.

The use of expressions in ORDER BY is not 100% portable. But using expressions like ORDER BY LOWER(column1), ORDER BY SUBSTRING(column1 FROM 1 FOR 6), and ORDER BY CAST(column1 AS CHAR...) can help speed or clarity.

```
SELECT column1 FROM Table1
```

returns a result set in order by column1 if Table1.column1 is clustered or otherwise preordered.

```
SELECT column1 FROM Table1 WHERE column1 > -32768
```

returns a result set in order by column1 if column1 is indexed and the DBMS makes use of the index.

```
SELECT DISTINCT column1 FROM Table1
```

returns a result set in order by column1 if column1 is not unique.

"Omit ORDER BY" is a popular tip, and it actually has an effect—but the effect is unreliable. This is fine if the ordering is for cosmetic purposes, or if the number of rows is tiny, but in other cases. . . . Judge the tip's merits for yourself.

Character Sorts

"Let justice be done, though the heavens fall."
—Attributed to an ancient Roman statesman

Sorts of character strings can be fast and wrong, or somewhat slower and less wrong, or much slower and 100 percent right. Three points along this continuum are labeled: **binary sort**, **dictionary sort**, and **dictionary sort with tie-breaking.** If it's a simple matter of knowing what's right and wrong, and knowing how much wrongness is tolerable, then you have some choice about which type of sort you want. Okay, maybe that's not simple. Yet we must try.

Binary sorts—also called *repertoire order sorts* or *codeset sorts* or (in IBM-speak) *sorts of bit data*—are merely sorts of the codes that are used to store the characters. For example, the Windows 1252 code page has this order:

- Control characters

- Some punctuation characters

- Digits

- Some more punctuation characters

- Uppercase letters

- More punctuation characters

- Lowercase letters

- Yet more punctuation characters and anything with accent marks

Since digits are in order 0 to 9 and letters are in order A to Z; code page 1252 is correct if the input is carefully controlled. Suppose you have a list of people's names. Can you ensure that (a) all names begin with a capital letter and contain only one capital letter, (b) accented names like Chrétien will be entered as Chrétien, and (c) the code page is not Unicode? Then use binary sort. Binary string comparisons are twice as fast as dictionary-order string comparisons on average, and that affects sort time (GAIN: 8/8).

Dictionary sorts are much closer to what a user would expect to see in an English dictionary. For example, the basic Sybase dictionary sort has this order:

- All punctuation, but each punctuation mark still has a different value. (Note that this is not the way real dictionaries work. They treat all punctuation the same, and multiple spaces map to one space.)

- Digits.

- Alphabet, with accented characters mapped to unaccented equivalents (for example 'ï' is treated like 'i').

Dictionary sorts require a conversion step before comparison, because no code page stores characters in the desired order. It's also fairly easy to add one additional step and say that lowercase characters shall map to uppercase equivalents, which makes for a variant called case-insensitive dictionary sorts. Basic

A Lilliputian Difficulty with Unicode

"Quinbus Flestrin . . . being afterwards commanded . . . to destroy and put to death not only all the Big-Endian Exiles, but likewise all the People of that Empire, who would not immediately forsake the Big-Endian Heresy. . . ."
—Jonathan Swift, *Gulliver's Travels*

Big-endian: A binary data transmission/storage format in which the most significant bit (or byte) comes first.
Little-endian: A binary data transmission/storage format in which the least significant bit (or byte) comes first.

A binary comparison is a byte-by-byte comparison. That's fine as long as one character equals one byte. But in Unicode, one character equals two bytes, or more. Take the Turkish character i, whose Unicode representation is 0130 hexadecimal. If storage is big-endian, it looks like this:

```
01 30
```

That's still fine, but if storage is little-endian, it looks like this:

```
30 01
```

And that's not fine—this letter will incorrectly sort in front of A (Unicode 0041 hexadecimal)!

dictionary sorts are a middle ground, reasonably right but with some compromises for the sake of speed.

Now suppose we *refuse* to compromise. Let's say we've gathered a list of nouns, and proper nouns have a capital letter. The list contains words that are the same except for capitalization and accents, such as smith/Smith and naive/naïve. How can we sort this list? Before we start, we must know about two gotchas:

- Although we want words with accents to follow words without accents, we want to find them either way. That is, the search condition WHERE word = 'naive' should return both 'naive' and 'naïve' since—for search purposes—these are two variant ways to represent the same word; they are not DISTINCT.

- Although we want words with lowercase letters to follow words with uppercase letters, we don't want 'smith' to follow 'Soho'. Correct order would be:

```
Smith
smith
Soho
```

For both these reasons, the following rules about accents and capitals can apply *only when the unaccented and uncapitalized forms are equal.* That's why the uncompromising sort method is called a dictionary sort "with tiebreaking." There can be up to three passes in this type of sort:

- Primary sort

  The primary sort orders by the letters as mapped to some canonical form—for example, A comes before B comes before C and so on.

- Secondary sort

  The secondary sort looks for accent distinction if primary sort values are equal.

- Tertiary sort

  The tertiary sort looks for case distinction if primary and secondary sort values are equal.

A dictionary sort without tiebreaking is the same thing as a primary sort alone.

Indexes Too

Column definitions will affect sorting for ORDER BY, but also sorting for indexes. Watch out for two implications:

Implication #!:

If column1 has a dictionary-order sort, it won't merely mean that ORDER BY column1 is slower; it also means that all index updates are slower (GAIN: 8/8 if binary sort is used instead of dictionary sort).

Implication #2:

Because indexes exist mainly to support WHERE rather than ORDER BY, keys in indexes don't need to be secondary-sorted. They are in order by primary sort and by ROWID.

Character Sort Support

For a reality check, take a look at Table 3–2, which shows the DBMSs that support the principal modes of character ordering.

Notes on Table 3–2:

- In all columns, "Yes" means the DBMS supports the feature. An asterisk following ("Yes*") means the DBMS treats the feature as the default. We call an option supported if there is any way at all to specify it in either the column definition or the SELECT statement. However, the column is

Table 3–2 *DBMS Support for Character Sorts*

	Case Sensitive	Nonaccent Preferred (Secondary)	Uppercase Preferred (Tertiary)	Optional Dictionary Sort	Optional Binary Sort
IBM	Yes*	No	No	No	Yes*
Informix	Yes*	No	No	No	Yes*
Ingres	Yes*	No	No	Yes*	No
InterBase	Yes*	No	No	Yes	Yes*
Microsoft	No*	Yes	Yes	Yes*	Yes
MySQL	No*	No	No	Yes*	Yes
Oracle	Yes*	Yes	Yes	Yes	Yes*
Sybase	Yes*	Yes	Yes	No	Yes*

"No" if the only way to specify the feature is by reinstalling the DBMS or rebuilding the database. For example, for Sybase we say "Yes*" under binary sort, but nowhere else, because Sybase's excellent character-sort support is presented only as an installation option that cannot be changed. Table 3–2 applies only for English, with an 8-bit character set.

- Case-Sensitive column

  Are string comparisons case sensitive? That is, are SMITH and smith equal or are they unequal strings?

- Nonaccent Preferred (Secondary) column

  If all other characters are equal, does the DBMS sort nonaccented characters before accented characters? That is, does naive come before naïve?

- Uppercase Preferred (Tertiary) column

  If all other characters are equal, does the DBMS sort uppercase letters before lowercase letters? That is, does Naïve come before naïve?

- Optional Dictionary Sort column

  This column is "Yes" if the DBMS can do a dictionary sort at runtime.

  :: IBM and Ingres do a dictionary sort on CHAR columns by default.

  :: Informix does a dictionary sort on NCHAR columns if you install with the EN_GB.8859-1 db_locale.

  :: InterBase supports the SQL Standard COLLATE clause, which lets you specify various collations at runtime.

  :: Microsoft does a dictionary sort on CHAR columns by default and supports the SQL Standard COLLATE clause, which lets you specify various collations at runtime.

  :: MySQL does a dictionary sort on all character and TEXT columns by default.

  :: Oracle provides an NLSSORT function, which lets you specify various collations at runtime.

  :: Sybase has an installation option that causes the DBMS to do a dictionary sort on all character columns. If this option is chosen, Sybase won't do binary sorts.

- Optional Binary Sort column

  This column is "Yes" if the DBMS can do a binary sort at runtime.

:: IBM supports a FOR BIT DATA attribute for character columns. CHAR() FOR BIT DATA columns are sorted with a binary sort by default.

:: Informix does a binary sort on CHAR columns by default.

:: Ingres has an installation option that lets you set up a collation to do a binary sort on all character columns. If this option is chosen, Ingres won't do dictionary sorts.

:: InterBase does a binary sort on NCHAR columns by default and supports the SQL Standard COLLATE clause, which lets you specify various collations at runtime.

:: Microsoft supports the SQL Standard COLLATE clause, which lets you specify various collations at runtime.

:: MySQL does a binary sort on BLOB columns by default and also supports a BINARY attribute for character columns. CHAR() BINARY columns are sorted with a binary sort by default.

:: Oracle does a binary sort on CHAR columns by default.

:: Sybase does a binary sort on all character columns by default. If the default isn't changed during installation, Sybase won't do dictionary sorts.

Table 3-2 shows that support for character sorts is sometimes weak. Let's see what we can do about that.

Collations

Another way to measure DBMS support of ORDER BY is to look at collations. A **collation,** or **collating sequence,** is a set of rules that determines the result when character strings are compared. In standard SQL, the default collation for a character set is the collation that will normally be used to compare and sort strings—but you can override this by adding an explicit COLLATE clause either to a column definition or to an ORDER BY clause. For example, suppose your DBMS provides a collation called German, which handles strings according to the rules of German rather than English. If you will always want the values of a character column to be collated with the German collation, you can define the column to have German as its default collation to enforce this:

```
CREATE TABLE Table1 (
  german_column VARCHAR(10) COLLATE German,
  ... )
```

On the other hand, if you'll only want the column's strings to be handled as German strings occasionally, you can define the column in the usual manner and just use the COLLATE clause in ORDER BY when necessary:

```
CREATE TABLE Table1 (
   german_column VARCHAR(10),
   ... )

SELECT * FROM Table1
    ORDER BY german_column COLLATE German
```

In this example, collation German is an object in the catalog, but ultimately the collation depends on vendor support.

It's good to have a choice of collations for supporting rules that apply outside North American English. The Big Eight don't provide consistent support for collation syntax; however, we can observe common threads.

- IBM

  Makes two principal collations available: a dictionary sort and a binary sort. IBM does dictionary-order string comparisons using the default character set (IBM-1252) for all character columns unless the FOR BIT DATA attribute is specified.

- Informix

  Makes two principal collations available. The main collation is associated with CHAR/VARCHAR; the optional collation is associated with NCHAR/NCHAR VARYING. It's possible to change a CHAR's collation at runtime with:

  ```
  ... ORDER BY CAST(char_column AS NCHAR...)
  ```

  Incidentally, it's also possible to use CAST to cast to the same character set you started with, as an alternative to the TRIM function.

- Ingres and Sybase

  Provide no ability to change a character column's collation at runtime.

- InterBase and Microsoft

  Support the SQL Standard COLLATE clause, with several collations available for each character set supported. Microsoft uses the Windows locale-specific API functions to support choices and thus offers excellent collation support.

- MySQL

  Makes two principal collations available: a dictionary sort and a binary sort. MySQL does dictionary-order string comparisons using the default character set (ISO-8859-1 Latin1) for all character columns other than BLOB, unless the BINARY attribute is specified.

- Oracle

  Provides excellent collation support by allowing you to specify collations with the Oracle-specific scalar function:

  ```
  ... NLSSORT(<string>,'NLS_SORT=<collation name>')
  ```

In most cases, the support for secondary and tertiary sorting is weaker than in English. (Microsoft and Oracle are the exceptions.) For example, IBM, Ingres, and MySQL do not put the German "Sharp S" character (ß) in the right place. (Neither do InterBase and Oracle unless you specify the German collation; neither does Informix unless you specify db_locale EN_GB.8859-1.) And in all cases, the use of a non-English collation leads to a slowdown unless your list is very small. That's not attributable to bias, mind—it's just a fact that the English alphabetization rules are simpler.

Table 3–3 shows the built-in collations supported by the Big Eight. As usual, we're showing only those options that come with the DBMS as regularly installed and are therefore always available. Built-in collations are better because the optimizer knows about them.

Collations Shouldn't Depend on Character Sets

DBMSs tend to promote the idea that a given collation can only apply to a single character set. This idea is based on the mistaken belief that characters cannot be compared with each other if they come from different sets.

How is this belief mistaken? Well, we've all heard of "the set of even numbers" and "the set of odd numbers," and everyone knows that they are distinct sets—they have *no* members in common. However, everyone *also* knows that the expression "3 > 2" is undoubtedly true. It's possible to perform odd and even number comparisons using the rules for "the set of integers" since the even and odd sets are subsets of the set of integers.

The same applies for character sets. All character sets are subsets of The One Big Character Set, which in standard SQL is called SQL_TEXT. In practice, SQL_TEXT is usually Unicode.

Table 3–3 *DBMS Support for Built-in Collations (West European)*

	Spanish I	Spanish II	German I	German II	Danish/ Norwegian	Swedish/ Finnish	Icelandic	Irish
IBM	No	Yes	No	No	No	No	No	No
Informix	No	No	No	No	No	No	No	No
Ingres	No	No	No	No	No	No	No	No
InterBase	Yes	No	Yes	No	Yes	Yes*	Yes	No
Microsoft	Yes	Yes	Yes	Yes	Yes	Yes	Yes	No
MySQL	No	No	No	No	No	Yes*	No	No
Oracle	Yes	Yes	Yes	Yes	Yes*	Yes	Yes	No
Sybase	No	No	Yes	No	No	No	No	No

Notes on Table 3–3:

- In all columns, "Yes" means the DBMS provides full and correct support for the collation, "Yes*" means the DBMS's support for the collation has a flawed primary sort, and "No" means there is no support at all for the collation.

- Spanish I and Spanish II columns

  Spanish I or "Traditional Spanish" treats CH and LL as separate letters, but Spanish II or "Modern Spanish" does not. Currently, some Latin American phone books still use Spanish I, but the latest Castilian dictionaries use Spanish II. Ñ is a separate letter in both.

- German I and German II columns

  German I treats ä, ö, and ü as if they're a, o, and u, but German II treats them as ae, oe, and ue. German I is for lists of words; German II is for lists of names. For that reason, the two collations are sometimes called "German dictionary order" and "German phone book order," respectively.

- Danish/Norwegian and Swedish/Finnish columns

  Danish/Norwegian and Swedish/Finnish collations differ at the primary level. If you see a collation labeled "Nordic" or "Scandinavian," it is inadequate.

:: InterBase's and MySQL's support for Swedish/Finnish shows a flawed primary sort. V and W should not be differentiated, but both DBMSs treat them as separate letters.[1]

:: Oracle's support for Danish/Norwegian shows a flawed primary sort. Aa should sort with Å after Z. Instead, Oracle puts Aa at the beginning of a list.

- Icelandic column

The Icelandic alphabet contains two characters more than the other Nordic alphabets.

- Irish column

Folk in Ireland are generally happy with the English collation, but Irish phone books have a quirk. Names that begin with M' or Mc or Mac come before all other names that begin with M. This convention was once the habit of North American phone books too, but the habit appears to be fading.

The Bottom Line: Character Sorts

Sorts of character strings can be fast and wrong, or somewhat slower and less wrong, or much slower and 100 percent right. Decide how much wrongness is tolerable in a specific situation, because you do have some choice about which type of sort you end up with.

Binary sorts are sorts of the codes that are used to store the characters. Binary sorts are fast but are prone to error unless your input is carefully controlled.

Dictionary sorts give you a result that is very close to what you'd see in an English list, which is no good if you're sorting non-English words. They're slower than binary sorts—they require a conversion step before comparison—so are a middle ground, reasonably right but with some compromises for the sake of speed.

---

1. A personal experience—We presented a paper on "Finnish Collation" at the Helsinki Business Polytechnic in March 2002. During the presentation, we polled our Finnish audience on the question, Should V = W in a Finnish primary sort? Ninety-five percent of the respondents voted "Yes." But on the same day, we found that the Helsinki telephone book ignores this rule; it has separate sections for names beginning with V and with W.

A dictionary sort with tiebreaking is the slowest—but also the most accurate—sort. These sorts take up to three passes to come up with a properly sorted list.

One way to force the right kind of sort is to specify a specific collation for the ORDER BY clause. Other options are declaring a column with a binary sort attribute, such as FOR BIT DATA with IBM and BINARY with MySQL. If all else fails, define your column as a binary string column—for example, with Sybase:

```
CREATE TABLE Table1 (
  column1 BINARY(10),
  ...)
```

Other Options

Leaving off the ORDER BY clause and forcing the type of sort you want to use (usually via a collation) are two methods you can use to speed up sorts, but each involves depending on features that may not be supported by the DBMS. Let's look at three things you can do that don't involve DBMS vagaries: sort keys, encouraging index use, and preordering.

Sort Keys

If you need secondary sorts or exotic collations, the speed goes down, and the DBMS support gets dicey. Both these problems are solvable—just add a column that contains a sort key to the table.

A **sort key** is a string with a series of one-byte numbers that represent the relative ordering of characters. The string has three parts: the primary number, the secondary number, and the tertiary number. Parts are separated by 01 hexadecimal. For example, the sort keys for 'naive' and 'Naïve' look like this:

	Character Weights Primary	Diacritic Weights Secondary	Case Weights Tertiary
naive	0E 70 0E 02 0E 32 0E A2 0E 21 01	01	01 01
Naïve	0E 70 0E 02 0E 32 0E A2 0E 21 01	02 02 13 01	12 01 01

Notice that:

• The primary parts of the two sort keys are the same.

- The secondary parts are different to reflect that ı and ï have different weights.
- The tertiary parts are different to reflect that n and N have different weights.

The MS Windows NT API has a function for converting a character string to a sort key. The function's name is LCMapString. The LCMapString input string can be in any of the character sets supported by Windows NT, and the function's output sort key has appropriate weights for the locale, which are roughly adequate for most common languages. Listing 3–1 shows a simplified version of a program for populating a table with sort keys.

Listing 3–1 *Populating a Table with Sort Keys*
```
locale_id = an ID representing country/collation/etc.
...
DECLARE Cursor1 CURSOR FOR
   SELECT character_column FROM Table1;

OPEN Cursor1;

for (;;) {
  FETCH Cursor1 INTO :character_string;
  if (NO_DATA_FOUND) break;
  LCMapString(locale_id, character_string, sort_key);

  UPDATE Table1 SET
      sort_key_column = :sort_key
      WHERE CURRENT OF Cursor1;
  }
...
```

Note that, for the code in Listing 3–1 to work, you must define sort_key_column as a character column with a default sort type of "binary sort." Since it's binary, it works as quickly as any binary sort, which is to say, more quickly than a dictionary sort. Once you've populated a table with sort keys, you can use this SQL statement to get a sorted list:

```
SELECT * FROM Table1
   ORDER BY sort_key_column
GAIN: 8/8
```

Encouraging Index Use

People often associate sorting with indexing. Partly that's because at one time sorting *was* indexing—dBASE II seems to have performed sorts by creating indexes. Nowadays, sorting is a separate activity, and only transient associations exist between the two. (For example, the DBMS may perform a sort while processing a CREATE INDEX statement.)

If the DBMS uses an index on `column1`, the natural result is that the rows will come out in order by `column1`. So it's tempting to replace this SQL statement:

```
SELECT * FROM Table1
    ORDER BY column1
```

with this one:

```
SELECT * FROM Table1
    WHERE column1 >= ''
    ORDER BY column1
GAIN: 5/8
```

The idea here is that ORDER BY works a bit faster if some preordering occurs before the sort. And, in fact, a gain occurs when the WHERE clause is used. There are, however, three things to note about this trick:

- You still can't omit the ORDER BY clause because there is no guarantee that the DBMS will use the index.

- The WHERE clause eliminates NULL values—not necessarily the result you want.

- In Oracle, there is no such thing as a truly descending index (the keyword DESC is allowed but ignored), so you can use this idea only for ascending sorts.

There is a variation on the trick, though. Suppose you have a compound index on (`column1, column2`). You want to *retrieve* by `column2`, but *sort* by `column1`. Here's how:

```
SELECT column1, column2 FROM Table1
    WHERE column1 > 0
      AND column2 = <result you want>
    ORDER BY column1
```

As we saw in Chapter 2, "Simple Searches," this is called using a redundant expression. It works particularly well if the DBMS chooses to use the index on (`column1, column2`) as a covering index (discussed in Chapter 9, "Indexes").

A second variation on the trick works if your DBMS supports clustered indexes. In that case, you can sort the columns of a table's cluster key in a way that supports your favorite ORDER BY option. When a **clustered index** exists, the rows are in order by the cluster key—this is guaranteed.

This is not to say that you should try to force the DBMS to use an index merely because it helps with ORDER BY. The DBMS can choose another path. Exceptionally, you might want to override the DBMS's path choice if your main interest is to get the first rows onto the user screen as quickly as possible. Microsoft specially allows for that possibility with its FIRSTFASTROW hint. This is particularly important if you want to limit the number of rows.

A question can arise whether you should change your ORDER BY clause to suit existing indexes or make new indexes to support your ORDER BY plans. In both cases, we would have to say "No." If you did either one, you'd be crossing the boundary between "taking advantage of a side effect" and "depending on a side effect." Anyway, recall from the discussion of secondary sorts earlier in this chapter, that a column's index keys may not be in the same order that you will need when you sort the column.

DBMSs can use compound indexes. For example:

```
SELECT column1, column2
  FROM Table1
  ORDER BY column1
```

will be faster if a compound index—(`column1, column2`)—is on `Table1` (GAIN: 5/8 with compound index).

DBMSs can misuse noncompound indexes. For example:

```
SELECT column1, column2
  FROM Table1
  ORDER BY column1, column2
```

will be slower if a noncompound index—(`column1`)—is on `Table1` (GAIN: -3/8). To improve the sort speed, remove the index entirely or replace it with a compound index (GAIN: 3/8).

Preordering

We have touched a few times on the point that ORDER BY goes more quickly if the incoming data is presorted—but not a lot more quickly, so this section involves ideas that pay off in only a minority of cases.

The obvious ways to preorder by `column1` are either (a) declare that `column1` is the clustered index key, or (b) export in sorted order and reimport. The primary advantage here is that fewer disk seeks should occur when the fetch direction is always forward. A further gain could occur if you split the sorted table into two, since some DBMSs can perform sorts in parallel if they're on two separate tables.

The less obvious way to preorder is to add a "rough key" column to the table. The procedure to form rough keys is analogous to the one we showed you for sort keys in Listing 3–1. The difference is that the rough key must be a single integer that contains only some primary-sort information for the first few characters of a column. If you decide to use this idea, keep this tip in mind: A 32-bit integer can store up to five uppercase Latin characters, given six bits per character.

Is the second of these two statements really faster than the first?

```
SELECT * FROM Table1
    ORDER BY real_column

SELECT * FROM Table1
    ORDER BY rough_key, real_column
GAIN: 5/8
```

The answer is definitely "Yes" if duplication of column values is rare. Is the saved time worth the trouble of making the rough key column? The answer is "Maybe yes" if absolutely every SELECT on the table has an ORDER BY `real_column` clause tacked on to it.

The Bottom Line: Other Options

Secondary sorts and exotic collations are not universally supported. They also make sorts slower. The solution is to add a column containing a sort key to the table and use that in your ORDER BY clauses.

A sort key is a string with a series of one-byte numbers that represent the relative ordering of characters. You can use the MS Windows NT API function `LCMapString` to convert a character string to a sort key.

A sort key column should be a CHAR column with a default binary sort.

ORDER BY works faster if some preordering occurs before the sort. Encourage preordering by using indexes, especially primary key and clustered indexes. One way to encourage the DBMS to use an index is to add redundant expressions to your queries.

Another way to preorder is to add a rough key column to the table. Rough keys are analogous to sort keys except that rough keys are defined as a single integer that contains only some primary-sort information for the first few characters of a column.

Parting Shots

The fastest sorts are the ones that do the least. If you can tolerate wrong answers, you can get higher throughput. That's a general maxim, which we'll be repeating in other contexts (for example, see Chapter 15, "Locks"). You can compensate for deficiencies that your DBMS may have and it is sometimes possible to use the side effects of other clauses to ease ORDER BY's job. So sorts don't have to be a worrisome thing.

4

GROUP BY

Because GROUP BY can involve a sort, much of what we said about ORDER BY columns in the previous chapter applies for GROUP BY arguments too—keep 'em short and keep few of 'em. Beyond that, you should watch out for some other things when you write a grouping query. In this chapter, we'll look at optimizing GROUP BY and its related HAVING clause, as well as the SQL Standard set functions.

Refresher

The GROUP BY clause can explicitly appear in a SELECT statement, as in this example:

```
SELECT column1 FROM Table1
  GROUP BY column1
```

Grouping also happens implicitly if there is a HAVING clause or a set function, as in this example:

```
SELECT COUNT(*) FROM Table1
  HAVING COUNT(*) = 5
```

In standard SQL—and with InterBase and Microsoft—a GROUP BY column may be followed by a COLLATE clause:

```
SELECT column1 FROM Table1
  GROUP BY column1,
           column2 COLLATE SQL_Latin1_General
```

In a nonstandard SQL extension supported by Ingres, Microsoft, MySQL, Oracle, and Sybase, a GROUP BY column may contain an expression:

```
SELECT LOWER(column1) FROM Table1
  GROUP BY LOWER(column1)
```

And in ANSI SQL:1999, IBM, Microsoft, and Oracle, a GROUP BY clause may contain CUBE or ROLLUP to indicate another level of grouping, like this:

```
SELECT column1, column2 FROM Table1
  GROUP BY CUBE (column1, column2)
```

The SQL Standard says that the correct name for an **aggregate function** is "**set function**," and the required set functions are AVG, COUNT, MAX, MIN, and SUM. In contrast, DBMS vendors prefer the term "aggregate function," and some provide extra built-in functions—for example, for standard deviation (STDEV) and/or variance (VAR)—in addition to the standard set functions. Some DBMSs also allow users to create their own aggregate functions. For example:

```
SELECT AVG(column1), STDEV(column1), UDF1(column1)
  FROM Table1
  WHERE column1 > 55
  GROUP BY column1
  ORDER BY column1
```

Most of the features we've mentioned are supported by most DBMSs. Table 4-1 shows the SQL Standard requirements and the level of support the Big Eight have for GROUP BY.

Table 4–1 *ANSI/DBMS GROUP BY Support*

	Basic GROUP BY	Expressions	CREATE VIEW	COLLATE Clause	CUBE/ ROLLUP	Max Columns	Max Bytes
ANSI SQL	Yes	No	Yes	Yes	Yes	N/S	N/S
IBM	Yes	No	Yes	No	Yes	>=20	254
Informix	Yes	No	Yes	No	Yes	>=20	>=2000
Ingres	Yes	Yes	Yes	No	No	>=20	>=2000
InterBase	Yes	No	No	Yes	No	>=20	>=2000
Microsoft	Yes	Yes	Yes	Yes	Yes	>=20	>=2000
MySQL	Yes	Yes	No	No	No	>=20	>=2000
Oracle	Yes	Yes	Yes	No	Yes	>=20	1969
Sybase	Yes	Yes	Yes	No	No	>=20	>=2000

Notes on Table 4-1:

- Basic GROUP BY column

  This column is "Yes" if the DBMS supports basic GROUP BY syntax like:

  ```
  SELECT column1, MIN(column2) FROM Table1
    GROUP BY column1
  ```

- Expressions column

  This column is "Yes" if the DBMS supports expressions in GROUP BY, like this:

  ```
  SELECT UPPER(column1) FROM Table1
    GROUP BY UPPER(column1)
  ```

- CREATE VIEW column

  This column is "Yes" if the DBMS lets you put GROUP BY in a CREATE VIEW statement, like this:

  ```
  CREATE VIEW View1 AS
    SELECT column1, COUNT(column1) FROM Table1
      GROUP BY column1
  ```

- COLLATE Clause column

  This column is "Yes" if the DBMS supports ANSI SQL-style COLLATE clauses, or Oracle-style NLSSORT() function calls, or a CAST to a different character set with a different collation in GROUP BY, like this:

```
SELECT column1, MIN(column2) FROM Table1
  GROUP BY column1 COLLATE SQL_Latin1_General
```

- CUBE/ROLLUP column

  This column is "Yes" if the DBMS supports CUBE and ROLLUP for summarizing, like this:

```
SELECT column1, column2 FROM Table1
  GROUP BY CUBE (column1, column2)
```

- Max Columns column

  Shows how many columns may be listed in the GROUP BY clause.

  For Sybase, our tests showed it was possible to group at least 20 columns. This differs from Sybase's response to JDBC's getMaxColumnsIn-GroupBy call, which returns 16.

- Max Bytes column

  Shows the maximum allowed length, in bytes, of grouped values.

Optimal GROUP BY Clauses

We've already mentioned that GROUP BY performs better if you keep the number of grouping columns small. One way you can do so is to avoid grouping redundant columns, as in this example:

```
SELECT secondary_key_column, primary_key_column, COUNT(*)
  FROM Table1
  GROUP BY secondary_key_column, primary_key_column
```

Because primary key columns are unique and may not contain NULL by definition, the mention of secondary_key_column in this example is redundant. The problem is that if you take secondary_key_column out of the GROUP BY clause, you'll get an error message. All DBMSs except MySQL and Sybase will tell you that you can't have secondary_key_column in the select list if it's not also in the GROUP BY list. This is how to write a query that's legal and that's faster:

```
SELECT MIN(secondary_key_column), primary_key_column, COUNT(*)
  FROM Table1
  GROUP BY primary_key_column
GAIN: 4/7
```

WARNING	Don't do this for Ingres; it shows a loss. The gain shown is for only seven DBMSs.

Here are two ways to speed up GROUP BY when you're joining tables.

Reduce before you expand

GROUP BY tends to reduce row counts, and JOIN tends to expand row counts. Because a DBMS must evaluate FROM and WHERE clauses before GROUP BY clauses, this tip is not easy to put into practice, but there is a way. You can make a join happen late by replacing it with a **set operator**. (The SQL Standard set operators are UNION, EXCEPT, and INTERSECT.) For example, replace Statement #1 with Statement #2:

```
Statement #1:
SELECT SUM(Table1.column2), SUM(Table2.column2)
  FROM Table1 INNER JOIN Table2
       ON Table1.column1 = Table2.column1
  GROUP BY Table1.column1

Statement #2:
SELECT column1, SUM(column2), 0
  FROM Table1
  GROUP BY column1
INTERSECT
SELECT column1, 0, SUM(column2)
  FROM Table2
  GROUP BY column1
GAIN: 2/2
```

Portability	Informix, Ingres, InterBase, Microsoft, MySQL, and Sybase don't support INTERSECT. The gain shown is for only two DBMSs.

GROUP on the same table

When you're grouping joined tables, the GROUP BY column should be from the same table as the column(s) on which you're applying a set function. We're passing this advice along because some vendors think it's important enough to mention in their documentation.

Also to do with joins and GROUP BY, you can improve performance by avoiding joins altogether. Consider this SELECT:

```
SELECT COUNT(*) FROM Table1, Table2
   WHERE Table1.column1 = Table2.column1
```

If `Table1.column1` is unique, you could replace the join with a subquery. Transform the SELECT to:

```
SELECT COUNT(*) FROM Table2
  WHERE Table2.column1 IN
    (SELECT Table1.column1 FROM Table1)
GAIN: 4/6
```

WARNING   Don't do this for Oracle; it shows a loss. The gain shown is for only six DBMSs (see Portability note).

Portability   MySQL doesn't support subqueries. The gain shown is for only six DBMSs.

HAVING

Most DBMSs do not merge WHERE and HAVING clauses. This means the following statements are logically the same but won't run at the same speed:

```
Query with WHERE and HAVING:
SELECT column1 FROM Table1
  WHERE column2 = 5
  GROUP BY column1
    HAVING column1 > 6
```

```
Query with WHERE only:
SELECT column1 FROM Table1
  WHERE column2 = 5
    AND column1 > 6
  GROUP BY column1
GAIN: 3/8
```

The "Query with WHERE only" runs faster on three of the Big Eight. You should use this type of query except in the rare cases where you need to defer the filtering implied by column1 > 6—for example, if the comparison is hard to evaluate.

Alternatives to GROUP BY

If you're writing a query that doesn't involve set functions, you can use DISTINCT as an alternative to GROUP BY. DISTINCT has three advantages: It's simpler, it's legal to use in expressions, and—with some DBMSs—it's faster. So instead of using Query #1, use the alternative Query #2:

```
Query #1:
SELECT column1
    FROM Table1
    GROUP BY column1

Query #2:
SELECT DISTINCT column1
    FROM Table1
GAIN: 4/8
```

The Bottom Line: Optimal GROUP BY Clauses

GROUP BY performs better if you keep the number of grouping columns small.

Avoid grouping redundant columns by using set functions.

When you're grouping joined tables, reduce before you expand. You can make a join happen late by replacing it with a set operator.

When you're grouping joined tables, the GROUP BY column should be from the same table as the column(s) on which you're applying a set function.

You can improve performance on some grouped joins by replacing the join with a subquery.

Most DBMSs do not merge WHERE and HAVING clauses. Write your queries with only a WHERE clause wherever possible.

Use DISTINCT instead of GROUP BY if your query doesn't involve set functions.

Sorting

Suppose you have an unsorted list and a sorted list, as shown in Table 4-2.

Consider 'Belgrade' in Table 4-2's unsorted list. How does the DBMS know if there is a duplicate? Answer: The DBMS must compare 'Belgrade' with both 'Sofia' and 'Budapest' because it can't be sure about duplicates until all the entries in the list have been checked.

Now consider the same question for 'Belgrade' in Table 4-2's sorted list. This time the answer is that the DBMS must compare 'Belgrade' with 'Budapest' alone—as soon as it has compared [n] to [n + 1], the DBMS is done. This means that grouping is fast if the list is sorted. A good strategy, then, is to sort the list for grouping purposes.

Another good strategy is to make a hash list so that equality can be determined with a single hash lookup. We looked at grouped output from the Big Eight and saw that seven of them returned the results in sorted order—a clear indication that they used sorts for grouping. The eighth DBMS—Informix—used hashing.

Because most DBMSs do sort before grouping, you can help the process by listing GROUP BY and ORDER BY columns in the same order. For example, don't write your query like this:

```
SELECT * FROM Table1
  GROUP BY column1, column2
  ORDER BY column1
```

Table 4-2 *Two Lists, Unsorted and Sorted*

Unsorted List	Sorted List
Belgrade	Belgrade
Sofia	Budapest
Budapest	Sofia

Write it like this instead:

```
SELECT * FROM Table1
  GROUP BY column1, column2
  ORDER BY column1, column2
GAIN: 2/7
```

WARNING   Don't do this for Informix; it shows a loss. The gain shown is for only seven DBMSs.

Indexes

Given that it helps GROUP BY to work on a sorted list, let's consider whether it's advantageous to have the list sorted in advance. In other words, let's consider indexes.

Most DBMSs will use indexes for grouping, but the GROUP BY clause has a lower priority than JOIN or WHERE clauses. For example, this SQL statement does *not* use an index to speed up the GROUP BY clause:

```
SELECT column1 FROM Table1
  WHERE column2 = 55
  GROUP BY column1
```

The reason no index is used should be clear: The DBMS must process the WHERE clause first, and it does so via an index on column2. But after the DBMS has done that, there is no point in looking at the index on column1 because the column1 index is on the whole table—not on the filtered result of the WHERE clause. Because of this, indexes are useful only for very simple grouping. Luckily, a significant number of SQL statements are that simple, so DBMSs have introduced optimizations for the following cases.

GROUP BY alone

GROUP BY itself will use an index if the grouping columns appear in the same order as the index columns. Indexes with DESC columns won't be useful. For example, this SELECT is faster if column1 is indexed:

```
SELECT column1 FROM Table1
  GROUP BY column1
GAIN: 4/8 if column1 indexed
```

MIN/MAX functions

A MIN or MAX function will use an index if the function is alone in the select list and there is nothing after the FROM clause. If there's an index, MIN() can work by getting the first value in the index, and MAX() can work by getting the last value in the index (or by getting the first value in a descending index, in the case of IBM). For example, DBMSs work very quickly with:

```
SELECT MIN(column1) FROM Table1
GAIN: 6/8 if column1 indexed
```

Alas, this statement is much harder and slower:

```
SELECT MIN(column1), MAX(column1)
   FROM Table1
```

For queries like this, it's better either to split the statement in two with UNION or use two separate SELECTs, like this:

```
SELECT MIN(column1) FROM Table1

SELECT MAX(column1) FROM Table1
GAIN: 8/8
```

COUNT functions

A COUNT function will use an index if only one column (or *) is referenced in the query and no clauses follow the FROM clause, for example:

```
SELECT COUNT(*) FROM Table1
GAIN: 2/8 if indexed
```

On average the gain is around 2/8. (Recall that this doesn't mean that DBMSs are 2/8 faster; it means that two of the Big Eight are faster, and the rest show no change.) One of the DBMSs that shows no change for this example is Oracle. The lack of a gain is because Oracle indexes don't include NULLs. Thus, for any query whose results might differ if NULLs are present, Oracle can't use an index. This is one of the prices that Oracle pays in return for smaller indexes and faster updates. It can help if you specify that all your grouping columns are NOT NULL. In theory, it would also help if you use COUNT(column) instead of COUNT(*) because COUNT(*) includes NULLs—but in practice it won't help, because COUNT(*) has a special optimization of its own, which we'll look at later in this chapter. (By the way, COUNT(*) usually works far better if you've updated statistics recently.)

SUM/AVG functions

A SUM or AVG function will use an index if you make sure that only one column is referenced in the query and that the column is indexed, as in this example:

```
SELECT SUM(column1) FROM Table1
  WHERE column1 > 5
```

Note that the search condition here is what's important for a covering index (described in Chapter 9, "Indexes"). But SUM and AVG functions don't show a gain if the DBMS uses indexes. In fact, there will often be a loss. This is unfortunate, but what you lose with SUM and AVG will be more than made up by the gains that you'll see with COUNT, MAX, and MIN.

The Bottom Line: Sorting

A good grouping strategy is to sort the list first. Grouping is fast if the list is sorted.

Most DBMSs sort before grouping. You can help the process by listing GROUP BY and ORDER BY columns in the same order.

Most DBMSs will use indexes for grouping. But the GROUP BY clause has a lower priority than JOIN or WHERE clauses so indexes are useful only for very simple grouping.

GROUP BY will use an index if the grouping columns appear in the same order as the index columns.

Set functions will use an index if the function is alone in the select list and there is nothing after the FROM clause. For COUNT, MAX, and MIN you'll see a gain if an index is used. For AVG and SUM, you'll sometimes see poorer performance with an index, but the gains on the other set functions outweigh the loss.

Set Functions and Summary Aggregates

In the last section we looked briefly at how you can force the DBMS to use indexes to speed up MIN and MAX, and we mentioned that COUNT is an unusual function because it has a special optimization of its own. In this section, we'll look at this special optimization and the set functions in greater detail. We'll also discuss summary aggregation.

COUNT

DBMSs keep statistics that are associated with each table. One of these statistics is the table size, a figure that the optimizer uses for (among other things) determining the driver in a join. (The **driver** is the table that the DBMS examines first when evaluating an expression. For example, if a join is based on the expressions Table1.column1 = 5 AND Table1.column2 = Table2.column2 and the evaluation plan is to read Table1, then lookup Table2 rows based on values in Table1's rows, then Table1 is the driver.) If the statistics are 100% up to date, then the DBMS could retrieve this value, and the response to a statement like:

```
SELECT COUNT(*) FROM Table1
```

would be instantaneous. Statistics become out of date as soon as a row is inserted, updated, or deleted, so this happy state of affairs is rare.

DBMSs also keep more permanent statistics, such as the number of pages, or the highest serial number for a table's serial-number column. For example, with MySQL you can get a statistic called LAST_INSERT_ID. Such numbers always reflect rows that have been deleted, so COUNT(*) can't use them. But they can serve as substitutes for COUNT(*) if you can accept a small amount of error. Remember that in the dBASE Dark Age, it was considered perfectly normal that a "row count" included the table's deleted rows.

The COUNT(DISTINCT column) function is an awful performer. If it's alone in the select list, you have a workaround. For example, this statement:

```
SELECT COUNT(DISTINCT column1)
  FROM Table1
  WHERE column2 > 55
```

can be replaced by:

```
SELECT DISTINCT column1
  FROM Table1
  WHERE column2 > 55
GAIN: 5/8
```

Once you have the result set for the alternative SELECT, get the result set size using the ODBC function `SQLGetDiagField`. If you can do this, it's several times quicker.

Portability   This tip is not portable. Many DBMSs will reject the SQLGetDiagField call.

The statistics-based COUNT(*) optimizations are useless if there is a WHERE clause. That is, this statement:

```
SELECT COUNT(*) FROM Table1
```

normally goes many times faster than:

```
SELECT COUNT(*) FROM Table1
  WHERE column1 = 55
```

In cases where the search condition is necessary, you can sometimes speed things up again by counting the column only—that is, change the query to:

```
SELECT COUNT(column1) FROM Table1
  WHERE column1 = 55
GAIN: 1/8
```

The reasoning here is that the DBMS will use a covering index if one is available.

SUM Trouble

Summing up a long list of FLOAT columns can result in a loss of precision under two circumstances: (a) where the exponent varies wildly, and (b) where much subtraction occurs because values are negative. It can also result in a perceived loss of precision when numbers that we think of as "exact" are handled as floats. (For example, the number .1 added ten times does *not* result in the number 1 when floating-point arithmetic is used, though we may subconsciously expect that result.)

COUNT Mumbo Jumbo

Some people swear that you can speed up COUNT(*) by replacing the function with a logical equivalent. We failed to find any evidence for this assertion. As far as we can tell, the following statements are exactly the same:

```
SELECT COUNT(*) FROM Table1
```

```
SELECT COUNT(1) FROM Table1
```

```
SELECT SUM(1) FROM Table1
```

We tried out all three variants on the Big Eight and found no performance distinction among them.

If you consciously decided to use FLOATs, then you know this is part of the game. If you consciously decided to define your column as a DECIMAL but your DBMS silently stores that as a FLOAT (see Chapter 7, "Columns"), you might regard the precision loss as significant. You can solve this problem by casting the SUM to a data type with more precision, such as DECIMAL or DOUBLE PRECISION. If you do this, note that it's important to CAST the number *within the expression*, not within the SUM. That is, rather than using this statement:

```
SELECT CAST(SUM(column1) AS DECIMAL(10))
  FROM Table1
```

use this statement instead:

```
SELECT SUM(CAST(column1 AS DECIMAL(10)))
  FROM Table1
GAIN: 3/6
```

Portability   MySQL and Ingres don't support CAST. The gain shown is for only six DBMSs.

Precision will also be slightly better if you say SUM(x + y) instead of SUM(x) + SUM(y) because the total number of additions will be smaller. On the other hand, precision is better if you say SUM(x) − SUM(y) instead of SUM(x − y) because the total number of *subtractions* will be smaller.

You can also have a problem with SUM—for example, SUM(column1)—if column1 is an INTEGER. This time it isn't a problem with precision (in fact, a precision loss never occurs if you use exact numeric data types). The problem goes like this:

```
INSERT INTO Table1
   VALUES (2000000000)    /* 2 billion */

INSERT INTO Table1
   VALUES (2000000000)    /* 2 billion */

SELECT SUM(column1)
   FROM Table1            /* 4 billion ... error? */
```

Four DBMSs—Ingres, InterBase, Microsoft, and Sybase—return an "overflow" error in such a case. Once again, you can avoid the problem by using CAST:

```
SELECT SUM(CAST(column1 AS BIGINT))
   FROM Table1            /* if BIGINT is legal */

SELECT SUM(CAST(column1 AS DECIMAL(10)))
   FROM Table1            /* if you prefer standard SQL */
```

Similar considerations apply if you want to pick your own precision for AVG functions, rather than depending on the arbitrary precision that the DBMS picks. Some DBMSs add a few positions (usually three or more) after the decimal point—so if, for example, column1 is defined as DECIMAL(5,3) the result of AVG(column1) is at least DECIMAL(8,6). Other DBMSs (e.g., IBM and Informix) return a FLOAT result.

Multiple Aggregation Levels

Reports frequently include both detail and summary information. That's what the CUBE and ROLLUP keywords are for. You should use GROUP BY CUBE (...)

Fast MAX

An ideal way to compute the MAX aggregate function is described in A.K. Dewdney's article "On the spaghetti computer and other analog gadgets for problem solving" (*Scientific American*, June 1984, page 19). The article suggests that, for each numeric value in the set that you want to sort, you cut a strand of uncooked spaghetti to a length matching the value. Hold all the strands together loosely in your fist, and rap them on a horizontal surface. Instantly the longest strand will be apparent. Measure it.

Unfortunately, only the MAX is visible—not the MIN, SUM, AVG, or COUNT of the set. This illustrates that if you design the system for a specific query, you can get fantastic results . . . and make every other query slower.

or GROUP BY ROLLUP (. . .) if you want detail/summary reports—if your DBMS supports this new SQL:1999 feature. If it doesn't, you can get multiple levels by UNIONing the detail rows with the summary rows, like this:

```
SELECT column1 AS col1, SUM(column2)
  FROM Table1
  WHERE column1 IS NOT NULL
  GROUP BY column1
UNION ALL
SELECT 'Total' AS col1, SUM(column2)
  FROM Table1
ORDER BY col1
```

Portability   MySQL doesn't support UNION. All other DBMSs can do this, but you should use CUBE/ROLLUP with IBM, Microsoft, and Oracle.

You can achieve the same effect with a subquery—for example, SELECT ... FROM (SELECT ...)—but if your DBMS will support the table subqueries enhancement, then it will probably support CUBE and ROLLUP too. A similar trick is useful if you want to treat each occurrence of NULL as a distinct value.

Expressions

Here are three SQL statements. Feel free to show off by guessing which one is illegal according to SQL Standard rules.

```
Statement #1
SELECT MAX(LOWER(column1)) FROM Table1
  GROUP BY column1

Statement #2
SELECT LOWER(column1) FROM Table1
  GROUP BY LOWER(column1)        /* Hint: this one! */

Statement #3
SELECT column1 FROM Table1
  GROUP BY column1 COLLATE SQL_Latin1_General
```

Doubtless you correctly guessed that Statement #2 is illegal because GROUP BY columns can't be in expressions—except COLLATE expressions. Unfortunately, many DBMSs won't support COLLATE, so they have to support other kinds of expressions, such as LOWER. After all, it's frequently necessary to have some choice over how the DBMS decides what's a duplicate and what's not. Do remember, though, that GROUP BY is evaluated *before* the production of the select-list columns, so you can't do this:

```
SELECT LOWER(column1) AS alias_name
  FROM Table1
  GROUP BY alias_name
  ORDER BY alias_name
```

In this example, `alias_name` is illegal in the GROUP BY clause. It is, however, legal in the ORDER BY clause because ORDER BY is evaluated *after* the production of the select-list columns.

Expressions are also helpful with the MIN and MAX functions. For example, assume `Table1` contains two rows with these values: {Sam, SAM}. This query:

```
SELECT MIN(column1)
  FROM Table1
```

can return either 'Sam' or 'SAM', because both values are equal in a primary sort comparison. To ensure a consistent result, use this expression in the select list instead:

```
SELECT MIN(UPPER(column1))
  FROM Table1
```

The Bottom Line: Aggregates

Summing up a long list of FLOAT columns can result in a loss of precision. You can solve this problem by casting the SUM to a data type with more precision. If you do, make sure to CAST the number within the expression, not within the SUM.

Use CAST to avoid "overflow" problems with SUM and AVG.

Precision will be slightly better if you say SUM(x + y) instead of SUM(x) + SUM(y).

Precision will be slightly better if you say SUM(x) – SUM(y) instead of SUM(x – y).

Use CUBE or ROLLUP to produce detail/summary reports. If the DBMS doesn't support this feature, you can still get multiple levels by UNIONing the detail rows with the summary rows.

Expressions are helpful with the MIN and MAX functions, to ensure a consistent result set for character strings.

Parting Shots

The temptation is always strong to store aggregate values somewhere in the database—in a summary column, a summary row, or even a summary table. In a data warehouse, this is a natural inclination and everyone realizes that it's faster to look up a calculated value than to recalculate the value. In an **Online Transaction Processing (OLTP)** environment, stored summaries are rarer for the following reasons: (a) updates that happen in two places are prone to error; and (b) if a specific query is really frequent, then it will be cached anyway.

The temptation is occasionally strong to calculate aggregate values on the client instead of on the server. This is possible if you have a read-only result set and you can program in a host language. (We have seen this recommended as a tip in some MySQL-related books.) In many shops, client-side aggregating is forbidden because it doesn't save enough to make up for the extra programming time and network transmission time.

The temptation should be strong to avoid GROUP BY and aggregate functions entirely. We can only hope that some of what we've said here will make them more palatable.

5

Joins

There was once a simple rule for joins—Index all the columns. As DBMSs have grown more sophisticated, and different join plans have become part of every DBMS's repertoire, the ways to optimize have become more varied and more subtle. Now, to get the most out of your DBMS, you need to know what the special situations are, and what the DBMS is getting up to.

The first thing to keep in mind is, when your work requires you to join information from multiple tables, you don't want to do the joins yourself. What you *do* want is to provide the optimum conditions so that your DBMS will perform the best **join** on its own—because it makes a big difference.

For example, if two tables, called Table1 and Table2, both have 1,000 rows and this SQL statement is executed:

```
SELECT * FROM Table1, Table2
    WHERE Table1.column1 = Table2.column1
```

then, effectively, the DBMS is supposed to do this:

- Process the FROM clause, which says—Make a temporary table that is a **cartesian join** of all the rows in both Table1 and Table2. This step results in a 1,000,000-row temporary table. (A cartesian join, or **cartesian**

product, of two sets, say A and B, is the set of all ordered pairs {a, b} where a is a member of set A and b is a member of set B. In database terms, a cartesian product joins all rows in `Table1` with all rows in `Table2`. Thus if `Table1` has the values {T_a1, T_b1} and `Table2` has the values {T_a2, T_b2} then the cartesian product is {(T_a1, T_a2) (T_a1, T_b2) (T_b1, T_a2) (T_b1, T_b2)}. Cartesian products are useful for explanation, but when we see an operation that "goes cartesian" we usually criticize the optimizer.)

- Then process the WHERE clause, which says—Filter the rows in the temporary table that have the same value in the columns named `column1`.

The temporary table's size is the product of the sizes of the two original tables, which means the processing time goes up geometrically if `Table1` and `Table2` get bigger (this is known as a **cartesian explosion**). The DBMS must use a strategy that comes up with the same results as if there was such an explosion, but without the horrific response times that the formal requirement implies.

Fortunately, three such strategies, or join plans, exist. In order of importance, they are: nested-loop joins, sort-merge joins, and hash joins. In this chapter, we'll show you how these join plans work, and how you can make a big difference to the response time your DBMS can produce when using them. We'll also talk about another strategy you can use to improve join performance: avoiding the join altogether by using a join index. Because of the geometric effects of joins, we are no longer talking about shaving a few percentage points off of a timing. Getting joins to work just right can result in queries working several times faster than they would if you were ignorant of their workings. In our examples, we'll mostly use what's called "old style join syntax" as we expect that's what most readers will be familiar with. But we'll also examine "ANSI style join syntax" and show you how it compares with the old style.

Join Plan Strategies

The type of join plan used by a DBMS depends on indexes, table sizes, and **selectivity.** (Selectivity is the measure of the distinct values in an index; see Chapter 9, "Indexes.") Table 5–1 shows the strategies normally used by the Big Eight.

Table 5–1   *Join Plans Used by DBMSs*

	Nested-Loop	Sort-Merge	Hash
IBM	Yes	Yes	Yes (hybrid)
Informix	Yes	Yes (hybrid)	Yes
Ingres	Yes	Yes	Yes
InterBase	Yes	Yes	No
Microsoft	Yes	Yes	Yes (hybrid)
MySQL	Yes	No	Yes
Oracle	Yes	Yes	Yes
Sybase	Yes	Yes	Yes

Nested-Loop Joins

"A coward dies a thousand times before his death.
The valiant never taste of death but once."
—William Shakespeare, *Julius Caesar*

A **nested-loop join** is based on some variation of the nested-loop pseudocode shown in Listing 5–1. Let's call the table in the outer loop the "**outer table**" and the table in the inner loop the "**inner table.**" This is straightforward terminology, and better than the terms "driven table" and "driving table"—the term "driving table" is synonymous with "outer table," but we find that confusing. While studying Listing 5–1, keep this in mind:

- Usually the word "matches" means "equal to" because the huge majority of joins are **equijoins** (joins using the equals operator).

- Usually the word "pass" means "add values from both rows to a temporary table," but quite often the DBMS only needs to gather the **row identifiers (ROWIDs)** for the matching rows.

Listing 5–1   *Nested-Loop Pseudocode*
```
for (each row in Table1) {              /* outer loop */
  for (each row in Table2) {            /* inner loop */
    if (Table1 join column matches Table2 join column) pass
    else fail
  }
}
```

Just using the technique shown in Listing 5-1 results in a huge improvement because the temporary table that results isn't a one-million-row Cartesian join—the code filters before adding rows. But there are still a million comparisons to do, so we must get even more sophisticated.

Consider that the important factor now is not the number of comparisons—comparisons are relatively cheap—but the number of **page reads**.[1] When we think of the loop in terms of pages, it looks like the pseudocode shown in Listing 5-2.

Listing 5–2 *Nested-Loop Page Reads*
```
for (each page in Table1) {              /* outer loop */
  for (each page in Table2) {            /* inner loop */
    for (each row in Table1-page) {      /* cheap stuff */
      for (each row in Table2-page) {
        if (join column matches) pass
        else fail
      }
    }
  }
}
```

And now, a first aha! moment. If there are 11 pages in the DBMS cache, and the inner table (Table2) has only 10 pages, then after the DBMS has iterated once through the inner loop, *the Table2-page is in the cache* when the second iteration begins. In that case, the total number of page reads is not the product of the tables' sizes, but merely the sum of the number of pages in both Table1 and Table2. Result: end of geometric explosions. We can learn two lessons from this:

Lesson for the DBMS maker   When two tables differ greatly in size, the smaller table should be the inner table because there's more chance to fit all the pages in the cache, and caching matters only for the inner table.

Lesson for you   Fitting more rows into small tables has a major effect on some join speeds. Concentrate on making the "small" table smaller.

---

1. A page is a fixed-size (usually 4KB, 8KB, or 16KB) disk storage unit holding multiple rows; see Chapter 8, "Tables."

Actually, in a sequential pass through a file, it's common to read multiple pages at a time. That doesn't affect the logic of what we're saying here at all, but you may as well know that people don't talk about "paged nested-loop joins." Instead they talk about "blocked nested-loop joins" because a group of pages is often called a "block."

If the cache is too small, the DBMS can look for an index to alleviate the problem. If an index is doing its job, then there's no need to scan every row in the inner table. It's enough to look up the value in the table's index. If the table has a three-layer index, of which two layers are unlikely to be in the cache, then we can estimate that the number of page reads will be:

```
(number of pages in outer table) + (number of pages in inner table * 2)
```

And from this, we learn two more lessons:

Lesson for the DBMS maker	The table with the good index should be the inner table.

Lesson for you	Having an index on one table can help a lot—but having indexes on both tables is not quite as important. With a pure nested-loop join plan, one of the tables will be the outer table and the DBMS can go through all its pages sequentially.

What's a Good Index?

In Chapter 9, "Indexes," we'll talk about several kinds of indexes. Generally, the index that gets the most points for a nested-loop inner table is a B-tree with good selectivity, preferably with few layers, and preferably the cluster key on a clustered index or else a primary-key index.

So far we've looked only at the general case where entire tables are joined. That's frequent for reports, but a query in a short transaction usually takes this pattern:

```
SELECT * FROM Table1, Table2
   WHERE Table1.column1 = Table2.column1
     AND Table1.column2 = <literal>
```

The `AND Table1.column2 = <literal>` expression in this example is known as a **restrictive expression.** If you apply a restrictive expression, the number of rows decreases (because not all rows in a table will be `true` for the expression). In contrast, `WHERE Table1.column1 = Table2.column1` is a **join expression.** If you apply a join expression, the number of rows increases (because several rows in `Table2` might match the ones in `Table1`). Because of this, it's important to ensure that you **restrict** before you join.

Given that, which should be the outer table in this example? Answer: `Table1`, because if `Table1` is the inner table, the DBMS would have to apply the restriction every time a row comparison is made in the inner loop—which is still (`outer * inner rows`) times. Two more lessons can be learned from this:

Lesson for the DBMS maker	If a table has a restrictive expression on it, that table should be the outer table.

Lesson for you	Use restrictive expressions on joins whenever you can, because that will reduce the number of iterations of the outer loop.

There are some joins that can be replaced by an `INTERSECT . . . CORRESPONDING` clause, and that works well enough if both tables have restrictive clauses (which can make nested-loop joining difficult because the DBMS has to apply a restriction every time a row comparison is made in the inner loop as well as the outer loop). However, because many DBMSs don't support INTERSECT, we won't discuss this option further.

Instead, let's take another look now at the join expression, which so far we've seen only as `Table1.column1 = Table2.column1`. Joins, of course, can

Swim with the Current

A DBMS will choose inner and outer tables based on these criteria (in order by ascending importance):

- The smaller table should be inner, if it's very small.
- The table with the best index should be inner.
- The table with a restrictive clause should be outer.

Don't fight it. If `Table1` is smaller and has a good index, then put your restrictive clauses on `Table2`—`Table2` should be the outer table anyway.

A good example of this situation is the case where a primary key must be joined to a foreign key:

```
SELECT *
  FROM Primary_key_table, Foreign_key_table
  WHERE Primary_key_table.key = Foreign_key_table.key
```

A salesperson will have more than one sale; a teller will have more than one transaction; a product will have more than one stock; and a primary key will have more than one foreign key—not a reliable rule, but a good guess. Another good guess is that the primary key has a unique index on the joining columns, while the foreign key doesn't. Most often, then, the DBMS will pick `Primary_key_table` as the inner table.

Swim Against the Current

In a nested-loop join, `Big_table` should be the outer table. But if there's a restrictive expression on `Small_table`, then the DBMS will choose `Small_table` as the outer table.

Some IBM experts propose fixing this by putting an unnecessary restrictive expression on `Big_table`. For example:

```
SELECT * FROM Small_table, Big_table
  WHERE Small_table.column1 = Big_table.column1
    AND Small_table.column2 > 10      /* this is meaningful */
    AND Big_table.column2 > ''        /* makes Big_table outer */
```

This tip comes from a reliable source, but as we saw in Chapter 2, "Simple Searches," redundant conditions cause losses more often than gains.

get a little more complicated than that. First of all, there might be an ANDed expression, as in:

```
SELECT * FROM Table1, Table2
   WHERE Table1.column1 = Table2.column1
     AND Table1.column2 = Table2.column2
```

In this case, it's not enough to ensure that `column1` and `column2` in the inner table are indexed. Instead, you need to make a compound index on (`column1, column2`) in the inner table (GAIN: 7/8 if compound index rather than two separate indexes). It's also important to make sure that the joined columns in `Table1` and `Table2` have exactly the same data type and the same size (GAIN: 7/8 if the data types are exactly the same). That's not a trivial efficiency matter—many DBMSs won't even use the index if there's a size mismatch.

What if the inner table is too big to fit in a cache and has no useful index? Or what if there's a restrictive clause on the inner table too? Well, then you're in trouble! The only bright spot in this situation is if you're using Microsoft or Sybase. These DBMSs will internally "create temporary table which is clustered by the join key" then "populate temporary table by selecting the join columns and using the restrictive clause." Other DBMSs, more prosaically, simply make a temporary index on the inner table. That might sound like a solution, but it's better to have a permanent index than a temporary index that gets created and dropped whenever the query comes along.

Another thing you can do if both tables are indexed is encourage the searches to occur in index order. For example, suppose you have this query:

```
SELECT * FROM Table1, Table2
   WHERE Table1.column1 = Table2.column1
```

For this example, assume that `Table1.column1` contains these values: {15, 35, 5, 7}. If lookups of `Table2.column1` occur in that order, then the disk heads are jumping around. But if you force the DBMS to search `Table2.column1` in numeric order, that problem goes away. To do this, change the query to:

```
SELECT * FROM Table1, Table2
   WHERE Table1.column1 = Table2.column1
     AND Table1.column1 > 0
GAIN: 4/7
```

> **WARNING**   Don't do this for Informix; it shows a loss. The gain shown is for only seven DBMSs.

Remember that this works only if `Table1.column1` is indexed and the index is used by the DBMS. The values found are now {5, 7, 15, 35}, and the lookups in the inner loop will be going forward in the index, which is good for caching and which makes read-aheads more useful.

A variation of this trick when the inner table is not indexed, is to encourage the searches to occur in ascending ROWID order. This can be done if ROWIDs are accessible to the programmer, but a DBMS can also do this sort of thing automatically.

Here are our final three lessons about nested-loops:

> When your join contains an ANDed expression, make a compound index on the inner table's join columns.

> Make sure that the joined columns in your inner table and outer table have exactly the same data type and the same size.

> Search in index order.

The Bottom Line: Nested-Loop Join Plans

The choice of inner/outer tables depends on restricting expressions, then index qualities, then table sizes.

You can influence the choice or you can go with the flow. When conditions are good, nested-loops can produce result rows only two or three times more slowly than selections from a single unjoined table.

Nested-loops are the only strategy that works with weird conjunctions, such as LIKE joins.

Because they're flexible and easy to implement, nested-loop joins are supported by all DBMSs and are the default choice in most situations.

Typical OLTP queries will involve nested-loop joins 100% of the time, and even reporting queries will involve nested-loop joins more than 50% of the time.

IBM's Hybrid Join

When it comes to tricks with ROWID order in the inner table, IBM is currently the most advanced DBMS. Consider this SQL statement:

```
SELECT * FROM Customer Outer, Invoice Inner
    WHERE Outer.customer_name = Inner.customer_name
      AND Outer.customer_name = 'SMITH'
```

To resolve this query, IBM does the following:

- Sort data so outer table access will be in the order of the join column on the inner table.
- When accessing the inner table, get RID (the IBM name for ROWID) and attach it to the row from the outer table. This results in a temporary table with {outer table rows, inner table RID}.
- Sort the temporary table by inner table RID.

The result is that IBM repeatedly scans the inner table—but in order by inner table RID rather than rows. This means there will be prefetches and quick access.

Sort-Merge Joins

A **sort-merge join,** sometimes known as a *merge scan* or simply *merge join,* is a tad more complex than a nested-loop, but we can still describe sort-merge joins in the few lines of pseudocode shown in Listing 5–3.

Listing 5–3   *Sort-Merge Pseudocode*
```
sort (Table1)
sort (Table2)

get first row (Table1)
get first row (Table2)

for (;;until no more rows in tables) {        /* merge phase */

    if (join-column in Table1 < join-column in Table2)
      get next row (Table1)
```

```
elseif (join-column in Table1 > join-column in Table2)
  get next row (Table2)

elseif (join-column in Table1 = join-column in Table2) {
  pass
  get next row (Table1)
  get next row (Table2)
  }
}
```

Note: There is an assumption here that no duplicates exist. Duplicates make the sort-merge plan more complex and slow.

In the merge phase of a sort-merge join, the DBMS is always going forward. It never needs to get the same row twice, so this is a one-pass rather than a nested-loop—a big advantage. The downside is the cost of sorting. However, efficient sorts should be faster than comparisons of everything to everything. In fact it's provable that sort-merge is faster than nested-loop if both tables are large—just compare the number of page reads.

Even so, DBMSs will prefer nested-loops because they require less RAM, are more flexible, and have no startup overhead. So all we'll look at here is the ideal sort-merge query. It looks like this:

```
SELECT * FROM Table1, Table2
  WHERE Table1.column1 = Table2.column1
```

What makes this example ideal is that the comparison operator is equals and there are no restrictive expressions—there are only join expressions, which is typical, in fact, of a query you'd use to produce a report. For such queries, you might gain with sort-merge but be warned that there's extra hassle, which might involve your DBA. (For example, with Sybase you need to explicitly "enable" sort-merge, and with Oracle you must have a large value for SORT_AREA_SIZE in init.ora.)

A wonderful opportunity for the sort-merge occurs when Table1 and Table2 are already in order by the same key. That would be true in cases where column1 is the **clustered key** (that is, the column chosen to be the index key for a clustered index; see Chapter 9, "Indexes") in both tables. However, if only one table is indexed, then nested-loop can take advantage of that index just as readily as sort-merge can.

The Bottom Line: Sort-Merge Join Plans

Sort-merge is excellent when the query type is right, the RAM is sufficient, and the two tables are so similar that neither is an obvious driver.

If DBMSs would improve support of sort-merge by taking more advantage of existing indexes, sort-merges would be more important for OLTP work than they are currently.

Hash Joins

A **hash join** is another method for producing a joined table. Given two input tables `Table1` and `Table2`, processing is as follows:

- For each row in `Table1`, produce a **hash.** (A hash is a number—often a 32-bit integer—that is derived from column values using a lossy compression algorithm.) Assign the hash to a hash bucket.

- For each row in `Table2`, produce a hash. Check if the hash is already in the hash bucket. If it is, there's a join. If it is not, there's no join.

Thus, a hash join is a type of nested-loop join in which the inner table rows are looked up via a hash algorithm instead of via an index. Most DBMSs don't keep permanent hash tables so here we're talking about a temporary hash table that the DBMS creates in RAM just before beginning the loop and destroys after the end of the loop. For a hash join to work properly, the following conditions should all be true:

- Condition #1: There is enough RAM set aside so that the hash table fits entirely in memory. (Usually there isn't much RAM. Cloudscape will avoid hash joins if more than 1MB is needed. Oracle allows setting a fixed size with yet another of its init.ora parameters: HASH_AREA_SIZE.)

- Condition #2: The join is an equijoin.

- Condition #3: Inner table join-column values are unique and can be uniquely hashed. With long character strings, collisions and uncertainties could wreck the plan.

- Condition #4: The inner table is searched many times because the outer table is large and contains many rows that are not filtered out by whatever restrictive expression exists on the outer table.

It might appear at first glance that Condition #1 is a showstopper when the inner table has more than, say, 100,000 rows. In fact, though, all DBMSs will perform a trick to keep from overflowing the hash area—they will read partitions of the table. Thus, for example, a DBMS with a 400,000-row table to search reads only 100,000 rows at a time, makes the hash list, does the comparisons, then clears the hash list for the next read. It has to perform the nested-loop four times instead of just once, but that's a lot better than bringing in so many rows at once that the hash table overflows and disk swapping occurs.

The important condition is Condition #4. An in-memory hash lookup is always faster than an index lookup, true—but only by one or two I/Os for each iteration. Take our earlier example of a query with a restrictive expression:

```
SELECT * FROM Table1, Table2
   WHERE Table1.column1 = Table2.column1
     AND Table1.column2 = <literal>
```

If the AND Table1.column2 = <literal> expression is true 20 times, and it takes 20 I/Os to read Table2, then you're at breakeven point. The cost of setting up the hash list would not be made up by the savings in the inner loop when there are so few iterations of the inner loop.

The Bottom Line: Hash Join Plans

Hash joins beat sort-merge joins beat nested-loop joins when the join is an equijoin with no restrictive expression and the tables are large—even when there are indexes that hash joins and sort-merge joins ignore.

On the other hand, when there is any sort of restrictive expression, nested-loops can do the filtering *before* the joining, and will therefore beat both hash joins and sort-merge joins. Sort-merge is best only if there's lots of RAM for a sort, or there's been a presort, or if an efficient sorting mechanism is on disk.

Avoid the Join Strategies

You can sometimes avoid a join by transforming an SQL statement to a simpler equivalent. For example, here is an SQL statement that could benefit from constant propagation:

```
SELECT * FROM Table1, Table2
   WHERE Table1.column1 = Table2.column1
     AND Table1.column1 = 55
```

When the equals operator is in the restrictive clause and the same column is in both the joining clause and the restrictive clause, such a statement boils down to a non-join, like this:

```
SELECT * FROM Table1, Table2
   WHERE Table1.column1 = 55
     AND Table2.column1 = 55
GAIN: 5/8 if both columns indexed
```

There isn't a transform for every case though. The most difficult and most effective joining strategy is to do the joining in advance and store one piece of information; namely, which rows in Table1 would relate to rows in Table2 if there was an equijoin. There are several ways to blaze a trail that the DBMS can follow in such cases. We'll mention two: join indexes and composite tables.

Join Indexes

Some DBMSs (e.g., Informix, Microsoft, and Oracle) allow you to avoid joins by providing support for indexes that span multiple tables. Let's compare how two regular (one table per index) indexes stack up against a **join index** (two tables per index). Figure 5-1 shows two regular indexes, one for Table1, the other for Table2. In contrast, Figure 5-2 shows a join index on the same two tables.

Now, suppose we do the old standby join on Table1 and Table2:

```
SELECT * FROM Table1, Table2
   WHERE Table1.column1 = Table2.column1
```

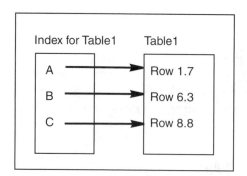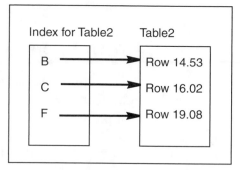

Figure 5–1   *Regular indexes for Table1 and Table2*

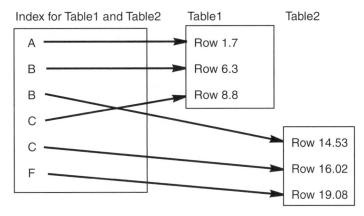

Figure 5–2   *Join index for Table1 and Table2*

When a join index is on the two tables, it's a trivial job for the DBMS to execute this statement. It needs only to scan the join index, and for each key value that points to a Table1 row, check whether the very next key has the same value and points to a Table2 row. If so, pass. In effect, this is a sort-merge join plan for which the sorting and merging have already been done! The number of I/Os needed is equal to the number of pages in the index, divided by the number of pages that the DBMS can read all at once given that this is a sequential scan.

Join indexes can be very helpful, but there is always a catch when you mingle information from two tables in one file: If you want only the information in Table1, then access will be slower because all this irrelevant data from Table2 is in your index. On average, scan time doubles and update time more than doubles. So the rule of thumb about join indexes is:

> If more than half of your queries on two tables are joins, and the join columns never change, and neither table is clustered, create a join index for the tables.

Composite Tables

You can also avoid joins by using a **composite table.** This is straightforward provided you avoid thinking of "composite indexes," which get confused with "compound indexes," which have nothing to do with "composite tables"—the composite we're talking about here is a table that contains column values derived from two (or more) other tables. The composite table can thus contain join information.

Let's put this example into SQL. Assume you have three tables and one index, defined as follows:

```
CREATE TABLE Table1 (
   column1 INTEGER PRIMARY KEY,
   column2 CHARACTER(50),
...)

CREATE TABLE Table2 (
   column3 INTEGER PRIMARY KEY,
   column4 CHARACTER(50),
...)

CREATE TABLE Composite (
   column1 INTEGER,
   column3 INTEGER,
   column2 CHARACTER(50),
   column4 CHARACTER(50),
...)

CREATE UNIQUE INDEX Index1
   ON Composite
      (column1, column3, column2, column4)
```

To keep the data in sync, if any rows of Table1 or Table2 are added or changed, the same changes must be copied to Composite. This is easy to do if your DBMS supports triggers. Then, when you need joined information from Table1 and Table2, instead of executing this SQL statement:

```
SELECT * FROM Table1, Table2
   WHERE Table1.column1 = Table2.column3
```

you can do this one instead:

```
SELECT * FROM Composite
   WHERE column1 = column3
GAIN: 8/8
```

Doing so lets you avoid the join at this time. In effect, it's still a join, but a join that was done earlier and so doesn't cost you the same amount of time. Index

`Index1` is a covering index, so all the information will actually come from the compound index. But even if your DBMS doesn't provide direct support for compound indexes, you can still use the composite table.

The composite table is just a baby step toward **denormalizing,** so a few words on that subject are in order. (To **denormalize** a table means to break the normalization rules deliberately, usually in an attempt to gain speed or save space.) It's sometimes suggested that a table would benefit from **denormalization** "if every query on it is a join query." But as we've seen, there are many kinds of joins, and some of them have almost no effect on query speed. The usual observation in OLTP shops is that the extra INSERT/UPDATE time needed to support the composite table would be as great as the time saved when querying—so it's no savings at all unless you do a lot of queries but rarely change your data. And those are just the performance issues—the design effects of abandoning normalization have to be considered as well. We won't discuss them here—such issues have been well covered in most basic DBMS design texts. But if you do decide to denormalize, here are some tips:

- Copy the columns from the primary key to the foreign key, not vice versa. That way you're only violating second normal form instead of first normal form. (For more on the normal forms, see Chapter 8, "Tables.")

- Take baby steps, moving only a few columns at a time, and also leaving the same values in the original positions for a while.

- Some common advice on denormalization: OLTP shops don't need to, **Decision Support System (DSS)** shops do need to.

The Bottom Line: Avoiding Joins

If more than half of your queries on two tables are joins, and the join columns never change, and neither table is clustered, create a join index for the tables if you can.

Denormalize and use composite tables to avoid joins if you work in a DSS shop.

Don't use composite tables to avoid joins if you work in an OLTP shop.

Three-Way Joins and Beyond

When more than two tables are joined, each join is scheduled and processed separately—there is no such thing as a nested-loop within a nested-loop, even though that might seem to be the obvious strategy. Partly that's because some joins can be processed in parallel (for example, Oracle does in-parallel joining), and partly it's because a nested-loop within a nested-loop would exacerbate the problem that simple joins have (that is, that the innermost table wouldn't stay in cache). Consider this SQL statement:

```
SELECT * FROM Table1, Table2, Table3
   WHERE Table1.column1 = Table2.column1
     AND Table2.column1 = Table3.column1
```

For a three-way join of `Table1`, `Table2`, and `Table3`, the strategy is to merge `Table1` and `Table2` to a single (`Table1_2`) table, and then merge (`Table1_2`) with `Table3`. The question—Which expression is evaluated first?—is answered in the usual way: The expression with the most points goes first (see Chapter 2, "Simple Searches"). After that, though, some shuffling occurs that depends on the closeness of the second expression to be evaluated to the first expression—so the expression with the *least* points might actually come in second place. A good idea is to specify join tables in both the FROM and WHERE clauses using the point rules described in Chapter 2, "Simple Searches"—but keep in mind that, when joins are involved, those rules are no more than a weak hint.

You can expect the DBMS optimizer to start going wrong if five or more joins are in the query (until recently Microsoft's admitted limit was four). You can get around such restrictions by making temporary tables from five-table joins and then joining the temporary tables, but the fact is that your guess will be no better than that of your DBMS vendor. For a multiway join, finding the shortest path is reminiscent of a traveling salesman problem and becomes more and more complex as you add tables.

For Microsoft and Sybase, there's a common recommendation: Add a redundant WHERE clause so that the optimizer will have more choices about paths. Here's an example:

```
SELECT * FROM Table1, Table2, Table3
   WHERE Table1.column1 = Table2.column1
     AND Table2.column1 = Table3.column1
     AND Table1.column1 = Table3.column1
/* the final AND is redundant but put it in anyway */
```

The thinking here is: If the optimizer is good, it will throw away the redundant clause, but if the optimizer is bad, it will benefit from the redundant clause because it now has a choice of all six possible join orders—including Table1 to Table3, and Table3 to Table1—which it wouldn't otherwise notice.

When we added the redundant WHERE clause to our example, we had to choose whether to add Expression #1 or Expression #2:

```
Expression #1:
... WHERE Table1.column1 = Table3.column1

Expression #2:
... WHERE Table3.column1 = Table1.column1
```

The best way to decide how to phrase a redundant WHERE clause is to figure out which table will be the outer table in your first join and base your decision on that. (You lose this choice if you use a USING or an ON clause.) Don't try to change clauses if you have a working query that contains an outer join.

Sybase and the Total Density Statistic

A table's **density** usually depends on the sensitivity of the index and is one of the items that the optimizer can gather during statistics or analysis. The density of a table is calculated as the fraction of rows that can be returned for a query. For example, if a table has 1,000 rows and density is 0.01, then 10 rows might match.

The Sybase optimizer uses a "Total Density" statistic when it needs to figure out the join order. Since the true cost of a multiway join depends heavily on the size of the outer table after each stage of the join (the smaller the better), Sybase just calculates the density for the order:

```
((Table1 JOIN Table2) then (Table2 JOIN Table3))
```

and compares the result with what would be returned for the order:

```
((Table2 JOIN Table3) then (Table1 JOIN Table2))
```

Sybase won't cost-compare more than four joins at once.

Old Style versus ANSI Style

Until June 2001, Oracle didn't support ANSI-style joins, but now that Oracle does, each of the Big Eight can work with either old-style joins, ANSI-style joins with USING, or ANSI-style joins with ON. Here are examples of each type:

```
old-style join:
SELECT * FROM Table1, Table2
   WHERE Table1.column1 = Table2.column1   /* old style */

ANSI-style join with USING:
SELECT * FROM Table1 JOIN Table2
   USING (column1)                         /* ANSI style */

ANSI-style join with ON:
SELECT * FROM Table1 JOIN Table2
   ON Table1.column1 = Table2.column1      /* ANSI style */
```

Portability	DBMS vendors prefer the second ANSI-style join, with an ON clause. Only MySQL and Oracle also support a join with a USING clause.

The terms "old-style" join and "ANSI-style" join are nobody's official terminology, and we use them only because we needed some names. The fact is that the old style is acceptable in SQL:1999, and the SQL Standard does not deprecate it. ("Deprecate" is a formal word. It means that the SQL Standard foundation document doesn't hint that the old style will be dropped from a future version of the official Standard.) So both styles are acceptable. There remains some debate about which style is "right" between those who prefer the old style (especially Oracle programmers) and those who prefer the ANSI style (especially Microsoft programmers). The only definite thing is that outer joins should be in ANSI style.

Does the style affect the performance? To answer this question, we wrote the same join two different ways, and tried them both out on the Big Eight. Watch the WHERE clause:

```
SELECT * FROM Table1 JOIN Table2
  ON Table1.column1 = Table2.column1
  WHERE Table2.column2 = 22               /* ANSI style */
```

```
SELECT * FROM Table1, Table2
  WHERE Table1.column1 = Table2.column1
    AND Table2.column2 = 22                    /* old style */
GAIN: 1/8
```

We found that with most DBMSs, these two statements ran equally fast. But with IBM, the old style is sometimes faster. The reason is hinted at in this quote:

> "When you use the ON clause to specify the join, you can use the WHERE clause as a post-join filter. The database server applies the post-join filter of the WHERE clause to the results of the outer join."
>
> —*IBM Informix Guide to SQL Syntax Documentation*

In other words, the restrictive expression is processed *after* the joining clause. That's what's supposed to happen logically. But if the clauses aren't optimized together at the same time, then the DBMS misses the best join plan: Make `Table2` the outer table, find rows in the outer table where `Table2.column2 = 22`, and then search for `Table1.column1 = Table2.column1` in the inner loop. Our conclusion, then, is that old style is never slower and can be faster.

While we're on the subject of syntax, we should note that it's traditional to put the joining clauses before the restrictive expression, as we've done in all our examples. However, even with rule-based or primitive optimizers, putting the clauses in a different order will not affect performance.

Outer Joins

Only one outer join type is supported by all DBMSs: LEFT joins. And only one syntax is supported by all DBMSs for left joins: ANSI style. Table 5-2 shows the SQL Standard requirements and which options are supported by the Big Eight.

Here's an example of an outer join:

```
SELECT Table1.column1
  FROM Table1 LEFT JOIN Table2
      ON Table1.column1 = Table2.column1
```

An outer join can be much slower than an inner join because `Table1` *must* be the outer table and `Table2` *must* be the inner table—otherwise, the join won't work. So even if `Table1` is smaller and better indexed and has a restrictive expression, it still can't be the inner table. And that means the DBMS can't pick the optimum join plan.

Table 5–2   *ANSI/DBMS Outer Join Support*

	Left	Right	Full
ANSI SQL	Yes	Yes	Yes
IBM	Yes	Yes	Yes
Informix	Yes	No	No
Ingres	Yes	Yes	Yes
InterBase	Yes	Yes	Yes
Microsoft	Yes	Yes	Yes
MySQL	Yes	Yes	No
Oracle	Yes	Yes	Yes
Sybase	Yes	Yes	No

If the DBMS applies a restrictive expression *after* the join is complete, there won't be any weird problems involving [NOT] NULL. For example, suppose `Table1` has a column called `column1` that contains the values {1, 3}. Meanwhile, `Table2` also has a `column1`, and its values are {1, 2}. A simple left join of these tables produces these result rows (assume all columns have a default value that is NULL):

Table1.column1	Table2.column1
1	1
3	NULL

A less-simple left join on the same tables can be done with this syntax:

```
SELECT Table1.column1, Table2.column1
   FROM Table1 LEFT JOIN Table2
       ON Table1.column1 = Table2.column1
   WHERE Table2.column1 IS NULL
```

The result of this query should be these result rows:

Table1.column1	Table2.column1
3	NULL

But that's not what Microsoft used to return! The plausible explanation was that Microsoft did the restrictive expression first. Good for performance; too bad it produced the wrong result. Fortunately, the current version of Microsoft produces the correct result.

If there's one thing that an outer join is definitely faster than, it's UNION. Before the introduction of outer join syntax, the simple left join had to be phrased as:

```
SELECT Table1.column1, Table2.column1   /* the inner part */
  FROM Table1, Table2
  WHERE Table1.column1 = Table2.column1
UNION ALL
SELECT column1, CAST(NULL AS INTEGER)   /* the outer part */
  FROM Table1
  WHERE Table1.column1 NOT IN
    (SELECT Table2.column1 FROM Table2)
```

If you see this syntax in some old program, replace it with a true left join. We tried that on the Big Eight and got a gain. Here's the equivalent left join statement:

```
SELECT Table1.column1, Table2.column1
  FROM Table1 LEFT JOIN Table2
      ON Table1.column1 = Table2.column1
GAIN: 6/7
```

Portability   MySQL doesn't support UNION or subqueries. The gain shown is for only seven DBMSs.

From the old Microsoft fiasco and the poor performance of the UNION, we glean two general rules:

- A DBMS optimizer will usually optimize only within a single clause (and when it optimizes two clauses at once it can bungle).
- A DBMS optimizer will always optimize only within a single SELECT.

Parting Shots

At the most general abstraction, one could say that the trick to speeding up joins is to give the DBMS lots of information—but not so much that it will be confused about which information to use. We've seen this over and over in this chapter—for example, sometimes we've said "Index here to improve the query," and in other cases, the advice has been "Don't index here because it will result in a useless path that you don't want the optimizer to take." So we can't leave you with some simple formula that will always speed up your joins. But there are some items that we do want to stress:

- Expect nested-loops.
- The best nested-loop is the one where all inner-table criteria are met.
- The most likely joins should turn out to be foreign-key/primary-key joins.

This is not really the end of our joining story. The favorite question is still to come in the next chapter—Should I join or should I subquery?

6

Subqueries

There seems to be a Law of DBMS Development that states—In version 1.0 the subquery support will be bad or nonexistent, and it will slowly get better.

Witness the IBM texts that tell you how bad subqueries were in the early days, and the fact that Sybase used to transform almost all subqueries to joins, and the fact that MySQL was seven years old before its developers announced a beta version with subquery support. The result is that subqueries get a bad reputation, which persists even after the product matures. In this chapter, we're going to tell you that subqueries are fast and reliable nowadays—but we expect you to be skeptical. So we'll take a hard look at the current state of affairs, performance-wise.

The topic of subqueries also tends to bring up several operating questions. When is it better to use a join rather than a subquery, and how would I flatten a query? What would induce a DBMS to choose a particular plan? What design and syntax choices can I exploit? We'll look at each one of these questions as well.

Refresher

A subquery is a SELECT statement with another SELECT inside it. It looks like this:

```
SELECT ...           /* outer or parent query */
  (SELECT ...)       /* subquery, inner query or subselect */
...
```

There are three possible plans to process a subquery:

- **flattened**. Transform the query to a join, then process as a join.
- **out-to-in**. For each row in the outer query, look up in the inner query.
- **in-to-out**. For each row in the inner query, look up in the outer query.

When processing is out-to-in, the outer query is the driver. When processing is in-to-out, the inner query is the driver.

Table 6–1 shows the SQL Standard requirements and the level of support the Big Eight have for subqueries.

Notes on Table 6-1:

- Basic Support column

    This column is "Yes" if the DBMS fully supports the [NOT] IN, [NOT] EXISTS, <comparison operator> ANY, and <comparison operator> ALL

Table 6–1 *ANSI/DBMS Subquery Support*

	Basic Support	Row Subquery	Table Subquery	Max Depth	Allow UNION	Types Converted
ANSI SQL	Yes	Yes	Yes	N/S	Yes	Yes
IBM	Yes	Yes	Yes	22	Yes	Yes
Informix	Yes	No	No	23	No	Yes
Ingres	Yes	No	No	11	No	Yes
InterBase	Yes	No	No	>=32	No	Yes
Microsoft	Yes	No	Yes	>=32	Yes	Yes
MySQL	No	No	No	N/A	N/A	Yes
Oracle	Yes	No	No	>=32	Yes	Yes
Sybase	Yes	No	No	16	No	Yes

predicates, and correctly handles subquery situations where the number of rows is zero.

- Row Subquery column

  This column is "Yes" if the DBMS supports row subqueries, for example:

  ```
  SELECT * FROM Table1
    WHERE (column1, column2) =
      (SELECT column1, column2 FROM Table2)
  ```

- Table Subquery column

  This column is "Yes" if the DBMS supports table subqueries, for example:

  ```
  SELECT *
    FROM (SELECT * FROM Table1) AS TableX
  ```

- Max Depth column

  Shows the maximum number of subquery levels supported.

- Allow UNION column

  This column is "Yes" if the DBMS allows UNION in a subquery.

- Types Converted column

  This column is "Yes" if the DBMS automatically casts similar data types during comparisons.

Join versus Subquery

When you write a join, you're letting the DBMS optimizer decide among a variety of plans, such as merge-sort, nested-loop, or hash; see Chapter 5, "Joins." But when you write a subquery, you are strongly hinting that you want a nested-loop. Both out-to-in and in-to-out queries are nested-loop plans—they merely differ in direction or driver choice. That's one point in favor of writing joins instead of subqueries, because it's better not to tell the DBMS what to do. The best option is to give the DBMS choices.

Nested-loops for subqueries can be different from nested-loops for joins. Listing 6–1 shows a join nested-loop, while Listing 6–2 shows a subquery nested-loop.

Listing 6–1 *Nested-Loop for Joins*

```
for (each row in driver) {
  for (each row in driven) {
    if "match" add to matchlist
  }
}
```

Listing 6-2   *Nested-Loop for Subqueries*

```
for (each row in driver) {
  for (each row in driven) {
    if "match" EXIT LOOP
  }
}
```

The difference between nested-loops for joins and nested-loops for subqueries is that a subquery needs to find only a single match, so it might be able to break out early from the inner loop. In contrast, a join needs all matches, so it must chug through all rows. (Because the subquery loop can abort early the result is sometimes called a "semijoin," but that's a rare word.) And that's one point in favor of writing subqueries, because a subquery loop will have fewer iterations.

To test whether subqueries can beat joins, we made two one-column (INTEGER) tables. Table1 had 1,000 rows, and Table2 had 10,000 rows. Each

Use IN

How can you encourage early breakout? Avoid the use of syntax like = (SELECT <query>). Use = ANY (SELECT <query>) expressions—or the commoner shorthand IN (SELECT <query>)—instead, because = (SELECT <query>) has to chug through the whole inner loop before it's certain that there is only one match. In other words, don't use forms like Query #1. Replace them with forms like Query #2 or Query #3:

```
Query #1        /* avoid this */
SELECT column1 FROM Table1
  WHERE column1 =
    (SELECT column1 FROM Table2)

Query #2        /* use this */
SELECT column1 FROM Table1
  WHERE column1 = ANY
    (SELECT column1 FROM Table2)

Query #3        /* or use this */
SELECT column1 FROM Table1
  WHERE column1 IN
    (SELECT column1 FROM Table2)
```

table was populated with random numbers between 100 and 1,000. There was no clustering or indexing. Then we tested this join and a similar-looking subquery against `Table1` and `Table2`:

```
Join:
SELECT MIN(Table1.column1)
   FROM Table1, Table2
   WHERE Table1.column1 = Table2.column1

Subquery:
SELECT MIN(Table1.column1)
   FROM Table1
   WHERE Table1.column1 IN
      (SELECT Table2.column1
          FROM Table2)
GAIN: 7/7
```

Portability	MySQL doesn't support subqueries. The gain on all tests shown in this chapter is for only seven DBMSs.

The result of the test was that the subquery was faster with every DBMS tested.

Here are some other arguments in the join-versus-subquery debate:

Pro join arguments

People who prefer joins over subqueries pose the following arguments:

- If the outer query's WHERE clause contains multiple ANDed/ORed conditions, the optimizer can arrange them better if everything is on one level—that is, if you flatten to a join. Optimizers tend to optimize each query separately.

- Some DBMSs (e.g., Oracle) can parallelize joins better than they can parallelize subqueries.

- When you do a join, data from both tables can be in the final select list. This isn't true for subqueries.

- Simply because people think joins are better, they use them more, and therefore DBMS vendors work harder to make joins better. It's a self-fulfilling prophecy!

Pro subquery arguments

On the other side, people who prefer subqueries over joins argue these points:

- Comparison rules might be more relaxed in subqueries. For example, SMALLINTs can be looked up in INTEGER subqueries without major penalties.

- Subqueries can contain GROUP BY, HAVING, and set functions. It's more cumbersome to join when such syntax exists, especially if the syntax is hidden within a view definition.

- Subqueries can appear in UPDATE statements. Most DBMSs can't update a join.

- Subqueries that use a comparison operator without ANY, and subqueries that use NOT EXISTS within NOT EXISTS (the "relational divide" problem), are not expressible using joins with classic syntax.

- In mature DBMSs, vendors utilize subquery optimizations similar to those that are used to optimize joins. For example, IBM was once unable to take advantage of indexes when doing in-to-out, but now IBM does use indexes in such situations.

Flattening

To flatten a query means to make everything one level. Based on our observations so far, there are clearly times when you should flatten a subquery. In this section, we'll discuss how the DBMS can flatten automatically, but first let's establish how you can do it yourself.

To flatten IN

Here's an example of a subquery using IN, and the flattened analogous query:

```
Subquery with IN:
SELECT * FROM Table1
  WHERE Table1.column1 IN
    (SELECT Table2.column1
      FROM Table2
      WHERE Table2.column1 = 5)
```

```
Flattened:
SELECT Table1.*
  FROM Table1, Table2
  WHERE Table1.column1 = Table2.column1
    AND Table2.column1 = 5
```

This simple flattening seems like it should be equivalent to the IN query, but it has a flaw that can be seen if `Table1` has these three rows: {1, 5, 5} and `Table2` has these three rows: {2, 5, 5}. Notice that the subquery-based SELECT would correctly return two rows: {5, 5}, but the flattened SELECT would return four rows: {5, 5, 5, 5}. Notice further that if the flattened SELECT is "corrected" by using SELECT DISTINCT instead of just SELECT, the join would return only one row: {5}. In other words, flattening can cause too many duplicate rows—and if you try to get rid of the duplicates, you can end up with too *few* duplicate rows. Sometimes you'll see this flaw if the DBMS flattens automatically. (By the way, DISTINCT can be expensive so don't use it if `Table2.column1` is uniquely indexed.)

To flatten NOT IN

Here's an example of a subquery using NOT IN, and the flattened equivalent query:

```
Subquery with NOT IN:
SELECT Table1.column1 FROM Table1
  WHERE Table1.column1 NOT IN
    (SELECT Table2.column1 FROM Table2)
```

```
Flattened equivalent:
SELECT Table1.column1
  FROM Table1 LEFT JOIN Table2
    ON Table1.column1 = Table2.column1
  WHERE Table2.column1 IS NULL
```

This type of flattening is rare, and has two flaws: it assumes that ON happens before WHERE as in the SQL Standard, and it assumes that `Table2.column1` has no NULLs (the `WHERE Table2.column1 IS NULL` clause is meant to find dummy rows produced by the outer join).

When is flattening automatic? The rules vary slightly between DBMSs and often seem to reflect some foible in the DBMS rather than some strategy. Amalgamating the rules followed by the various DBMSs, we can say that a flattening is almost certain to happen to subqueries in this scenario:

- Flattening is legal—that is, the subquery isn't in an UPDATE statement, contains no implied groupings, and so on.
- The outer query does not have any of {<>, NOT EXISTS, AND, OR, CASE} directly before the subquery.
- The inner query does not have a join or another inner query.
- There is not a one-to-many relation. (The DBMS might determine that by finding a UNIQUE index on the subquery column.)

If you think the DBMS is likely to flatten incorrectly, you can discourage it by changing the conditions. If you think the DBMS is likely to flatten correctly, then you face the question—Why code with a subquery in the first place? If it's going to be a join anyway, it would be clearer to code it as a join. In other words, if flattening is automatic, that's a reason to flatten manually! We think that's taking things a bit too far. Better to let the DBMS decide, and worry yourself about the portability. Keep in mind that the original subquery code is there because somebody thought it was better.

The Bottom Line: Join versus Subquery

The difference between nested-loops for joins and nested-loops for subqueries is that a subquery needs to find only a single match, so it might be able to break out early from the inner loop. In contrast, a join needs all matches, so it must chug through all rows.

One major point in favor of writing joins instead of subqueries is that it's better not to tell the DBMS what to do. By writing joins, you're giving the DBMS choices instead of forcing it to follow a specific plan.

One major point in favor of writing subqueries is that a subquery loop may have fewer iterations, so subqueries may be faster than joins.

Encourage the DBMS to break out of subquery loops early by using syntax like IN (SELECT <query>) rather than = (SELECT <query>).

Generally joins are better, but if, on average, several rows are in the driven query for each row in the driver (for example, a primary-to-foreign or other one-to-many relation), and especially if matching rows come first in the driven query, then subqueries are better.

Syntax Choices

You can make several syntax choices when writing subqueries. The major sub-query predicates are IN and EXISTS, but we'll also look at negation, duplicate elimination, double subqueries, and set operation alternatives.

IN

In a slight plurality of cases, the plan for IN subqueries is in-to-out—that is, the DBMS starts on the inside and drives to the outer query. We will generalize and say that in-to-out plans occur for subqueries that (a) begin with <comparison operator> [ANY | ALL] and (b) contain no correlations. Although far from reliable, this rule is easy to remember. Here's a simple example:

```
SELECT * from Table1
  WHERE Table1.column1 IN
    (SELECT Table2.column1 FROM Table2
      WHERE Table2.column1 = 5)
```

This example subquery has a restriction in it (WHERE Table2.column1 = 5), which is a signal that the subquery has few rows. That's what you want. If a sub-query is in-to-out, then the relationship should be few-rows-to-many.

Let's look at what one mature DBMS, IBM, does with this example. According to IBM's EXPLAIN facility, the general plan is as follows:

1. Evaluate the subquery to filter the WHERE Table2.column1 = 5 rows.

2. Sort the result in order by Table2.column1 (a preparation for step #3).

3. Eliminate duplicate occurrences of Table2.column1 values.

4. Save the result set in a work area, preferably in memory.

5. Loop:
   ```
   For (each Table2.column1 value in the work area result set)
     {
       Index-lookup for:
         ... WHERE Table1.column1 = <Table2.column1 value>
     }
   ```

For the loop in the fifth step, it's vital that Table1.column1 be indexed, but it's irrelevant if Table2.column1 is indexed.

You can throw a wrench into the works by changing IN (subquery) to NOT IN (subquery). Doing so makes the ratio many-to-few instead of few-to-many, and that means processing should be out-to-in. For an out-to-in query, IBM makes a temporary index on the work table and does the final step in reverse.

DISTINCT

The IBM plan for IN includes steps for sorting and eliminating duplicates. That makes sense because the best optimizations are ones that reduce the row count *in the driver*. In addition, a slight speedup occurs if the rows in the outer query are in order by Table1.column1, because the lookups will occur in ascending order by value. There is a way to force other DBMSs to follow a similar plan: It is legal to add the word DISTINCT in the inner query, like this:

```
SELECT * from Table1
  WHERE Table1.column1 IN
    (SELECT DISTINCT Table2.column1 FROM Table2
      WHERE Table2.column1 = 5)
GAIN: 2/7
```

Logically, DISTINCT is superfluous here, but we're looking for some common side effects of DISTINCT: (a) it causes ORDER BY, and (b) it reduces the number of rows in the inner query. In our tests, Table2.column1 contained integers, most of them duplicates, and it had a high likelihood that smaller numbers would match values in Table1. The explanation for the gain is that, by eliminating duplicates and by making it more probable that "matches" (i.e., small numbers) would appear early, DISTINCT sped things up with some DBMSs. Other DBMSs just ignored DISTINCT, so no harm was done.

Another side effect of DISTINCT, but more frequently seen with GROUP BY or HAVING, is **materialization**—that is, to evaluate some expressions, the DBMS will create a temporary table, put the rows from the original table(s) into the temporary table, and select from the temporary copy. Scanning is faster if the inner loop happens on a materialized "view" of the table, which is smaller than the table itself. Materialization is also a factor that discourages the DBMS from flattening. As we've suggested before: If DISTINCT is a do-nothing operator because there's no duplication, then the relation is not one-to-many, and therefore a join is probably better than a subquery.

Though DISTINCT takes time, the rows are short if you're just retrieving one column in the subquery. But DISTINCT does involve a sort, so do consider the sort tips provided in Chapter 3, "ORDER BY."

EXISTS

The sort of subquery that [NOT] EXISTS introduces has a notable characteristic: It contains correlations. Again, we could say that technically it doesn't have to and we're generalizing shamelessly, but we really do want to talk about queries of the general form:

```
Query #1:
SELECT * FROM Table1
  WHERE EXISTS
    (SELECT * FROM Table2
      WHERE Table1.column1 = Table2.column1)
```

Query #1 at least is better than the alternative expression:

```
Query #2:
SELECT * FROM Table1
  WHERE 0 <
    (SELECT COUNT(*) FROM Table2
      WHERE Table1.column1 = Table2.column1)
GAIN: -4/7
```

The reason the COUNT(*) alternative (Query #2) is slower than Query #1 is that a subquery's nested-loop breaks out as soon as there's a match. That's like stopping the count when you reach the number one. Not that anybody would really consider the COUNT(*) alternative, but it illustrates nicely the maxim—Don't ask for more precision than is needed to answer the question. The condition > 0 (or 0 <) is often a hint of an underlying "Yes/No" question.

Some DBMSs will repeat a correlated subquery for each occurrence of the outer row. You can check if your DBMS is one of them by doing a simple test: Double the number of outer rows, and see if the statement takes about twice as long. We did this with the Big Eight (GAIN: -2/7). The result shows that two of the Big Eight do slow down if the outer query gets bigger. For such DBMSs, it's good if you can put a significant restriction on the outer query. Doing so won't harm performance overall.

EXISTS (SELECT * ...)

*We want to dispose of a popular superstition that says—Instead of using SELECT * in an EXISTS subquery, you should use a short and specific select list. To test this "tip," we tried these three variants on some large tables:*

```
SELECT * FROM Table1
  WHERE EXISTS
    (SELECT * FROM Table2)

SELECT * FROM Table1
  WHERE EXISTS
    (SELECT column1 FROM Table2)

SELECT * FROM Table1
  WHERE EXISTS
    (SELECT 5 FROM Table2)
```

All three queries took the same amount of time.

Indexing both `Table1.column1` and `Table2.column1` is advantageous because either one might be the object of an index-lookup.

IN or EXISTS?

If IN and EXISTS have different plans, and if IN can be transformed to EXISTS, which should you use: IN or EXISTS? Consider these two equivalent queries:

```
SELECT * FROM Table1
  WHERE Table1.column1 IN
    (SELECT Table2.column1 FROM Table2)

SELECT * FROM Table1
  WHERE EXISTS
    (SELECT * FROM Table2
      WHERE Table1.column1 = Table2.column1)
```

Which query is better? It's impossible to say by just looking at them, but if the scenarios were slightly different, or if we knew a little more about the tables, we'd be able to make some tentative guesses:

- If `Table1` has many rows and `Table2` has few rows, use IN (GAIN: 2/7).
- If the outer query has an additional restrictive expression (e.g., `WHERE Table1.column2 = 5`), use EXISTS (GAIN: 2/7).
- If the outer query is `WHERE NOT ...`, use NOT EXISTS (GAIN: 3/7).

For each scenario, the derivation follows from the reasoning we've gone through to this point.

Double INs

Sometimes a subquery will add sets together. Here's an example:

```
SELECT * FROM Table1
  WHERE EXISTS
    (SELECT * FROM Table2
       WHERE Table1.column1 = Table2.column1
     UNION
     SELECT * FROM Table3
       WHERE Table1.column2 = Table3.column1)
```

There are two problems with this example. First, many DBMSs don't support UNION in a subquery. Second, it's slow! It's better to transform queries like this one to a SELECT with an outer query that contains two IN subqueries. Here's how:

```
SELECT * FROM Table1
  WHERE Table1.column1 IN
    (SELECT Table2.column1 FROM Table2)
    OR Table1.column2 IN
      (SELECT Table3.column1 FROM Table3)
GAIN: 2/3
```

Portability   Informix, Ingres, InterBase, and Sybase don't allow UNION in subqueries. The gain shown is for only three DBMSs.

Here's another example. Query #1 could be transformed to Query #2:

```
Query #1
SELECT * FROM Table1
  WHERE Table1.column1 IN
    (SELECT Table2.column1 FROM Table2)
    AND Table1.column2 IN
        (SELECT Table2.column2 FROM Table2)

Query #2
SELECT * FROM Table1
  WHERE (Table1.column1, Table1.column2) IN
      (SELECT Table2.column1, Table2.column2 FROM Table2)
```

But this transform works only if the DBMS supports row subqueries—a rare feature. If your DBMS doesn't support row subqueries, you can still get the effect of the transform by using arithmetic or concatenation, like this:

```
SELECT * FROM Table1
  WHERE Table1.column1 || ',' || Table1.column2 IN
      (SELECT Table2.column1 || ',' || Table2.column2
          FROM Table2)
GAIN: 4/6
```

WARNING   Don't do this for Sybase; it shows a loss. The gain shown is for only six DBMSs.

Here's a final example. Query #1 transforms into Query #2:

```
Query #1:
SELECT * FROM Table1
  WHERE Table1.column1 IN
      (SELECT Table2.column1 FROM Table2
          WHERE Table2.column1 IN
              (SELECT Table3.column1 FROM Table3))
```

```
Query #2:
SELECT * FROM Table1
  WHERE Table1.column1 IN
    (SELECT Table2.column1 FROM Table2)
    AND Table1.column1 IN
        (SELECT Table3.column1 FROM Table3)
GAIN: 7/7
```

It's better to merge two subqueries into one.

TOP

Some DBMSs support a nonstandard SQL extension TOP <number> clause for the SELECT statement. TOP (or its equivalent) finds the first [number] rows that match the SELECT requirements. For example, Microsoft lets you do this:

```
SELECT * FROM Table1 X
  WHERE X.column1 IN
      (SELECT TOP 5 Y.column1 FROM Table2 Y
          WHERE Y.column2 = X.column2
          ORDER BY Y.column1 DESC)
```

The example looks only for the first five rows that are true for the subquery, then evaluates the rest of the query with that data. (Microsoft also allows ORDER BY in a subquery if a TOP clause is in the select list.) Table 6–2 shows the TOP equivalent support provided by the Big Eight.

Table 6–2   *DBMSs and TOP Equivalent*

	SELECT clause that limits rows returned
IBM	FETCH FIRST <number>
Informix	FIRST <number>
Ingres	No support
InterBase	No support
Microsoft	TOP <number>
MySQL	LIMIT <number>
Oracle	SAMPLE (<number>)
Sybase	No support

> ALL

Conditions of the form > ALL (subquery) have a slight portability problem. If the subquery has zero rows, then most DBMSs correctly say the condition is true—but some incorrectly say the condition is false. Fortunately, none of the Big Eight have this flaw.

Be that as it may, > ALL conditions should be replaced by > ANY conditions with a MAX in the subquery. For example, Query #1 should be replaced by Query #2:

```
Query #1:
SELECT * FROM Table1
  WHERE column1 > ALL
     (SELECT column1 FROM Table2)

Query #2:
SELECT * FROM Table1
  WHERE column1 > ANY
     (SELECT MAX(column1) FROM Table2)
GAIN: 5/7
```

The idea in this example is that if Table2.column1 is indexed, then the DBMS may have an optimal way to find MAX(column1). (Note that these queries can return different results if Table2 is empty, or if Table2.column1 contains NULLs.)

Set Operations

A subquery is a type of set operation. Suppose you have a set of rows from an outer query (OUTER) and a set of rows from an inner query (INNER). For IN subqueries, (OUTER) values must contain (INNER) values. For NOT IN subqueries, (OUTER) values must *not* contain (INNER) values. Both of these operations could also be done with *explicit* set operators, namely INTERSECT and EXCEPT. Many DBMSs don't support INTERSECT or EXCEPT, although all DBMSs except MySQL support another set operator: UNION. Table 6–3 shows the SQL Standard requirements and the level of support the Big Eight have for the set operators. Notes on Table 6–3:

• Oracle and Sybase call EXCEPT the MINUS operator.

Table 6–3 *ANSI/DBMS Support for Set Operators*

	UNION	EXCEPT	INTERSECT	UNION JOIN
ANSI SQL	Yes	Yes	Yes	Yes
IBM	Yes	Yes	Yes	No
Informix	Yes	No	No	No
Ingres	Yes	No	No	No
InterBase	Yes	No	No	No
Microsoft	Yes	No	No	No
MySQL	No	No	No	No
Oracle	Yes	Yes	Yes	No
Sybase	Yes	Yes	No	No

It matters little whether a DBMS supports INTERSECT, but the EXCEPT operator is useful for transforming NOT IN. For example, Query #1 can be transformed to Query #2:

```
Query #1:
SELECT column1 FROM Table1
  WHERE Table1.column2 NOT IN
      (SELECT column2 FROM Table2)

Query #2:
SELECT column1 FROM Table1
EXCEPT
SELECT column1 FROM Table1
  WHERE Table1.column2 IN
      (SELECT column2 FROM Table2)
GAIN: 2/3
```

Portability Informix, Ingres, InterBase, and Microsoft don't support EXCEPT. The gain shown is for only three DBMSs.

The gain happens because IN conditions use indexes. NOT IN conditions don't use indexes.

The Bottom Line: Syntax Choices

In general, in-to-out plans occur for subqueries that (a) begin with <comparison operator> [ANY | ALL] and (b) contain no correlations.

If a subquery is in-to-out, then the relationship should be few-rows-to-many.

The best optimizations are ones that reduce the row count in the driver.

Add DISTINCT to the inner query, even when it's logically superfluous. DISTINCT causes ORDER BY, and it reduces the number of rows in the inner query.

Scanning is faster if the inner loop happens on a materialized view of the table, which is smaller than the table itself. DISTINCT helps here as well.

Materialization is a factor that discourages the DBMS from flattening.

If DISTINCT is a do-nothing operator because there's no duplication, then the relation is not one-to-many. A join is probably better than a subquery in such cases.

[NOT] EXISTS subqueries generally contain correlations.

If you can put a significant restriction on the outer query, that's good—even if the restriction has to be repeated in the inner query.

Because you can't break out of the outer loop when using [NOT] EXISTS, it's more effective to reduce the number of outer-loop iterations.

Use IN for subqueries when the outer table has many rows and the inner table has few rows.

Use EXISTS for subqueries when the outer query has a search condition in addition to the subquery condition.

Use NOT EXISTS for subqueries that have a WHERE NOT outer query.

Don't write queries that contain two subqueries. It's better to merge two subqueries into one.

Conditions of the form > ALL (subquery) have a portability problem. Replace > ALL conditions with > ANY conditions that have a MAX function in the subquery.

The EXCEPT operator is useful for transforming NOT IN subqueries. EXCEPT provides a gain because it changes NOT IN to IN. IN conditions use indexes. NOT IN conditions don't use indexes.

Parting Shots

When you use subqueries, you are giving the DBMS a weak "hint" about processing plans, but the DBMS still has plenty of scope for decision making. Each of the possible plans may be best for certain situations so a blanket statement like "always flatten" would be facile. But when you know the situation, and you know how to influence the plan, you can do some of the decision making yourself.

7

Columns

When you're defining a column, the first question you should ask is—What data is possible or impossible for this column? For example, a "phone number" column should accommodate all possible phone numbers but no impossible ones; a "book title" column should accommodate uppercase conversion but not addition. Your second question should be—Given the answer to the first question, what data type is both efficient and portable for this column? For example, an elapsed-minutes column might be defined as INTEGER rather than INTERVAL because INTEGER is smaller and is more easily cast to a C data type.

This chapter is all about how you can choose the data type and size for a column without growing dependent on any DBMS's foibles. After discussing the general questions of column size and size variability, we'll look at the main built-in SQL data types: characters, temporals, numbers, bits, and "large objects" such as BLOBs. Then we'll consider factors that cause overhead regardless of data type, such as nullability and column order within a table definition. In our discussions, we'll highlight both storage and performance issues.

How Big Is the Size Factor?

"Drake's formula looks scientific, but the result can be anywhere from 0% to 100%."
—Peter D. Ward and Donald Brownlee, *Rare Earth;*
Why Complex Life Is Uncommon in the Universe,
Copernicus Springer-Verlag, New York

These days, disk drives are cheap, and reducing disk space is not in itself a performance issue anymore. What is important is the answer to this question—If I make every column smaller, will every application get faster, and if so how much? Alas, the answer depends so much on the application, we have to hedge and hum. . . . Yes, but, if.

The most important factor in performance is the number of reads and writes the DBMS makes. The minimum input/output unit is the **page**. Rows of data never overlap page boundaries (except with InterBase and Oracle), so a 10% reduction in row size won't always cause a 10% reduction in the number of pages. Still, if the row size is small and the average is calculated over many tables, that reduction in size should be true. Given this, if you reduce row sizes by 10%, a 1,000-page table will be reduced to 900 pages. Extrapolating, let's further assume that an index with 1,000 pages will thus be reduced to 910 pages (because there will be more keys in an index page, but the reduction is a bit less than 10% because the ROWID part of an index key never changes in size). The effect on performance is good:

- Sequential scans will read 10% fewer pages.

- Indexed scans will read $\log_2(9) = 3.17\%$ fewer pages, or one less page 3.17% of the time on average.

- Multiple-row fetches will read fewer rows because the probability of two rows being in the same page is greater.

- A **data-change statement** (INSERT, UPDATE, or DELETE) will write the same number of pages. Fewer pages doesn't translate to fewer writes because a typical OLTP transaction causes a single page write, and that fact is unaffected by the number of rows in a page.

So—reducing column sizes might cause the number of I/Os to go down 10%, or 0%. But if all four of the preceding scenarios are equally probable, the number of I/Os goes down 6% on average.[1]

What about non-I/O? Let's assume that about 50% of CPU time is devoted to fixed-overhead calculations like stack pushes or conditional jumps. The rest of the time is spent doing in-memory copying (which will go down 10%), sorting (which will go down 10% because more keys fit in temporary memory), and operations on columns (which will go down 10% because of the on-chip cache and more than 10% for operations on character columns).

In simplified terms, then, let's conclude that for an example scenario where the row size goes down 10%, the CPU time goes down 5%. Yes, many assumptions went into this conclusion—as we said at the start, hedge hum. . . . Yes, but, if! But we can draw this generalization from our conclusion—If opportunities exist to reduce row size by 10%, you now have plausible reasons to conjecture that CPU time will correspondingly be reduced by 5%. (We ran a very simple 10-character versus 9-character test on the Big Eight and got an average speed gain of 6.5%.) Of course you will have to measure real data afterward to know for sure, but the conjecture will help you decide whether it's worth trying to reduce row size at all.

Fixed or Variable?

"And if the bed was too large, Procrustes stretched his guest
on a rack until he fitted. . . ."
—Plutarch, "Theseus The Athenian Adventurer"

When should a column be fixed-size? When should it be variable-length? Does the distinction make any difference?

The best-known example of a fixed-size SQL data type is CHARACTER (or CHAR), as opposed to CHARACTER VARYING (or VARCHAR), which may vary

---

1. We haven't taken caching into account for these calculations because, although the existence of a cache reduces the number of read/writes, the probability that a page is in cache is slightly greater if files are smaller. Did you know that "seek" takes seven milliseconds on MS Windows NT even if the disk head doesn't move? We did not take no-wait writing into account for similar reasons.

in size. In fact, several other data types have fixed- and variable-length equivalents, such as ANSI SQL's BIT versus BIT VARYING, IBM's GRAPHIC versus VARGRAPHIC, Sybase's BINARY versus VARBINARY, and so on. But sometimes the storage method for a column depends not so much on the defined data type, as on the column's nullability attribute, or even on the data type of *other* columns. To be specific:

- For Microsoft 6.5 and Sybase, if a column can contain NULL, then it is also variable-length. That is, a column defined as VARCHAR(15) NOT NULL is variable-length—but so is a column defined as CHAR(15) NULL.
- For MySQL, if *any* column in a table is defined as variable-length, then all columns are. So if you define one column as CHAR(15) and another as VARCHAR(15), you end up with two variable-length columns. (On the other hand, if all character columns have four bytes or fewer, you end up with all fixed-size columns regardless of data type definition.)
- For all other DBMSs or situations, the column's data type declaration is definitive.

All DBMSs store the size of a variable-length column in a separate value that is between one and four bytes long. Because of this overhead, it is worthless to ask for variable-length if the average size of the column's data will be less than four bytes, or if the average size doesn't vary. The result would be a swelling of row size—not a shrinking. However, in all other circumstances, variable-length columns are shorter, sometimes by a large factor. They are also more accurate. For example, in a CHAR(8) column, it's not possible to tell whether this string:

'NANCY   '

contained trailing spaces originally, or whether the spaces were added as filler. With a VARCHAR(8) column, though, you would know that the trailing spaces were not added by the DBMS.[2]

---

2. This applies to all DBMSs except InterBase, which uses **Run-Length Encoding (RLE)** for compression. RLE has the effect of reducing lengths for columns that have a large number of repeating bytes, such as spaces or NULLs. However, InterBase will expand to full defined sizes when reading or transmitting.

The argument against a variable-length column is that it takes longer to update. Let's be clear here. It does *not* take longer to read a row with variable-length columns, because all DBMSs use size values rather than null-terminators (like C). It *does* take longer to *update* a row with variable-length columns though, and the reason is shifts. (A **shift** is the movement of rows caused by a change in the row size. When the length of a row is changed due to an UPDATE or DELETE operation, that row and all subsequent rows on the page may have to be moved, or shifted.)

Consider a table with three columns defined as CHAR(3), VARCHAR(10), and VARCHAR(10), respectively. Figure 7–1 shows what a page for such a table might look like.

Suppose the second column of the first row shown in Figure 7–1 is updated from ABCDE to ABCDEF. How will the DBMS fit the larger string in? Well, first it shifts the next column (containing WOMBATS) forward one byte to make room for the new string. This causes the WOMBATS column to overflow into the next row, so the DBMS then shifts that row down, and so on all the way down the page. If no free space is at the end of the page, there's a page overflow, and the DBMS then has to make room by taking an entire row of the page and migrating it to another page. So by adding *one* character to a column value, you can cause thousands of bytes to move, and can even cause an extra page write (or more, where logs are involved).

Shifts, particularly forward shifts, are so severe that the time lost by one UPDATE is greater than the time saved by making the column a few bytes smaller. Don't focus on one column when you think about this! It's not really a matter of whether the column can change size—it's a matter of whether the *row* can change size. So even if you define a column (say, column1) to be fixed-size solely because you're worried about UPDATE speed, but you define a later column (say, column2) to be variable-length, shifts can still occur.

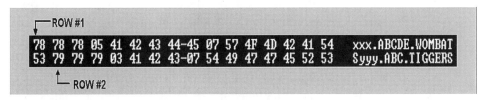

Figure 7–1 *A page*

How can you prevent shifts? Obviously, one way is to use fixed-size data types exclusively. But even that won't always work. For example, in Microsoft, rows affected by UPDATE triggers or replicated by certain options will cause a "DELETE followed by an INSERT (elsewhere)" instead of an "UPDATE in place"—that is, shifts happen anyway.

Another way, which won't reduce the number of shifts within a page but will at least reduce the overflows, is to declare at the outset that a certain amount of the page should be left free initially, in case rows expand (this option is variously called PCTFREE or FILLFACTOR; see the section "Free Page Space" in Chapter 8, "Tables").

A third way to prevent shifts, which works if values tend to be small at first and grow later, is to start by putting a filler in a variable-length column. For example:

```
INSERT INTO Table1 (variable_column)
  VALUES ('plain       -')
 /* do this initially */

... time passes ...

UPDATE Table1 SET
  variable_column = 'Rain in Spain'
 /* no forward shift occurs */
```

Unfortunately, the filler characters can't be all spaces because of a bug, which we'll talk about later.

Finally, to prevent shifts, some DBMS vendors recommend that you not index variable-length columns.

The Bottom Line: The Size Factor

If (maximum size > (mean size + 4 bytes)) and there are many reads for every UPDATE, use variable-length data types because you'll save time and space.

If a column can contain NULL and the DBMS is Microsoft or Sybase, use variable-length data types because you have no choice.

Other considerations to take into account are whether the column is indexed, whether all rows are equally important, and whether triggers are used. We'll discuss these matters in other chapters.

If you use variable-length columns, set aside a small amount of free space per page to allow for swelling.

Once you decide to make a column variable-length, you could also decide to give it an absurd size because the defined length doesn't affect storage size. Don't do that—the DBMS might have to allot the full defined length in temporary uses. For example, when InterBase sends rows from the server to the client, the packet size is determined based on the defined column sizes, not the average or actual sizes. So never define column lengths greater than you really possibly need. Remember that you can always ALTER TABLE later—you won't have fun, but you can do it.

Characters

The SQL Standard provides four data types for columns that contain character string data: CHAR, VARCHAR, NATIONAL CHARACTER (or NCHAR), and NATIONAL CHARACTER VARYING (or NCHAR VARYING). DBMSs that support these data types may set their own maximum lengths for each. Table 7–1 shows the SQL Standard requirements and the level of support (data type and maximum size in characters or bytes) the Big Eight have for character data types, while Table 7–2 shows how the SQL Standard and the DBMSs treat trailing spaces and data truncation for character columns.

Notes on Table 7–1:

- The figures in Table 7–1 show the maximum-possible defined length of an SQL character column. For example, the largest CHAR column possible with Ingres is CHAR(2000), which lets you insert strings up to 2,000

Table 7–1 *ANSI/DBMS Support for Character Data Types*

	CHAR	VARCHAR	NCHAR	NCHAR VARYING	Other
ANSI SQL	Yes	Yes	Yes	Yes	No
IBM	254 bytes	32KB	No	No	No
Informix	32KB	255 bytes	32KB	255 bytes	2KB
Ingres	2KB	2KB	No	No	No
InterBase	32KB	32KB	32KB	32KB	No
Microsoft	8KB	8KB	8KB	8KB	No
MySQL	255 bytes	255 bytes	255 bytes	255 bytes	64KB
Oracle	2KB	4KB	2KB	4KB	No
Sybase	16KB	16KB	16KB	16KB	No

characters long, the largest possible VARCHAR column with MySQL is VARCHAR(255), which lets you insert strings up to 255 characters long, and so on. The maximum length often depends on the page size, as with Sybase. The SQL Standard lets vendors set the maximum sizes of each data type.

- The defined length and the length in bytes is the same if—and only if— the character size is one byte. This, of course, depends on the character set being used.

- Informix calls the NCHAR VARYING data type NVARCHAR. Informix also supports LVARCHAR, for variable-length character data up to 2KB long.

- MySQL also supports BLOB (for case-sensitive character values larger than the CHAR/VARCHAR maximum) and TEXT (for case-insensitive character values larger than the CHAR/VARCHAR maximum). BLOB and TEXT maxima are 65,535 characters.

Notes on Table 7–2:

- Strips Trailing Space from VARCHAR column

  This column is "No" if the DBMS follows the SQL Standard and does not strip trailing spaces from a string assigned to a variable-length column.

Table 7–2 *ANSI/DBMS Support for Character String Operations*

	Strips Trailing Space from VARCHAR	**Warning on Truncate**
ANSI SQL	No	Yes
IBM	No	Yes
Informix	No	No
Ingres	No	Yes
InterBase	No	Yes
Microsoft	No	Yes
MySQL	Yes	No
Oracle	No	Yes
Sybase	Yes	No

:: Informix does not strip trailing spaces on INSERT, but it does strip them when you SELECT from a VARCHAR column; not a very useful trait.

- Warning on Truncate column

  This column is "Yes" if the DBMS follows the SQL Standard and returns a truncation warning or error if you assign a too-long string to a character column.

  :: Sybase will provide a truncation error if SET STRING_RTRUNCATION is on.

Because we're trying to determine whether it's best to define columns with a fixed-size data type or a variable-length data type, we'll ignore the distinctions between, say, CHAR and NCHAR and concentrate on the question—Should CHAR or VARCHAR be used to define columns? The main difference between the two is that CHAR is fixed-size while VARCHAR is variable-length—a consideration we've already dealt with. But there are five other differences to consider as well.

One: Changes to maximum size

Until recently, VARCHAR's maximum length was often shorter than CHAR's. For example, in Microsoft 6.5, a VARCHAR column couldn't be longer than 255 characters. If you're upgrading an old application, it's time to see whether more columns should be VARCHAR now.

Two: Trailing spaces

If you insert this string:

```
'X'
```

into a CHAR(5) column, the DBMS will pad with four trailing spaces and store this string:

```
'X    '
```

On the other hand, if you insert:

```
'X  '
```

into a VARCHAR(5) column, an ANSI SQL DBMS will keep the trailing spaces and store:

```
'X   '
```

That is, a VARCHAR column does not lose meaningful information about trailing spaces. However, several DBMSs are not SQL Standard-compliant (see Table 7-2). With those DBMSs, it's impossible to determine how many spaces were inserted originally.

Three: Concatenation

Because of the space padding requirement, concatenating CHAR columns involves extra work. For example, suppose you have two columns, forename and surname, each defined as CHAR(20). The concatenation of forename with surname, for example:

```
SELECT forename || surname
  FROM Table1 ...
```

would result in a string that looks like this (except with MySQL and Sybase):

```
'Paul              Larue              '
```

Probably not the result you're looking for! To get the DBMS to return the logical result:

```
'Paul Larue'
```

you'd need to amend your query to:

```
SELECT TRIM(forename) || ' ' || TRIM(surname)
  FROM Table1 ...
```

Four: Data type conversion

CHAR and VARCHAR are two different data types, so expressions of the form char_column = varchar_column involve data type conversions. Some DBMSs won't use indexes if conversions are necessary, so be consistent when defining columns that might be compared or joined.

Five: Truncation

If you make a mistake and insert ABCDE into a CHAR(4) column, don't expect to see an error or warning message. Some DBMSs will silently truncate your string to ABCD and you'll lose possibly vital data (see Table 7–2).

Length Specification

Whether you choose to use CHAR or VARCHAR, you'll also have to decide on a length specification for the column. When defining length, most people err on the side of caution. For example, they find the longest value in the original input data and then double that value for the resulting column length. Here are some length-specification hints, relevant to columns that contain names:

- The longest name in the Bible is *Maher-shalal-hash-baz* (21 characters; Isaiah 8:1).

- The longest legal URL is 63 characters.

- The longest taxonomic name, *Archaeosphaerodiniopsidaceae*, has 28 characters. The famous long words *antidisestablishmentarianism* and *floccinaucinihilipilification* have 28 and 29 characters, respectively.

- The names of American states and Canadian provinces can be abbreviated to two-letter codes, and the names of countries can be abbreviated using the three-letter ISO codes for nations. (It's best not to use the ISO two-letter nation codes because of duplication that could cause confusion. For example, the two-letter ISO code for the Cayman Islands is *KY*, which is also the abbreviation for Kentucky.)

- That famous long Welsh name, *Llanfairpwllgwyngyllgogerychwyrndrobwll Llantysiliogogogoch*, can be abbreviated to *Llanfair PG*.

Variant Character Sets

You can use CHARACTER SET clauses to support variant character sets, but it's more convenient to use this convention:

- Use CHAR/VARCHAR for the basic Western European character set (variously called ISO 8859-1 or Windows 1252 or Latin1).

- Use NCHAR/NCHAR VARYING for the alternate national-language set.

The obvious alternate NCHAR/NCHAR VARYING set is Unicode, and that's what you'll always get with Microsoft, Oracle, and Sybase. Unicode is the Java default, so conversions to/from Java host variables are easy, but for most ODBC and **ActiveX Data Objects (ADO)** drivers, there's extra overhead. Here are some other Unicode considerations:

- There are actually two different Unicode sets. One uses two bytes for each character; the other uses up to three bytes per character.
- With Intel processors, 16-bit operations are penalized. For example it takes about three times longer to compare two 16-bit values than to compare two 8-bit values.
- Responsible DBMSs will use Unicode for system table names.
- There is no guarantee that you can use collation options with Unicode.

Speaking of collation—the fastest collation is binary. A binary collation is usually managed by either defining a column with a FOR BIT DATA/BINARY attribute or by forcing a binary collation in some other way—preferably with the ANSI SQL COLLATE clause. (For a discussion of collations, see Chapter 3, "ORDER BY.") You should not, however, use a binary collation if there are Unicode characters and the storage is big-endian.

If you do use a national-language character set, you'll be happy to know that all DBMSs except InterBase support the LOWER and UPPER functions correctly despite a strange SQL-92 requirement that only "simple Latin letters" should be converted.

The Bottom Line: Characters

Some DBMSs won't give you an error or warning message if you insert a too-large value into a character column. They'll just silently truncate, and you'll lose possibly vital data.

Use CHAR/VARCHAR for the basic Western European character set (ISO 8859-1 or Windows 1252). Use NCHAR/NCHAR VARYING for the alternate national-language set, which will often be Unicode.

In the past, VARCHAR's maximum length was often shorter than CHAR's. If you're upgrading an old application, it's time to see whether more columns should be VARCHAR now.

An SQL-compliant DBMS will pad with trailing spaces, if necessary, when inserting into a CHAR column. It will not strip trailing spaces when inserting into a VARCHAR column, so a VARCHAR column does not lose meaningful information about trailing spaces.

Because of the space padding, concatenating CHAR columns involves extra work.

Expressions of the form char_column = varchar_column involve data type conversions. Be data type consistent when defining columns that might be compared or joined.

Recommendation: Prefer VARCHAR/NCHAR VARYING for character string data.

Temporals

The SQL Standard provides four data types for columns that contain temporal data: DATE, TIME, TIMESTAMP, and INTERVAL. Table 7–3 shows the SQL Standard requirements and the level of support (data type and storage size in bytes) the Big Eight have for these data types, while Table 7–4 shows the minimum and maximum temporal values/value sizes allowed for each data type.

Table 7–3   *ANSI/DBMS Support for Temporal Data Types*

	DATE	TIME	TIMESTAMP	WITH TIME ZONE	INTERVAL	DATETIME
ANSI SQL	Yes	Yes	Yes	Yes	Yes	No
IBM	4	3	10	No	No	No
Informix	4	No	No	No	11	11
Ingres	12	No	No	No	No	No
InterBase	8	8	8	No	No	No
Microsoft	No	No	No	No	No	8
MySQL	3	3	4	No	No	8
Oracle	7	No	11	13	11	No
Sybase	No	No	No	No	No	8

Notes on Table 7–3:

- Informix calls the TIMESTAMP data type DATETIME and requires precision qualifiers to be added to it, as with INTERVAL. The DATETIME data type takes between 5 and 11 bytes of storage, depending on the qualifier. Informix supports both SQL Standard INTERVAL options. INTERVAL YEAR TO MONTH uses 4 bytes of storage, while INTERVAL DAY TO SECOND requires up to 11 bytes.

- Ingres calls the TIMESTAMP data type DATE.

- Microsoft and Sybase call the TIMESTAMP data type DATETIME.

- Oracle's DATE and TIMESTAMP data types both include a TIME. The TIMESTAMP data type size ranges from 7 to 11 bytes, depending on the precision. If WITH TIME ZONE is added, TIMESTAMP requires 13 bytes of storage. Oracle supports both SQL Standard INTERVAL options. INTERVAL YEAR TO MONTH uses 5 bytes of storage, while INTERVAL DAY TO SECOND requires 11 bytes.

Table 7–4   *ANSI/DBMS Temporal Ranges*

	DATE Min	DATE Max	TIME Precision Default	TIMESTAMP Precision Default	Fractional Seconds Specifiable
ANSI SQL	0001-01-01	9999-12-31	N/S	N/S	Yes
IBM	0001-01-01	9999-12-31	Second	Microsecond	No
Informix	0001-01-01	9999-12-31	Millisecond	Millisecond	Yes
Ingres	0001-01-01	9999-12-31	Second	Second	No
InterBase	0001-01-01	9999-12-31	Second	Second	No
Microsoft	1753-01-01	9999-12-31	Millisecond	Millisecond	No
MySQL	0001-01-01	9999-12-31	Second	Second	No
Oracle	01-JAN-4712 BC	31-DEC-4712 AD	Microsecond	Microsecond	Yes
Sybase	1753-01-01	9999-12-31	Millisecond	Millisecond	No

Notes on Table 7–4:

- DATE Min column

  Shows the minimum date allowed by the DBMS in DATE, TIMESTAMP, or equivalent columns.

  :: MySQL's TIMESTAMP has a minimum date portion of `'1970-01-01'`. MySQL's DATETIME has a minimum date portion of `'0001-01-01'`.

- DATE Max column

  Shows the maximum date allowed by the DBMS in DATE, TIMESTAMP, or equivalent columns.

  :: MySQL's TIMESTAMP has a maximum date portion of `'2037-12-31'`. MySQL's DATETIME has a maximum date portion of `'9999-12-31'`.

- TIME Precision Default column

  Shows the default fractional seconds precision supported by the DBMS in TIME, TIMESTAMP, or equivalent columns. This column is "second" if the DBMS doesn't accept a time with a fractional seconds portion, such as `TIME '15:30:10.25'`.

- TIMESTAMP Precision Default column

  Shows the default fractional seconds precision supported by the DBMS in TIMESTAMP or equivalent columns. This column is "second" if the DBMS doesn't accept a time with a fractional seconds portion, such as `TIMESTAMP '2002-02-10 15:30:10.25'`.

- Fractional Seconds Specifiable column

  This column is "Yes" if the DBMS supports a fractional seconds precision definition for TIME, TIMESTAMP, or equivalent columns, as in:

  ```
  CREATE TABLE Table1 (
     column1 TIME(2)
     ...)
  ```

  which ensures that every `column1` value will be a time with a fractional seconds precision of two digits—for example, `TIME '15:30:10.25'`.

The main SQL Standard data types for temporal information are DATE, TIME, and TIMESTAMP. There is also an INTERVAL data type, supported only by Informix and Oracle; a TIME WITH TIME ZONE data type, supported only by

Minimum Date Value

Looking at Table 7–4, you'll see that the minimum date value varies a lot. The explanations for the various minimum year figures chosen are:

- "0001" (1 AD) is the first allowable year according to the SQL Standard.
- "1582" is the year the Gregorian calendar was first used in some Catholic countries.
- "1753" is the year the Gregorian calendar became official in England and America.
- "4713 BC" is the year from which we count Julian days. The start date of the Julian period was calculated by Julius Scaliger, who proposed that days should be counted in decimal, without regard to months or years. Astronomers adopted this system and took noon GMT-4712-01-01 Julian (that is, January 1, 4713 BC) as their zero point. (Note that 4713 BC is the year –4712 according to the astronomical year numbering.)

In fact, the differences are unimportant, because the DBMSs that support dates such as '0001-01-01' are merely projecting the Gregorian calendar backward in time as if it was in force in 1 AD. This assumption, which is called *prolepticism*, is false—so calculations that use old dates are specious.

PostgreSQL, and the PostgreSQL makers say you shouldn't use it; and a TIMESTAMP WITH TIME ZONE data type, supported only by Oracle, although IBM has a CURRENT TIMEZONE niladic function: subtracting CURRENT TIMEZONE from a local time converts the local time to Universal Coordinated Time (UTC). So there isn't much diversity here, except for precision and the curious business of the minimum date value.

DATE, TIME, and TIMESTAMP are all fixed-size fields so the size factor doesn't really come into play. The only significant decision you need to make for temporal data is whether you should use a combined date plus time data type, such as TIMESTAMP—even if you only need the time, or only need the date. Interestingly, if you use TIMESTAMP instead of DATE or TIME, you often aren't using any additional space because many DBMSs use a combined column internally anyway, as shown in Table 7–3.

In addition to the size factor, there are two other main advantages to using TIMESTAMP for temporal data:

- Comparisons are easier to write when everything has the same data type.

- There won't be any erroneous "date minus date" calculations by people who forget to take the time into account. One can always reformat later. (By the way, the same advice applies for any situation where there is a major and a minor component. For example, it's better to have a single "height" column containing 64 instead of a "feet" column containing 5 and an "inches" column containing 4.)

The Bottom Line: Temporals

If you use TIMESTAMP instead of DATE or TIME, you often aren't using any additional space because the DBMS uses a combined column for storage, internally. On the other hand, TIMESTAMPs sometimes take more space to store, partly because the default precision of a TIMESTAMP column includes a fractional seconds portion; information that is rarely necessary. Searches for the date component of a TIMESTAMP will be slow. The optimizer won't see that particular date values occur frequently because the time is stored along with it.

Dates and times are just different magnitudes of the same property—and we don't use two different columns to store the "integer" and "decimal" parts of a number, do we? Temporal comparisons and transfers are easier if there is only one data type. Furthermore, a TIME doesn't really mean anything unless the date is known as well.

TIMESTAMP (or its non-standard SQL-extension equivalent, DATETIME) is supported by more DBMSs than the other temporal data types.

Recommendation: Prefer TIMESTAMP for temporal data.

Numbers

There are three kinds of numbers: integers, floats (approximate numbers), and fixed-decimal numbers. (Technically, integers are a type of fixed-decimal number with a scale of zero, but storage methods for integers and decimal numbers differ so we'll talk about them separately.) There is also a number type that auto-increments—we'll call this a *serial*. All DBMSs except Oracle use similar numeric formats, so in our discussion of numeric data types, we'll talk about the "normal" DBMSs first and relegate Oracle's treatment of numbers to a sidebar.

Integers

The SQL Standard provides two data types for columns that contain integers: INTEGER (or INT) and SMALLINT. Table 7–5 shows the SQL Standard requirements

Table 7–5 *ANSI/DBMS Integer Support*

	INTEGER	SMALLINT	BIGINT/LONGINT	TINYINT/INTEGER1
ANSI SQL	Yes	Yes	No	No
IBM	4	2	8	No
Informix	4	2	8	No
Ingres	4	2	No	1
InterBase	4	2	No	No
Microsoft	4	2	8	1
MySQL	4	2	8	1
Oracle	Yes	Yes	No	No
Sybase	4	2	No	1

and the level of support (data type and size in bytes) the Big Eight have for these data types.

Notes on Table 7–5:

- INTEGER column

    A 32-bit binary (four bytes) allows for the range –2147483648 to +2147483647. ANSI and Informix disallow the value –2147483648 (hexadecimal 80000000).

- SMALLINT column

    A 16-bit binary (two bytes) allows for the range –32768 to +32767. ANSI and Informix disallow the value –32768 (hexadecimal 8000).

- BIGINT/LONGINT column

    A 64-bit binary (eight bytes) allows for the range –223372036854775808 to +9223372036854775807. Informix calls this data type INT8.

- TINYINT/INTEGER1 column

    An 8-bit binary (one byte) allows for the range –128 to +127. Microsoft and Sybase support unsigned TINYINT only, with a range from 0 to +255. MySQL supports both signed TINYINT (range –128 to +127) and unsigned TINYINT (range 0 to +255).

- Oracle accepts columns defined as INTEGER or SMALLINT but treats all numbers differently from other DBMSs; see the sidebar "Oracle Numbers."

Any number that has a scale of zero (no digits after the decimal point) should be in an integer column, because integer arithmetic is faster than arithmetic with a decimal point. In fact, the fastest arithmetic occurs with the specific SQL data type INTEGER because on a 32-bit machine (such as a Pentium), 32 bits is the native word size. Thus, for example:

```
CREATE TABLE Table1 (
   column1 SMALLINT)

INSERT INTO Table1 ...

SELECT column1 * 1234
  FROM Table1
```

is slower than:

```
CREATE TABLE Table1 (
   column1 INTEGER)

INSERT INTO Table1 ...

SELECT column1 * 1234
  FROM Table1
GAIN: 5/8
```

although the difference is unnoticeable unless millions of calculations happen.

The INTEGER data type is also the default data type of any literal that contains all digits. Consider the expression:

```
... WHERE column1 = 555
```

If column1 is a SMALLINT, the DBMS will have to cast its value to INTEGER before it can make the comparison with the integer literal 555.

The other integer data types have special advantages though:

- SMALLINT is the only other SQL Standard data type and is just half the size of INTEGER.
- TINYINT is the smallest and is still large enough for personal information, but beware: Even seemingly restricted data like "number of wives" or "height in centimeters" could cause overflow. (Solomon had 700

wives, and Goliath was six cubits and a span, or about 290 centimeters tall.)

- BIGINT is appropriate for numbers larger than two billion, though working with compilers that can't handle such large numbers could be troublesome.

Here's another consideration: At the beginning of this chapter, we said it's important to choose a data type that won't allow impossible values for a column. For example, if you have a list of mileages between world cities, using SMALLINT (and perhaps UNSIGNED if the DBMS allows it) gives you a free check constraint—it should be impossible to insert the absurd value 35000. We still hold to this advice, with one caveat—It Won't Always Work. That is:

> "On some systems, for example, the numeric operations for some data types may silently underflow or overflow."
>
> —*PostgreSQL Interactive Documentation*

> "When asked to store a value in a numeric column that is outside the column type's allowable range, MySQL clips the value to the appropriate endpoint of the range and stores the resulting value instead. Conversions that occur due to clipping are reported as 'warnings' for ALTER TABLE, LOAD DATA INFILE, UPDATE, and multi-row INSERT [but not for single-row INSERT]."
>
> —*MySQL Reference Manual* (Square bracket comment ours)

If input errors are a serious worry, only an explicit CHECK constraint will do the job right.

If you decide to define `column1` as INTEGER, don't just consider whether the largest possible value is less than or equal to 214783647, but also whether `SUM(column1)` will be less than or equal to 214783647. A DBMS will normally decide that the sum of an INTEGER column is a BIGINT or a DECIMAL—but it could just overflow instead.

Why are telephone numbers stored in CHAR(12) columns instead of BIGINT columns? The answer is that, although a CHAR(12) column is longer, there are built-in functions for all the operations that are likely to be performed on telephone numbers: LIKE, SUBSTRING, SIMILAR, and so on. Meanwhile, all the built-in numeric operators (+ – / *) are useless for telephone numbers. The general rule in such cases is that a column should have a non-numeric data type if all appropriate operations for it are non-numeric. A similar generality can be stated for the temporal data types.

Recommendation: Prefer INTEGER for integers unless maximum values—including those from arithmetic operations—exceed the INTEGER range.

Floats

The SQL Standard provides three data types for columns that contain floats: REAL, FLOAT, and DOUBLE PRECISION (or DOUBLE). Table 7–6 shows the SQL Standard requirements and the level of support (data type and precision) the Big Eight have for these data types.

Notes on Table 7–6:

- The letters IEEE mean "according to the IEEE 754 Standard for Binary Floating-Point Arithmetic." Informix and PostgreSQL use "the native C float," which coincidentally corresponds to IEEE 754 for any common C compiler.

- IEEE single storage is 32 bits (four bytes). It allows for seven-digit precision, with a usual range from –3.402E+38 to –1.175E–37 for negative numbers, zero, and from +1.175E-37 to +3.402E+38 for positive numbers.

- REAL and FLOAT(n)—where n <= 23—are usually synonymous and refer to a 32-bit floating-point number, IEEE single precision. InterBase, though, allows you to define a column with a specific precision for FLOAT, for example:

```
CREATE TABLE Table1 (
   column1 FLOAT(20))
```

Table 7–6   *ANSI/DBMS Float Support*

	REAL	FLOAT	DOUBLE PRECISION
ANSI SQL	Yes	Yes	Yes
IBM	IEEE single	IEEE double	IEEE double
Informix	IEEE single	IEEE double	IEEE double
Ingres	IEEE single	IEEE double	IEEE double
InterBase	IEEE single	IEEE single	IEEE double
Microsoft	IEEE single	IEEE double	IEEE double
MySQL	IEEE double	IEEE single	IEEE double
Oracle	Yes	Yes	Yes
Sybase	IEEE single	IEEE double	IEEE double

but ignores the precision specified. InterBase FLOAT(n) is always 64-bit IEEE double precision even though FLOAT alone is always 32-bit IEEE single precision.

- IEEE double storage is 64 bits (eight bytes). It allows for 15-digit precision, with a usual range from −1.798E+308 to −2.225E-307 for negative numbers, zero, and from +2.225E-307 to +1.798E+308 for positive numbers.

- DOUBLE PRECISION and FLOAT(n)—where n BETWEEN 24 AND 53—are usually synonymous and refer to a 64-bit floating-point number, IEEE double precision. For MySQL, REAL is synonymous with DOUBLE, rather than with FLOAT.

- Oracle accepts columns defined as REAL, FLOAT, or DOUBLE PRECISION, but treats all numbers differently from other DBMSs; see the sidebar "Oracle Numbers."

The official SQL term for FLOAT, REAL, and DOUBLE PRECISION values is "approximate numeric" but "floating point" or simply "float" is common. The key point for all such values is that the decimal point is *floating*. (If the decimal point is *fixed*, see the next section.) You should use float literals when working with floats. For example, use this type of expression:

```
UPDATE Table1 SET
    float_column = 1.25E02
```

instead of:

```
UPDATE Table1 SET
    float_column = 125
```

Portability MySQL won't accept a float literal unless it has a two-digit exponent. That is, the literal 1.25E02 is acceptable, but 1.25E2 is not. All other DBMSs allow you to drop the leading zero.

Floating-point operations are fast if they go through the computer's **Floating Point Unit (FPU),** but a compiler can make the cautious assumption that no FPU is present. In that case, floating-point operations are slow because they are emulated instead of performed with the FPU. When you install a DBMS, the installer should detect the FPU automatically and bring in the right code, whether FPU dependent or emulated, so make sure you rerun the install program after hardware upgrades or moves.

Take another look at Table 7-6 and the precisions shown for the float data types. The range of IEEE single-precision float is from –1.175E-37 to +3.402E+38, to 7 decimal digits precision, although some DBMSs are more cautious in stating the actual range supported. The range of IEEE double-precision float is from –2.225E-307 to +1.798E+308, to 15 decimal digits precision. Again, some DBMSs give a slightly smaller range. These sizes are shown in Table 7-7.

Table 7-7 shows that the range of a single-precision float is –1.175E-37 to +3.402E+38. In reality it isn't possible to store all the real numbers in that range in a four-byte space; it isn't even possible to store all the integers in that range in four bytes (the range of a four-byte INTEGER is from –2.14E9 to +2.14E9). So for most numbers in the single-precision range, you'll need to use whatever number is closest that *can* be represented in a single float. In other words, a floating-point number is exact in bit combinations—that is, all bit combinations are exact—but it might not be exactly the same as the number that was inserted originally. Hence the name *approximate*.

The question that arises from this is—Is it better to use DOUBLE PRECISION for float columns or REAL? (We'll ignore FLOAT entirely because REAL and DOUBLE are just synonyms for predefined sizes of FLOAT.)

We checked the Big Eight to see what happens if the same number is stored both ways. First, we created this table:

```
CREATE TABLE Table1 (
    real_column REAL,
    double_column DOUBLE PRECISION)
```

Table 7-7 *IEEE 754 Floats*

	Precision in Bits (effective mantissa size)	Precision in Decimal Digits (inexact)	Min	Max
Single Precision	<=23	7	–1.175E-37	+3.402E+38
Double Precision	>=24 AND <=53	15	–2.225E-307	+1.798E+308

Then we inserted the same number into both columns and selected:

```
INSERT INTO Table1 VALUES (0.01, 0.01)

SELECT * FROM Table1
  WHERE real_column = 0.01
/* result is zero rows, "incorrect" */

SELECT * FROM Table1
  WHERE double_column = 0.01
 /* result is one row, "correct" */
```

Most DBMSs returned the "correct" result for the second SELECT, but were unable to find a row where real_column contained the value 0.01. Due to their greater precision, DOUBLE PRECISION columns return the expected result more frequently than do REAL columns.

Recommendation: Prefer DOUBLE PRECISION for floats.

Decimals

The SQL Standard provides two data types for columns that contain fixed-decimal numbers: DECIMAL and NUMERIC. Table 7–8 shows the SQL Standard requirements and the level of support (data type and maximum precision in digits) the Big Eight have for these data types.

Table 7–8 *ANSI/DBMS Decimal Support*

	DECIMAL	**DECIMAL Precision**	**NUMERIC**	**NUMERIC Precision**
ANSI SQL	Yes	N/S	Yes	N/S
IBM	Yes	31	Yes	31
Informix	Yes	32	Yes	32
Ingres	Yes	31	Yes	31
InterBase	Yes	18	Yes	18
Microsoft	Yes	38	Yes	38
MySQL	Yes	254	Yes	254
Oracle	Yes	38	Yes	38
Sybase	Yes	38	Yes	38

Notes on Table 7–8:

- IBM, Informix, Ingres, Microsoft, Oracle, and Sybase store decimal values as packed decimal values; see the sidebar "Oracle Numbers."
- InterBase stores decimal values inside SMALLINTs, INTEGERs, BIGINTs, or FLOATs, depending on the defined size. The longest string of 9s that could fit in a BIGINT is 999999999999999999 (eighteen 9s) so DECIMAL(18) is the largest precise fixed-decimal number that such a trick can accommodate.
- MySQL stores decimal values as unpacked floating-point numbers—that is, MySQL decimals are stored as strings, using one character for each digit of the value, plus another character for the sign and decimal point if applicable. The maximum number of digits that can be specified is 254, but the actual range for both DECIMAL and NUMERIC is the same as for a double-precision float (see DOUBLE PRECISION in Table 7–6).

A fixed-decimal number is one that has a fixed-decimal precision. For example, DECIMAL(7,2) has a precision of seven digits, with a fixed scale—the number of digits after the decimal point—of two digits. If the data type of a column is DECIMAL, then the actual precision must be at least as big as the defined precision. If the data type of a column is NUMERIC, then the actual precision should be exactly the same as the defined precision, but in practice most DBMSs treat NUMERIC as a synonym for DECIMAL.

Any numeric literal can take three forms, as shown in Table 7–9. Notice that Table 7–9 shows that the number 17.7 is a DECIMAL—not a FLOAT. This can confuse C programmers because in C the literal value 17.7 is a float.

All DBMSs except for InterBase and MySQL store DECIMAL values as a packed string of decimal digits, usually with two decimal digits per byte; see

Table 7–9 *Forms of a Numeric Literal*

Form	Data type	Example
Digits and no decimal point	INTEGER	537
Digits with decimal point	DECIMAL	17.7
Exponential notation	FLOAT	1.32E15

the sidebar "Oracle Numbers." InterBase, as mentioned earlier, stores decimal values inside integers, while MySQL stores them as unpacked strings.

The primary advantage of DECIMAL is that it is easy to cast to CHAR, because the number isn't stored in binary form. The primary disadvantage is that DECIMAL values must be converted to binary form before some arithmetic operations can be performed on them.

In general the conversion requires only your patience—the DBMS handles multiple-digit arithmetic slowly, but it gets there. One exception exists, though: MySQL avoids the slowness of multidigit arithmetic by converting to floats when one of the operands is decimal. So this work around is primarily of interest to MySQL users:

- Define two INTEGER columns instead of one DECIMAL column. For example, instead of Definition #1, use Definition #2:

```
Definition #1:
CREATE TABLE Table1 (
   column1 DECIMAL(7,5),
   ...)
```

```
Definition #2:
CREATE TABLE Table1 (
   column1_pre_decimal_point INTEGER,
   column1_post_decimal_point INTEGER,
   ...)
```

To add 7.35 to such a divided number, add 35 to column1_post_decimal_point. If the result is greater than 100, subtract 100 and carry one, then add seven plus the carry to column1_pre_decimal_point. The work around sounds awful—but it works more quickly than a decimal addition.

We still live in an era where the question—Should I use floats for decimals?—makes some sense, but the era is fast approaching its end. The fact is that most sensible bean-count values (i.e., money) can be stored and manipulated as integers now, and with 64-bit processors the values are trillions. The only reason to use floats for dollars is that some host languages still have no equivalent for DECIMAL. It is notable that all the DBMSs that support a MONEY data type store MONEY internally as a DECIMAL with a predefined scale.

Recommendation: Prefer DECIMAL for fixed-decimal numbers and for most floats.

Oracle Numbers

Taking a different path from the other DBMSs, Oracle uses a single storage method—**packed decimal**—for all kinds of numbers. The format consists of two parts:

- An exponent: size—1 byte.
- A mantissa: size—up to 20 bytes, packed decimal, possibly includes a 1-byte sign.

Leading and trailing zeros are not stored.

Packed decimal is a number representation where each number is expressed as a sequence of decimal digits, with each decimal digit encoded as a 4-bit binary number (or nibble). In some cases, the right-most nibble contains the sign (positive or negative).

Oracle's system is good for up to 38 digits of decimal precision. The exponent represents the number of digits before the decimal point. Technically, the decimal point "floats," but all integers on the number line between $-1.0E38$ and $+1.0E38$ can be represented. Here's how Oracle stores the decimal number 523:

```
Exponent in byte #0: 2
Mantissa in byte #1: 5
                     2
Mantissa in byte #2: 3
         filler:     _
```

That is, 523 is stored in a format similar to 5.23×10^2. One byte is used for the exponent (2), and two bytes are used for the three significant digits of the mantissa (5, 2, 3). Blank filler is added to the second byte to fill it completely.

The system's range is as big as the ranges for SMALLINT, BIGINT, and REAL, so Oracle can accept column definitions for any of those data types. But the storage is always the same. Because Oracle is only simulating a float by using a wide integer, though, details that are specific to the IEEE 754 specification—for example, **Not a Number (NaN)**—can't be represented.

The differences between Oracle and other DBMSs when it comes to numbers can be summarized as follows:

- Number size
  Oracle numbers are variable-length. Other DBMSs' numbers are fixed-length.

- Storage format
  Oracle uses one storage format for numbers. Other DBMSs use at least three storage formats for numbers.

- Biggest integer supported
Oracle's biggest integer is 1.0E38. Other DBMSs' biggest integer is 9.2E18 (BIGINT).
- Biggest float supported
Oracle's biggest "float" is 1.0E38. Other DBMSs' biggest float is 1.7E308 (DOUBLE).

The differences are so large, many of the recommendations that apply for other DBMSs do not apply to Oracle. Here are some Oracle-specific recommendations instead:

- Avoid multiply and divide because the packed decimal numbers will have to be converted before they can be operated on.
- Allow free space on each page because rows are all variable-length.
- Don't worry about floating-point storage because it's not there.

It is easier to convert decimal numbers to and from packed decimal representation than binary representation, but packed decimal is often converted to binary for arithmetic processing.

Serials

The SQL:1999 Standard does not provide a data type for columns that contain "serial" numbers but most DBMSs do provide support for auto-incremented, or monotonic, values. Table 7-10 shows the level of support the Big Eight have for serial data types.

Table 7–10   *ANSI/DBMS Serial Support*

	Data Type	Sequence Generator
ANSI SQL	N/A	N/A
IBM	INTEGER AS IDENTITY	N/A
Informix	SERIAL, SERIAL8	N/A
Ingres	TABLE_KEY	N/A
InterBase	N/A	GEN_ID function
Microsoft	INTEGER IDENTITY	N/A
MySQL	INTEGER AUTO_INCREMENT	N/A
Oracle	N/A	CREATE SEQUENCE
Sybase	NUMERIC(10,0) IDENTITY	N/A

Notes on Table 7–10

- Data Type column

  What is the serial attribute and/or data type?

  This column is "N/A" if no serial data type is supported and otherwise shows the name of the serial data type and necessary serial attribute, if required. For example, Informix supports serial data on columns defined with the SERIAL or SERIAL8 data types, while Sybase supports serial data on columns defined as NUMERIC(10,0) IDENTITY.

- Sequence Generator column

  What is the sequence generator?

  This column is "N/A" if serial data is supported via the serial attribute and/or data type shown in the Data Type column and otherwise shows the name of the function or statement the DBMS uses to generate sequences. For example, Oracle's CREATE SEQUENCE statement creates a SEQUENCE object. The next version of the SQL Standard is expected to support a SEQUENCE object as well.

The various "serial" data types are usually 4-byte integers, with values assigned by the DBMS. The idea is that the DBMS will increment the value for each row you INSERT. Serial data types are useful for ensuring that each row of a table has a unique identifier. For example, you could create a table with Informix's nonstandard SQL-extension serial data type:

```
CREATE TABLE Table1 (
   column1 SERIAL PRIMARY KEY,
   column2 INTEGER)
```

Because the value of `column1` increases each time you INSERT a value into `column2`, the uniqueness of each row is guaranteed.

The problem with serials is that they can cause trouble with concurrency control; see Chapter 15, "Locks."

Recommendation: Prefer INTEGER for serials and do your own value assignments.

The Bottom Line: Numbers

All DBMSs except Oracle use similar numeric formats, so look for our Oracle-specific recommendations only if you use Oracle.

Any number with a scale of zero (no digits after the decimal point) should be in an INTEGER column. INTEGER is the default data type of any literal that contains all digits. SMALLINT is the only other SQL Standard data type and is usually just half the size of INTEGER. TINYINT is the smallest integer data type and is still large enough for most personal information. BIGINT is appropriate for numbers larger than two billion though working with compilers that can't handle such large numbers could be problematic.

Floating-point operations are fast if they go through the computer's FPU. When you install a DBMS, the installer should detect the FPU automatically and bring in the right code, whether FPU dependent or emulated, so make sure you rerun the install program after hardware upgrades.

The primary advantage of DECIMAL is that it is easy to cast to CHAR, because the number isn't stored in binary form. The primary disadvantage of DECIMAL is that it must be converted to binary form before some arithmetic operations can be performed on it.

Serial data types are useful for ensuring each row of a table has a unique identifier. The problem with serials is that they can cause trouble with concurrency control.

Recommendation if you don't use Oracle: Prefer INTEGER for integers unless maximum values—including those from arithmetic operations—exceed the INTEGER range. Prefer DECIMAL for fixed-decimal numbers and for most floats. Prefer DOUBLE PRECISION for floats where DECIMAL isn't appropriate. Prefer INTEGER for serials and do your own value assignments.

Recommendation if you use Oracle: Data type doesn't really matter because all numbers are stored the same. Avoid multiply and divide because the packed decimal numbers will have to be converted before they can be operated on. Allow free space on each page because rows are all variable-length. Don't worry about floating-point storage because it's not there.

Bits

The SQL Standard provides two data types for columns that contain bit strings: BIT and BIT VARYING. It also provides one data type for columns that contain "logical" bits: BOOLEAN. Table 7–11 shows the SQL Standard requirements and

Table 7–11 *ANSI/DBMS Bit Support*

| | "String of Bits" Data Types | | | | "Logical" Data Types | |
	BIT	BIT VARYING	BINARY	VARBINARY	BOOLEAN	BIT
ANSI SQL	Yes	Yes	No	No	Yes	No
IBM	No	No	254 bytes	32KB	No	No
Informix	No	No	32KB	2KB	1 byte	No
Ingres	No	No	2KB	2KB	No	No
InterBase	No	No	No	No	No	No
Microsoft	No	No	8KB	8KB	No	1 byte
MySQL	No	No	No	No	No	1 byte
Oracle	No	No	2KB	No	No	No
Sybase	No	No	8KB	8KB	No	1 byte

the level of support (data type and maximum size in bytes) the Big Eight have for these data types.

The word "bit" can mean different things depending on what DBMS you look at, so we've divided the BIT data types into two categories. In Table 7–11, the "string of bits" data types are the SQL Standard BIT and BIT VARYING (with a length argument equal to the fixed and maximum number of *bits,* respectively) plus the nonstandard SQL extensions BINARY and VARBINARY (with a length argument equal to the fixed and maximum number of *bytes,* respectively). The values in each of these data types should be just a bunch of zeros and ones—raw data that has no meaning to the system. Sometimes people store character data in "string of bits" columns to evade the character set or collation rules associated with a character string data type.

The "logical" data types shown in Table 7–11 are the SQL Standard BOOLEAN and the nonstandard SQL extension BIT. The values in logical columns represent true/false/unknown conditions. It is unfortunate that Microsoft and Sybase call this data type BIT because it is unrelated to the true SQL Standard BIT data type. The correct word really is BOOLEAN.

Notes on Table 7–11:

- "String of Bits" Data Types columns
  - :: While IBM does not provide either a BINARY or VARBINARY data type for bit or binary string data, the DBMS provides the same functionality through the FOR BIT DATA attribute. A column defined as CHAR(8)

FOR BIT DATA is equivalent to a column defined as BINARY(8), and a column defined as VARCHAR(8) FOR BIT DATA is equivalent to a column defined as VARBINARY(8).

:: Informix's CHAR data type is really a fixed-length "string of bits" type. If you want collations and dictionary sorts, you have to use Informix's NCHAR.

:: Ingres, Microsoft, Oracle, and Sybase all have a binary string data type. Ingres uses the terms BYTE and BYTE VARYING, Microsoft and Sybase call them BINARY and VARBINARY, and Oracle has a RAW data type (fixed-size only).

- "Logical" Data Types columns

:: Informix's BOOLEAN doesn't provide full SQL Standard BOOLEAN support, although it does allow you to store three values: 0/1/NULL.

:: The Microsoft/Sybase BIT data type is for logical data but allows only two values—0/1—to be inserted. The SQL Standard logical data type, BOOLEAN, requires support for three values: true/false/unknown.

:: While MySQL does have a BIT data type, it is only a synonym for CHAR(1)—a fixed-size character string one character long. This provides no support for bit strings, nor does it provide true support for logical data.

The Bottom Line: Bits

BIT and BIT VARYING are unsupported data types, at least in the SQL Standard style.

BINARY and VARBINARY are handy retainers for data too small to be BLOBs, and too meaningless to be CHARs but are nonstandard SQL extensions. Most DBMSs provide support for binary strings under one name or another.

Recommendation: If portability is a major concern, store bit and binary strings in BLOBs. Use the DBMS's nonstandard binary string data type if space is at a premium.

The BOOLEAN data type is also unsupported in the SQL Standard style. The DBMSs that have a BOOLEAN (Informix), BOOL (MySQL), or BIT (Microsoft and Sybase) data type don't provide true Boolean support.

Recommendation: Take a leaf from MySQL's book. The BOOLEAN data type can be replaced with CHAR(1), which takes the same amount of space (one byte) and requires no conversion effort when used with an API. Add a CHECK constraint to limit the acceptable data, and you'll have better—and more portable—Boolean support than is otherwise possible. BOOLEANs will be worth something only when they can operate according to the SQL Standard, which isn't the case now.

Large Objects

The SQL Standard provides three data types for columns that contain **large object (LOB)** data: BINARY LARGE OBJECT (or BLOB) for binary data and, for character data, CHARACTER LARGE OBJECT (or CLOB) and NATIONAL CHARACTER LARGE OBJECT (or NCLOB). Table 7–12 shows the SQL Standard requirements and the level of support (data type and maximum segment size) the Big Eight have for these data types.

Notes on Table 7–12:

- BLOB column

  Shows the maximum size of a BLOB if the DBMS supports this data type.

  :: Microsoft and Sybase support IMAGE for binary data up to 2GB long; really a synonym for BLOB.

  :: MySQL supports BLOB for case-sensitive character values up to 65,535 characters long; really a synonym for CLOB (or a large VARCHAR) and not a true BLOB.

Table 7–12   *ANSI/DBMS Large Object Support*

	BLOB	CLOB	NCLOB	Other	Maximum Length In or Out
ANSI SQL	Yes	Yes	Yes	No	N/S
IBM	2GB	2GB	No	No	64KB
Informix	4TB	4TB	No	2GB	2GB
Ingres	2GB	2GB	No	No	2KB
InterBase	4GB	No	No	No	64KB
Microsoft	No	No	No	2GB	8KB
MySQL	64KB	No	No	2KB	24MB
Oracle	4GB	4GB	4GB	No	64KB
Sybase	No	No	No	2GB	32KB

- CLOB column

  Shows the maximum size of a CLOB if the DBMS supports this data type.

  :: Microsoft and Sybase support TEXT for character values up to 2GB long; really a synonym for CLOB.

  :: MySQL supports BLOB for case-sensitive character values up to 65,535 characters long; really a synonym for CLOB (or a large VARCHAR) and not a true BLOB.

- NCLOB column

  Shows the maximum size of an NCLOB if the DBMS supports this data type.

  :: Microsoft supports NTEXT for Unicode character values up to 2GB long; really a synonym for NCLOB.

  :: MySQL supports TEXT for case-insensitive character values up to 65,535 characters long; really a synonym for NCLOB (or a large NCHAR VARYING).

- Other column

  Shows the maximum size of a LOB if the DBMS supports other data types for large object data.

  :: Informix supports TEXT for character data up to 2GB long and BYTE for binary data up to 2GB long. The DBMS can access these "simple" LOB data types in one piece.

  :: Microsoft supports IMAGE as a synonym for BLOB, TEXT as a synonym for CLOB, and NTEXT as a synonym for NCLOB.

  :: MySQL supports BLOB as a synonym for CLOB and TEXT as a synonym for NCLOB. MySQL also supports LONGBLOB as a synonym for a CLOB up to 2GB long and LONGTEXT as a synonym for an NCLOB up to 2GB long.

  :: Sybase supports IMAGE as a synonym for BLOB and TEXT as a synonym for CLOB.

- Maximum Length In or Out column

  Shows the maximum segment size allowed for a single INSERT (in) or SELECT (out) operation on a LOB column.

  :: For Oracle, the maximum segment size is dependent on the operating system but cannot exceed 4GB.

The normal situation in data storage is that rows fit inside pages. Because pages have fixed sizes, no column can be longer than the page size. For example, Microsoft's page size is 8KB, and it turns out that the maximum length of a CHAR or VARCHAR column is 8KB. LOBs can be larger because the LOB value does not go on the page with the rest of the row. Instead, the page contains a pointer to a data page, or a page series. The pages to which the pointer points are usually stored far away—probably in a different file. For example, suppose you have this table:

```
CREATE TABLE Table1 (
    column1 CHAR(5),
    column2 BLOB,
    column3 CHAR(5)
    )
```

If you were to INSERT a row into Table1 so that column1 contains XXXXX, column2 contains the text of this book in the BLOB, and column3 contains YYYYY, you'd end up with the situation shown in Figure 7-2. (There are exceptions—for example, if the BLOB is small, then InterBase will try to fit the value in the main file.)

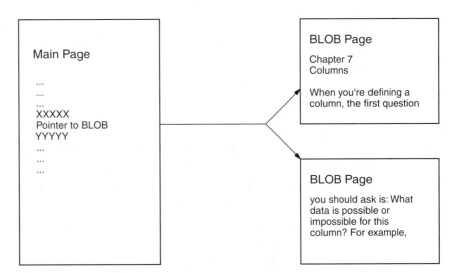

Figure 7-2 *How a LOB is stored*

LOB pages are a linked list (veterans of dBASE will see a similarity to the infamous "memo" column here). The pages can stretch out till the crack of doom, but typically the addressing space on a 32-bit machine is 2GB—which is why so many DBMSs list 2GB as the maximum LOB size. This method can waste a great deal of space. For example, with most DBMSs, if you store a NULL in a LOB, you still take up a whole page. One exception to this is InterBase, which uses RLE compression so the space used is only about 500 bytes. If you use two LOBs, you need two LOB pages. It's impractical to declare a single memory variable with a length of 2GB or to send a single 2GB message over a network. So the DBMS must provide special scalar functions for handling LOB-to-file retrievals, or for reading and writing only a chunk of a LOB at a time.

LOBs, then, have several disadvantages:

- They waste space.
- They require extra page reads.
- They don't allow all the string-manipulation functions that CHAR/VAR-CHAR allow.
- Some tools have trouble understanding LOBs.

So when would you want to use a LOB? The obvious answer is when the value for a column is longer than the maximum CHAR/VARCHAR length and, of course, when the data being stored doesn't represent character data (such as a picture). But many people also use LOBs to take advantage of the fact that LOBs are stored outside the main file. Thus, for example, you could also use a LOB for a column that is rarely used in SELECT and has all of these characteristics:

- Its length is variable.
- Its average length is at least a few hundred bytes.
- It is never used in WHERE, GROUP BY, or ORDER BY clauses.

The effect of making such a column a BLOB or a CLOB will be that (a) more rows fit in the main table (which speeds up access in the common case), and (b) changes to the LOB column won't cause shifting because the LOB is stored in a page of its own.

One other thing we should mention—LOBs can be different from other data types not only in the way they are stored, but also in the way they are buffered. For example, IBM will usually transfer large objects directly between the disk and the server's output message area without using the buffer pools that are used for transferring other data columns. Because of this, LOBs actually have very little effect on IBM's memory consumption despite their (usually) very large size. The downside, of course, is that the number of things you can do with a LOB is severely limited.

The Bottom Line: LOBs

The normal situation in data storage is that rows fit inside pages. Because pages have fixed sizes, no regular column can be larger than the page size.

LOBs can be larger than a page because the LOB value does not go on the page with the rest of the row. Instead, there is a pointer to a data page or a page series. LOB pages are a linked list.

LOBs have several disadvantages. They waste space, they require extra page reads, they don't allow all the string-manipulation functions, and some tools have trouble understanding them.

LOBs have the advantage that they are stored outside the main file, so (a) more rows fit in the main table (which speeds up access in the common case) and (b) changes to the LOB column won't cause shifting because the LOB is stored in a page of its own.

Recommendation: Prefer LOBs for images and character columns whose data is longer than the maximum CHAR/VARCHAR length. Prefer LOBs for variable-length columns, with an average length of at least a few hundred bytes, that are rarely used in SELECT and are never used in WHERE, GROUP BY, or ORDER BY clauses.

NULLs

When you're creating a table, you can expect that each variable-length column you define will take at least one byte (and up to four bytes) extra storage for a size or offset value. The other likely per-column overhead is the storage for NULL. Because NULL is not equal to any other value, it can't be stored in the space allotted for the column—extra storage is required for a special flag indicator that says "this is NULL" or "this is not NULL." For example, in IBM or Ingres databases, this flag is one byte long and precedes the column, while in MySQL databases the flag is one bit per nullable column, rounded up to the nearest byte. And as we said earlier, nullable columns in Sybase databases and older versions of Microsoft are automatically variable-length.

This is horrific: What should be a mere "constraint" has become an unchangeable "physical storage descriptor." As a result, you will often have a hard time changing a column from nullable to NOT NULL, or vice versa.

NULL is the only constraint that affects storage. That's a little disappointing, because other constraints could also be used to good effect. For example:

- If a column was defined with:

  ```
  ... DEFAULT 'a very long value'
  ```

  a BOOLEAN flag could be used to indicate that a value equals the DEFAULT value.

- If a column was defined with a CHECK constraint, for example:

  ```
  ... CHECK (column1 in 'red', 'pink', 'fuschia')
  ```

  a TINYINT number could be used to map to each value, for example:

  ```
  0 (means 'red')
  ```

  The MySQL people already have moved one step in this direction with a data type that they call ENUM, because it's like C's enum operator.

Both of these suggestions are examples of storing a short code to represent a long value. This practice is rapidly becoming archaic because you can do a better job with a **user-defined data type (UDT)**.

The Bottom Line: NULLs

NULL costs overhead. Because NULL is not equal to any other value, it can't be stored in the space allotted for the column—a special flag indicator that says "this is NULL" or "this is not NULL" must also be stored.

Microsoft and Sybase are anti-NULL DBMSs.

Recommendation: Prefer NOT NULL for performance and portability reasons.

---

3. Amusing side issue—Because the default can change if ANSI_NULL_DFLT is set, a script of CREATE TABLE statements could have different effects with different Microsoft databases. Therefore Microsoft books recommend you use NULL explicitly—for "portability." In other words, you must violate the SQL Standard so that you'll be portable.

Microsoft & Sybase versus NULL

"NULL is not the same as a blank string."—Everybody

One could get the impression that Microsoft and Sybase databases are hostile environments for NULLs. Here are some indicators.

Nullable is not the default

With any other DBMS, and with Standard SQL, if you do this:

```
CREATE TABLE Table1 (
    column1 INTEGER)
```

then `column1` can contain NULL by default. With Microsoft and Sybase, `column1` is NOT NULL by default. To make `column1` accept NULLs, you can create your table like this:

```
CREATE TABLE Table1 (
    column1 INTEGER NULL)
```

but this is not standard SQL syntax.[3]

NULL causes variable-length

We mentioned the implications of this early in this chapter.

NULL means blank

It's not possible to store a blank string in a Sybase database. If you do this:

```
UPDATE Table1 SET
    variable_column = ''      /* no space between '' */
```

Sybase will silently change the statement to:

```
UPDATE Table1 SET
    variable_column = ' '     /* one space between '' */
```

The reason? The only way to store a NULL is to store a completely empty string! (That's why nullable columns must be variable-length.) Therefore a truly blank column can't be stored because—contrary to what we all learned—blank means NULL. Previous versions of Microsoft also had this problem, as does Oracle.

Indications of this anti-NULL attitude crop up elsewhere. For example, a look at Microsoft's ODBC specification reveals that they love to return a blank string as a signal that a value is unknown.

This is a shame. The reasonable default assumption should be that a column can contain NULL. That is both sensible and conforms to the SQL Standard. Nevertheless, given Microsoft's and Sybase's attitude, NOT NULL must be the preference for performance reasons.

Column Order Within Rows

"If the aforesaid pickaninny's a king he takes precedence over you, and if he's not—
then what's he doing here?"

—The Prince of Wales to Germany's angry ambassador, regarding Tonga's king

There are potential advantages to storing all nullable or variable values at the
end of the row:

- Oracle won't waste storage space on a NULL for a variable-length column at the end of a row.

- Any DBMS can calculate the column's offset within the row more quickly if no variable-length columns are before it that have to be skipped.

You need not change your table definitions to realize these advantages if
the DBMS will automatically figure out the best column order when you execute CREATE TABLE (as, for example, Microsoft does) or if the DBMS has different
criteria (for example, with IBM there's a slight advantage in putting the
most *volatile* column at the end; see the section "IBM Logging" in Chapter 14,
"Data Changes"). So put columns in the order that users will expect to see
them when they SELECT *. Typically, this means that related columns are
grouped together, and the primary key is on the left, followed by columns that
are frequently used for searches.

Here's another tip. One table with 50 columns is better than 50 tables with
one column each because:

- The per-column storage overhead is less than the per-row storage overhead.

- The position of the fiftieth column might be determinable at parse time.

- Fewer entries are in the system catalog.

Therefore, if you have a miscellaneous pile of N static (read-only) system
values, store them horizontally (in one table) rather than vertically (in N tables).
This switch to a horizontal rather than vertical viewpoint is sometimes called
pivoting.

The Bottom Line: Column Order

Storing all nullable or variable values at the end of the row may have advantages, but you need not change your table definitions—some DBMSs will automatically figure out the best column order when you execute CREATE TABLE and other DBMSs have different criteria.

Recommendation: Put columns in the order that users will expect to see when they execute SELECT *: generally, related columns grouped together, and the primary key on the left, followed by columns that are frequently used for searches.

Parting Shots

We conducted an experiment using these two slightly different table definitions:

```
CREATE TABLE Table1 (
    column1 INTEGER NOT NULL,
    column2 CHAR(64) NOT NULL,
    column3 INTEGER NOT NULL,
    column4 INTEGER NOT NULL)

CREATE TABLE Table2 (
    column1 DECIMAL(3),
    column2 CHAR(64) NOT NULL,
    column3 INTEGER NOT NULL,
    column4 INTEGER NOT NULL)
```

The purpose of the experiment was to see whether the two definitions for column1—INTEGER NOT NULL and DECIMAL(3)—would make a difference to performance, especially with Microsoft. We thought it would. Our reasoning was:

- The fact that column1 is the first column in the table is irrelevant if it's DECIMAL(3), because Microsoft will make it a variable-length column and therefore—since Microsoft shifts variable-length columns to the end of the row—the column order for Table2 will actually be {column2, column3, column4, column1}.

- The fact that Table2.column1 is DECIMAL(3) means it will be stored as a three-byte string.

We weren't testing to see whether operations on column1 would go faster. Instead we were testing to see whether accesses involving column3 would go faster! Our suspicion was that column3 would be misaligned. On an Intel machine, if (offset within page) is not divisible by four, there is a penalty for reading a four-byte integer. So we inserted 10,000 rows into both tables, then scanned for column3 = 51700 (which was always false). And—as expected—the scan worked faster on Table1, where column1 was defined as INTEGER NOT NULL (GAIN: 4/8).

Data type *does* make a difference!

8

Tables

Performance depends on time. Time is physical. To see how table access depends on time, we must look at the physical storage of tables. The physical storage is on disk or in memory. You can influence physical storage when you CREATE TABLE and ALTER TABLE, and you can be influenced by physical storage when you SELECT, INSERT, UPDATE, and DELETE. These issues relate to the proper design of tables (the "logical" level), but to comprehend the issues you need to know how DBMSs use disks and memory (the "physical" level).

This chapter addresses the storage hierarchy, which is the way rows are grouped: in pages, extents, files, and tablespaces. That will naturally lead to a discussion of partitions, fragmentation, and the most important relational design issue: normalization. Because the SQL Standard only concerns itself with "rows" and "tables" and not with their physical mapping, this chapter is not about SQL:1999. However, it is about a *de facto* standard, because all DBMSs operate similarly.

Unfortunately, there is no standard terminology. For example, what most people call a "page" is a "data block" to Oracle users, and what most people call "partitioning" is "fragmentation" to Informix users, and the definition of "extent" is another thing that's far from fixed. We'll just have to ask you to look at the definitions of these terms in this chapter and in the glossary (Appendix B), and please avoid assuming that our choice of definition is the one that you're accustomed to from your experience of a particular DBMS.

The Storage Hierarchy

You can doubtless think of many examples of storage hierarchies in ordinary life. For example, people live in neighborhoods, which are in towns, which are in regions, countries, continents, and so on up the line. The relations are generally many-to-one, although there are occasional one-to-one correspondences (e.g., Australia is both a country and a continent), and occasional exceptions (e.g., a person can straddle a city boundary).

Figure 8–1 shows the storage hierarchy—the physical constructs of a database. The hierarchy of physical objects suggests that—with occasional one-to-one correspondences or exceptions—data rows live in pages, which are in extents, which are in files, tablespaces, and databases. There is a reason for each level of grouping. To see what the reason is, we'll go through each of those objects in order, up the line.

Pages

Depending on the DBMS, a page is also called a **data block,** a **block,** a **blocking unit,** a **control interval,** and a **row group.**

A page is a fixed-size hopper that stores rows of data. Pages have four common characteristics, which are not true by definition but are always true in practice. They are:

- All pages in a file have the same size. Indeed for some DBMSs, it is true that all pages in all files have the same size, but the usual case is that you have a choice when making a new object.

- The choice of page sizes is restricted to certain multiples of 1024 (1KB), in a range between 1024 and 65536—that is, between 1KB and 64KB.

- The optimum page size is related to the disk system's attributes. Smaller page sizes like 2KB were once the norm, but disks' capacity tends to increase over time, so now 8KB is reasonable, while 16KB is what we'll upgrade to soon.

- Pages contain an integral number of rows. Even for the rare DBMSs that allow large rows to overflow into later pages, the very strong recommendation is that you should avoid overflow.

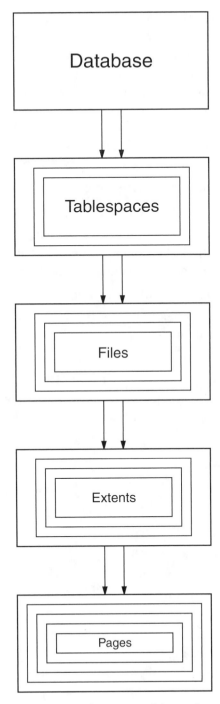

Figure 8–1 *Physical constructs; the storage hierarchy*

One other thing about pages is usually true in practice and is always recommended—All rows in a page are rows for the same table. It is true that IBM and Microsoft allow mixing rows from different tables into the same page, while Oracle allows mixing in a special condition called *clustering*, but these exceptions have advantages in special cases only. Table 8-1 shows what the Big Eight do with pages. The most interesting fact is how slight the differences are.

Notes on Table 8-1:

- Default Page Size column

    Shows the DBMS's default page size, in KB.

- Other Allowed Page Sizes column

    If the DBMS allows you to change the default page size when creating an object, this column shows the page size options (in KB) available. This column is "No" if the DBMS doesn't allow you to change the page size.

- Overflow Allowed column

    This column is "Yes" if the DBMS allows a too-large row to span more than one page.

- Mixing Allowed column

    This column is "Yes" if the DBMS allows rows from different tables to be on the same page, is "Clu" if that's possible but only for a clustered file, and "No" otherwise.

Table 8-1   *DBMSs and Pages*

	Default Page Size	Other Allowed Page Sizes (KB)	Overflow Allowed	Mixing Allowed
IBM	4KB	4,8,16,32	No	Yes
Informix	4KB	No	No	No
Ingres	2KB	2,4,8,16,32,64	No	No
InterBase	1KB	2,4,8	Yes	No
Microsoft	8KB	No	No	Yes
MySQL	1KB	No	No	No
Oracle	8KB	2,4,8,16,32	Yes	Clu
Sybase	2KB	2,4,8,16	No	No

Now that we know what a page *is*, let's look at what a page is *for*:

- A page is a minimal unit for disk I/O.

  That doesn't mean that DBMSs read and write one page at a time—in fact most DBMSs will read several pages at once—but a page is the smallest amount that a DBMS *could* read, and the smallest amount that a DBMS *usually* writes. There is no such thing as a disk read of a mere row! The objective is to make a page I/O synonymous with an I/O of the minimal unit that the disk drive uses. For example, on MS Windows NT with more than 64MB RAM, a common sector size is 512 bytes, there is one sector per cluster, and 8KB is an optimum read size (assuming the **NT File System, NTFS**). On a hand-held machine, a 1KB page is better for footprint reasons.

- A page is a unit for locking.

  It's no longer the minimal unit for locking, because most DBMSs allow locking at the row level too. But page locking is traditional and convenient. We'll talk more about page locks in Chapter 15, "Locks."

- A page is a unit for caching.

  A **read** is a transfer from disk to memory. Once the DBMS has a page in memory, it will want to keep it there for a while. It keeps the page in a **buffer,** or **buffer pool**—an in-memory copy of a bunch of pages, with a fixed size. The DBMS maintains the buffer pool itself (it does not rely on the operating system, though any caching by the operating system is a nice bonus); it generally reads several pages at once into the buffer and throws out individual pages according to a **Least-Recently-Used (LRU)** algorithm. (If the cache holds 100 pages, and you have a 101-page table, then repeated full-table scans will defeat the LRU algorithm. There are nonstandard ways to tweak the cache size or to lock tables in cache.)

- A page is a unit for administration.

  By that we mean that DBMSs store a significant amount of housekeeping information in a page, outside the row data. This housekeeping information will include a header (which may contain row offsets, overflow pointers, identifications, last modified date, NULL bits, some indication of size, etc.), some free space, and sometimes a trailer.

Because a page is a minimum unit, when you ask for a single row, the DBMS will access a page. The only thing you'll see is the single row, but now you know what's really going on. And you can use that knowledge. Here's what it implies:

- Big rows waste space.

  Given that the size of the header and trailer is usually about 100 bytes, a 2KB page has about 1,950 bytes for storing row data. So if your row size is 1,000 bytes, you can fit one row per page, and there will always be 950 bytes of free space. But halve the row size to 500 bytes, and you can fit three rows per page (500 * 3 = 1500) and still have 450 bytes of free space left over. Halve the row size again, and even less space will be wasted.[1]

- Two get in for the price of one.

  When you access two rows on the same page, the second access is free. Well, maybe not free, but the point is you've already paid for it—the DBMS has the whole page in the cache. You can't specify which page a row goes into, but you can improve your luck by doing two INSERTs together, by fetching in the DBMS's default order instead of asking for ORDER BY, or by **sequencing** (that is, forcing rows to be close together by using SERIAL data types or IDENTITY columns or auto-incrementing objects). Most obviously, you could just shorten rows so that more are in a page.[2]

Both of these implications suggest that making rows smaller is a good thing. But there is a limit to all good things, and the limit is 512 (it's just a housekeeping thing, having to do with the way some DBMSs store page header information in a fixed space). To sum it up, your aim should be to have at least 10 rows per page, but fewer than 512 rows.

---

1. The precise overhead is different with each DBMS. For example, Ingres requires 38 bytes per 2KB page plus two bytes per row, while Oracle requires between 84 and 107 bytes per page.

2. Or you can make your pages larger. For some DBMSs, it's only an option at install time (for example, with Oracle it's an init.ora parameter). Therefore we do no more than mention the possibility.

LOB Pages

An exceptional situation arises when a column is defined as a BLOB or another LOB data type such as TEXT, IMAGE, or CLOB. Recall (from Chapter 7, "Columns") that BLOB columns are rarely on the same page as the other columns of a table—they get pages of their own. With many DBMSs, BLOBs are even automatically in a file of their own—the best method.

With most DBMSs (MySQL is an exception), BLOB pages can't be shared. You can't store two BLOBs on one page, and you can't store BLOB and non-BLOB columns on one page. Therefore any BLOB that isn't NULL will involve a lot of overhead space: the pointer from the main page (about 10 bytes), the page header (about 80 bytes per BLOB page), and the unused space at the end of the last BLOB page (a few thousand bytes on average).

If a table has LOBs in it, you should avoid table scans, and you should avoid SELECT * . . . statements.

Extents

An **extent** is a group of contiguous pages. Extents exist to solve the allocation problem. The allocation problem is that, when a file gets full, the DBMS must increase its size. If the file size increases by only one page at a time, waste occurs because:

- The operating system must update the file allocation tables. The amount of updating is about the same whether the addition is one page or eight pages.
- If file A grows, then file B grows, then file A grows again, and so on; the operating system will have to maintain a succession of short (one page) chains: ABABABAB. This is a type of fragmentation. As we've hinted before, fragmentation is bad; we'll discuss it later in this chapter.
- The DBMS must update the data dictionary every time a file grows.

Suppose, though, that the DBMS adds *eight* pages when the file gets full, instead of only one page. That solves the allocation problem. Call that eight-page amount an extent, and you now have a definition of what an extent is, in its primary meaning. Notice that in the primary meaning, extents are units of allocation, not units of I/O as pages are.

Now suppose that, in the CREATE TABLE statement, you were able to define two things: (a) an initial extent size (how much to allocate during CREATE) and (b) a "next" extent size (how much to allocate each subsequent time when the file gets full). Well, you can. Here's an example using Informix's non-standard SQL extension syntax:

```
CREATE TABLE Table1 (
    column1 INTEGER,
    column2 VARCHAR(15),
    column3 FLOAT)
    EXTENT SIZE 20 NEXT SIZE 16
```

Depending on the DBMS, you can usually define the initial and next extent sizes, but most people make no specification and just use default values. Typical default values are: 16x4KB pages (IBM), 8x8KB pages (Microsoft)—or 1MB for certain tablespaces (Oracle). Clearly Oracle is different. Oracle believes that it's a good idea to preallocate a large amount of file space. This makes the allocation problem a rare phenomenon.

To see extents in action, we used Ingres to create a table with ten rows per page and 16 pages per extent. Then we timed INSERT speed. We found that INSERT speed was consistent except for a small hiccup (7% slower) on every 10th row (i.e., at each page end) and a slightly larger hiccup (20% slower) on every 160th row (i.e., at each extent end). It is possible to predict an average INSERT time, but the worst case is much worse than the average. All because of extents.

Read groups

A **read group** is a group of contiguous pages. For many DBMSs, a read group is the same thing as an extent, but there's a logical difference. A read group is the number of pages that are *read together*, while an extent is the number of pages that are *allocated together*. Table 8-2 shows the usual name and default size of a read group for the Big Eight.

Consider IBM. Table 8-2 tells us that IBM's default page size is 4KB, and the default read group size is 16 pages. This SQL statement forces IBM to perform a table scan:

```
SELECT * from Table1
  WHERE column1 LIKE '%XX%'
```

Table 8–2 *DBMSs and Read Groups*

	Vendor's Term	Usual or Recommended Size
IBM	Extent	16x4KB pages
Informix	Extent	16x4KB pages
Ingres	Read Group	8x2KB pages
InterBase	None	4KB
Microsoft	Extent	8x8KB pages
MySQL	Read Group	16x1KB pages
Oracle	Extent	8x8KB pages
Sybase	Extent	8x2KB pages

When executing this SELECT, IBM reads 16 pages at a time into the buffer. This is faster than reading 16 pages, one at a time. It's the right thing to do because all pages must be examined in order to resolve the query. It would be wrong to keep all the pages in cache, though, because pages read during a table scan are unlikely to be needed again soon.

So a read group is a unit of I/O, but not the minimal unit—the page is the minimal unit, and the page is also the administrative unit for caches. It comes down to this: If most of your SELECTs involve table scans, then you want the read group size to be double the default amount. If the only way to accomplish this is to double the extent size, so be it. Increasing the read group size will also mean that more space is needed in memory for the buffer pool.

> **Tip** If the extent size is not the same as the read group size, then it should be an exact multiple of the read group size.

Files

A **file** is a group of contiguous extents. And that's about it.

Surprisingly, a file is not a physical representation of a table. It could be, but usually it isn't because of one of the following:

- Most DBMSs allow mixing of extents. That is, the first extent in a file can contain pages for `Table1`, and the second extent in the same file can

How Important Is It to Be in Cache?

Consider the famous Oracle cost-based optimizer I/O formula:

```
I/O = (Disk I/O * 1) + (CPU I/O ÷ 1000) + (Net I/O * 1.5)
```

In this formula, "Disk I/O" means "access to the disk drive" and has a weight of one. "CPU I/O" means "access to a cache copy" and has a weight of 0.001. "Net I/O" means "access over the network" and has a weight of 1.5. In Chapter 17, "Cost-Based Optimizers," we try to figure out what this formula is good for. Right now, we only need to know that Oracle considers a disk access to be 1,000 times more expensive than a cached access.

contain pages for `Table2`. This is true even for those DBMSs that do not allow mixing within a page.

- A few DBMSs, as an option, don't bother with files at all. Usually this is a Unix option. The idea is that by performing I/O on the operating system's "nonblock raw device" one can avoid the overhead of the file system's features, such as caching. (After all, if the DBMS does its own caching well, the operating system's cache is redundant.) Many people are unaware that Windows NT allows raw I/O without files; Sybase tested the option once and found that raw I/O is about 2% faster than I/O via files.

- Files can be split across more than one drive, either because the file's simply too big or to enhance the advantage of partitioning. (**Partitioning** is the process of splitting a database object—usually a tablespace, table, or index—into two or more physical locations, or partitions; see the following section.)

Partitions

A **partition** is a group of contiguous extents. Often a partition is a file, but it doesn't have to be.[3] Suppose you have four extents, numbered {1, 2, 3, 4}. Figure 8–2 shows what a two-partition system could look like.

---

3. Informix calls a partition a **fragment**. We think that is a horrible choice of words, and we will never use the word "**fragmentation**" when we mean "partitioning."

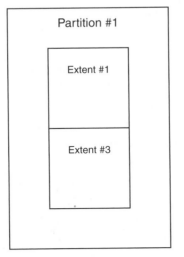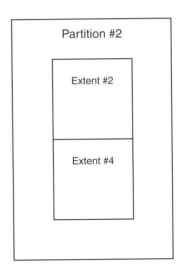

Figure 8–2   *A two-partition system*

Partitions are bad if there are few extents and few database users. Why? Because the fundamental principle is that rows should be crammed together. That helps caching and reduces the number of page writes.

Partitions are good if—and only if—there are many extents and many database users. Why? Two reasons, actually. The first is that in a multiuser environment, partitioning reduces contention. The second is that in a multidisk-drive environment, partitioning increases parallelism.

How does partitioning reduce contention? Suppose that User AMY and User BOB are both doing an INSERT. User AMY arrives first and locks the final page of the final extent. (In practice the DBMS starts by looking for free space within the file, but this example is realistic enough.) Now User BOB arrives and—here's the trick—locks the final page of the final extent *in the other partition*. BOB is not locked out because AMY and BOB do not have to contend for the same end page.

How does partitioning increase parallelism? Suppose that the partitions are on different independent disk drives (Disk #1 and Disk #2) and that the DBMS must read a page in Extent #1 (stored on Disk #1) and also a page in Extent #2 (stored on Disk #2). In this case, the DBMS can issue simultaneous "seek and read" commands for the two pages. Because the drives work independently, the time to perform both commands is the same as the time to perform only one command. In fact you can realize some of partitioning's advantages with any multithreaded operating system even if the partitions are areas within a single file on a single disk drive, but if you have the hardware to do it, you should keep partitions as separated as they can be.

Balanced partitions are best. If there is a 50/50 chance that a user will want Partition #1 instead of Partition #2, and there is a 50/50 chance that a desirable page is in Partition #1 instead of Partition #2, then there's balance. Obviously there would be more contention if User AMY and User BOB were more likely to go for the same partition, or if Page #1 and Page #2 were more likely to be on the same partition.

In other words, it is wrong to say—Let's separate the much-used records from the little-used records. That's fine if the little-used records are being shuffled off to a slow or remote storage medium, but we're talking about two storage areas on the same disk, or two disk drives of equal quality. Balanced partitions are best.

IBM, Informix, Ingres, Microsoft, Oracle, and Sybase support partitioning with non-standard extensions to the CREATE TABLE or ALTER TABLE statements (InterBase and MySQL don't support partitioning). You should be able to specify under what conditions an INSERT will head for Partition #1 rather than Partition #2. For example, with Informix's non-standard SQL-extension syntax, you can specify conditions like:

```
... BY EXPRESSION
      branch_number < 7 IN Partition1,
      transaction_time < TIME '11:00:00' IN Partition2
```

This attempt to use logic is vain, because there is no guarantee that the conditions are changeless. If they were, you would probably use separate tables instead of separate partitions. A simple hash algorithm that ensures random or round-robin distribution of rows is all you really need.

Partitioning is normal in all big shops except data warehouses. Partitioning is unpopular for data warehouses because:

- Reducing locks is unimportant when transactions are read-only.
- Reports are sorted, but partition algorithms can destroy order.
- Sequential processing is faster if all rows can be accessed with one scan.

Naturally, even data warehouses do some distribution in order to encourage parallel queries (putting joined tables and their indexes on different drives,

Manual Partitioning

Even if your DBMS doesn't support partitioning, you can simulate it by splitting your table into multiple tables with duplicate row definitions. Typical criteria are geographic (e.g., "Branch #1 in this table and other branches in that table") or temporal (e.g., "1999 transactions in this table and later transactions in that table").

This sort of thing works as long as the primary key contains a code that tells you what table to look in, and you're willing to UNION searches with conditions that span the partitioning criteria. The advantage is that you can do most of your work with smaller tables. The disadvantage is that rows might have to move from one table to another when a value changes. Eventually such systems fall apart and are replaced by automatically partitioned systems.

say). Real partitioning, though, is for OLTP. People over-generalize and say that sequential queriers put similars together while ad-hoc queriers distribute them randomly, but that's an aide-memoire rather than a true observation.

Tablespaces

A **tablespace** (also called a **dbspace** by some DBMSs, e.g., Informix) is a file, or a group of files, that contains data. For example, this non-standard Oracle SQL-extension statement creates and associates a tablespace with a 10MB file:

```
CREATE TABLESPACE Tb
  DATAFILE '\disk01\tb.dbs' SIZE 10M;
```

Here's another example, using IBM's syntax:

```
CREATE TABLESPACE Tb
  MANAGED BY DATABASE
  USING ('d:\data1')
```

This IBM tablespace has no preset size limitation. It can grow up to the size allotted for the file named `d:\data1`.

A tablespace can contain a single table, or it can be shared either between one table and its indexes or between multiple tables. In other words, it's possible to mix extents from different objects in the same tablespace. Mixing brings some advantages for administration but has no great performance effect.

The typical reasons for dividing databases into tablespaces are:

- So that different users will have access to different physical areas
- So that users' data will be separate from system data
- So that extents with different sizes will be separate
- So that partition schemes can be tailored to table or application
- So that backups or maintenance can be done on only part of a database
- So that database backups and restores can be run in parallel

The Bottom Line: Storage Hierarchy

A page is a fixed-size hopper that stores rows of data. A page is a minimal unit for disk I/O, a unit for locking, a unit for caching, and a unit for administration.

All pages in a file have the same size. The choice of page sizes is restricted to certain multiples of 1024, between 1KB and 64KB. The optimum page size is related to the disk drive's cluster size; 8KB is the current usual page size.

Pages contain an integral number of rows. All rows in a page are rows for the same table.

When you ask for rows, the DBMS gets pages.

Big rows waste space. Keep row size small—but not too small. Aim for a minimum of 10 rows and a maximum of 511 rows per page.

When you access two rows on the same page, the second access is free—that is, access to Row #1 is free if the page is still in the buffer pool since you accessed it for Row #2. Use this fact to help performance: do two INSERTs together, fetch in the DBMS's default order, make rows smaller or pages larger.

LOB columns are rarely on the same page as the other columns of a table—they get pages of their own. If a table has LOBs in it, avoid table scans and SELECT * ... statements.

An extent is a group of contiguous pages that are allocated together.

A read group is a group of contiguous pages that are read together.

If the extent size is not the same as the read group size, then it should be an exact multiple of the read group size.

A file is a group of contiguous extents.

A partition is also a group of contiguous extents. Often a partition is a file, but it doesn't have to be.

Partitions are bad if there are few extents and few database users. Partitions are good if there are many extents and many database users because partitioning reduces contention and increases parallelism.

If you have the hardware to do it, keep partitions physically separated.

Don't make assumptions that are only true for not-yet-partitioned databases. For example, ignore the observation that some tables have rows in order by date of insertion.

Start partitioning before you have 100 users or one million rows or two disk drives. Don't worry about tables that are small or are used by only a small group of users. Strive for balance. Balanced partitions are best.

A tablespace is a group of files.

It's possible to mix extents from different objects in the same tablespace. Mixing brings some advantages for administration, but has no great performance effect.

Heaps

In this section, we'll look at a particular storage structure called a **heap.** A heap, or **heap-organized table,** is a structure for storing data in an unstructured manner. When you add something to a heap, it goes wherever free space is available, which probably means "at the end"—existing data is not moved to make free space available for new data. Heaps are the default structure. They're certainly the simplest type.

ROWID

Here is a nonstandard Oracle SQL-extension statement that seeks out a particular data row:

```
SELECT column1 FROM Table1
  WHERE ROWID = '00001F20.00A3.0001'
  FOR UPDATE OF column1
```

In this statement, the ROWID value has three parts: (a) the page number within a file, (b) the row number within the page, and (c) the file number within the list of database files that Oracle keeps in the system catalog. In other words, the Oracle ROWID is a row identifier—it uniquely describes a row of a heap-organized table to the DBMS. Other DBMSs have different formats and use different terms, as shown in Table 8–3. But the name doesn't matter—the important thing is that most DBMSs have a row identifier that you can use in SQL statements, and we'll call this the "ROWID" throughout this book.

The question is—Should you?

The Oracle statement shown earlier is the fastest possible SELECT. With any other column, the DBMS has to take the column value and find the address by looking it up. With a ROWID, the column value *is* the address. Therefore, one way to go through a table is like this:

```
SELECT ROWID FROM Table1

SELECT * FROM Table1
  WHERE ROWID = ?
```

The first SELECT statement gets all the row identifiers into a program buffer so that you can then access each individual row with the second SELECT.

Using ROWID speeds up SELECT. On the other hand, the Oracle statement can also fail or can cause an error to appear in the database. The obvious danger is that another user could delete the row, which makes the row identifier invalid. The greater danger is that another user could delete the row, then INSERT a new row at the same location—which makes the row identifier a valid, but false, pointer. Some further dangers are specific to the DBMS or table type you're using:

- Informix won't support true row identifiers if there's partitioning.

Table 8–3   *DBMSs and ROWID*

	ROWID Equivalent
IBM	RID
Informix	ROWID
Ingres	tid
InterBase	No support
Microsoft	RID
MySQL	_rowid
Oracle	ROWID
Sybase	RID

- Microsoft will let rows change location if there's a clustered index.

- PostgreSQL doesn't document how its row identifiers work so if something goes wrong you can't hold them responsible.

This is hardly surprising to anyone who understands relational theory. The fact is that row identifiers are not an SQL feature—they are a trap door for getting away from SQL. They are useful—if they weren't then DBMSs wouldn't allow them—but the only completely safe use of ROWID is inside a serialized transaction. (A **serialized transaction** is a transaction that prevents or avoids data changes by other users, and you shouldn't use one until you've read Chapter 15, "Locks.") Inside a transaction, row identifiers can be used for navigation—for example, to simulate subqueries and outer joins with application program code when the DBMS doesn't support such advanced features.

Incidentally, row identifiers are "**pseudocolumns**" rather than real columns. They take up no space in the row. They do not appear if you say SELECT * ... because SELECT * ... only gets defined columns. You must specify row identifiers explicitly to get them.

Migration

We saw in the last chapter that variable-length columns are common. Even if you think you use fixed-size data types, there's no way to avoid variable-length columns that works with all DBMSs.

Suppose you have a situation in which Row #1 on Page #1 contains one variable-length column with value NULL. This UPDATE is executed:

```
UPDATE Table1
  SET column1 = 'abcdefg'
```

This is called an **expanding UPDATE** because the row is clearly getting bigger. This is a problem because no free space is between Row #1 and Row #2 on the same page (because column1 is variable-length). Therefore, before the DBMS can modify Row #1, it must shift Row #2 down. Incidentally, because shifting takes time, it takes more time to update variable-length columns if you use large (16KB or more) page sizes. But that's not our immediate concern.

Our real concern is—What if Page #1 is already full? Pages are fixed-size— the DBMS can't make them bigger. And the DBMS can't simply shift rows forward in all subsequent pages—that could cause a single-row UPDATE to take hours. So the DBMS must find some free space in another page and put the new data in that page. In theory there are different ways to do this, but we found that DBMSs prefer these choices:

- The row that gets moved is the row that's being updated—*not* the row that would otherwise be shifted past the end of the page. This choice saves time because if the DBMS moved a different row, it would have to get a lock on it before the UPDATE could proceed.

- The new row location will probably be close to the old one, but it's not possible to guarantee that. Most DBMSs will either look for space within the same extent or will search through a list of pages that have free space in them (Oracle calls this list the **freelist**). However, if all pages are full, the DBMS has to allocate a new extent and put the changed row at the end.

- The DBMS puts in a pointer at the original row location. The pointer is the row identifier of the new location. So even if the new row location is Page #7 Row #7, you can still access it at Page #1 Row #1 (the DBMS will automatically follow the pointer). That means if you accessed the row using a row identifier, you are safe because the original ROWID is still valid. There is also no need to change index keys because they can continue to point to the original location. However, all subsequent accesses of this row will take twice as long, until the table is reorganized.

The whole process of finding a home for an expanding UPDATE is called **migration.** As well as causing slow access due to pointers, migration causes space to be wasted. That's because the row is gone from the original page. All that's left is a pointer, so there's more free space now in the original page.

Fragmentation

In the long term, after a database has been subjected to data changes for a few weeks, it begins to show signs of **fragmentation.** A group of pages is fragmented if:

- Excess free space is on many pages because of deletions or **shrinking updates** or migrations.

- The logical order of rows (the ROWID order) is not the same as the physical arrangement because of pointers left by migrations.

- Pages or extents for different tables are interleaved.

Fragmentation is easy to identify: SELECT all the ROWIDs and look at their page-number components. If some pages have surprisingly few rows, then be suspicious. Programs that do such monitoring are often supplied as DBMS utilities.

The DBMS can try to reduce fragmentation automatically, by reclaiming wasted space. For example, we know that Oracle keeps a freelist of reusable areas. But reclaiming only delays the evil day. It is not possible to stop fragmentation, and eventually you must rebuild the database or run a utility to reorganize the pages. (Incidentally, reorganizing will do nothing to reduce the fragmentation caused by the operating system. You must also run the operating system's defragger. You won't have to do this if you allocate huge extents at the start.)

The effect of fragmentation is that, on average, Row [n] gets moved farther away from Row [n + 1]. Is such a phenomenon important? That depends very much on your disk drive. Consider these specifications from a high-performance IBM drive:

- Track-to-track seek time (to an adjacent track): 1 millisecond.

- Full stroke seek time (from one end of disk to other end): 15 milliseconds.

- Other factors (average latency, settle time, transfer rate): 7 milliseconds.

From these figures, we can calculate that a nearby disk access takes (7ms + 1ms) 8 milliseconds, while a far away disk access takes (15ms + 7ms) 22 milliseconds—or nearly three times as long. Such extreme cases would be rare though, because two randomly placed rows are normally separated by less than the width of the disk and also because **elevator seeking** happens. The term "elevator seeking" is an operating system term that means "traveling through a disk's physical locations in the manner of an elevator, instead of jumping backward or forward for each request." The term comes from the elevator analogy, which goes like this—A building is analogous to a disk drive, a building floor is analogous to a disk track, and a building elevator is analogous to a disk head. If you are alone in the building and you press "13th floor," the elevator goes directly to it[4] and the only factor is seek time. But when a dozen people are getting on or off and going up or down, the scenario changes: The elevator is constantly traveling from the building top to building bottom and back, opening on floors along the way. Then the major factor is not seek time (that's going to happen anyway) but the number of times that the doors open for floors you don't want. The analogous term for this factor is "head contention"—that is, the number of jobs that want to use the drive head at the same time.

The bottom line is that fragmentation does waste space and does cost time, but it would be more noticeable on a laptop (which is single-user) than on a very large machine with a heavy load. If there are occasional cleanups for both the DBMS and the operating system, and performance in single-user mode is not important, then your only remaining worry is that **migrated rows** take twice as long to read.

Free Page Space

When you create a table or index, you can usually set an attribute to control how much free space a page should contain initially. This attribute goes by various names. For example, Oracle calls it **PCTFREE** (percent to leave free), while Ingres calls it **FILLFACTOR** (percent to fill). Table 8–4 shows the PCTFREE equivalent for the Big Eight.

Table 8–4 *DBMSs and Free Space Attribute*

	PCTFREE Equivalent
IBM	PCTFREE
Informix	FILLFACTOR
Ingres	FILLFACTOR
InterBase	No support
Microsoft	FILLFACTOR
MySQL	No support
Oracle	PCTFREE
Sybase	FILLFACTOR

4. Unless you're in North America where, in the words of the poet:
"The architect he skipped direct/From twelve unto fourteen ..."
—Ogden Nash, "A Tale of the Thirteenth Floor"

Consider how Oracle does an INSERT.

1. Calculate size of new row.

2. Find the "last" page. (This is for the simplest case, a heap. When Oracle is adding to a heap, the DBMS is looking at pages in the last extent or the freelist.)

3. Look at the page header to find out how much space is available.

4. ```
If (available space < PCTFREE)
        If (there are no more pages)
            Allocate new extent
            Goto Step #2
```

5. Copy new row into page, update page header, and stop.

Given that PCTFREE just causes space to be wasted in every page, why would you want a PCTFREE greater than zero? That's easy: to avoid migration. If free space is in a page, then an expanding UPDATE will just grow into it, rather than migrating. It's generally accepted that migration is such an awful thing that you should be willing to accept 10% waste space in every page in return for reduced migration. Therefore, for example, Oracle's default PCTFREE setting is 10%—that is, Oracle reserves 10% of each page for updates to existing rows, by default.

Hold on, though. Remember that migration happens only if there is an expanding UPDATE. But expanding UPDATEs *can't happen* if (a) the table is read-only or (b) all the table's columns are fixed-size and there is no plan to ALTER TABLE to amend the column sizes. Under either of these conditions, you should override the default and set PCTFREE to equal zero (or FILLFACTOR to equal 100). Incidentally, if a table is read-only, then it's also good practice to use larger page sizes. Incidentally (again), if all columns are fixed-size, then the amount of per-page overhead space is slightly less. Remember that a column is not truly fixed-size unless it's defined as NOT NULL, and remember too that InterBase and Oracle use variable-length for almost every situation.

You can dispense with PCTFREE entirely if you allocate free space in selected rows at INSERT time—that is, by putting a filler in variable-length columns—as suggested in Chapter 7, "Columns."

The bottom line is: avoid migration. Here's how:

• Add a bit of filler when you do the original INSERT.
```

- Use PCTFREE (or its equivalent).

- Don't do DELETE plus INSERT. Do UPDATE instead.

- Put DELETEs and shrinking UPDATEs before expanding UPDATEs or INSERTs. Arrange batches in ROWID order.

- If columns will be changed regularly, define them as fixed-size fields, not variable-length fields.

The Bottom Line: Heaps

Most DBMSs have a row identifier that you can use in SQL statements. While using ROWID allows you to write the fastest possible SELECT, ROWID also poses two dangers. The first is that another user could DELETE the row, which makes the row identifier invalid. The second, and greater, danger is that another user could DELETE the row and then INSERT a new row at the same location, which makes the row identifier a valid, but false, pointer.

The only completely safe use of ROWID is inside a serialized transaction.

The process of finding a home for an expanding UPDATE is called migration. Migration causes slow access due to pointers. It also wastes space.

A group of pages is fragmented if (a) excess free space is on many pages because of deletions, shrinking UPDATEs, or migrations, (b) the logical order of rows is not the same as the physical arrangement because of pointers left by migrations, or (c) pages or extents for different tables are interleaved. Fragmentation wastes space and costs time.

The DBMS can try to reduce fragmentation automatically by reclaiming wasted space. But it is not possible to stop fragmentation, and eventually you must rebuild the database or run a utility to reorganize the pages.

When you create a table or index, you can usually set an attribute to control how much free space a page should contain initially. Use this feature to avoid migration, which is a larger problem than wasted space.

Because expanding UPDATEs can't happen if (a) the table is read-only or (b) all the table's columns are fixed-size, set PCTFREE to zero (or FILLFACTOR to 100) in these cases.

If a table is read-only, it's good practice to use larger page sizes.

Clusters

In the last section, we discussed affairs that relate to heap storage structures. We won't talk about the other important kind—clusters—in detail until we've given you a good grounding in indexes, in Chapter 9. We will take a moment, though, to mention clusters here.

A **cluster** is a structure for storing data in a specific order.[5] The main idea behind clusters is that rows should be kept in order according to some column value, such as the primary key—this is called the *cluster key*. A sequenced file has obvious advantages for access, so let's just consider the impacts on file organization.

To begin with, it looks like INSERTs are harder with a cluster (because you have to make room between existing rows to fit in the new value according to cluster key order). But there is an offsetting effect: Two subsequent INSERTs probably won't go to the same place, so the contention problem that heaps have isn't as great.

Consider Oracle's clusters. Besides the two effects we've already mentioned, Oracle throws in a mixing feature. If two tables have columns with values in the same range—think of primary key and foreign key tables—then you can order them both in the same file. The upshot is that a primary key row and its matching foreign key row will probably end up in the same page, because the primary key and the foreign key have the same value and therefore sort to the same place. So when you access two joined rows, there is only one disk access. *This destroys the claim that joins are inherently slow.* Other DBMSs (e.g., IBM) allow mixing, but mixing makes no sense unless you can combine it with a feature that allows rows to be clustered near each other when they have similar contents.

You would expect Oracle clustering to be popular. It is not. It has a severe flaw: To use clustering, you must allocate a fixed size (e.g., two pages) for each cluster key. If the size is too big, space is wasted. If the size is too small, overflows happen. (Oracle calls this problem "collisions.") Oracle clustering is thus inappropriate except for a narrow set of applications. Still, this is an implementation problem only—the idea itself is excellent. We regard the concept as worth mentioning because eventually Oracle gets it right, and if they don't, then somebody else will.

The Bottom Line: Clusters

INSERTs are harder with a cluster because you have to make room between existing rows to fit in the new value according to cluster key order. But two

---

5. In this section, we are talking about a type of cluster that we call "weak" clustering; see Chapter 9, "Indexes."

subsequent INSERTs probably won't go to the same place, so clusters reduce contention.

The Normal Forms

Given what we've seen so far, wouldn't it be wonderful if there was a standard way to: (a) reduce row lengths by splitting rows vertically, (b) isolate different data on different files so it could be partitioned, and (c) mitigate fragmentation by cramming truly similar data into the same pages? Well, there is a standard way. It's called normalization.

Some people think that normalizing is like Latin—supposedly, learning Latin helps you think clearly and look good, but it's an optional subject. Well, if that's so, it's odd that so many plumbers and engineers—people who slept through all the artsy stuff in school—insist on using normalization. Perhaps it's time to take a second look at the subject.

Consider Table 8-5, which shows an unnormalized "table" called `Diplomatic_1`. `Diplomatic_1` contains the following information: the name of a diplomat, the language the diplomat speaks, the number of years the diplomat has spoken the language, the diplomat's title, the diplomat's length of service with the diplomatic corps, the diplomat's salary, the group with which the diplomat is affiliated, and the name of the person who heads the group. Each diplomat has a unique name, so the `name` column can be used as the table's primary key, as indicated by the fact that the `name` heading is underlined in Table 8-5. (In practice, a key can usually be constructed in more than one way—for example, a social security number is another value that can uniquely identify an individual.)

Requests of the form "Tell me something about a diplomat" are easily answered by the structure of the data shown in Table 8-5. But answers to requests like "Which diplomats speak Greek?" and "Change the diplomat in charge of the FTA" are far more difficult. Normalization changes the organization of a table so that you can use its data more flexibly.

The first step in normalizing is based on the relational rule that each column of a table may contain only one, atomic, value per row. Looking at Table 8-5, it's easy to see that the `language`, `years_used`, `work_group`, and `head_honcho` columns violate this rule, because a diplomat may speak multiple languages and may be affiliated with multiple groups. If we add new rows by duplicating the nonrepeating values for each combination of repeating values though, Table 8-5 will be represented in **first normal form (1NF)**. (A 1NF

Table 8-5 *Diplomatic_1 Table*

name ====	language	years_used	title	service_length	salary	work_group	head_honcho
Axworthy	French German	3 2	Consul	4	30,000.00	WHO IMF	Greene Craig
Broadbent	Russian Greek	1 3	Diplomat	2	25,000.00	IMF FTA	Craig Crandall
Campbell	French Spanish Italian	2 1 3	Consul	3	28,000.00	EA	Temple
Craig	French Greek Russian Spanish	1 5 2 9	Ambassador	8	65,000.00	IMF	Craig
Crandall	French	9	Ambassador	3	55,000.00	FTA	Crandall
Greene	French Spanish Italian Japanese	3 7 1 4	Ambassador	9	70,000.00	WHO	Greene
Temple	French Russian	4 2	Ambassador	2	60,000.00	EA	Temple

table contains only scalar values.) The `Diplomatic_2` table shown in Table 8-6 is the `Diplomatic_1` table normalized to first normal form.

Take another look at Table 8-6. Now that `Diplomatic_2` is in first normal form, the `name` column is no longer sufficient to uniquely identify a row, because several rows may exist for a diplomat who speaks multiple languages or is affiliated with more than one group. One solution to this problem is to create a new, compound primary key—for example, (`name`, `language`, `work_group`) combined—to uniquely identify a single row of `Diplomatic_2`.

Table 8-6 appears to be a step backward. Not only does it require more space to present the data, but responding to requests such as "Change Temple's title" and "Add Campbell to another group" is now more time consuming. This problem is addressed by the remaining normalization steps, which are based on the concept of dependence and the relational rule that—in every row of a table—each column must be dependent on every part of the primary key.

Briefly, the concept of **dependence** has two rules. First, if the value of `column1` uniquely determines the value of `column2`, then `column2` is **functionally dependent** on `column1`. Second, if the value of `column1` limits the possible values in `column2` to a specific set, then `column2` is **set dependent** on `column1`. For example, because each diplomat has only one title, `name` will uniquely determine `title`—therefore, `title` is functionally dependent on `name`. Further, `work_group` is set dependent on `name`, because each diplomat is assigned to one or more of a specific set of groups.

The concept of dependence tells us that the `title`, `service_length`, and `salary` columns are not dependent on the entire primary key—(`name`, `language`, `work_group`)—of `Diplomatic_2`; they are dependent on `name` alone. Because this violates the relational rule, let's create a new table—containing only `name`, `title`, `service_length`, and `salary`. The key for this table will, once again, be `name`. Let's call the new table `Diplomats`.

Of the remaining `Diplomatic_2` columns, `years_used` is determined by both `name` and `language` and therefore doesn't properly belong to `Diplomats`, so let's create another new table—called Languages—using just these three columns. The Languages table's key is (`name`, `language`). Because Languages also contains the `name` column, it is still possible to associate a diplomat's language experience with his or her other data.

Splitting a table like this prevents it from having columns that are dependent on only part of the table's key. A first normal form table that also has no partial key dependence is said to be in **second normal form (2NF)**. (A 2NF table is a 1NF table that contains only columns that are dependent upon the

Table 8-6 *Diplomatic_2 Table*

name	language	years_used	title	service_length	salary	work_group	head_honcho
Axworthy	French	3	Consul	4	30,000.00	WHO	Greene
Axworthy	German	2	Consul	4	300,00.00	IMF	Craig
Broadbent	Russian	1	Diplomat	2	25,000.00	IMF	Craig
Broadbent	Greek	3	Diplomat	2	25,000.00	FTA	Crandall
Campbell	French	2	Consul	3	28,000.00	EA	Temple
Campbell	Spanish	1	Consul	3	28,000.00	EA	Temple
Campbell	Italian	3	Consul	3	28,000.00	EA	Temple
Craig	French	1	Ambassador	8	65,000.00	IMF	Craig
Craig	Greek	5	Ambassador	8	65,000.00	IMF	Craig
Craig	Russian	2	Ambassador	8	65,000.00	IMF	Craig
Craig	Spanish	9	Ambassador	8	65,000.00	IMF	Craig
Crandall	French	9	Ambassador	3	55,000.00	FTA	Crandall
Greene	French	3	Ambassador	9	70,000.00	WHO	Greene
Greene	Spanish	7	Ambassador	9	70,000.00	WHO	Greene
Greene	Italian	1	Ambassador	9	70,000.00	WHO	Greene
Greene	Japanese	4	Ambassador	9	70,000.00	WHO	Greene
Temple	French	4	Ambassador	2	60,000.00	EA	Temple
Temple	Russian	2	Ambassador	2	60,000.00	EA	Temple

entire primary key.) Both Diplomats (Table 8–7) and Languages (Table 8–8) are in second normal form.

The situation with the Diplomatic_2.work_group column is slightly different. We have already noted that a diplomat's name determines the set of groups with which that diplomat is affiliated. This information is independent of the languages spoken by the diplomat, so a table with the work_group column shouldn't have language in its primary key. But work_group *does* uniquely determine a group's head_honcho.

Remember the Law of Transitivity from Chapter 2, "Simple Searches"? Well, it applies to dependence as well. That is, if column2 is dependent on column1 and column3 is dependent on column2, then it is also true that column3 is dependent on column1. This is known as a transitive dependence—column3 is **transitively dependent** on column1, via column2.

In our example, head_honcho is transitively dependent on name, because name determines a set of values for work_group, and head_honcho is functionally dependent on work_group. A second normal form table that has no transitive dependence is said to be in **third normal form (3NF)** and thus fulfills the relational requirement that—in every row of a table—all columns must depend directly on the primary key, without any transitive dependencies through other columns. (A 3NF table is a 2NF table whose non-key columns are also mutually independent; that is, each column can be updated independently of all the rest.)

Because each work_group has only one head_honcho, let's finish our normalization design by creating two more new tables. The first, called Groups, will contain the columns work_group and head_honcho. The Groups table's primary key is work_group. (head_honcho could also be a key if each diplomat managed only

Table 8–7   *Diplomats Table*

name ====	title	service_length	salary
Axworthy	Consul	4	30,000.00
Broadbent	Diplomat	2	25,000.00
Campbell	Consul	3	28,000.00
Craig	Ambassador	8	65,000.00
Crandall	Ambassador	3	55,000.00
Greene	Ambassador	9	70,000.00
Temple	Ambassador	2	60,000.00

Table 8–8 *Languages Table*

name	language	years_used
====	=======	
Axworthy	French	3
Axworthy	German	2
Broadbent	Russian	1
Broadbent	Greek	3
Campbell	French	2
Campbell	Spanish	1
Campbell	Italian	3
Craig	French	1
Craig	Greek	5
Craig	Russian	2
Craig	Spanish	9
Crandall	French	9
Greene	French	3
Greene	Spanish	7
Greene	Italian	1
Greene	Japanese	4
Temple	French	4
Temple	Russian	2

Table 8–9 *Groups Table*

work_group	head_honcho
=========	
EA	Temple
FTA	Crandall
IMF	Craig
WHO	Greene

Table 8–10 *Affiliations Table*

name	work_group
====	=========
Axworthy	WHO
Axworthy	IMF
Broadbent	IMF
Broadbent	FTA
Campbell	EA
Craig	IMF
Crandall	FTA
Greene	WHO
Temple	EA

one `work_group`.) And finally, because each diplomat is affiliated with one or more groups, we'll create an `Affiliations` table, using the columns `name` and `work_group`. `Affiliations` forms the association between the `Diplomats` and `Groups` tables and is "all key"—that is, `Affiliations` has no additional dependent columns, because the only thing dependent on both `name` and `work_group` is the fact that they are associated. Table 8-9 shows the third normal form `Groups` table, and Table 8-10 shows the third normal form `Affiliations` table.

At this point, our normalization process is complete. All tables are in third normal form, and requests such as those listed earlier can easily be dealt with.

Here are some tips for good database design:

- Don't use an existing database as the basis for a new database structure—you don't want to inadvertently duplicate awkward or inconsistent table definitions.

- Avoid unnecessary duplication of data—make sure each table represents just one subject.
- Define a primary key for every table—not only will it uniquely identify a row, you'll use it to join tables. A primary key must have unique, NOT NULL values that, preferably, change only rarely.
- Define unique keys and foreign keys for your tables.

Breaking Normalization Rules

Still on the subject of normalization, strictly speaking, an error isn't a performance problem unless you correct it. So the following observations won't convince the true cowboys in the crowd, because they only affect performance when results must be correct. Um, that still sounds nontrivial, so let's observe two scenarios.

Scenario #1: BREAK 1NF

InterBase, Informix, and Oracle have supported arrays for many years, and now ARRAY is an SQL:1999 data type. Another SQL:1999 collection data type, ROW, is supported by Informix. Suppose we have a table that contains addresses. We want to split the address column into four parts because—when the data is printed—four lines are used for the address. (In effect, we want to break first normal form.) So, instead of using Definition #1, we make our Addresses table with either Definition #2 or Definition #3:

```
Definition #1:
CREATE TABLE Addresses (
  identifier INTEGER PRIMARY KEY,
  address CHARACTER(100),
  ... )

Definition #2:
CREATE TABLE Addresses (            /* Use ARRAY data type */
  identifier INTEGER PRIMARY KEY,
  address CHAR(25) ARRAY[4],
  ... )

Definition #3:
CREATE TABLE Addresses (            /* Use ROW data type */
  identifier INTEGER PRIMARY KEY,
  address ROW (r1 CHAR(25),
               r2 CHAR(25),
```

```
        r3 CHAR(25),
        r4 CHAR(25)),
...  )
```

At this point, someone needs an answer to the question—How many addresses are in New York? We can no longer answer the question with this query:

```
SELECT * FROM Addresses
  WHERE address LIKE '%New York%'
```

Instead, we'll have to use one of these queries to get the answer . . . which takes considerably longer to execute. (Yes we tried it, on Informix, whose ROW data type complies with the SQL Standard.)

```
SELECT * FROM Addresses       /* for the ARRAY data type */
  WHERE address[1] LIKE '%New York%'
     OR address[2] LIKE '%New York%'
     OR address[3] LIKE '%New York%'
     OR address[4] LIKE '%New York%'

SELECT * FROM Addresses       /* for the ROW data type */
  WHERE address.r1 LIKE '%New York%'
     OR address.r2 LIKE '%New York%'
     OR address.r3 LIKE '%New York%'
     OR address.r4 LIKE '%New York%'
```

And herein lies the problem with breaking 1NF just to make the printing job easier. Not only are the collection type queries slower, they're not even strictly correct—New York could have been split over two or more lines.

Scenario #2: BREAK 2NF

Now, suppose we create two more tables, as follows:

```
CREATE TABLE States (
  state_code CHARACTER(2) PRIMARY KEY,
  state_name CHARACTER(25))

CREATE TABLE Cities (
  identifier INTEGER PRIMARY KEY,
  city_name CHARACTER(25),
  state_code CHARACTER(2))
```

One of the rows in Cities contains a state_code value of AL. We can look up AL in the States table to determine that AL means Alaska. But we find that when we print addresses we must do joins to display the name of the state:

```
SELECT identifier, city_name, state_name
  FROM Cities, States
  WHERE Cities.state_code = States.state_code
```

Because we don't want to waste time doing the join, we duplicate the state_name in the Cities table and end up with the tables shown in Table 8-11 and Table 8-12.

With the new Cities table, we don't have to join any more. We can simply execute this SQL statement:

```
SELECT identifier, city_name, state_name
  FROM Cities
```

We've broken second normal form (state_name is dependent on state_code, not just identifier)—but performance will obviously improve.

Time passes. . . .

At this point, we find that some user, who didn't understand the system, thought state_name in the Cities table is an updatable column. So she changed it to Saudi Arabia—but forgot to update state_code as well. To prevent that from happening again, we add a CHECK constraint to Cities:

```
ALTER TABLE Cities
  ADD CONSTRAINT State_Check CHECK (
      (state_code, state_name) =
          (SELECT state_code, state_name FROM States))
/* this could also be done with a FOREIGN KEY constraint */
```

Table 8-11 *Cities Table*

identifier	city_name	state_code	state_name
1	Riyadh	AL	Alaska
2	Medina	AL	Alaska
3	Mecca	AL	Alaska

Table 8-12 *States Table*

state_code	state_name
KY	Kentucky
AL	Alaska
NY	New York

This is inevitable. Whenever redundant columns are added, errors creep in, and we correct them by adding constraints or triggers. (By the way, not all DBMSs will accept the syntax of this CHECK constraint.) So let's take stock:

- All the rows in the `Cities` table are slightly larger. As we know from the last chapter, this means when we SELECT from `Cities` alone, the selection is slower.

- The `Cities` table is subject to a new constraint. That means INSERTs will be slower. In fact, because the constraint references a far table, INSERTs could slow down by just as much as we saved by not joining on the SELECTs.

- One other thing. `AL` doesn't stand for `Alaska`—it stands for `Alabama`. When we fix that, we'll have to remember to fix it in two places.

The point we want to make here is that denormalizing only *appears* to make things faster. That is, when we deliberately denormalized, we failed to make an improvement overall. In fact, it appears that denormalizing improved one thing, but caused an offsetting problem to pop out somewhere else.

Relational proponents like to notice that sort of thing. They say it proves that you might as well try to optimize for a broad range of cases, because when you optimize for a single case, you muck things up elsewhere. And here we can address the claim that "it is practical" to denormalize. That's true—but "it" is a singular pronoun. Normalizing is an attempt to optimize generally. Denormalizing is an attempt to normalize for a particular application, to introduce a bias.

By following normalization rules, you will be splitting a table—for example, where the original table was `Table1 (column1, column2, column3, column4)`, you end up with `Table1 (column1, column2, T2_ID)` and `Table2 (T2_ID, column3, column4)`. The advantages of this arrangement are three-fold:

- Tables are narrower. Therefore, scans are quicker.

- There are more tables. Therefore partitioning is easier.

- Irrelevant information is separated out. Therefore a data change affecting `column4` won't block a transaction affecting `column1`—locks will be less frequent.

The Bottom Line: Normalization

> "There is basically no need for OLTP denormalization today."
> —Richard Yevich and Susan Lawson, *DB2 High
> Performance Design and Tuning,* Prentice Hall PTR

Normalizing means smaller rows. Smaller rows mean faster retrievals because (a) the chance of overflowing the operating system cache is smaller, (b) a single page read retrieves more records into cache, and (c) byte-by-byte comparisons involve less bytes. On the other hand, (a) fragmentation is more likely as rows are updated or deleted, (b) string comparisons always involve an initial read of the size (the parser cannot decide in advance how many repetitions to plug into the loop that it produces), and (c) row position within a file can't be calculated in advance because row start is not a simple matter of saying (row size * row number).

Normalizing also has these effects: (a) table scans for a particular column are twice as fast (on average) because the number of rows per page is greater, (b) parallel queries are possible, (c) fetch and lock times are reduced, and (d) INSERTs are slowed by primary-key/foreign-key integrity checks.

Normalizing helps design and programming, and it makes things more efficient too (at least as far as 3NF, which is easy to reach with case tools). The downside is that too many slow joins happen if you ask for all information related to an entity—but really, you should be thinking about making the join faster or cutting out unnecessary joins rather than opting to denormalize.

Views

To this point, we've talked only about physical representations, as if all tables are base tables. Does it matter if a table is a view? To find out, we tested three well-known propositions.

Portability	MySQL doesn't support views. The gains shown in this section are for only seven DBMSs.

Proposition one

A query of a view takes longer to prepare because it requires an extra lookup in the system catalog.

Calculated Fields

When you introduce redundancy, you risk error (because two occurrences of the value will be out of sync). The solution is to add a trigger, which will ensure that any change to A will also cause a change to B. So the question is—Is the calculation cost greater than the maintenance cost? We've already noted that SELECTs are more common than UPDATEs. But arithmetic is cheap. Is there any sort of calculation that takes so long that it's worth some trouble to avoid it? Yes—a calculation that involves multiple rows (and therefore involves multiple I/Os). The top three uses of calculated fields are:

- To avoid the one-column join
  For example, you might have "Error 50" and the short explanation is "Lamination Drier Overheated." But you must always explain Error 50 when you display—that is, it's a lookup of a code.
- To avoid the double join
  For example, you have a hierarchy A → B → C and you frequently join A → C without needing B (by "hierarchy," we mean many-to-one table relationships here).
- To avoid the transaction join/join-and-sum
  For example, with a general ledger you have a running total—you don't want to get the balance by looking at all the withdrawals and deposits since day one.

Simpler calculations aren't worth the trouble.

It turns out this proposition is true. To test it, we created a view on a simple table:

```
CREATE VIEW View1 AS
  SELECT * FROM Table1
```

Then we timed the relative speed of Query #1 as opposed to Query #2:

```
Query #1:
SELECT * FROM View1

Query #2:
SELECT * FROM Table1
GAIN: 7/7
```

Proposition two

It is faster to execute a prepared query on a **materialized view** twice, than to materialize the view twice. (A materialized view is a view whose rows take up space.)

It turns out this proposition is true too. To test it, we created a materializable view on a simple table:

```
CREATE VIEW View1 AS
  SELECT SUM(column1) AS sum_column1
    FROM Table1
```

Then we timed the relative speed of Query #1 as opposed to Query #2:

```
Query #1:
SELECT SUM(column1) FROM Table1

Query #2:
SELECT * FROM View1
GAIN: 2/7
```

Note: We ran each query twice so that the prepared plan might still be in cache.

Proposition three

It is madness to use a view of a join or a union, unless you intend to use all columns.

It turns out this proposition is also true, provided that a primary-key/foreign-key relationship exists between the tables. To test it, we created these two tables, as well as a view on a join of Table1 and Table2:

```
CREATE TABLE Table1 (
    column1 INT PRIMARY KEY,
    column2 INT)

CREATE TABLE Table2 (
    column1 INT REFERENCES Table1,
    column2 INT)

CREATE VIEW View1 AS
  SELECT Table1.column1 AS column1,
         Table2.column2 AS column2
    FROM Table1, Table2
    WHERE Table2.column1 = Table1.column1
```

Then we timed the relative speed of Query #1 as opposed to Query #2:

```
Query #1:
SELECT DISTINCT column1 FROM View1

Query #2:
SELECT DISTINCT column1 FROM Table2
GAIN: 7/7
```

Not a single DBMS detected what we were doing and threw away the join clause. Each one performed the useless join and so it's true—You should avoid views of joins if you only need columns from one side of the join.

The Bottom Line: Views

A query of a view takes longer to prepare than a query of a table.

It is faster to execute a prepared query on a materialized view twice, than to materialize the view twice.

Don't query a view of a join or a union unless you intend to use all columns.

Parting Shots

Data independence doesn't (yet) exist. We can decry that fact, or we can live with it. We certainly shouldn't encourage it.

Standardization at the physical level does (sort of) exist. Vendors hide this by using different terminology for everything, but the fact remains: there are pages and extents and read groups and files and partitions and tablespaces. There is, in fact, a Storage Hierarchy.

Migration is a serious problem. Fragmentation is too, but takes a long time to show itself.

Normalization is a good thing. No good thing is all good.

9

Indexes

"Indexes make SELECTs faster, but they make UPDATEs slower."
—Common knowledge

The common knowledge about indexes is true—but it's too vague for our purposes. In this chapter, we'll try to be more precise about indexes. Specifically, we'll look at these questions:

- What precisely is an index?
- How much does an index accelerate a SELECT?
- What do you, as an application programmer, need to know about the costs, the alternatives, the work arounds, the rules, and the concepts of dealing with indexes?

The pleasant thing to note about the technology of indexing is that it's mature. Nearly all DBMSs (including the Big Eight) depend on the **B-tree** structure for their indexes. B-trees have been around for over 30 years, so their use is very well known. Many DBMSs also use the **bitmap (bitmap index),** an interesting technology but by no means a new idea either. A few also use hashes for indexing, though hashes are typically hidden from the end user. Thus, despite vendors' attempts to differentiate their products, index implementations are the same. They have to be, because it's been established through years of practice what the better techniques are. That's good news for you! When you switch DBMSs, you won't have to relearn everything, and when you grow old, the kids will still understand you when you tell your index war stories.

Refresher

We said in Chapter 1, "Facilis Descensus Averni," that we assume you're already familiar with (among other things) indexes, but here's a quick summary of index basics to refresh your memory.

Because the SQL Standard doesn't deal with physical storage of database objects or data, no official "standard" syntax exists for creating an index. However, because the foundation of a good DBMS's performance is its indexes, all DBMSs support the creation of indexes in some way, usually via the nonstandard SQL-extension CREATE INDEX statement. The *de facto* standard syntax, supported by each of the Big Eight is:

```
CREATE [ UNIQUE ] INDEX <Index name>
  ON <Table> ( <column> [, ...] )
```

CREATE INDEX makes an index on one or more columns of a table. By default, the values are indexed in ascending (ASC) order, but you can index them in descending order by adding the keyword DESC somewhere, usually after the column name. If you want to prohibit duplicate values in the indexed column(s), add the keyword UNIQUE to your CREATE INDEX statement.

Strictly speaking, it's the DBA who sets the rules for creating and dropping indexes. Nevertheless, common practice is to give programmers the right to say if an index is necessary. And certainly the database's users have the right to employ indexes. In fact, they would have a hard time avoiding them. Typically a DBMS will read an index to handle these situations:

* An expression of the form <column> <predicate> <literal> in a WHERE clause.
* An expression of the form <column> = <column> in an ON clause.
* DISTINCT, UNION, and ORDER BY.
* Sometimes, to evaluate a column expression in the select list.

- To avoid sorts. Sorts are generally fairly expensive, and the time needed to do a sort grows exponentially with the size of a table.
- To maintain UNIQUE, PRIMARY KEY, and FOREIGN KEY constraints.

An index helps the DBMS solve a query faster by allowing it to avoid a sequential search, or full table scan. It's a well-known fact that this SQL statement:

```
SELECT * FROM Table1
  WHERE column1 = 5
```

will be evaluated much faster if `column1` has a distributed set of indexed values—and provided that `Table1` is fairly large. So indexing speeds up SELECT. The price you pay for this is that INSERT, UPDATE, and DELETE will be slower on the indexed columns. Thus, if your code contains many SELECT statements with the same column in the WHERE clause, you should ensure that column is indexed. And if your code contains massive data-change statements involving the same column, it's a good idea to make sure it's (at least temporarily) not indexed. (Note that we're not talking about indexes used by the DBMS to enforce constraints here—we just mean explicitly created indexes that don't involve the access path needed to make the data change.)

B-trees

Two types of searches are possible when you're retrieving data from your database. An internal search occurs when you're searching a file that fits into your computer's internal memory. When you need to retrieve data from a very large file, though, the search is called an *external search* because the entire file doesn't fit into the available RAM. B-tree structures lend themselves nicely to external searching—they make it possible both to search and to update a large file with guaranteed efficiency.

All DBMSs depend on B-trees—they are the default structures built when you create an index and are also the structures that will be used to enhance retrieval in most cases. Each of the Big Eight use the B-tree. Informix alone says explicitly that it uses a variant called the B+tree, but the rest of the Big Eight do too. None of the Big Eight use the other important variant, the B*-tree.

A B-tree is essentially just a sorted list of keys, which are {data, pointer or row locator} combinations. The actual structure of a B-tree consists of a number

Characteristics of B-trees

A B-tree of order m is a tree with the following characteristics:

- Every node has at most m children.
- Every node, except for the root and the leaves, has at least (m/2) children.
- The root has at least two children, unless it is a leaf.
- All leaves appear on the same level and carry no information.
- A nonleaf node with k children contains (k-1) keys.
- A leaf is a terminal node (one with no children).

A B+-tree is an improved B-tree that allows you to efficiently search a file both sequentially and randomly. All records of the file are stored in the B+-tree's leaves, with only a few of the keys duplicated in the branch nodes. A B+-tree's leaves are always at least half full—a new key enters the nonleaf part of the tree whenever a leaf splits. B+-trees are B-trees with two common features: (a) all keys are in the leaf nodes even if that means they are repeated in more than one layer, and (b) there are pointers from leaf to leaf.

A B*-tree is an even better form of B-tree. It has these characteristics:

- Every node except the root has at most m children.
- Every node, except for the root and the leaves, has at least ((2m-1)/3) children.
- The root has at least two and at most (2[(2m-2)/3]+1) children.
- All leaves appear on the same level.
- A nonleaf node with k children contains (k-1) keys.

The important characteristic is the second one—the fact that at least two-thirds of the available space in every node is always used. This uses space efficiently and makes searches faster. On the downside, it slows down INSERT because nodes tend to need more attention as they fill up. B*-trees are B-trees with one difference: A split is not a 50/50 fission. Instead the DBMS will attempt to shift keys into adjoining leaf blocks so that pages are fuller and the need to make new pages is less frequent. This makes splits affect multiple pages. B*-tree use is very rare.

Note: We will follow common usage and use "B-tree" to mean the "B+-tree" variant of the B-tree, as most DBMS vendors do.

of nodes stored as items in the B-tree's file. Each node contains a portion of the sorted list of keys in the B-tree, along with pointers to other nodes. The **root node** for a given B-tree is where all searches through that tree begin. Figure 9–1 shows a simplified example of this principle.

In a B-tree, records are stored in locations called *leaves*. The name derives from the fact that records always exist at endpoints—there is nothing beyond them. The maximum number of children per node is known as the *order* of the tree. A practical B-tree can contain thousands, millions, or billions of records.

The four characteristics that describe a B-tree are: sortable, selective, subset, balanced.

- *Sortable* because you travel through a B-tree's keys in order, as when you use >= or BETWEEN in a WHERE clause, or when you use ORDER BY to sort a result set. A BLOB, which has no inherent sortability, is not appropriate for a B-tree index.

- *Selective* because you want to get only some of the rows. Selectivity is defined as:

  `(number of distinct values) / (total number of values)`

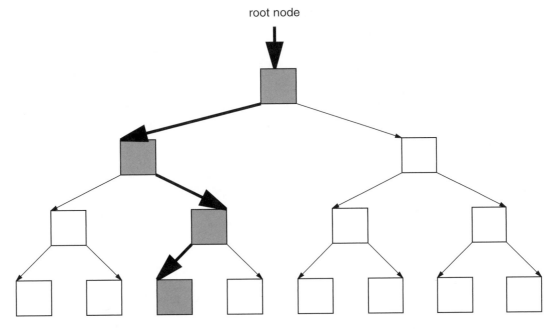

Figure 9–1   *Searching a B-tree*

and is often expressed as a percentage. Thus, for a sex column in a 100-row table, selectivity is 2%—there are only two possible distinct values and (2/100) is 2%. The usual recommendation is not to make a B-tree if selectivity is a low value, so sex is an example of an inappropriate choice.

- *Subset* because the key value (the part of an index key other than the pointer) is completely derived from the column value in the data row. Thus, if a row is {'Abc', 15}, then a full index also has {'Abc', 15}—though possibly truncated and not necessarily in that order.

- *Balanced* because the distance from the root to the leaf is always the same. Figure 9–2 shows an example of an unbalanced tree.

Confusingly, it's traditional to diagram a tree upside down—the root is sometimes called the "top layer" and the leaf is the bottom. The interesting thing to note about the tree shown in Figure 9–2 is that a direct pointer leads

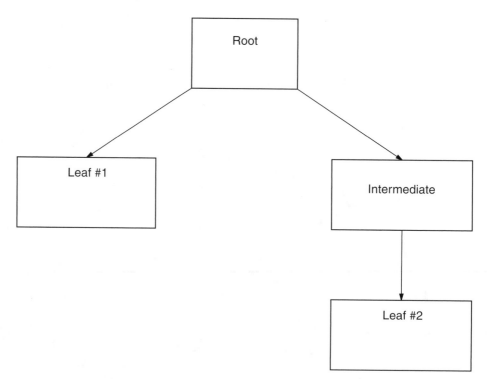

Figure 9–2   *An unbalanced tree*

from the root to leaf page #1, but an intermediate node is between the root and leaf page #2, which is what makes the tree unbalanced. Therefore, eponymously, Figure 9-2 is not a B-tree—B-trees are *always* balanced.

In a B-tree, all the keys are grouped inside fixed-size pages. The keys in the root page point to intermediate pages, the keys in the intermediate pages point to leaf pages, and the keys in the leaf pages point to data rows. That, at least, is what happens when three levels (or three layers) are in the index, and the index is not clustered (the "clustered index" exception is something we'll talk about later). Figure 9-3 shows a three-level B-tree.

Searching a B-tree

Suppose you have the table and index shown in Figure 9-4 (we'll call this our example database) and execute this SQL statement:

```
SELECT * FROM Table1
  WHERE column1 = 'OTTO'
```

To evaluate this query, the DBMS starts by scanning the index's root page. It scans until it's pointing to a key value that is greater than or equal to OTTO (in

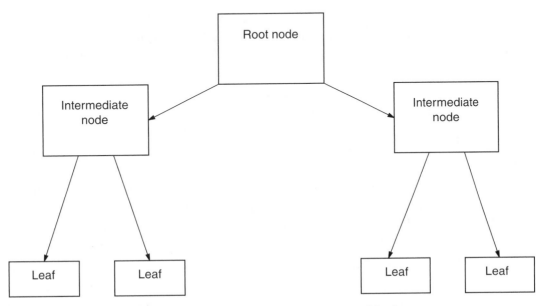

Figure 9–3   *Three-level B-tree showing root, intermediate, and leaf pages*

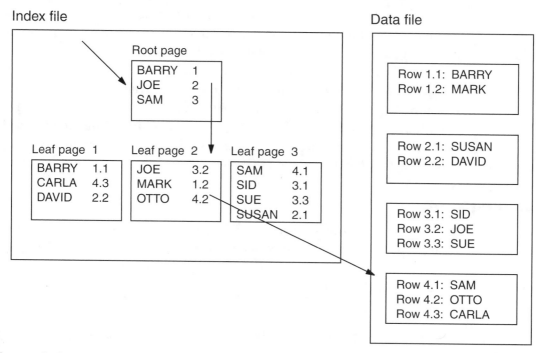

Figure 9–4 *Example database with B-tree index*

this case, SAM). Now OTTO, if it exists, is on the path that is pointed to by the key just before that (in this case, JOE), so the DBMS loads leaf page #2. Then it scans leaf page #2, looking again for the first value that is greater than or equal to OTTO (in this case, OTTO). This second scan tells the DBMS to load data page #4. Once it has done so, it finds OTTO in the second row in that page.

Two things are worth noting about this system:

- The DBMS is scanning keys that are known to be in order, so it can do a binary search—not a sequential search—of the keys in the page. (A binary search is possible even if there are variable-size keys because the page header contains offset pointers.) Thus it makes no difference whether keys are at the start or at the end of the page—search time is the same.

- Your search didn't specify how many rows you wanted. Therefore, unless the DBMS somehow knows that OTTO can only occur once, it will continue scanning. In this case, it will follow the leaf pointer and get the next leaf block—a wasted disk access, because the next leaf page actually begins with SAM.

The notes here are about exceptions and details. The fundamental point is much simpler: The DBMS needed two page reads to find the key. This figure is fixed—the number of index levels equals the number of reads, always, except that you can be fairly confident that the root page is in a cache. (There is actually one exception: If the DBMS is scanning leaf pages sequentially, there is no need to visit intermediate or root pages so the reads are fewer.)

For example, suppose you execute this query:

```
SELECT column1 FROM Table1
  ORDER BY column1
```

and the DBMS decides to resolve the query by going through all the keys in the index, sequentially. In that case, with most DBMSs, the transit is from leaf page to leaf page directly and not via the upper (i.e., intermediate or root) index levels. This is because there are pointers from one leaf page forward to the next leaf or from one leaf page back to the previous leaf.

The critical thing, then, is the number of layers—not the total index size—and that's why it's good to have big pages. Typically an index page size is 8KB. It's this mandate—Keep the number of layers small!—that influences several of the design and updating decisions that programmers must make. A rule of thumb is that the number of layers should never exceed five. If there are more than five layers, it's time for drastic measures like partitioning. (This rule is somewhat arbitrary, as all "rules of thumb" are—we're just passing on the general consensus from many diverse sources.)

Inserting into a B-tree

When you INSERT a new row, or UPDATE with a new value for an indexed column, the result includes the insertion of a new key value into the index. Usually the insert of a new key value is simple:

* The DBMS scans the index pages until it finds a key value that is greater than the new key value.

* Then it shifts forward all following data in the page to make room for the new key value.

- Then it copies the new value into the page. (The shifting should mean that it's slightly slower to insert a key at the start of a page than at the end—which means that it's bad to INSERT in a descending sequence. However, the difference is barely measurable.)

What if a key value insert isn't simple? For example, what happens with our example database (Figure 9–4) if the following SQL statements are executed?

```
INSERT INTO Table1 VALUES ('MARY')

INSERT INTO Table1 VALUES ('OMAR')
```

The page doesn't contain enough room on which to fit these new key values. To make them fit, the DBMS must take some keys out of the current page and put them in a new page—for example, at the end of the index file.[1] This process is called **splitting**. The rules for splitting are as follows:

- At the leaf level, splits should only occur when there is no chance of fitting the new key in the current page.

- Splits should be 50/50. That is, after the split happens and the new key is added, the total number of bytes in the keys of the current page should be about the same as in the new page. There are exceptions to this rule: (a) when the new key would otherwise go at the end of the page, the current page is left alone and only the new key goes into the new page and (b) the definition of a "full" page depends on switches like PCTFREE/FILLFACTOR.

- A pointer to the new leaf page must be added into the appropriate page at the intermediate level.

- For reasons that have to do with locking, a split must not cascade. That is, a split on the leaf must not cause a split in the intermediate level. To ensure this, the DBMS will split a nearly full intermediate-level page first, before it reads the leaf page. This means that unnecessary splits are sometimes made at high levels.

---

1. This, of course, is a very simplistic description of what could actually happen. As with data pages, allocation of new index pages is usually more complex; involving the DBMS's freelist or other storage hierarchy rules.

- If variable-length fields are present, the calculations become more complicated because the split cannot occur right in the middle of the page, and because the new key might be so big that a single split will not free enough room.

Figure 9-5 shows what the example database looks like after the INSERTs. The effect of INSERT is much like the effect of dripping grains of sand, one grain at a time, onto the top of a pile. For a long time nothing happens, but eventually the addition of one more grain causes an avalanche, the shape of the pile changes, and a new equilibrium is reached.

Because of splits, the speed of data-change statements (INSERT, UPDATE, DELETE) may vary unpredictably. To reduce that unpredictability, you can

Index file

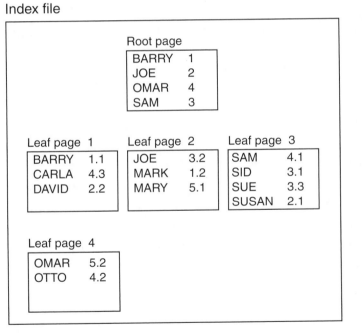

Data file

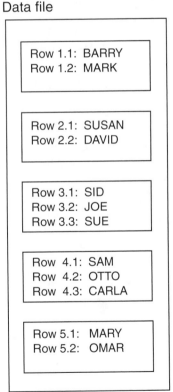

Figure 9–5   *Example database after INSERTs**

---

*Figure 9-5 shows the same database as in Figure 9-4, after two INSERTs and a split. Notice that not all leaf pages are full, and notice that leaf page #4 should logically follow leaf page #2.

instruct the DBMS to leave a little bit of space in every page and therefore make splits unlikely. This is done with PCTFREE or FILLFACTOR (see the section "Free Page Space" in Chapter 8, "Tables"). But PCTFREE/FILLFACTOR and their ilk affect only the free space left during index creation or rebuilding. During data-change operations, splitting occurs only if there is absolutely no chance of fitting the new key in the page.

Because of the rules of splits, a page will be less than 100% full after a large number of random key insertions (because of waste space at the end of the page), but more than 50% full (because a split makes pages 50%[2] full and then there's room for some INSERTs that won't cause a split). The rule of thumb to follow here is to assume pages are 70% full if insertions are random, or more than that if insertions are done in an ascending sequence.

Deleting from a B-tree

There are two ways to delete keys from B-trees: the obvious way, and the Microsoft/Oracle way.

If the DBMS treats deletions as merely insertions in reverse, the deletion rules are:

- Scan the index until the key whose value equals the deleted value is found. This involves comparing both key value and data pointer because sometimes the same value can occur in different rows.
- Shift all following keys in the page upward over the key being deleted.
- If the key was the first in the leaf page, update the key value in the intermediate page. Some cascading may occur, and there is an opportunity for a reverse split—that is, two logically adjacent pages could now be merged if both are less than 50% full. Actually, though, no such thing happens.

Microsoft and Oracle don't do deletions the obvious way. For these DBMSs, the deletion rules are:

- Scan the index to find the key . . . so far so good.

---

2. This is an approximation. As stated earlier, the definition of a "full" page is influenced by switches like PCTFREE/FILLFACTOR.

- Mark the key as deleted—but don't move anything! The key is still there and is still used for ordering, but it's become a "ghost" row.

The obvious advantage of the Microsoft/Oracle way is that the expense of shifting and cascading is eliminated—for now. (An additional and perhaps more important reason has to do with a special type of lock called a "key range lock," which we'll discuss in Chapter 15, "Locks.") That's all very well, and the space is reused when a new value will fit in the same place or when a low-priority background thread clears up the page. However, it does mean you shouldn't repeatedly change an indexed column to an ever-newer value. Consider this snippet of code, part of a program to make an index grow indefinitely:

```
for (i=0; i<1000000; ++i) {
  num=rand();
  EXEC SQL UPDATE Table1 SET column1 = :num;
  }
```

We ran a program containing a loop like this after inserting 10,000 rows into Table1. When the program finished, the index had at least doubled in size. So although the old tip—Do DELETE before INSERT—is still good, it isn't as powerful as it once was.

Let's do one more change to our example database (Figure 9-5). We'll DELETE with this SQL statement:

```
DELETE FROM Table1
  WHERE column1 = 'CARLA'
```

Now, assuming the DBMS has deleted the obvious way, the example database won't have any ghost rows but will still look rather messy. Figure 9-6 shows what it looks like now; this is what is known as a *fragmented database*.

Fragmentation

So far, we've done two INSERTs and one DELETE on the example database, and the result is a horrible mess! Look at everything that's wrong with Figure 9-6:

- The leaf pages are out of order. At this stage, if the DBMS wants to go through the pages in logical order by key value—a common requirement

Index file

Data file

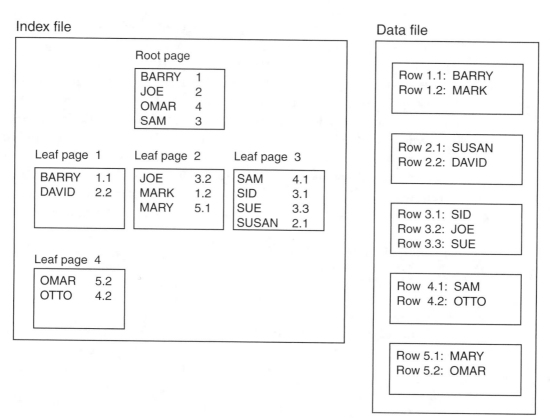

Figure 9–6   *Example database after DELETE—fragmented*

for a range search, an ORDER BY, or a GROUP BY—it must jump from leaf page #2 to page #4 and then back to page #3. The situation won't affect searches for a single row with an equals operator, but that hides the effect only for a while. As we learned in Chapter 8, this problem is called *fragmentation*.

- The leaf pages vary in fullness. Leaf pages #1 and #4 are only 50% full. Leaf page #3 is 100% full, and the next insertion will almost certainly cause a split. This problem is called **skew**.

- And finally, the root looks ready for a split on the very next insertion, regardless of what gets changed. Remember, splits in upper layers happen "in anticipation" so a split may occur even when the leaf page won't overflow. And a split on the root is an especially bad thing, because after a root split happens, there is one more layer—and when there is one more layer, there is one more I/O for every index lookup. And when *that* happens, everything takes 50% longer. That's unfair in this case, because the leaf pages aren't really full, or even 70% full on average.

Hey, we admit this isn't a real example. In particular, by limiting the page size so the maximum number of rows per page is four, and by making changes in precisely the wrong places, we've made it look very easy to cause a mess. In fact, though, on a real database, the rule of thumb is that you don't have to worry about fragmentation and skewing until the number of rows you've changed or added is equal to more than 5% of the total number of rows in the database. After that, it's probably time to rebuild. Tools are available to check how messy an index looks, but they're vendor-specific so we'll skip them and proceed right to the rebuilding step.

Rebuilding a B-tree

If you've followed us this far, you know that rebuilding will be an inevitable part of database life until DBMSs learn how to rearrange indexes automatically during regular activity. Skew and fragmentation cause a need for cleanup. There are two ways to do it: ALTER INDEX/REBUILD or DROP INDEX/RECREATE.

ALTER INDEX/REBUILD

We're being vague with our syntax here because it varies, but most DBMSs support some type of nonstandard SQL extension that will "rebuild" an index. The important thing is that rebuilding doesn't really happen. What does happen is shown, in pseudocode, in Listing 9–1.

Listing 9–1 *Pseudocode of ALTER INDEX/REBUILD*

```
for (each leaf page)
 if (first index key in page could fit in prior leaf page)
  if (insert wouldn't overflow past index's free page space)
   shift this index key to the prior leaf page
   shift following keys up; adjust intermediate-page pointers
   repeat
for (each intermediate page)
 do approximately the same things as for leaf-page loop
```

We have left out some important matters in Listing 9-1, such as what to do if a page becomes empty and the index can be shrunk. But the important thing is that the algorithm will fix skew. It won't, however, fix fragmentation. Table 9–1 shows the command each of the Big Eight provides for index rebuilding.

DROP INDEX/RECREATE

Although it's reasonable to guess that it will take 100 times longer than ALTER INDEX/REBUILD, sometimes the only way to fix an index is to drop the index (with the nonstandard SQL-extension statement DROP INDEX) and then re-make it with CREATE INDEX. And even that won't be enough unless you also run an operating system defragger program. We can only say that DROP INDEX/ RECREATE should be more frequent than it is, but there is no rule of thumb and no consensus about this.

In this context, let's address some general issues about "bulk changes"— changing many keys at once. Long ago, someone had the insight that if bulk changes were made in order by key value, the process would go much more quickly because the DBMS would always be going forward to a later page in the index. It would never have to backtrack, and therefore the heads would not thresh back and forth on the disk drive.

This is relevant to CREATE INDEX because, as it happens, all DBMSs have optimized CREATE INDEX so that the DBMS will sort the keys before putting them in the index. That's why you'll often see the tip—Load data first, make index second. Presorting the keys yourself is so much better that you'll even see this tip—If you're going to change more than 5% of the keys, drop the index first and create it again when the changes are over. (Of course, you'll

Table 9–1   *DBMS ALTER INDEX/REBUILD Support*

	Rebuild Command
IBM	REBUILD INDEX utility
Informix	none: vendor recommends DROP INDEX and re-create
Ingres	MODIFY … TO MERGE
InterBase	ALTER INDEX INACTIVE/ACTIVE
Microsoft	DBCC DBREINDEX
MySQL	none: vendor recommends OPTIMIZE TABLE
Oracle	ALTER INDEX … REBUILD
Sybase	dbcc reindex

make sure that the relevant table can't be used by another transaction while you're doing this!)

In an ideal world, you would sort the rows you were about to process (e.g., by UPDATE statements), so that the DBMS could update the index in key order, but within a page—doing deletions before insertions so that room would be guaranteed for the new keys. The latest version of Microsoft's DBMS does such sorting automatically. Finally, most DBMSs will allow options like "disable index" (e.g., MySQL, Oracle) or "defer index key write" (e.g., MySQL). These options are confessions of weakness on the DBMS maker's part, but that is no reason to disdain them.

> **Tip** Just before a peak period, anticipate by rebuilding your index even if it's not fragmented. Use PCTFREE/FILLFACTOR, so that lots of space will be in each index page when the split times come.

The Bottom Line: B-trees

All DBMSs depend on B-trees—they are the default structures built when you create an index and are also the structures that will be used to enhance retrieval in most cases.

A B-tree is sortable because you travel through a B-tree's keys in order.

A B-tree is selective because you want to get only some of the rows.

A B-tree is a subset because the key value (the part of an index key other than the pointer) is completely derived from the column value in the data row.

A B-tree is balanced because the distance from the root to any leaf is always the same.

When searching a B-tree, the DBMS is scanning keys that are known to be in order, so it can do a binary search—not a sequential search—of the keys in the page. Thus it makes no difference whether keys are at the start or at the end of the page—search time is the same.

The number of B-tree index levels equals the number of index page reads, always, except that you can be fairly confident that the root page is in a cache.

The critical thing is the number of B-tree layers—not the total index size—and that's why it's good to have big pages. Keep the number of layers small!

A rule of thumb for B-trees is that the number of layers should never exceed five. If there are more than five layers, it's time for drastic measures like partitioning.

The rules for index splitting are:

- At the leaf level, splits should only occur when there is no chance of fitting the new key in the current page.

- Splits should be 50/50—after the split, the total number of bytes in the keys of the current page should be about the same as in the new page.

- A pointer to the new leaf page must be added into the appropriate page at the intermediate level.

- A split must not cascade.

Because of splits, the speed of data-change statements may vary unpredictably. To reduce that unpredictability, you can instruct the DBMS to leave a little bit of space in every page and therefore make splits less likely.

Because of the rules of splits, a page will be less than 100% full after a large number of random key insertions (because of wasted space at the end of the page) but more than 50% full (because a split makes pages 50% full and then there's room for some INSERTs that won't cause a split). The rule of thumb to follow is to assume pages are 70% full if insertions are random, or more than that if insertions are done in an ascending sequence.

Don't repeatedly change an indexed column to an ever-newer value.

You don't have to worry about fragmentation and skewing until the number of rows you've changed or added is equal to more than 5% of the total number of rows in the database. After that, it's probably time to rebuild.

Skew and fragmentation cause a need for cleanup. There are two ways to do it: ALTER INDEX/REBUILD or DROP INDEX/RECREATE (syntax deliberately vague).

If bulk changes are made in order by key value, the process goes much more quickly because the DBMS is always going forward to a later page in the index. So—load data first, make index second.

If you're going to change more than 5% of the keys, drop the index first and create it again when the changes are over.

Just before a peak period, anticipate by rebuilding your index even if it's not fragmented. Use PCTFREE/FILLFACTOR, so that each index page will have lots of space when the split times come.

Types of Indexes

In this section, we'll talk about the various kinds of indexes—compound indexes, covering indexes, unique indexes, clustered indexes—you might encounter, and how you can take advantage of them.

Compound Indexes

A **compound index** is an index whose keys contain values derived from more than one data column. The terms *compound index*, **composite index,** and **multicolumn index** all mean the same thing and are equally valid. Each of the Big Eight support compound indexes.

Figure 9–7 shows some keys from an index that is based on two columns: surname and given_name. Notice that the keys are in order by the left-most column (surname) so a search on given_name alone will not be advantageous.

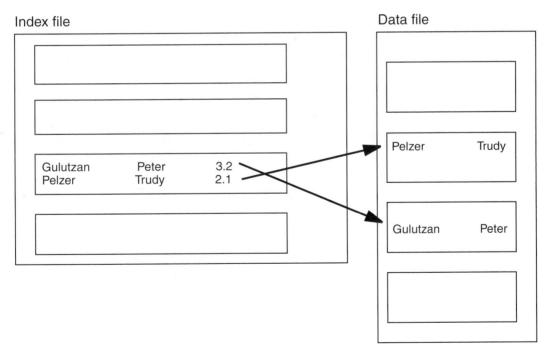

Figure 9–7   *An extract from a compound index*

Similarly, a telephone book may contain both a surname and a given name, but we would be foolish to look for Peter or Trudy in a phone book. It follows then, that a compound index is good when you want to search for, or sort by (a) the left-most column or (b) the left-most column and any of the other column(s)—and under no other circumstance.

Why would you want to make a compound index instead of making two indexes—one on surname and the other on given_name—and letting the DBMS merge the results? That is, why don't we have this scenario:

1. There are two indexes, one on surname and one on given_name.

2. The search is:
   ```
   SELECT * FROM Table1
     WHERE surname = 'smith'
       AND given_name = 'willy'
   ```

3. The DBMS searches the first index and comes up with, for example, these five matches:
   ```
   7, 35, 102, 448, 930
   ```

4. The DBMS searches the second index and comes up with, for example, these three matches:
   ```
   16, 102, 137
   ```
   Notice that the two lists of matches are in order, which is a natural result of the fact that in a B-tree keys are sorted by key value first, row locator second.

5. The DBMS merges the two ordered sets and comes up with the matching value:
   ```
   102
   ```

Apparently this method is so obvious that people simply assume that it will happen. In fact it normally doesn't[3]. What really happens at step 4 is that, instead of reading the second index, the DBMS reads each of the data rows—

---

3. Some versions of IBM and Sybase actually do use this method, but here we're talking about the normal case where merges don't happen.

{7, 35, 102, 448, 930}. Each time it reads a row, the DBMS looks at the value in the given_name column to see if it is willy.

The error of thinking that the DBMS will take the sensible route and make full use of all indexes available for the query is probably what leads to the phenomenon of "over indexing" (making indexes for every column that appears in queries). Over indexing is useless. Most DBMSs pick only one index as a driver.

The way to make use of an index on a second column is to put that column in a compound index. In that case, the DBMS takes this approach:

1. There is a compound index on (surname, given_name).

2. The search is:
   ```
   SELECT * FROM Table1
     WHERE surname = 'smith'
       AND given_name = 'willy'
   ```

3. The DBMS searches the compound index and comes up with one match:
   ```
   102
   GAIN: 7/8
   ```

The general recommendations that apply for all DBMSs, then, are:

- Use compound indexes if queries often contain the same columns, joined with AND.

- Use compound indexes if you have any key based on a one-character column.

- Use up to 5 columns in a compound index. You can be sure that the DBMS will allow at least 16, but 5 is regarded as the reasonable maximum by some experts.

- The left-most column should be the one that occurs in queries most often. This should also be the column that is the most selective.

And one more recommendation that applies to an obsolete DBMS but does no harm now:

- The order of columns in the WHERE clause should be the same as the order in the compound index.

Covering Indexes

Suppose you have a compound index (we'll call it Index_name_sex) on Table1's columns (name, sex). You execute this SQL statement:

```
SELECT sex FROM Table1
   WHERE name = 'SAM'
```

When you do so, the DBMS will use index_name_sex for the search because name is the left-most column in the index key. But once it has found the key {SAM, M}, the DBMS says, "Whoa, there's no need to get the data row," because sex is right there in the key. So the DBMS is able to return M directly from the index. When, as in this case, everything in the select list is also in the index that will be used, the index is called a **covering index.**

Ordinarily, using a covering index will save one disk read (GAIN: 6/8). The gain is automatic but only if the columns in the select list exactly match the columns in the covering index. You lose the gain if you select functions or literals, or if you put the column names in a different order.

Affairs get even better if you can persuade the DBMS to use a covering index regardless of whether it's searching for anything. For example, suppose you search Table1 without a WHERE clause, as in:

```
SELECT name FROM Table1
   ORDER BY name
```

Will the DBMS do the "smart" thing and scan the covering index, instead of scanning the table and then sorting? Answer: Sometimes. But Cloudscape won't use covering indexes unless it needs them for the WHERE clause anyway, and Oracle won't use an index if the result might involve NULLs. So there's a gain if you assume that NULL names don't matter and you change the search to:

```
SELECT name FROM Table1
  WHERE name > ''
  ORDER BY name
GAIN: 7/8
```

Even if you don't care about either selecting or ordering, a gain might still be achieved using a covering index. If the rows in the table are large, and the index keys are small, then it stands to reason that a scan of the entire index will be quicker than a scan of all the rows in the table. For example, if you want to list the sex column, don't use Query #1. Use Query #2 instead.

```
Query #1:
SELECT sex FROM Table1
 /* this causes a table scan */

Query #2:
SELECT name, sex FROM Table1
 /* this causes an index scan */
GAIN: 2/8
```

By using Query #2 even though you don't care about name, you speed up the search by selecting an unnecessary column. In this example, you're really using the index, not as a tool to enhance access to the table, but as a substitute for the table. Thus it's a cheap way to get some vertical partitioning.

The benefits of "treating the index as a table" are often significant, provided you keep a few sobering facts in mind:

- DBMSs never use covering indexes when there are joins or groupings.

- The index selection can't be used for UPDATE statements.

- Adding frequently changed columns to indexes strictly to make them covering indexes violates the principle that indexes should not be volatile.

Unique Indexes

Recall that index selectivity is calculated as follows:

```
(number of distinct values) / (total number of values)
```

Selectivity can be less than one if NULLs are indexed, or it can be less than one if duplicate keys are allowed. When selectivity equals one, you have perfect selectivity—and a **unique index.** The name is misleading—it's not the index that's unique; it's the keys in the index that are unique. But nobody's confused about the main thing: Unique indexes are good, and optimizers love 'em. Here's some good reasons to make your indexes unique:

- The Microsoft and Sybase optimizers give more points to indexes that have a selectivity equal to one or close to one. (Actually the cost-based optimizer depends on statistics to detect selectivity, but the rule-based optimizer just looks at the index's UNIQUE flag.) In fact, these optimizers won't even use an index that has a selectivity less than 0.1.

- If the DBMS knows in advance that a value can have only one occurrence, it can exit the loop quickly after it has found that value. It won't bother reading and checking again.

So, when the keys really are unique, should you always make the index with CREATE UNIQUE INDEX instead of just CREATE INDEX? Yes—with two exceptions.

The first exception is that you don't want to create an index at all if the DBMS will create one automatically due to a UNIQUE or PRIMARY KEY clause in the table constraints. Most DBMSs will make unique indexes automatically to enforce constraints, so you don't have to. Table 9-2 shows which DBMSs automatically create indexes when you define a constraint and whether redundant index creations are blocked.

The second exception is that you don't want to enforce uniqueness if the database is in an early stage and not all values are known yet. You might think that you could just do this:

```
INSERT INTO Table1 (unique_column)
  VALUES (NULL)
```

But—surprise!—IBM, Informix, Microsoft, and Sybase won't let you have two NULL keys in a unique index, while Ingres and InterBase won't accept any NULLs at all (see Table 10-1 in Chapter 10, "Constraints"). Get used to it: Portable programs can't use both NULLs and unique indexes.

Notes on Table 9-2:

- UNIQUE Index column

  This column is "Yes" if the DBMS automatically creates an index when you define a UNIQUE constraint.

- PKEY Index column

  This column is "Yes" if the DBMS automatically creates an index when you define a PRIMARY KEY constraint.

- FKEY Index column

  This column is "Yes" if the DBMS automatically creates an index when you define a FOREIGN KEY constraint.

Table 9-2 *DBMSs and Auto-Creation of Indexes*

	UNIQUE Index	PKEY Index	FKEY Index	Stops Redundant CREATE INDEX
IBM	Yes	Yes	No	No
Informix	Yes	Yes	Yes	Yes
Ingres	Yes	Yes	Yes	No
InterBase	Yes	Yes	Yes	No
Microsoft	Yes	Yes	No	No
MySQL	Yes	Yes	No	No
Oracle	Yes	Yes	No	Yes
Sybase	Yes	Yes	No	No

Redundant Indexes

Before creating an index, check to see if a similar index is already there. Most DBMSs create an index silently and automatically when you define a PRIMARY KEY or UNIQUE constraint. Some do the same for a FOREIGN KEY constraint.

The auto-creation is sometimes a mistake. For example, suppose you have Table2 with an existing compound index using (column1, column2). Now suppose you do this:

```
ALTER TABLE Table2 ADD CONSTRAINT Constraint1
    FOREIGN KEY (column1) REFERENCES Table1
```

With some DBMSs, this SQL statement results in a new index even though an index is already on (column1, column2).

Redundant indexes will, of course, take up extra disk space and slow down UPDATEs, but the real worry is that the optimizer will get confused when there are several equivalent possible paths. So be prepared to drop redundant indexes.

- Stops Redundant CREATE INDEX column

  This column is "Yes" if the DBMS stops you when you try to create a redundant index.

Unique indexes can cause optimizer confusion. Here's a way to confuse a simple optimizer:

- Define two indexes as follows:
```
CREATE UNIQUE INDEX Index1
   ON Table1 (sex, social_security)

CREATE INDEX Index2
   ON Table1 (surname)
```
- Now search for:
```
SELECT * FROM Table1
  WHERE surname = 'JONES'
    AND sex = 'M'
```

See the problem? Because sex is associated with a unique index, Index1 will be chosen as the driver even though Index2 is doubtless more selective. Luckily, none of the Big Eight are so stupid—provided they're in cost-based rather than rule-based mode—and none of the world's database programmers are so stupid either because they know and follow this maxim—When defining a compound index, put the most selective key on the left.

Clustered Indexes

Clustered indexes have been around since SQL was in its cradle, and six of the Big Eight—IBM, Informix, Ingres, Microsoft, Oracle, and Sybase—support them. There are two varieties, which we will call by the nonstandard names "weak" and "strong." In both varieties, the objective of clustering is to store data rows near one another if they have similar values. For example, suppose you have a one-column table—call it Table1—that has these values in column1:

```
'Jones'
'Smith'
'Jones'
'Abbot'
'Smith'
'Jones'
```

This is disorganized. If the rows could be reorganized so that this was the order:

```
'Abbot'
'Jones'
'Jones'
'Jones'
'Smith'
'Smith'
```

then there would be a better chance that all `'Jones'` rows are on the same page. If all `'Jones'` rows are on the same page, this query is faster because there are fewer pages to fetch:

```
SELECT * FROM Table1
  WHERE column1 = 'Jones'
```

This query is also faster, because of presorting:

```
SELECT * FROM Table1
  ORDER BY column1
```

In a cluster, data rows are lined up the way we want them for a range search, an ORDER BY or a GROUP BY. Not only is this good for selections, it also reduces the number of "hot spots"—a potential problem that we'll discuss in Chapter 15, "Locks."

Clustering speeds up queries even if rows aren't 100% in order.

Provided that there is any ordering, queries will be faster on average—provided that the **cluster key** (`column1` in our earlier example) is important. The DBMS can use a clustered index to find out what the row order should be (an index is a handy structure for the purpose because indexes are ordered). You just have to tell the DBMS that you want a clustered index and that you want `column1` to be the cluster key. There can, of course, be only one clustered index per table because the data rows can only be sorted in one order.

In contrast, when a table has only a **nonclustered index,** pages and data rows are not stored in an order based on the index key, but rather in a heap—like the pile of papers on an untidy person's desk. Usually a new row is just dumped wherever it can fit in the file—that's why it's called a *heap.*

The difference between a **weak-clustered index** and a **strong-clustered index** is the fierceness with which the DBMS maintains cluster-key order. Most DBMSs have weak-clustered indexes, and they only guarantee to make a good-faith attempt to maintain order. Two of the Big Eight—Microsoft and Sybase—have strong-clustered indexes, and they maintain order forcibly, even when this requires a lot of reorganizing of both index keys and data rows. (Oracle has both weak-clustered indexes and index-organized tables; index-organized tables are in fact strong-clustered indexes, but Oracle doesn't call them that.) Because their effect is major, we will examine strong-clustered indexes more closely.

Strong-clustered indexes

The concept is simple: The leaf level of a strong-clustered index doesn't contain mere index keys. Instead, the leaf level contains the data rows themselves. Figure 9–8 and Figure 9–9 illustrate this by showing a conventional "data heap and separate" structure (Figure 9–8) and a radical "clustered index with integrated data" structure (Figure 9–9) containing the same data.

The pointer from an index key to a data row is called a **row locator.** The structure of the row locator depends on whether the data pages are stored in a

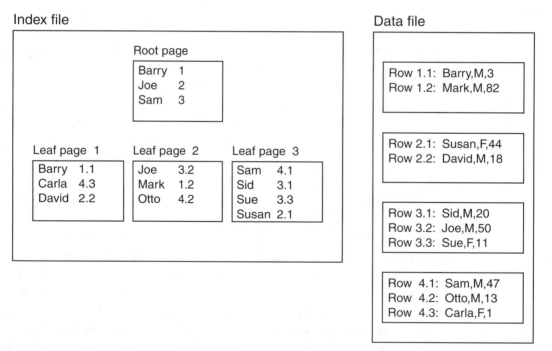

Figure 9–8 *A heap-and-index structure*

Combined index and data file

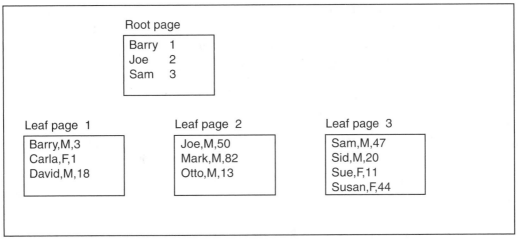

Figure 9-9 *A clustered index*

heap or are clustered. For a heap, a row locator is a pointer to the row. For a table with a strong-clustered index, the row locator is the cluster key.

Strong clustering certainly looks like a winning idea. Assume you have two tables based on Figure 9-8 and Figure 9-9 and execute this query on each:

```
SELECT * ...
  WHERE column1 = 'SUSAN'
```

Which query is faster? Well, the DBMS will need three I/Os if it has a heap (two I/Os to scan the index and one more to get the data row)—but only two I/Os if it has a cluster (two I/Os to scan the index and zero needed to get the data row). It doesn't really matter even if the data rows in the leaf page are likely to be twice as big as the index keys, because—remember the earlier talk about the number of layers being the important criterion?—doubling the key size doesn't double the access time.

This advantage appears for strong-clustered indexes *only*. With either a weak- or a strong-clustered index, data rows are in order. But the fact that the expression WHERE column1 = 'SUSAN' works with one less I/O is an additional effect that appears only with strong-clustered indexes.

To sum it up, both varieties of clustered indexes are good for GROUP BY, ORDER BY, and WHERE clauses. Strong clusters are also good for long keys (because a strong-clustered index on a long key takes no extra space for the leaf level). An extra benefit if the DBMS is Microsoft is automatic garbage collection (Microsoft doesn't have automatic garbage collection for ordinary heap tables).

INSERTs are harder with strong clusters because you have to make room between existing rows to fit in the new value according to cluster key order. But two subsequent INSERTs probably won't go to the same place, so clusters reduce contention.

UPDATEs are harder with strong clusters because any change in the cluster key means the row order can change too. But you are less dependent on ROWID with clusters; access using the cluster key is almost as quick.

There is no question that any changes that affect the cluster key will be huge and slow, because when the key value changes, the whole row must move in order to stay in order. However, there is a simple remedy: Never update the cluster key. In fact, under the hood, there is no such thing as an UPDATE of a cluster key—the DBMS translates such an UPDATE to a DELETE followed by an INSERT.

Choice of clustered key

The conventional advice is that you should have a clustered index for almost any table that's not tiny or temporary. This means you have to pick a set of columns for the cluster key—and it better be a good pick, because it is extremely inconvenient to change the cluster key after the table is full of data. By definition, there can only be one cluster key because the rows can only have one order. So what columns should form the cluster key? Good news. Many have asked that question before, and a body of sage counsel can guide the picking. Unfortunately, there's also bad news—priorities differ depending on whether the DBMS has strong or weak clustering.

When clustered indexes are strong, the primary key can be the cluster key. This saves time and confusion, and is often the default behavior, so we'll just defer this piece of sage counsel to Chapter 10, "Constraints." In situations where the primary key isn't there or isn't an obvious choice for a cluster key, you should explicitly state that the primary key is nonclustered. Then choose a cluster key with these characteristics:

- It shouldn't be volatile.

- It shouldn't be a "serial" data type—that is, the key should not auto-increment.

- It should be short (preferably an integer).

- It should be unique. (Some DBMSs—for example, Microsoft—will add a **uniquifier** integer if the key is not unique, but that's worth avoiding.)

- It should be the column on which you'll most often want to do range searches.

- It might as well have the order in which you'll want to get results.

However, when clustered indexes are weak, the rule "the primary key can be the cluster key" is weak too. Here are two rules for choosing the cluster key for a weak-clustered index, especially popular among IBM experts:

- Base the cluster key on a foreign key. The effect of clustering is that most rows with the same value for the foreign key will be together. Therefore a search like this:

```
SELECT ... WHERE foreign_key_column = 70
```

has a good chance of picking up all the matching rows with one page read. Primary-key/foreign-key joins will be faster for a similar reason. Notice that this advantage exists precisely because foreign keys, unlike primary keys, are not unique.

- Base the cluster key on the column with which you most often will do range searches or sequential passes. For example, if you will frequently do this type of search:

```
SELECT ... WHERE column1 BETWEEN 70 AND 150
  ORDER BY column1
```

then `column1` is a good choice for the cluster key.

Beware, though, if the possible cluster key is a monotonically sequential, or serial key—for example, an integer whose values always go up and always go up by the same amount, when you INSERT. The problem with monotonics (which are sometimes hidden behind names like "identity" or "timestamp" columns—see Chapter 7, "Columns") is that the nth row and the (n + 1)th row will both fit in the same page—so there might be contention for the same resource. Usually, in multiuser systems, you want rows to be dispersed.

This above all—The benefits of clustered indexing depend on a monster assumption; namely, that you want to retrieve and sort by the cluster key far, far more often than with any other key.

Secondary indexes to a strong-clustered index

Consider this scenario. You've defined `Table1` with a strong-clustered index—the cluster key is `column1`—and inserted the following data:

Table1.column1	Table1.column2
1	Willy
10	Margaret
100	Fiona

Now you want to add a secondary index—a nonclustered index on `column2`. Here's the problem. Because each row of the table is in an index leaf page, it can move within the page whenever another row is inserted or deleted above it, and it can even move to a different page if there's an index split. If that happens, the `column2` pointers are useless because the pointer part of an index key (aka row locator or **bookmark**) is normally a row identifier (aka ROWID or RID). Recall from Chapter 5, "Joins," that a row identifier is a physical address, such as {File number, Page number, Row number within page}. But the physical address of the row can change—so a ROWID is unreliable.

One solution to this problem—the old Oracle8 solution—is to disallow the creation of any nonclustered indexes to a strong-clustered table.[4] This has the unfortunate effect of limiting the usefulness of strong-clustered indexes, and in fact they're rarer in Oracle shops than in Microsoft shops. You can write your own schemes for doing "manual joins," and so on, but that's no fun.

Another solution—the Microsoft solution—is to make the row locator be the cluster key. That way, when the DBMS looks up `column2`, it ends up with the cluster key value that uniquely identifies the row: the value of `column1`. For example, suppose you ask for information about `Fiona`:

---

4. The latest Oracle incarnation—Oracle9i—now allows secondary indexes to clustered tables. Oracle uses the term "index-organized tables" where we use "strong-clustered index" and insists that the cluster key be the table's primary key—but the differences are at a detailed level, and we won't go into them here.

```
SELECT * FROM Table1
  WHERE column2 = 'Fiona'
```

Now the DBMS can look up the data row in the clustered index, by searching for the column1 value—an elegant solution. If the clustered index and the secondary index both have three levels, the DBMS needs (3 + 3) six I/Os to reach the data row, given the column2 value.

The search would be faster if there was a ROWID. In fact, a heap is "as good" (same I/O) if you're always looking for a unique value. So let's suppose this—You have a table with only two unique or nearly unique indexes. Access is equally likely via either index, so you're better off with a heap.

This may sound counter-intuitive, so let's examine the situation more closely. Here, once again, are our assumptions:

- Both indexes are unique, or nearly so.
- Both indexes have three levels.
- Both indexes are equally likely to be chosen.

Now, if you're looking up in a heap and the number of index levels is always three, then the average I/O count for the lookup is four—three I/Os to access via either index and one I/O to access the heap page, given the ROWID. On the other hand, if you're looking up in a cluster, the time to look up with the cluster key is three I/Os, and the time to look up via the secondary index is six as shown earlier. The average when *either* index is equally likely is thus 4.5 I/Os—((3 I/Os + 6 I/Os)/2). This is more than the four I/Os needed for a heap, and so a heap is better if access is equally likely with either index. Still, Microsoft recommends clustered indexes "always."

While we're on the subject of strong-clustered indexes, here are some tips on their use:

- Remember that a nonclustered index on a table points to the leaf page of the table's clustered index (because the clustered index's leaf page is the same as the data page). It is therefore a duplication if you have a column in the nonclustered index that's also in the clustered index. For example, suppose you have a strong-clustered index on (emp_id, sex) and are considering adding another index on (surname, sex). Don't. Since sex is already "covered" in the clustered index, make the nonclustered index on (surname) alone.

- A covering index is even more important because you're not just saving one I/O, you're saving three or four.

- If you want quick access to a table's cluster key columns alone, then make a nonclustered index of the same columns. The index must be a covering index, because you don't want to access the actual data rows. The index must also have a short key, because the advantage lies in the fact that the nonclustered index should have fewer layers than the clustered index. This tip will work, but if the clustered index is so big that it has too many levels, you should solve that problem with normalizing or partitioning, which we discussed in Chapter 8, "Tables."

The Bottom Line: Types of Indexes

A compound index is an index whose keys contain values derived from more than one data column. A compound index is good when you want to search for, or sort by (a) the left-most column or (b) the left-most column and any of the other columns.

Over indexing is useless because the DBMS often picks only one index as a driver. The way to make use of an index on a second column is to put the column in a compound index.

Use compound indexes if queries often contain the same columns, joined with AND.

Use compound indexes if you have any key based on a one-character column.

The left-most column in a compound index should be the one that occurs in queries most often. It should also be the most selective column.

When everything in the select list is in the index that will be used, the index is called a *covering index*. Ordinarily, using a covering index will save one disk read, but only if the columns in the select list exactly match the columns in the covering index. You lose the gain if you select functions or literals, or if you put the column names in a different order.

Whenever possible, persuade the DBMS to use a covering index regardless of whether it's searching for anything.

If the rows in the table are large, and the index keys are small, persuade the DBMS to use a covering index.

The benefits of "treating the index as a table" are often significant. Just remember that (a) DBMSs never use covering indexes when there are joins or groupings, (b) the index selection can't be used for UPDATE statements, and (c) adding frequently changed columns to indexes strictly to make them covering indexes violates the principle that indexes should not be volatile.

Index selectivity is calculated as:

```
(number of distinct values) / (total number of values)
```

Selectivity can be less than one if NULLs are indexed, or it can be less than one if duplicate keys are allowed. When selectivity equals one, you have perfect selectivity—and a unique index.

If the DBMS knows in advance a value can occur only once, it can exit the loop quickly after it has found that value. It won't bother reading and checking again. So unique indexes can save time.

Be prepared to drop redundant indexes.

When defining a compound index, put the most selective key on the left.

There are two main types of cluster indexes: "strong" clusters and "weak" clusters.

Strong clusters have these characteristics:

- The leaf level of a strong-clustered index doesn't contain index keys. Instead, the leaf level contains the data rows themselves.

- All data rows are in order.

- Strong clusters are good for GROUP BY, ORDER BY, and WHERE clauses, and for long keys.

- INSERTs are harder with strong clusters because you have to make room between existing rows to fit in the new value according to cluster key order. But two subsequent INSERTs probably won't go to the same place, so clusters reduce contention.

- UPDATEs are harder with strong clusters because any change in the cluster key means the row order can change too. But you are less dependent on ROWID with clusters; access using the cluster key is almost as quick.

- Updates that affect the cluster key will be huge and slow.

- The primary rule for choosing a strong cluster key is—Let the cluster key be the primary key.

- The secondary rule for choosing a strong cluster key (for situations where the primary key isn't an obvious choice) is—Choose a cluster key with these characteristics: (a) not volatile, (b) short and preferably an integer, (c) unique, (d) on which you'll most often want to do range searches, and (e) in the order in which you'll want to get results.

- If you want quick access to a table's strong cluster-key columns alone, make a nonclustered index of the same columns. The index must be a covering index and must have a short key.

Weak clusters have these characteristics:

- Data rows may be in order, but the DBMS does not guarantee this.

- Weak clusters are good for GROUP BY, ORDER BY, and WHERE clauses.

- The primary rule for choosing a weak cluster key is—Base the cluster key on a foreign key or base the cluster key on the column with which you most often will do range searches or sequential passes.

Beware of the cluster key that is monotonically sequential. The problem with monotonics (aka serials) is that the nth row and the $(n + 1)$th row will both fit in the same page—so there might be contention for the same resource. Usually, in multiuser systems, you want rows to be dispersed.

The benefits of clustered indexing depend on a monster assumption—that you want to retrieve and sort by the cluster key far, far more often than with any other key. Choose your cluster keys accordingly.

Bitmap Indexes

All DBMSs use B-trees, but about 50% of them also offer an extra option: a bitmap index. Bitmap indexes are good for getting statistics out of large numbers of rows with static data. Specialist "warehouse database managers" like IBM Red Brick Warehouse are best in this field, but most of the large general

DBMS vendors support bitmap indexes too.[5] In this section, we'll look at the simple bitmap indexes supported by Informix, Oracle, and Sybase (IBM bitmap indexes look quite different).

A bitmap index consists merely of multiple lines of bits. A line of bits is called a **bit vector** (a **vector** is any one-dimensional array). Suppose you have a table, Table2, with a column called sex and a bitmap index on sex. The sex column can have three possible values: M or F or NULL. Table2's data is shown below:

Table2.sex

F

M

F

F

Because there are three possible values for the Table2.sex column, the bitmap index for the column contains three bit vectors. Each entry in a bit vector is one bit long. Because Table2 contains four rows, the length of each bit vector is four bits. A bit value of one means true. A bit value of zero means false. (If all vectors have a zero bit, the row in that position is a deleted row.) The bit vector is in order by row number, and the position of a bit in its vector matches the position of the row in the data table. Here is the bitmap index result for Table2.

M vector	F vector	NULL vector
0 (M is false)	1 (F is true)	0 (NULL is false)
1 (M is true)	0 (F is false)	0 (NULL is false)
0 (M is false)	1 (F is true)	0 (NULL is false)
0 (M is false)	1 (F is true)	0 (NULL is false)

---

5. Except for Microsoft, but there are rumors that Microsoft will get into the act soon, taking some technology from Microsoft FoxPro's Rushmore technology.

Thus for row #2 in Table2 the bitmap index stores three redundant statements: M is true, F is false, NULL is false. Despite the redundancy, the storage is efficient: Three 4-bit vectors are only 12 bits, or 1½ bytes. In theory, three 8,192-byte pages would be enough to store the "index entries" of 65,536 rows of data.

Suppose the size of Table2 expands to 65,536 rows, and you want to know whether any males are recorded in the table. So you do this search:

```
SELECT * FROM Table2
  WHERE EXISTS
    (SELECT * FROM Table2
      WHERE sex = 'M')
```

Listing 9–2 shows an assembly routine that scans the relevant index page and tells you (in theory) how long this search would take. On a Pentium, the loop shown in Listing 9–2 takes two cycles per row. A 1GHz Pentium can do one billion cycles per second. Assuming the worst case—that there are no males—a scan requires (4 cycles / 1 billion cycles per second) * (8192 bytes / 4 bytes per 32-bit word)—that is, one quarter-millionth of a second, approximately. Well, anything that can scan 65,000 rows in one quarter-millionth of a second, plus the time for one page I/O, is *fast*. Even though no DBMS uses an optimized assembler, you can see that bitmap indexes are great for certain types of questions.

Listing 9–2 *Assembly routine to scan bitmap index*

```
mov     ebx,offset start_of_page
rept    8192/4 <
        mov     edx,[ebx]           ;1 cycle
        add     ebx,4               ;4 bytes tested at a time
        test    edx,0ffffffffh      ;1 cycle
        jnz     exists
        >
mov     eax,false                   ;nothing found
ret
exists:
mov     eax,true                    ;something found
ret
```

The Bottom Line: Bitmap Indexes

We think it's inevitable that every SQL DBMS will support bitmap indexes soon, so we're sure that the following tips will be handy.

Remember that B-trees are considered effective by optimizers if selectivity is greater than 0.1. If your queries use "key values" with lower selectivity than 0.1, the best way to speed them up is with bitmap indexes.

B-trees and bitmap indexes do not combine well. When you search via a B-tree, you get a list of ROWIDs in index-key order. When you search via a bitmap, you get a list of bits in ROWID order. Because the lists differ in structure, ANDs, ORs, and NOTs require extra conversion steps.

Assembly-language instructions for AND, OR, and NOT all take only two cycles for each 32-bit word in a bit vector. However, no fast assembly-language instruction tells you "how many bits are on in the word" or "which bit is on in the word." Therefore a DBMS is fast at Boolean logic but relatively slow at finding particular rows.

Bitmap indexes are particularly useful for queries that contain [NOT] EXISTS, UNIQUE, or GROUP BY.

Bitmap indexes are occasionally used for joins, but that's part of an internal process that the application programmer can't influence.

Bitmap indexes are particularly useless when a column can be any one of thousands of possibilities. Have you ever noticed that "income" reports or questionnaires contain no gross averages or individual figures but only boxes (e.g., [] 1500–3000 [] 3001–6000 [] more)? That kind of pregrouping is a big aid for bitmap index construction.

A common recommendation is that a column is a candidate for a bitmap if the number of possible distinct values is less than 1% of the total number of rows. For example, if the column is `color` and the value can be any one of the values in a 256-color display or NULL, the number of rows in the table should be at least 25,700 before you put `color` in a bitmap index.

Bitmap indexes are best for large (because a bit of storage is efficient), non-normalized (because there will be many repetitions), static (because updating one row means updating multiple bit vectors) tables.

Other Index Variations

Thus far we've discussed only the index structures supported by every DBMS (or at least the majority of major DBMSs). But a few interesting or inspiring features are implemented by only some DBMSs. We think that each one is worth a heads-up.

- DESC values. Used by: IBM.

  Useful if there is an ORDER BY <column> DESC clause, but not essential. For example, Oracle allows you to specify the keyword DESC when you're creating an index, but ignores it. All Oracle indexes are purely ascending, and Oracle handles the descending situation by scanning backward, using back-pointing pointers in the leaf blocks.

- Low-level access. Used by: Informix.

  Sometimes the routines that the DBMS uses to scan or update the index are available as a C library, usually with a name like "ISAM API" or "Tree Access."

- Function keys. Used by: Informix, Microsoft, Oracle, PostgreSQL.

  It's wonderful to be able to do this:

  ```
  CREATE INDEX Index1
    ON Table1 (LOWER(column1))
  ```

  so that:

  ```
  SELECT * FROM Table1
    WHERE LOWER(column1) = 'x'
  ```

  will blaze. But don't try it until you know what "nondeterministic" means; see Chapter 11, "Stored Procedures."

- Reverse keys. Used by: IBM, Oracle.

  Question—Why would you want to store CHUMLEY as YELMUHC, thus putting the key in the Ys rather than the Cs? Answer—If the latter part of the key value is more changeable than the front part, then a reverse key will lead to greater dispersal. That reduces hot spots and makes access slightly faster.

- Hashes. Used by: Ingres, Informix, Oracle, PostgreSQL.

  Because the efficiency of hashing in certain contests against B-tree searching is extremely good, it's surprising that so few DBMSs use it except for internal purposes—for instance, when deciding which partition a row goes into.

- Full-text indexing. Used by: Microsoft, MySQL.

  Easy to use (you probably think that Google.com is simple and quick), but updates are hard (you also probably notice that adding a URL to Google takes a few weeks).

Index Key Values

The general rule for indexes is that a key value is an exact copy of the column value in the data row. That is, if the data column has a 16-bit SMALLINT value, then so does the key. And if the data column is variable-length, then so is the key. The rule that copies are exact has just two common exceptions.

The first and most notorious exception to the rule that key and column value copies are exact is that Oracle—and Oracle alone—refuses to store NULLs. Oh, the DBMS will put NULLs in compound keys if other columns are NOT NULL, but Oracle doesn't have much use for NULL keys. So if you have a table (Table1), containing two columns (column1, column2), and column2 is indexed, then:

- Oracle can do:

  `INSERT INTO Table1 VALUES (5, NULL)`

  much more quickly, because the DBMS doesn't have to update the index at all.

- Oracle can do:

  `SELECT * FROM Table1 WHERE column2 < 5`

  a bit more quickly, because the index on column2 has fewer keys and therefore might have fewer levels.

- Oracle cannot do:

  `SELECT * FROM Table1 WHERE column2 IS NULL`

  quickly, because the DBMS can't use an index for any case where column2 IS NULL might be true.

This is a good trade off. Unfortunately, it causes an attitude difference between Oracle programmers and everybody else: Oracle programmers will think nullable columns are good, while programmers for other DBMSs will think that NOT NULL leads to performance improvements.

The second exception to the rule that key and column value copies are exact is that index keys might be truncated—sometimes silently, sometimes explicitly.[6] This is a reasonable thing, because it's good to keep key size small, and a few dozen bytes should be enough to differentiate two similar but different key values. The only effects you, the programmer, see are:

- The order of the keys isn't necessarily the order that should appear for an ORDER BY clause.

- The value of using compound indexes is less because the right-most columns can disappear.

- Some queries, especially those that contain `column1 = column2` comparisons, will take longer because not everything is in the index.

On the other hand, accuracy is not affected. Usually truncation becomes an issue when the total index key size is more than 100 bytes, which should be rare.

> **Tip** It is a mistake, when calculating data-row size, to think thusly:
>
> The free space in the page is 8,000 bytes, and the row size is 798 bytes, and one of the columns is CHAR(38), so I'll change that column to CHAR(40). After all, it's free because—even though the row size is two bytes bigger—I'm still fitting the same number of rows (10) in the page.
>
> What's forgotten is that every index key based on the column will also be bigger.

While we're on the subject of shortening keys, here's a brief note about **compression**—that is, making index keys shorter by throwing bytes away from the front or from the back.

Front compression depends on the fact that keys are in order, and so the first n bytes of key #2 are probably the same as the first n bytes of key #1. The first

---

6. For example, MySQL allows indexes to be defined on the left-most n characters of a column. PostgreSQL, on the other hand, has now dropped support for partial indexes.

n bytes of key #2 can thus be replaced with a single byte that means "the first n bytes are the same as those of the previous key." For example, here are four key values:

```
Johnson    Johnson    Jonathan    Jones      (total 27 bytes)
```

If each key begins with a byte meaning "number of bytes that are the same," these four keys can be stored like this:

```
0Johnson   7                      2nathan    3es        (total 19 bytes)
```

Back compression depends on the fact that most keys are distinguishable after a few characters. That is, if two keys are different, then that will be clear after a small number of characters, so there's no need to store the bytes that don't establish the differences between key values. (This is called a *lossy compression* because information is lost, but what's lost can be recovered when the original data row is read in.) If the four example keys were back-compressed instead of front-compressed, this would be the result:

```
Joh        Joh        Jona        Jone       (total 14 bytes)
```

Both front compression and back compression can save lots of space. The downside is that compression can slow down index scans—extra CPU time is often required to reconstruct the key column values. Compression also incurs additional storage overhead (usually four bytes). Because of this, not all DBMSs use compression. DBMS makers don't like the effects of compression on locking, CPU time, cascading changes, complexity, and difficulty doing binary searches.

At first glance, it may look like our claim—that there are only two exceptions to the rule that index keys are exactly like data keys—is mistaken. The apparent error is this: keys are supposed to be in order. To maintain order, keys must be compared with each other frequently. In a comparison, some conversion is commonly necessary. For example, a case-insensitive index might have these keys: {a, B}. For comparison purposes, such an index must convert B to b—that is, ask for LOWER(B) before checking if the value is greater than a. In that case, why doesn't the DBMS store b instead of B? The reason is that it doesn't want to lose information that might be useful for a covering index.

The Bottom Line: Index Key Values

The general rule for indexes is that a key value is an exact copy of the column value in the data row. The two exceptions to this rule are (a) the case of NULLs (Oracle won't store NULL so Oracle programmers think nullable columns are good, while programmers for other DBMSs think that NOT NULL leads to performance improvements) and (b) the fact that index keys might be truncated or compressed.

Usually truncation becomes an issue when the total index key size is more than 100 bytes, which should be rare. In that case, (a) the order of the keys isn't necessarily the order that should appear for an ORDER BY clause, (b) the value of using compound indexes is less because the right-most columns can disappear, and (c) some queries will take longer because not everything is in the index. So keep the size of index keys small.

Parting Shots

Don't let the selectivity get lower than 10% for a B-tree. Use a bitmap index if selectivity goes below 1%.

A compound index should have no more than five columns.

A B-tree should have no more than five layers. If it gets beyond that, partition.

With Microsoft, every permanent big table should have a clustered index. With Oracle, the necessity is much less urgent.

Expect inconsistent performance if you have NULLs in your index keys, or if you UPDATE indexes frequently.

In a typical mixed environment, tables should have no more than five indexes. In a DSS environment, go higher—maybe up to 12 indexes per table. In a pure OLTP environment, go lower—make just enough indexes for a primary key and one or two foreign keys.

Just before the end of the month (or when you know there will be a flurry of activity), rebuild the indexes—leaving a big PCTFREE or a small FILLFACTOR (i.e., leave lots of room in the index pages so splits won't happen). Just after the end of the month (or when you're expecting report requests), add a few indexes—your shop is changing from an OLTP to a DSS for a while.

When all else is equal, do DELETEs before INSERTs within a transaction.

Never index a volatile column. A volatile column is one that will see changes to x% of the occurrences in the course of a week. Unfortunately, nobody can agree on the value of x. Clearly, though, the calculation should be based on this equation:

```
(I/Os saved by faster lookup) minus (I/Os wasted due to frequent splits)
```

10

Constraints

As a programmer, you create database constraints so that garbage won't go in, and therefore less garbage will come out—you hope. Is garbage-free data itself an optimization? Can it give the optimizer and the user better information to help in evaluating SELECTs? Or will the constant error testing hinder INSERTs, UPDATEs, and DELETEs? In this chapter, we'll address the good and bad effects of constraints on optimization.

Portability   MySQL does not support triggers or constraints (unless they're implicit NOT NULL constraints or explicit PRIMARY KEY and UNIQUE constraints). The gains shown throughout this chapter are for only seven DBMSs unless the test specifically uses only those three constraint types.

NOT NULL

The NULL "value" is a concept required by relational theory's data integrity rules. That is, relational theory recognizes that, in some situations, a datum is not available, not known, or inapplicable. NULL is used to represent all three of these cases. It's important to remember that NULL does not equate to a blank or a zero: it's something else entirely. Though a blank is equal to another blank and a zero is equal to another zero, a NULL is never equal to anything, not even another NULL.

NOT NULL constraints are used to enforce a rule that a column must always contain valid and applicable data—in short, that a column may not contain NULL. In the SQL Standard, this syntax:

```
... <column>...NOT NULL
```

is just a shorthand form for:

```
... CHECK (<column> IS NOT NULL)
```

That is, NOT NULL constraints are just CHECK constraints according to the SQL Standard. With most DBMSs, though, NOT NULL constraints are effectively quite different from ordinary CHECK constraints in these ways:

- NOT NULL constraints are usually unnamed and can't be dropped.
- Defining a column as NOT NULL has an effect on the way that the column values are stored.
- NOT NULL constraints are sometimes compulsory.

NOT NULL affects storage because it is impossible to store a NULL value in the column itself. For instance, if a column is defined as SMALLINT, then it may contain any negative or positive number that fits in 16 bits—but there is no room for a reserved 16-bit value that could mean NULL. Therefore the DBMS must have a flag outside the column itself that says either "this is NULL" or "this is not NULL." In Microsoft, this flag is part of a bit list at the start of the row. In IBM and most other DBMSs, the flag is a byte at the start of the column. Either way, a column that can contain NULL takes more space to store than does a NOT NULL column.

A column that can contain NULL also takes slightly longer to retrieve, because you must always add a check for a NULL indicator to your program before processing the value itself. The severest effect is seen with Sybase, because Sybase silently changes fixed-size columns (such as CHAR) into variable-length columns (such as VARCHAR) if they can contain NULL. The result is that with unindexed columns, most DBMSs handle columns that can contain NULL *slower* than NOT NULL columns. On the other hand, with indexed columns, Oracle handles nullable columns *faster*.

Some DBMSs have one or more gotchas that make columns that can contain NULL unwieldy. For example:

- They make the assumption that all column definitions imply NOT NULL.

- They require that primary keys be explicitly declared NOT NULL.[1]

- They refuse to allow multiple occurrences of NULL when a column is defined as UNIQUE. Some DBMSs have conflicting rules in this area because they treat a UNIQUE constraint differently from a UNIQUE INDEX key. Of the Big Eight, only IBM does this. With IBM, a UNIQUE constraint column must be defined as NOT NULL and therefore disallows any NULL values. A column that is part of a UNIQUE INDEX key, though, is allowed one NULL value.

- They do not allow NOT NULL constraints to be dropped. This is a tricky area because, although the SQL Standard doesn't distinguish between NOT NULL in a column definition and a NOT NULL constraint, some DBMSs do. The difference lies in distinguishing between NOT NULL as a column attribute that cannot be changed and CHECK (`<column>` IS NOT NULL) as a constraint that can be dropped. The SQL Standard considers the two to be the same. That is, with SQL:1999, these two definitions both result in a named constraint that can be dropped:

```
Case #1:
CREATE TABLE Table1 (
    column1 INTEGER NOT NULL)

Case #2:
CREATE TABLE Table1 (
    column1 INTEGER,
    CHECK (column1 IS NOT NULL))
```

IBM, Ingres, and InterBase consider Case #1 and Case #2 to be different. For these DBMSs, the first CREATE TABLE statement results in a column (column1) with a NOT NULL attribute, and this attribute may not be changed—a clear violation of the SQL Standard. These DBMSs also support the second CREATE TABLE statement, which results in a named

---

1. Early versions of MySQL required that all columns in any index must be defined as NOT NULL. This defect does not exist in MySQL version 3.23.

constraint that can be dropped—as the SQL Standard requires. Informix, Microsoft, Oracle, and Sybase correctly conform to the SQL Standard for both Case #1 and Case #2. MySQL is SQL Standard-compliant for Case #1—that is, MySQL lets you use the ALTER TABLE statement to change a nullable column to NOT NULL and vice versa. However, MySQL doesn't support named CHECK constraints and so is not SQL Standard-compliant for Case #2.

All four of these gotchas are flat-out violations of SQL:1999, but we can't do anything about that. Until these "rogue DBMSs" conform to the SQL Standard, portable programs should contain NOT NULL declarations in all or most column definitions. Table 10-1 shows which of the Big Eight treat NULL in a non-conformant fashion.

Notes on Table 10-1:

- Auto NOT NULL column

    This column is "Yes" if the DBMS assumes that `column1` in this table definition is a NOT NULL column rather than a "NULL allowed" column as required by the SQL Standard:

    ```
    CREATE TABLE Table1 (
        column1 INTEGER)
    ```

Table 10–1   *ANSI/DBMSs and NULL Gotchas*

	Auto NOT NULL	Drop NULL	Multiple NULL	Force NOT NULL PKEY Column	Force NOT NULL PKEY Table
ANSI SQL	No	Yes	Many	No	No
IBM	No	No	One	Yes	Yes
Informix	No	Yes	One	No	No
Ingres	No	No	Zero	Yes	Yes
InterBase	No	No	Zero	Yes	Yes
Microsoft	Yes	Yes	One	No	No
MySQL	No	Yes	Many	No	Yes
Oracle	No	Yes	Many	No	No
Sybase	Yes	Yes	One	No	Yes

- Drop NULL column

  This column is "No" if the DBMS doesn't allow you to drop a NOT NULL constraint as required by the SQL Standard.

- Multiple NULL column

  This column is "Zero" if the DBMS doesn't allow any NULLs in a UNIQUE column; "One" if the DBMS allows only one NULL in a UNIQUE column; and "Many" if the DBMS allows multiple NULLs to be inserted into a UNIQUE column as required by the SQL Standard. (Note: By "UNIQUE column," we mean a column that is part of a UNIQUE constraint or a column that is part of a UNIQUE INDEX key. We do not mean a column that is part of a PRIMARY KEY constraint, though such columns are also constrained to contain only unique values. The difference between the two is that the SQL Standard allows UNIQUE columns to contain NULLs but disallows any NULLs in PRIMARY KEYs.)

- Force NOT NULL PKEY Column column

  This column is "Yes" if the DBMS requires an explicit NOT NULL constraint when you define a PRIMARY KEY column constraint. That is, the DBMS requires this definition:

  ```
  CREATE TABLE Table1 (
     column1 INTEGER NOT NULL PRIMARY KEY)
  ```

  rather than this definition as required by the SQL Standard:[2]

  ```
  CREATE TABLE Table1 (
     column1 INTEGER PRIMARY KEY)
  ```

- Force NOT NULL PKEY Table column

  This column is "Yes" if the DBMS requires an explicit NOT NULL constraint when you define a PRIMARY KEY table constraint. That is, the DBMS requires this definition:

  ```
  CREATE TABLE Table1 (
     column1 INTEGER NOT NULL,
     CONSTRAINT Constraint1 PRIMARY KEY (column1))
  ```

---

2. We should note that Entry Level SQL-92—the lowest conformance level—requires the explicit NOT NULL definition we're deploring here and in the next paragraph. Because each of the DBMSs that force this syntax declares its SQL compliance level to be Entry Level SQL-92, it is not in violation of the outdated Standard. But SQL-92 was superseded in 1999, and Core SQL:1999 specifies that NOT NULL is to be implied because non-nullability is inherent in the definition of a primary key just as uniqueness is.

rather than this definition as required by the SQL Standard:

```
CREATE TABLE Table1 (
    column1 INTEGER,
    CONSTRAINT Constraint1 PRIMARY KEY (column1))
```

NULL Indicators

Even if you define every column in every table as NOT NULL, you still need to add NULL indicator checks to your programs because there's still a possibility that NULLs might be returned. For example, these three SQL statements could return NULLs under some circumstances:

```
SELECT MAX(column1) FROM Table1

SELECT Table1.column1, Table2.column1
    FROM Table1 LEFT JOIN Table2
        ON Table1.column1 = Table2.column1

SELECT SUM(column1) FROM Table1
    WHERE column2 > 100
/* returns NULL if no column2 value is greater than 100 */
```

The Bottom Line: NOT NULL Constraints

To speed things up, define columns and domains with NOT NULL as often as possible.

Even if your definitions always include NOT NULL, make sure your program allows for the possibility of retrieved NULLs. Add NULL indicator checks for every OUTER JOIN retrieval and wherever it's possible that a query might be searching an empty table.

CHECK

A CHECK constraint is used to enforce a rule that a column may contain only data that falls within some specific criteria. To segue from NOT NULL constraints to CHECK constraints, let's ask the nasty question—Is it redundant to have both? At first glance, the answer appears to be "Yes." For example, suppose you have a table defined like this:

```
CREATE TABLE Table1 (
    column1 INTEGER NOT NULL,
```

```
...
CHECK (column1 < 10)
...)
```

Obviously a value that "must be less than ten" must automatically be NOT NULL anyway, right? Wrong. One of SQL's little-known details is that a CHECK constraint doesn't have to be `true`. It only has to be "other than `false`"[3]—which means a NULL would be accepted by the CHECK constraint. Therefore a NOT NULL constraint is not a redundancy in this example.

Portability   InterBase is the exception. With InterBase, the CHECK constraint would reject NULL. MySQL doesn't support CHECK constraints.

In general, you use CHECK constraints to ensure that the value of a column falls in a fixed range. This means that a constraint like:

```
... CHECK (column1 < 10)
```

is slightly suspect. In practice, most integer columns fall within an unsigned range—for example:

```
... CHECK (column1 BETWEEN 0 AND 9)
```

—or should be convertible to any fixed decimal—for example:

```
... CHECK (column1 >= -99999999 AND column1 <= +99999999)
```

Either because of poor performance or because the syntax is not portable, CHECK constraints should not contain:

- Column-to-niladic-function comparisons like:
  ```
  ... CHECK (date_column > CURRENT_DATE)
  ```
  (This is illegal in IBM, Microsoft, Oracle, and the SQL:1999 Standard.)

---

3. Actually, the SQL Standard doesn't really say this, but most people have interpreted it that way.

- Column-to-subquery comparisons like:

```
... CHECK (column1 IN (SELECT column1 FROM Table1))
```

(Such CHECKs could lead to trouble with some of the transaction isolation levels that are the subject of Chapter 15, "Locks.")

Foreign keys or stored procedures work better in both cases.

CHECK constraints should be defined on the column, rather than on the column's domain or user-defined type (UDT) definition. The reason is primarily that most DBMSs do not support domains, but also because a domain constraint is not directly associated with the column in the catalog and can therefore take longer to look up.

By the way, with most DBMSs, it's possible to define constraints with conflicting conditions—the DBMS won't stop you. For example, you would be allowed to define these constraints on the same table:

```
... CHECK (column1 BETWEEN 5 AND 10)
```

```
... CHECK (column1 < 2)
```

The result, of course, is that you could then INSERT only NULLs into column1 because no number satisfies both constraints simultaneously. Because the DBMS likely has no check for this situation, it's always a good idea to check all existing constraints on a table for conflicts before creating a new one.

It's technically possible that a CHECK constraint will not be violated at the time you update a row, but it will be violated by the time the SQL statement ends. This situation can arise because of CASCADEs, because of triggers, or because the constraint depends on values of other rows that are updated later in the same statement. Because of these possibilities, an SQL Standard-compliant DBMS will wait until the end of the statement before testing a constraint for violations. Thus, every row has to be accessed twice—once to change it, and a second time later on to test for constraint violations. If a data-change statement affects hundreds of rows, there is no guarantee that the updated row will still be in cache by the time the second access occurs.

The Bottom Line: CHECK Constraints

Don't try to save time by omitting a NOT NULL constraint if you've already added a CHECK constraint. Use NOT NULL and CHECK constraints together—

unlike a search condition, constraints just need to be "other than `false`" in order to be satisfied.

Instead of using CHECK constraints, use FOREIGN KEY constraints or stored procedures for these types of comparisons: (a) column to niladic-function and (b) column to subquery.

Define your CHECK constraints on columns, not on domains or UDT definitions.

FOREIGN KEY

A FOREIGN KEY constraint is used to enforce a rule that a column may contain only NULL or data that is also contained in a matching, primary key, column.[4] A foreign key should exactly match its referenced primary key, both in data type and in column size. Some DBMSs (for example, Informix, Microsoft, and Sybase) will not even let you define a column as:

```
CREATE TABLE Table2 (
    column1 INTEGER REFERENCES Table1,
    ...)
```

if `Table1`'s definition is:

```
CREATE TABLE Table1 (
    column1 SMALLINT PRIMARY KEY,
    ...)
```

This restriction makes sense when you consider that a data type is itself a range constraint. You can't possibly have a value of 1,000,000 in the foreign-key column if the primary-key values are SMALLINTs, and therefore must be less than 32,768.

This leads us to the observation that *any* constraint (except a NOT NULL or UNIQUE constraint) that applies to the primary key must apply to the foreign

---

4. We use "primary key" throughout this section for the sake of simplicity. The SQL Standard actually specifies that a foreign key must match a unique key. In practice, of course, the match is normally made to the type of unique key known as a primary key.

key as well. Therefore the following pair of CREATE TABLE statements contain an unnecessary CHECK constraint in Table2's definition:

```
CREATE TABLE Table1 (
    column1 SMALLINT,
    CHECK (column1 > 0),
    PRIMARY KEY (column1))

CREATE TABLE Table2 (
    column1 SMALLINT,
    CHECK (column1 > 0),
    FOREIGN KEY (column1) REFERENCES Table1)
```

In our tests, we found that some DBMSs will actually process the CHECK constraint when inserting or updating Table2, even though logically they don't have to—they're just wasting time. That is, these two data-change statements should take the same amount of time whether Table2's definition includes the CHECK clause or omits the CHECK clause:

```
INSERT INTO Table2 ...

UPDATE Table2 SET column1 ...
GAIN: 2/7 if the redundant CHECK on Table2 is omitted
```

But with two of the DBMSs we tested, the data changes went faster when Table2's definition did not include the redundant CHECK constraint.

Not only should foreign-key columns match primary-key columns with respect to data type and size, they should match in names too. One of the features of a foreign-key table should be that it's easy to join with a primary-key table. In fact, that's the original meaning of natural join: a join over foreign- and primary-key columns. Unfortunately, the meaning of NATURAL JOIN in current SQL is slightly different. In the SQL Standard, NATURAL JOIN merely means a join over columns with the same name. To make these definitions compatible, make sure that any column that is *not* part of the foreign key does not have the same name as some primary-key column. For example this pair of table definitions contains a bad column name:

```
CREATE TABLE Chains (
    chain_id INTEGER,
    city CHARACTER(20),
    PRIMARY KEY (chain_id))
```

```
CREATE TABLE Stores (
    store_id INTEGER,
    chain_id INTEGER,
    city CHARACTER(20),
    PRIMARY KEY (store_id),
    FOREIGN KEY (chain_id) REFERENCES Chains)
```

The mistake is that both tables contain a column named `city`. Therefore a search involving

```
... Chains NATURAL JOIN Stores ...
```

won't work naturally because the DBMS will try to join over two columns (`chain_id`, `city`) when there's only one reasonable joining column (`chain_id`). If it's too late to fix all the names in the database, then the recourse is to avoid any use of SQL's NATURAL JOIN—ON or USING clauses are a must. Another good check is to ask if your application ever does a join over something other than primary-key/foreign-key columns. If so, there's probably something wrong with either the database design or the application.

Here's one more check you should make—Does the same column appear in more than one foreign key? If so, it is a "servant of two masters," and the DBMS will have a hard time prejoining with a join index. Some DBMSs (but none of the Big Eight) will simply disallow constructions like:

```
CREATE TABLE Table3 (
    column1 INTEGER,
    FOREIGN KEY (column1) REFERENCES Table1,
    FOREIGN KEY (column1) REFERENCES Table2)
```

The Bottom Line: FOREIGN KEY Constraints

A foreign key is a column, or group of columns, that may contain only those values found in a similar set of unique (usually primary key) columns belonging to (usually) another table. The rule enforces data integrity: The rationale is that you can't have an order if there is no customer, you can't have an employee working in department "A" if there is no such department, you can't have a factory that makes widgets if you don't have widgets as a product, and so on.

Define all foreign-key columns to match their primary-key column exactly in data type, column size, and column name.

Save time by eliminating redundant CHECK constraints on foreign-key columns where the same constraint already exists on the matching primary-key column.

Avoid the use of NATURAL JOIN when two tables have columns with the same name that are not linked with a primary-key/foreign-key relationship.

Don't use the same column for multiple FOREIGN KEY constraints or your DBMS will have a hard time prejoining with a join index.

PRIMARY KEY

A PRIMARY KEY constraint is used to enforce a rule that a column may contain only unique, non-NULL data. This is to ensure that each row of a table can be uniquely identified. Too frequently, you will encounter the wrong sort of primary-key specification:

```
CREATE TABLE Table1 (
   column1 ... NOT NULL PRIMARY KEY,
   ...)
```

No gross harm results, but that's not the usual recommendation. To preserve orthogonality, this definition is often suggested instead:

```
CREATE TABLE Table1 (
   column1 ... NOT NULL,
   CONSTRAINT Constraint1 PRIMARY KEY (column1),
   ...)
```

We'll go a little further and ask—Is even that specification wrong? After all, primary-key columns can't contain NULL by definition, so specifying NOT NULL with standard SQL is a redundancy. Again, we couldn't find any evidence that gross harm results, but we'd still say that the only fully correct specification for a primary key is:

```
CREATE TABLE Table1 (
   column1 ... ,
   CONSTRAINT Constraint1 PRIMARY KEY (column1),
   ...)
```

Unfortunately, five of the Big Eight—IBM, Ingres, InterBase, MySQL, and Sybase—won't allow it (see Table 10–1).

In the SQL:1999 SQL/Foundation document, all tables are defined to have a primary key via functional dependencies, but this area is a little-known and complicated one that no DBMS has implemented. So everyone recommends that an explicit PRIMARY KEY definition should appear for every table defined. Everyone is right—but when you know that there will never be duplicates or foreign keys (e.g., with a one-row temporary table), making a primary key is unnecessary and costly.

In a reasonable world, you would be able to add the primary key and any matching foreign keys after the table exists. Adding the foreign key after table creation would solve the *cyclic references* problem. For example, the two table definitions shown in Listing 10-1 are illegal outside a CREATE SCHEMA statement. The elegant solution to the cyclic references problem is shown in Listing 10-2.

Listing 10-1   *Illegal cyclic references table definitions*

```
CREATE TABLE Table1 (
  column1 INTEGER PRIMARY KEY,
  column2 INTEGER FOREIGN KEY REFERENCES Table2)

CREATE TABLE Table2 (
  column2 INTEGER PRIMARY KEY,
  column1 INTEGER FOREIGN KEY REFERENCES Table1)
```

Listing 10-2   *Solving the cyclic references problem*

```
CREATE TABLE Table1 (
  column1 INTEGER,
  column2 INTEGER)

CREATE TABLE Table2 (
  column2 INTEGER,
  column1 INTEGER)

ALTER TABLE Table1
  ADD CONSTRAINT Constraint1
    PRIMARY KEY (column1)

ALTER TABLE Table2
  ADD CONSTRAINT Constraint2
    PRIMARY KEY (column2)

ALTER TABLE Table1
  ADD CONSTRAINT Constraint3
    FOREIGN KEY (column2) REFERENCES Table2
```

```
ALTER TABLE Table2
  ADD CONSTRAINT Constraint4
      FOREIGN KEY (column1) REFERENCES Table1
```

Portability   MySQL doesn't support FOREIGN KEY constraints. Sybase requires that you also have an explicit NOT NULL constraint for the PRIMARY KEY.

As well as being legal, the CREATE-then-ALTER formulation shown in Listing 10–2 represents the facts better. Columns are part of a table so they should be defined in the CREATE TABLE statement. Constraints are not part of a table so they should be defined separately. However, craving your indulgence, we admit that CREATE-then-ALTER is pie in the sky/soapbox talk—there is a practical difficulty in using the idea.

The practical difficulty is that if your DBMS supports clustered indexes, then the words "PRIMARY KEY" will cause the DBMS engine to think: "Aha, a primary key. How useful. I'll make this table a clustered index, and the clustering key will be the columns of the primary key." These are reasonable assumptions. The trouble is, the DBMS must know *at table-creation time* whether or not there is a primary key, because that decides the type of file structure the DBMS will use. Therefore it is *too late* to add or drop a primary-key specification after table creation.

You can avoid this difficulty by letting the cluster key be a nonprimary key or by defining a UNIQUE key later to serve as the primary key (it's a little-known fact that foreign keys can refer to unique keys other than the primary key). We're ignoring such work arounds here because they have no popularity.

The conclusion we've come to is that you should decide the primary key in advance. While deciding, you should take some performance factors into account. Alas, these factors lead to a dilemma.

First of all is the fact that the primary-key columns will automatically be index columns—all DBMSs perform an implicit CREATE INDEX when they see a PRIMARY KEY constraint. (Recall that the same is not true of foreign keys; see Table 9–1 in Chapter 9, "Indexes.") So, in keeping with our earlier discussion of what's the best sort of index key, the best sort of primary key consists of only one column, and that column should be defined as an INTEGER. It must not be a FLOAT—two FLOAT values can appear to be distinct when they are not, and the uniqueness checking would fail. Therefore:

A simple one-user shop should use ascending integers for a primary key.

Second of all is the fact that a serial sequence can cause **hot spots**. Hot spots are pages in either the index or data file that every job wants to access at the same time. Consider: If Sam and Mary are both adding rows to the same table, and Sam's inserted row is #5550001, then Mary's row will be #5550002— because that's the next in sequence and index keys are in sequence. So it's a near certainty that both Sam and Mary will want to lock the same index page. There are ways around the hot spot problem, such as reverse-key indexing and range locking; see Chapter 9,"Indexes," and Chapter 15,"Locks." But the simpler solution is to avoid hot spots entirely. Therefore:

A complex multiuser shop should use an out-of-order series of characters for a primary key. This key can be derived from (a) the time of day to the nearest millisecond or (b) the user's session identifier. Such keys are often defined as CHAR(12) or longer.

So far, our advice has assumed that you will be able to assign arbitrary values to your primary keys. Sadly, the easiest way to make arbitrary values unique is to use a serial sequence.

Here are other rules of thumb for defining primary keys:

- The primary-key column should be the first column in the table.
- The value should/should not have any meaning.

But these rules are mere conventions. What counts is that the primary-key column should be easy to form and assuredly unique. It should also, preferably, be a value that is very rarely changed.

The Bottom Line: PRIMARY KEY Constraints

A primary key is a unique, non-NULL column, or group of columns, that uniquely identifies a row of a table.

If you're programming for a simple one-user shop, use ascending integers for primary-key columns.

If you're programming for a complex multiuser shop, avoid hot spots—use an out-of-order series of characters derived from the time of day to the nearest millisecond or the user's session identifier for primary-key columns.

When defining a primary key, remember the most important criterion: the column chosen should be easy to form and assuredly unique.

UNIQUE

As well as primary-key constraints, you can add unique key constraints to your tables with UNIQUE (<column>) clauses in CREATE TABLE and ALTER TABLE, or with the nonstandard SQL-extension CREATE UNIQUE INDEX ... (<column>) statement. All DBMSs allow nonprimary unique keys, but IBM, Informix, Ingres, InterBase, Microsoft, and Sybase have an odd restriction—they don't allow two NULL values in a column if that column is defined with a UNIQUE constraint. (In fact, neither IBM, Ingres, nor InterBase allow *any* NULLs in a column defined with a UNIQUE constraint, although IBM does allow one NULL in a UNIQUE INDEX key.) It's as if these DBMSs think that "NULL = NULL"—which, as students of NULL theory know, is not the case. One should be able to have NULLs in unique keys as well as in foreign keys because values may be unknown initially—or they may be unspecifiable initially, as in cyclic references.

Even if all values are guaranteed in advance to be unique, your DBMS will check for uniqueness anyway (unless you turn the constraints off, as we'll discuss later in this chapter). To check for uniqueness, the DBMS has to look up the value in a B-tree and then update the B-tree. Happily, and contrary to the case of just a few years ago, it is now possible to execute this SQL statement with many DBMSs:

```
UPDATE Table1
   SET unique_column = unique_column + 1
```

Portability	Once there was a problem—and it's still a problem for Informix, Ingres, InterBase, and MySQL—that such updates would fail if two rows in Table1 contain sequential values.

For example, assume `Table1` contains these six rows:

	Table1.unique_column
Row #1	1
Row #2	2
Row #3	3
Row #4	4
Row #5	5
Row #6	6

To execute the UPDATE statement, the DBMS updates the first row of `Table1`, causing `unique_column` to equal 2. Then it tries to update the unique index, which already has a 2 in it (from Row #2). In the past, and with some DBMSs even now, the DBMS would fail at this point. The trick is that the uniqueness test must be made at the end of statement, not at the end of processing for each row, even though that's less convenient for the DBMS. This also applies for PRIMARY KEY constraints, because a PRIMARY KEY constraint is just a type of UNIQUE constraint. In practice, though, a primary key is non-volatile so the situation should not arise.

Rule-based optimizers will give some preference to unique indexes, knowing that they have guaranteed selectivity.

The Bottom Line: UNIQUE Constraints

If it's unique, define it as UNIQUE so the optimizer will know.

Triggers

The constraints we've discussed to this point—NOT NULL, CHECK, FOREIGN KEY, PRIMARY KEY, and UNIQUE—are known as *declarative constraints*. Triggers are not declarative because they contain procedural code. They're slightly less pure in the relational sense, and early DBMSs didn't support them, but today seven of the Big Eight support both declarative constraints and triggers.

In our tests, we found that triggers are slower than declarative constraints. For example, firing this trigger with a compound SQL statement:

```
CREATE TRIGGER Trigger1
   AFTER INSERT ON Table1
   REFERENCING NEW ROW AS New
   FOR EACH ROW
   BEGIN
     IF
       New.column1 NOT BETWEEN 1 AND 10
     THEN
       SIGNAL SQLSTATE = '23000'
     END IF
   END
```

is slower than leaving the checking up to the CHECK constraint in this table definition:

```
CREATE TABLE Table1 (
   column1 SMALLINT,
   CHECK (column1 BETWEEN 1 AND 10)
   ...)
GAIN: 4/7
```

However, before glibly saying "declarative constraints are better than triggers," we should note that the trigger has flexibilities that might be more important to you than performance. For example, a trigger statement can log an incident and return a customized warning, while all a declarative constraint can do in the same instance is return an error with a fixed error message. An old saw, which we've never heard before, goes—The more inflexible the server is, the more adaptable the client must be.

Nevertheless, the trigger involves so many steps that it can't be fast. Consider the steps shown in Listing 10–3.

Listing 10–3 *Steps involved in executing a trigger*

```
A trigger must:

Make a savepoint.

For each row: {
  Perform "before each row" trigger code.
  Copy the row as it exists before update, to a BEFORE IMAGE.
  Update the row.
  Copy the row as it exists after update, to an AFTER IMAGE.
  }

At end of statement (after constraints are checked): {
  For each row: {
    Perform "after each row" trigger code.
    If (fatal error) restore to savepoint.
  }

Cleanup.
}
```

Listing 10–3 shows that a trigger does two "for each row" loops. In theory the DBMS doesn't have to do the second loop if the trigger is only "before each row." In practice, though, before- and after-triggers are equally fast.

At this time, there is support only for INSERT, UPDATE, and DELETE triggers (except with Informix, which also provides SELECT triggers). To make a SELECT trigger, you can employ a trick that works like this—Suppose you want to keep a log of each time that a row from Table1, which contains the string WASHINGTON in a column named city, is retrieved. The solution is to mandate that all selections must go via a view of Table1, called View1, and to define View1 with an external function call. The SELECT statement would thus look like this:

```
SELECT * FROM View1
  WHERE city = 'WASHINGTON'
```

The CREATE VIEW statement would look like this:

```
CREATE VIEW View1 AS SELECT
      Table1.*,
      Function1(city) AS Function_return
   FROM Table1
```

And the CREATE FUNCTION statement would look like this:

```
CREATE FUNCTION Function1
   (parameter1 CHAR(10)) RETURNS SMALLINT
   LANGUAGE C
   PARAMETER STYLE GENERAL
   NOT DETERMINISTIC
   RETURN NULL ON NULL INPUT
   NO SQL
   EXTERNAL
```

Finally, the external function code would look like Listing 10-4.

Listing 10–4   *External function code for SELECT trigger*
```
short* __export __cdecl FUNCTION1 (char* c)
{
  static short return_value;
  HANDLE FileHandle;
  HANDLE MutexHandle;
  unsigned long ret;

  if (lstrcmp(c,"Washington")==0) {
    MutexHandle=CreateMutex(0,TRUE,"MUTEX");
    FileHandle=CreateFile(
        "T",
        GENERIC_WRITE,
        0,
        0,
        OPEN_ALWAYS,
        FILE_ATTRIBUTE_NORMAL,
        0);
    SetFilePointer(FileHandle,0,0,FILE_END);
    WriteFile(FileHandle,"it happened",11,&ret,0);
    CloseHandle(FileHandle);
    CloseHandle(MutexHandle);
    return_value=ret; }
```

```
else return_value=0;
return (&return_value); }
```

The matter is not simple—you must persuade the DBMS that the function is unpredictable and can change the column value. Otherwise, the DBMS will optimize the function call and only do it once. To persuade the DBMS not to optimize, write the function in a language the DBMS doesn't understand natively, make the column input/output (in fact the column isn't touched), and above all declare the function as NOT DETERMINISTIC.

A word of caution about NOT DETERMINISTIC functions. In real triggers, it is possible to call stored procedures with nondeterministic functions, but there is a peril. Our favorite one triggers an action that depends on the time of day, because "for some reason" time of day can't be used in a CHECK clause. Well, some people would think that reason is important—suppose the database becomes corrupt, and the recovery procedure involves rerunning a log of transactions. In such a case, the recovery isn't run at the same time of day as the original transaction—and thus a transaction that succeeded before the crash will fail during the recovery. Remember that some DBMSs handle functions in select lists when they open the cursor; others handle them when they fetch from the cursor.

The Bottom Line: Triggers

If speed is your only concern, use declarative constraints instead of triggers.

Use views with an external function call to write a SELECT trigger.

Declarative constraints differ from triggers in that constraint conditions guarantee that data always fulfills a specific requirement, while trigger conditions are enforced only when data changes. That is, constraints are passive requirements for correctness, while triggers are responses only to specific actions.

Because trigger checking happens after constraint checking, it's tricky to change the value of a table column within the trigger. That could lead to loops (because the change would cause another constraint check) or to subversions (because the change wouldn't go through the same checking that a regular data-change statement would go through). The SQL Standard has special rules that are designed to prevent such tricks.

Triggers fire on INSERT, UPDATE, or DELETE statements but not on "implied" inserts like the DBMS's nonstandard database LOAD statement and not on "implied" deletes like the DBMS's nonstandard table TRUNCATE statement.

Disabling Constraints

There are three ways to allay or prevent constraints: defer, disable, drop.

Defer

The standard way to allay or prevent constraints is to defer the constraint. To use this method, you first have to explicitly name the constraints on a table and define them as deferrable, like this:

```
CREATE TABLE Table1 (
   column1 SMALLINT,
   ...
   CONSTRAINT Constraint1 CHECK (
      column1 < 1000) DEFERRABLE INITIALLY DEFERRED)
```

A constraint defined as DEFERRABLE allows you to specify when you want the DBMS to check the constraint for violation—the choices are after the SQL statement is executed or at transaction end. The INITIALLY DEFERRED keywords ensure that the DBMS will defer checking the constraint either until transaction end or until you activate the deferrable constraints in your program with a SET CONSTRAINTS statement, like this:

```
SET CONSTRAINTS ALL IMMEDIATE
```

Remember that constraint deferring only happens within a transaction—as soon as you COMMIT, the DBMS will check for constraint violations. With deferrals, though, you can gain some control over the timing of constraint checks, which is especially an advantage if cyclic references are in your table definitions, or if there is an assumption that the transaction might have to be canceled with ROLLBACK anyway.

Portability   At the moment, SQL Standard-compliant deferral is supported only by IBM and Oracle. Informix supports the SET CONSTRAINTS statement, but all Informix constraints are deferrable by definition. Microsoft supports deferrable constraints, but not with standard SQL syntax.

Deferral Transaction End

If you defer constraints, do not wait for COMMIT to check for violations. If COMMIT fails, the transaction will ROLLBACK—and you won't get a chance to fix anything! So:

```
SET CONSTRAINTS ALL IMMEDIATE
```

is the statement you want.

Disable

The nonstandard way to allay or prevent constraints is to disable the constraint. For example, if you put this nonstandard Oracle SQL-extension statement in your program:

```
ALTER TABLE ...
  DISABLE <constraint list>
```

the constraints in the list cease to have any effect. The disablement happens over transaction boundaries.

Disablement is attractive for loading, because it is more efficient to do 1,000 INSERTs and then check all the data at once, than to do an INSERT followed by a constraint check one thousand times. Also, if you're doing a bulk UPDATE on a replicated database, or a database recovery, then the constraints have already been checked for the same data. In such cases, it becomes reasonable to hope that second checks are unnecessary. Keep in mind, though, that if you disable PRIMARY KEY or UNIQUE constraints, the DBMS won't update their associated indexes. At the moment, disablement is supported only by Oracle, but Microsoft has this equivalent nonstandard SQL-extension:

```
ALTER TABLE ... NOCHECK CONSTRAINT
```

Fine-Tuning

A bit of fine-tuning is possible with both the defer and the disable methods. By naming specific constraints, you can control the order of checking. Why? Because the first constraint you want to process is the one that's most likely to fail. The earlier a process fails, the less time has been wasted on it.

Drop

Another standard, but inconvenient, way to allay or prevent constraints is to drop the constraint, like this:

```
ALTER TABLE Table1
    DROP CONSTRAINT Constraint1 CASCADE
```

As with disabling constraints, this method helps speed the process of large-file INSERTs, bulk UPDATEs, and database recoveries. It also has the same disadvantage: Automatically updated indexes for PRIMARY KEY and UNIQUE constraints will be left out of sync with your data. But if you can't use constraint disablement, you can still drop constraints and then re-create them once your bulk work is completed.

The Bottom Line: Disabling Constraints

Of the three possible ways to allay or prevent a constraint—defer, disable, drop—only deferral and dropping the constraint are supported by standard SQL.

You can gain control over the timing of constraint checks by defining them as DEFERRABLE constraints. Deferred constraints can enhance performance especially when cyclic references are in your table definitions, or if there is an assumption that a transaction might have to be canceled with ROLLBACK anyway.

If you defer constraints, do not wait for COMMIT to check for violations. If COMMIT fails, the transaction will ROLLBACK—and you won't get a chance to fix anything! Always use SET CONSTRAINTS ALL IMMEDIATE before COMMIT.

To speed up data loading, bulk UPDATEs on a replicated database, and database recoveries, either disable or drop (and then re-create) your constraints.

To save time, ensure your DBMS checks the constraint that's most likely to fail first. Control the order of constraint checking by either deferring or disabling the constraints.

Client Validations

When a client (rather than the server) performs a constraint check, it's usually called a "validation" instead of a constraint. Validations may be inappropriate for business rules but are reasonable for verifying that input is formatted correctly and contains meaningful values.

Validations are redundant—the server will do them anyway. But that doesn't make validations a waste of time, because the client and server are on separate processors. By using validations, you aren't relying on the client; you're only helping throughput by ensuring that ridiculous transactions won't go across the network to the server.

Considering that bad data is less common than good data, is this filtering worthwhile? Absolutely, because a failed process takes *longer* than a successful one. Here's an example. In Oracle, constraint checking takes place during row processing, and constraints are checked a second time at end of statement if there are any interim violations. So a violated check gets processed twice as often as an unviolated check. Add on the fact that Oracle, if a statement fails at the end, has to roll back any changes made during the statement by restoring the original "before image" copy. So failures can cost more than successes.

Clients can check constraints that relate to a single instance of a row—for example, a check digit, a range, an absence, or a serial number. You must be warier of using clients to check whether a user has authorization, whether a withdrawal amount is too large, or the like, as these are all examples of business rules. For reasons we'll discuss elsewhere (see Chapter 16, "Clients and Servers"), it is rare nowadays to process many business rules on the client computer.

The Bottom Line: Client Validations

Having a client machine validate data rather than sending it to the server to be checked saves time by ensuring that ridiculous transactions won't go across the network to waste time on the server.

Clients can check constraints that relate to a single instance of a row—for example, a check digit, a range, an absence, or a serial number.

Clients shouldn't check constraints that relate to business rules—for example, whether a withdrawal amount is too large or a book has been catalogued.

Redundant SELECT Clauses

Here's an example of a redundant clause. Suppose that Table1 has a compound PRIMARY KEY consisting of (column1, column2). This SQL statement:

```
SELECT DISTINCT column1, column2
   FROM Table1
```

then has a redundancy—when all columns in a PRIMARY KEY or UNIQUE constraint are in a query's select list, and there are either no joins at all or the only joins are PRIMARY KEY to FOREIGN KEY, then the DISTINCT operator is redundant. You can improve performance by removing DISTINCT:

```
SELECT column1, column2
   FROM Table1
GAIN: 5/8
```

Once again, though, there are some caveats. It's dangerous to throw out the DISTINCT if:

- The constraint is deferrable—because the constraint could have been violated earlier in the transaction or, if your isolation level is READ UNCOMMITTED, another program could have violated the constraint.
- There is a possibility that the constraint could be disabled or dropped at some future time. (Remember that there is no way to make a trigger for ALTER TABLE.)
- There is a possibility that the query will select duplicate rows containing NULLs.

Optimizations like these require some extra trouble, because your program must check whether a constraint has been dropped and adapt accordingly. Unfortunately, there is no trigger for the ALTER TABLE . . . DROP CONSTRAINT statement, so you'll have to check the INFORMATION_SCHEMA for the information each time.

As optimizers improve, this technique will lose utility. So far, we are seeing some DBMSs that claim to do some constraint-related optimizations during SELECT. However, we've yet to see any DBMS that does the whole job, and we doubt that we will see any for a long while.

The Bottom Line: Redundant SELECTs

If a constraint exists with logic that duplicates a query's search condition, get rid of the redundant clause (unless NULLs are a possibility).

Parting Shots

A column constraint restricts the number of potential values that the column may contain, thereby giving the column more specificity. The DBMS optimizer likes specificity, so constraints are hints to the optimizer. For example, many DBMSs will prefer a UNIQUE column as a driver for joining.

Constraints are also hints to the programmer, because most DBMSs don't make full use of them. The simplest example is a CHECK constraint whose logic is repeated in the WHERE clause, like this:

```
CREATE TABLE Table1 (
   column1 SMALLINT,
   column2 CHARACTER(5),
   ...
   CHECK (column1 BETWEEN 15 AND 30))

SELECT * FROM Table1
  WHERE column2 = 'HARRY'
    AND column1 > 10
```

Clearly the AND column1 > 10 clause could be eliminated in the query (because it can never be false anyway)—if you can tolerate the possibility that column1 contains NULL. When applying this, remember that CHECK constraints have to be "other than false," but WHERE clauses have to be true.

Constraint checks happen at statement end. Data type checks happen at statement start. Therefore it's theoretically slow to say (using a constraint check):

```
CREATE TABLE Table1 (
  column1 SMALLINT,
  CHECK (column1 BETWEEN -9 AND 9))
```

as opposed to (using a data type check):

```
CREATE TABLE Table1 (
  column1 DECIMAL(1))
```

In practice, though, the CHECK constraint is better because it's more reliable. Some DBMSs will fail to return an error message if you insert values like 99 into a DECIMAL(1) column.

11

Stored Procedures

A stored procedure is something that is both *stored* (that is, it's a database object) and *procedural* (that is, it can contain constructs like IF, WHILE, BEGIN/END). Like a procedure in any language, an SQL stored procedure can accept parameters, declare and set variables, and return scalar values. A stored procedure may contain one or more SQL statements, including SELECT, so it can return result sets too. Listing 11–1 shows an example of a stored procedure declaration, in SQL Standard syntax.

Portability	MySQL does not support stored procedures. All gains shown in this chapter are for only seven DBMSs. Also, because stored procedures were around long before the SQL Standard got around to requiring them, every DBMS uses slightly different syntax to define stored procedures. A discussion of the differences is beyond the scope of this book.

Listing 11–1   *Stored procedure declaration, SQL standard syntax*

```
CREATE PROCEDURE        /* always CREATE PROCEDURE or FUNCTION */
  Sp_proc1              /* typically names begin with Sp_ */
(param1 INT)            /* parenthesized parameter list */
MODIFIES SQL DATA       /* SQL data access characteristic */
BEGIN
  DECLARE num1 INT;     /* variable declaration */
  IF param1 <> 0 THEN   /* IF statement */
    SET param1 = 1;     /* assignment statement */
  END IF;               /* terminates IF block */
  UPDATE Table1 SET     /* ordinary SQL statement */
    column1 = param1;
END
```

Refresher

We said in Chapter 1, "Facilis Descensus Averni," that we assume you're already familiar with (among other things) stored procedures, but here's a quick summary of syntax to refresh your memory.

Informix calls it **Stored Procedure Language (SPL);** Sybase and Microsoft call it Transact-SQL; Oracle calls it **Procedure Language extensions to SQL (PL/SQL);** the SQL Standard refers to **Persistent Stored Modules (PSM).** All these names refer to the same thing. It's easy to see this if you write the same stored procedure in several dialects and put the statements in columns side by side, with each syntax element occupying one row. We've taken the stored procedure declaration shown in Listing 11-1 and done this; the result is shown in Table 11-1.

Although no two columns of Table 11-1 are exactly alike, the important thing the table shows is how similar the statements are to one another, and to the SQL Standard. For example, if your background is Microsoft/Sybase, you just have to adapt to a few differences: Parameter and variable names do not begin with @; blocked statements are terminated explicitly (for example, IF ... END IF) as in Ada; the parameter list must be inside parentheses; semicolons are statement separators. Those are just details. We're confident that you'll be able to read our standard SQL PSM syntax examples regardless of your prior experience.

Table 11-1   *Listing 11-1's Stored Procedure in Four SQL Dialects*

ANSI SQL PSM	Informix SPL	Microsoft/Sybase Transact-SQL	Oracle PL/SQL
CREATE PROCEDURE Sp_proc1	CREATE PROCEDURE Sp_proc1	CREATE PROCEDURE Sp_proc1	CREATE PROCEDURE Sp_proc1
(param1 INT)	(param1 INT)	@param1 INT	(param1 IN OUT INT)
MODIFIES SQL DATA			
BEGIN			
DECLARE num1 INT;	DEFINE num1 INT;	AS DECLARE @num1 INT	AS num1 INT;
			BEGIN
IF param1 <> 0	IF param1<> 0	IF @param1<> 0	IF param1 <> 0
THEN SET param1 = 1;	THEN LET param1 = 1;	SELECT @param1 = 1	THEN param1 := 1;
END IF;	END IF;		END IF;
UPDATE Table1 SET	UPDATE Table1 SET	UPDATE Table1 SET	UPDATE Table1 SET
column1 = param1;	column1 = param1;	column1 = @param1	column1 = param1;
END	END PROCEDURE		END;

Determinism

> "But it sufficeth that the day will end, And then the end is known."
> —William Shakespeare, *Julius Caesar*

A function is **deterministic** if it always generates the same outputs, given the same inputs. For example, the SQL Standard built-in function UPPER is deterministic if UPPER('i') always returns I. Notice that there are two inputs here: the explicit argument 'i' and the constant environment setting 'code page = Western'. (If the code page were Turkish, the result of UPPER('i') would not be I.)

In contrast, a function is **nondeterministic** if it's possible that it might generate different outputs each time it is run, even if the inputs are always the same. This user-defined function is nondeterministic:

```
CREATE FUNCTION Sp_non_deterministic ()
RETURNS INTEGER
BEGIN
  IF CURRENT_TIME = TIME '11:00:00' THEN RETURN 1;
     ELSE RETURN 2;
  END IF;
END
```

Function Sp_non_deterministic will return a different result depending on an input value that is not determinable until execution, namely the time of day. Nondeterministic functions are bad.

- They are bad in CHECK clauses because you cannot be sure that you can rerun the same data-change statements and get the same results each time.

- They are bad in select lists because DBMSs like to say "if the query has the same syntax then use the same plan."

- They are bad in WHERE clauses because they cannot be indexed. There's no point in indexing a function that is subject to unpredictable change. The DBMS has to reevaluate the function every time.

Nondeterminism is a long name but a fairly simple idea. Clearly, you want to make sure your functions are deterministic, and you want to declare to the DBMS that they are deterministic. The problem area is external functions. They often depend on hidden factors (like the existence of a file) that the DBMS cannot detect.

Advantages of Stored Procedures

The advantages of stored procedures, in order by importance, are:

- Procedures are on the server so messages don't need to go back and forth to the client during the time the procedure is executed.

- Procedures are parsed once, and the result of the parsing is stored persistently, so there's no need to reparse for every execution.

- Procedures are in the catalog so they are retrievable, and procedures are subject to security provisions, in the same way as other SQL data.

- Procedures are in one place so code sharing is easy, and when changes happen there's no need to send code changes to clients.

Also, in theory, a procedural language is better adapted for procedural goals. So when you're working with scalar values rather than databases or sets, and one step happens after another, then constructs such as IF, DECLARE, BEGIN/END, FOR, WHILE, and so on, come into their own. Things get particularly interesting if the procedural language you're using is C or Java.

Less Traffic

Stored procedures mean less message traffic between clients and servers. The client must send some sort of message to initiate the procedure, and the procedure must return some sort of result when the procedure is over, but that's all—no message passing occurs within the procedure. So a stored procedure that contains [n] statements will need only two messages, while an ODBC application that contains [n] statements will need (2 * n) messages. This factor is significant because a message takes at least a few milliseconds (on a TCP/IP connection to the same computer), and most likely a few centiseconds (on a LAN), or even a few deciseconds (on a WAN or Internet connection). Against this, you must set the cost of loading a stored procedure from disk the first time, which takes a few milliseconds. Calculating these factors together, we can say that stored procedures are faster than direct passing of SQL statements when (a) more than two SQL statements in the stored procedure are executed, and (b) the stored procedure is accessed so frequently that it might already be in the operating system's cache.

A stored procedure is not the only thing that leads to less traffic. You can sometimes achieve similar effects with views or constraints. And you must remember that not all application programs need messages over a network—they could be **Common Gateway Interface (CGI)** programs called by the application server.

A message is not the same thing as a fetch. Beware of twaddle like "if a database has many rows, then stored procedures are good because the excess rows won't be transferred over the network for processing"—the rows won't be transferred anyway if you use WHERE clauses in your SQL statements! However, data-change (INSERT/UPDATE/DELETE) statements *can* cause useless messages if the DBMS feels obliged to return the number of rows that were changed. That's an SQL Standard requirement, but only Microsoft does it, and the message can be suppressed by telling Microsoft: SET NOCOUNT ON.

At the start of this section, we gave you four advantages to using stored procedures. Traffic reduction is more important than the other three combined. If you're on a network, you need stored procedures, and traffic reduction is the reason.

Semiprecompilation

The second advantage of stored procedures is that they're precompiled. This means that the DBMS only has to prepare a statement once, instead of preparing a statement every time it executes. To avoid building false hopes, we should emphasize that the precompilation is only partial, is only temporary, and is not a free lunch.

Let's take Informix as an example. We know that other DBMSs operate a bit differently, but they all operate under the same constraints. In a general fashion, here is what actually goes on.

When a CREATE PROCEDURE statement (for example, CREATE PROCEDURE Sp_proc1) is executed, Informix parses the statement and stores two things in the database catalog: a list of the objects (tables or other stored procedures) on which the procedure depends, and a list of tokens from the parsing. The token list is called *pcode*. It's a step away from an ASCII command but a long way from executable code. Pcode is somewhat like Java **bytecode**—it's interpretable, not executable. The pcode is kept in a BLOB field in the catalog's tables.

When EXECUTE PROCEDURE Sp_proc1 is run for the first time, Informix loads the procedure's pcode and makes a query plan. The query plan has to go in a cache, but the cache has only enough room for 16 query plans because query plans require a lot of RAM. If the cache already contains 16 query plans, Informix discards the least-recently-used query plan at this point. The precompilation advantage for stored procedures thus applies only to the last 16 procedures you've used. All other procedures must be reloaded and, in effect, precompiled again, because making the query plan is the bulk of the precompilation job.

When EXECUTE PROCEDURE Sp_proc1 is run and it's *not* the first time, Informix has a cached query plan ready to go. However, the DBMS must still check the dependency list because the stored procedure might refer to some object that has been altered or dropped since the first time the procedure was executed. The other thing that might have changed since the first time is the parameter values, so Informix reprocesses them too.

Now Informix locks the procedure. Usually stored procedures are not re-entrant because some of the variable information is stored outside the user's area. By ensuring that only one job at a time can execute, Informix ensures that executions of stored procedures are serializable.

And then Informix actually does the job.

Listing 11–2 shows a comparison test that we ran on a LAN, for a table with no rows in it. The point of the test was to see whether it was faster to SELECT data using direct SQL or via a stored procedure. The result of the test was that the "Direct SQL" execution was faster than the "stored procedure" execution. Our explanation for this is two-fold:

- First, the SQL statement was cached, so precompilation is true for both cases.

- Second, there is a call overhead for (a) finding Sp_proc1, (b) checking EXECUTE privileges, (c) saving current state, and (d) returning the result set to the caller.

So stored procedures do not enhance performance in every circumstance.

The result of Listing 11–2's test might lead us to say—If you're executing the same thing multiple times, then just PREPARE, don't use a stored procedure. But it's not that simple—the results of a PREPARE can disappear when a transaction ends. The results of a stored-procedure precompilation are more permanent.

Listing 11–2   *Test: Direct SQL versus stored procedure*

```
Stored Procedure
CREATE PROCEDURE Sp_proc1
   ...
   SELECT * FROM Table1;
   ...
...
CALL Sp_proc1
-- repeat CALL 1000 times
```

```
Direct SQL
SELECT * FROM Table1
-- repeat 1000 times
GAIN: 3/7
```

Because the DBMS remakes a plan the first time a procedure is called, you had better make sure the DBMS has all the necessary information when that first time happens. In particular:

- If a table needs indexes, make them before the first call. Don't execute CREATE INDEX within the procedure.

- Populate a table with realistic data before the first call, so the optimizer sees the histograms and knows the table sizes.

- Pass parameter values to the first call if the parameters are likely to be passed again in subsequent calls.

With any DBMS there are ways to force re-precompilation of stored procedures, and doing so occasionally won't harm anything. In most offices, it's easy: turn the machine off once a day.

Parameters

We've already noted that the DBMS rechecks the parameter values every time it executes a stored procedure, and that the DBMS takes parameter values into account for its query plan when it executes a procedure for the first time. The same cannot be said for local-variable values. Therefore if a procedure has a condition like this somewhere:

```
... WHERE column1 = num1
```

it's better if num1 is a parameter, not a variable.

Procedure parameter passing is "by value" (although you can simulate "by reference" passing using BLOBs and REFs). When parameter passing is by value, the DBMS usually makes a local copy so that the called procedure can make changes to the parameter without mucking up the original. That leads inevitably to the bad idea of declaring parameters to be "input/output" even when they're merely "input" parameters. The trick behind the idea is that an "input/output" parameter value is not recopied down the line if stored procedure #1 calls stored procedure #2—only the address is copied—so it saves you space and copying time.

The problem with the trick is that not all procedure calls are on the server's local stack. For example, if the server uses **Remote Procedure Call (RPC)** methods, then the parameter value *is* copied, and stored procedure #2 makes a *second* copy when it returns. Therefore you actually *lose* space and copying time by declaring the parameter to be an "input/output" parameter.

If you really want to avoid constant recopying of parameter values, you can either make judicious use of the SQL DEFAULT clause for column and domain definitions, or (more likely) you can use globals. Yes, there is no such thing (except in Microsoft's implementation), but you can simulate globals by storing values in temporary tables. People frequently do. Another form of global is one of the "global registers" that are accessible from any of the niladic functions—just keep in mind that most register values can't be changed by the user within a transaction.

Other Tips

The first tip to keep in mind when you're working with stored procedures is not to think of a compiler when you think of the precompiler. (A **precompiler** is a utility that converts SQL statements in a host program to statements a compiler can understand.) You are probably working with a primitive pcode interpreter, and the tricks that you take for granted with C—like constant propagation and invariant hoisting—are not supported here. For example, the stored procedure shown in Listing 11–3 is too optimistic.

Listing 11–3 *Optimistic stored procedure*

```
CREATE PROCEDURE Sp_proc1
(param1 INT)
MODIFIES SQL DATA
BEGIN
  DECLARE num1 INT;
  DECLARE num2 INT;
  SET num2 = 1;
  WHILE num2 <=3 DO
    SET num1 = param1;
    IF num1 > num2 AND param1 <> 1 THEN
        UPDATE Table1 SET column1 = 15 + num1 - 7;
    END IF;
    SET num2 = num2 +1;
  END WHILE;
END
```

Listing 11–3's procedure can be made about 50% faster if we ourselves—rather than expecting the DBMS to do it—take things out of the loop, fold, put declarations together in one statement, and avoid the assumption (which is true only in C) that if num1 > num2 is false then param1 <> 1 won't be tested. The improved procedure is shown in Listing 11–4.

Listing 11–4 *Improved stored procedure*

```
CREATE PROCEDURE Sp_proc1
(param1 INT)
MODIFIES SQL DATA
BEGIN
  DECLARE num1 INT, num2 INT;
  SET num1 = param1;
  SET num2 = 1;
  WHILE num2 <=3 DO
    IF num1 > num2 THEN
        IF param1 <> 1 THEN
            UPDATE Table1 SET column1 = num1 + 8;
        END IF;
    END IF;
  SET num2 = num2 +1;
  END WHILE;
END
GAIN: 5/7
```

The second stored procedure tip to keep in mind is to shift logic from WHERE clauses to IF clauses whenever possible. For example, if your procedure contains this code:

```
BEGIN
  UPDATE Table1 SET column1 = num1 WHERE num1 = 2;
END
```

change the code to:

```
BEGIN
  IF num1 = 2 THEN
    UPDATE Table1 SET column1 = 2;
  END IF;
END
GAIN: 5/7
```

Partly, the gain here happens because a falseness (when num1 <> 2) can be detected earlier. With IBM, the reason might be more subtle—IBM can actually compile the IF block, by converting it to C (or Java) statements and then invoking the appropriate compiler. But IBM can't compile the UPDATE statement, so any logic taken out of the UPDATE will be evaluated faster.

Listing 11–5 shows an example of a stored procedure that contains an SQL SELECT statement. We used InterBase for this example. InterBase does not conform to Standard SQL PSM as well as other DBMSs, but the code should still be easy to follow. Note especially these four things, marked by the comments in the Listing:

- Note 1: It is an InterBase requirement that all SQL statements be enclosed within a BEGIN ... END block.

- Note 2: It's a good idea to put a qualifier such as "Schema1." in front of the table name. This removes confusion if some other user, with a different default schema, calls the Select_proc procedure. Also, some DBMSs will look up an object faster if it's qualified, because they know what container to begin the search with. It's recommended that all objects used in a procedure should belong to the same schema.

- Note 3: The keyword SUSPEND is specific to InterBase. It means "return the fetched row to the caller."

- Note 4: No explicit CLOSE is in this procedure. The code depends on the DBMS to close cursors automatically when it exits. This method is safe, but in a more complex procedure it's important to remember to close early.

Listing 11–5 *An InterBase stored procedure using SELECT*

```
CREATE PROCEDURE Select_proc
(parameter1 INTEGER)
RETURNS (var1 CHAR(2), var2 CHAR(2), var3 CHAR(2))
AS
BEGIN                                         /* Note 1 */
FOR SELECT column1, column2, column3
    FROM Schema1.Table1                       /* Note 2 */
    WHERE column1 = :parameter1
    INTO :var1, :var2, :var3
  DO
  SUSPEND;                                     /* Note 3 */
END                                           /* Note 4 */
```

Once Listing 11-5's `Select_proc` procedure has been created, these two statements are equivalent:

```
SELECT column1, column2, column3
  FROM Schema1.Table1
  WHERE column1 = ?

EXECUTE PROCEDURE Select_proc
```

The interesting thing is that the EXECUTE PROCEDURE statement (or CALL statement, in ANSI SQL) will be faster than the SELECT statement *even if the stored procedure is not cached* (GAIN: 1/1). That's because "SELECT procedures" don't return result-set metadata.

The Bottom Line: Stored Procedures

When you use a stored procedure, you are depending on cache (which is limited) and access to the procedure (which may be serialized). Therefore it is a mistake to use stored procedures too frequently—that is, it is a mistake to use them except for the reasons discussed in this chapter. Stored procedures are like Santa Claus: You get presents for nothing—but you ought to be good anyway.

Don't declare parameters to be "input/output" when they're merely "input" parameters.

Result-Set Metadata

When you execute a SELECT statement, for example:

```
SELECT column1
  FROM Table1
```

you get back the values for column1 in a result set. What you may not realize is that you also get back the metadata about column1: its name, length, and other descriptive data. The DBMS passes this information automatically; usually the application program doesn't need it, so the passing is a waste of network packets. The CALL statement, on the other hand, won't return metadata. So when you're not repeating the SELECT multiple times, you'll save time by using CALL with a stored procedure instead.

Don't write stored procedures as if the precompiler has the built-in skills of a compiler. Take things out of loops, fold, put declarations together in one statement, and avoid testing assumptions on your own—don't expect the DBMS to do these things for you.

Shift logic from WHERE clauses to IF clauses whenever possible.

If a stored procedure contains an IF statement and is inside a trigger, take the condition out of the IF and put it in the trigger's WHEN clause.

If a stored procedure contains conditions like this:

```
IF <search condition> THEN
   SELECT * FROM Table1;
   ELSE SELECT * FROM Table2;
END IF;
```

then only one of the SELECTs (whichever SELECT is actually executed) will be precompiled and get a stored plan. To ensure that both plans are stored, put the SELECTs in procedures of their own and CALL as required, like this:

```
CREATE PROCEDURE Sp_proc1
   ... SELECT * FROM Table1 ...

CREATE PROCEDURE Sp_proc2
   ... SELECT * FROM Table2 ...

...
IF <search condition> THEN
   CALL Sp_proc1;
   ELSE CALL Sp_proc2;
END IF;
```

Two different connections will not use the same in-memory copy of a stored procedure. That's an argument for connection pooling; see Chapter 13, "JDBC."

Use VARCHAR parameters rather than CHAR parameters. Some DBMSs will automatically add space padding if the data type is CHAR, and that slows network access. However, if you have a long IN parameter and a long OUT parameter, you should combine them as a single INOUT fixed-size CHAR parameter. Reusing the same buffer for input and output will save memory on the server.

IBM recommends that you avoid putting COMMIT or ROLLBACK in the stored procedure. The transaction-end statements are especially bad if you're using distributed transactions and TP monitors. However, doing so will save one network message (if auto-commit is off).

Microsoft recommends that you avoid interleaving data-change statements with data definition statements. For example, do not mix CREATE and INSERT statements in a stored procedure.

Try to make sure that the stored procedure and the client application are operating with similar assumptions. For example, they should each have the same codepage.

Do not assume that frequently used stored procedures are cached. They can be invalidated due to many circumstances—for example, if the DBMS automatically updates the database statistics every hour, or the stored procedure contains SQL statements which are not executed every time the procedure is run, or there are too many stored procedures for the DBMS's fixed cache size.

Begin a stored procedure by testing whether a parameter is NULL. Some DBMSs (not the SQL Standard) allow callers to pass two arguments to a procedure that was defined with three parameters. In such a case, the third parameter value will be NULL. Among the Big Eight, only Ingres allows such uneven passing. (Other DBMSs allow uneven parameter passing when a parameter was defined with a DEFAULT NULL clause, but this is not standard SQL.)

Parting Shots

Are stored procedures cute? Well, they're a little Ada-like and wordy. Many things that you can do in C or Pascal, you can't do in SQL procedures. And most implementations are inefficient. And there is still a portability issue, though that's being resolved now that SQL:1999 has clarified all.

What should a procedure consist of? Answer: The entire transaction from inception to end. The reasoning here is that a stored procedure should enforce business rules, and a transaction is the performance of a set of business rules. It's common to see a transaction containing multiple procedures, but a pessimistic programmer will make stored procedures fairly large.

Should a procedure be public? Yes, but don't expect that the result will be that the DBMS keeps a single copy of the procedure in memory. Procedures may not be reentrant, or the logic and the meaning of unqualified names may not be the same for every user.

Should all SQL statements be in stored procedures? No, because of the bottlenecks discussed in this chapter, and because a program is hard to follow if all it does is CALL procedures.

Should all SQL views or constraints be in stored procedures? No, because the DBMS will optimize for views and constraints, and the code for that is compiled permanently. You are not going to get equivalent performance by replacing the DBMS's compilations with your own code.

Should stored procedures be used even if they harm performance? Yes. We haven't really addressed the security, clarity, and deployment issues here—that's beyond the scope of this book. But, together with performance, these issues add up to a powerful argument for using stored procedures.

The performance issue is a big factor. The judicious use of stored procedures, at the right times, in the right way, will make an application at least three times faster. Getting this part right is where the big payoffs are.

12

ODBC

On the Web, the www.sourceforge.net site hosts about 30 myriads of open source projects. One day we extracted the projects in sourceforge's category "DBMS Front End" and looked to see what the vendors were using to communicate with the DBMS engine. Table 12–1 shows the results.

As you can see, Table 12–1 shows that, as an API for DBMSs, ODBC is the clear leader. It's been #1 since Microsoft brought out ODBC 1.0 in August 1992. The

Table 12–1 *APIs Used by DBMSs*

API	Number of Projects
ODBC	62
JDBC	45
Oracle OCI	11
OLE DB	6
ADO	2
DAO	2
RDS	1
SQL DBI	1
Other	4

other APIs (especially JDBC) have their niches, and we'll certainly talk about them later in this book. But in any discussion of database programming, the ODBC API should get pride of place, and that's what we'll talk about in this chapter.

Several years ago, Microsoft lost enthusiasm for ODBC, so we don't expect major enhancements to ODBC from that quarter. As a result, there has been some uncertainty about its future. Let's clear that up: ODBC is doomed—but the core of ODBC will prosper and progress for years. There are several reasons why this is true and certain:

- ODBC is native.

  If you look in the documentation for IBM, Ingres, and Microsoft, you'll find that every one of these vendors claims to run ODBC natively. The word "native" means "no public API is beneath this API"—and that's a good thing. (By contrast, the Oracle ODBC driver is non-native because it has to call Oracle's true bottom layer, the Oracle Call Interface.) In general, a native API is a good thing because there can be no finger pointing when a problem comes along. Sometimes it's also suggested that a native API is inevitably faster than a non-native API, but that's false—the cost of pushing parameters on a stack and issuing an assembly language CALL statement is too trivial to be worth considering.

- Core ODBC is standard.

  The ANSI/ISO SQL Standard document (SQL/Call-Level Interface ISO/IEC 9075-3) describes an interface that is, to all effects and purposes, the same as core-level ODBC. Yes, there are differences; yes, the differences could grow—nevertheless, the fact remains that Microsoft doesn't own the specification that people actually use and depend upon. If you looked at a program written with the IBM API, you'd exclaim: "But this is an ODBC program!" To which the comebacks would be: (a) No it isn't, because ODBC is a Microsoft trademark; (b) No it isn't, because it contains some IBM-specific enhancements; (c) Yes it is, because it adheres to the SQL/CLI Standard, and the differences between SQL/CLI and ODBC are less than the differences between, say, Borland C and Microsoft C.

- Microsoft is aboard.

  Microsoft has only recommended its newer methods as better, without ever threatening to pull the plug on ODBC. Microsoft too says that one can run ODBC natively and is committed to aligning ODBC with the SQL:1999 Standard.

Refresher

We said in Chapter 1, "Facilis Descensus Averni," that we assume you're already familiar with (among other things) programming with an SQL API such as ODBC, but here's a quick summary of ODBC basics to refresh your memory. All of our examples will work equally well with ODBC 3.x and standard SQL/CLI except where noted.

Primarily, ODBC is a specification of the format for calls and parameters that an application program can include, as well as a specification of the activities that the called routines—i.e., the ODBC driver—must perform when the call happens. Microsoft provides installation utilities and a driver manager for the Windows platform; however, one can dispense with the fripperies— "ODBC" programs run on Unix too.

ODBC programs can be pure client-side, when they're front ends. ODBC programs can also be pure server-side, when they're CGI. Or ODBC programs can be between the extremes—the routines themselves are in a middling ODBC driver that can be middleware or might be completely inside the DBMS. (In this chapter, we'll use the term "DBMS" to mean everything that the function includes, no matter how indirectly.)

Every SQL call (at least when it's in a C/ODBC program) has these characteristics:

- It begins with the letters SQL.

- It refers to a handle of a resource. A resource is an **env** (environment), a **dbc** (database connection), a **stmt** (statement container), or a **desc** (descriptor for SQL statement parameters). These resources have a hierarchy, shown in Figure 12-1.

Listing 12-1 shows the ODBC "hello-world" program. This simplest of all ODBC programs builds, and then tears down the minimum scaffolding that a program will always have: an env, a dbc, and a stmt. An ODBC program that passes any input parameters to SQL statements, or retrieves any result sets from SQL, will have descs too.

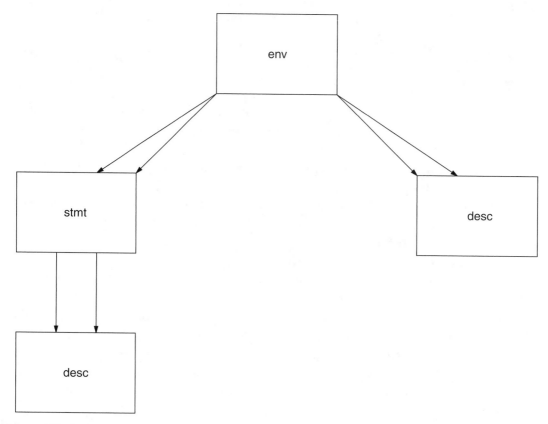

Figure 12–1   *Hierarchy of ODBC resources*

Listing 12–1   *The simplest ODBC program*

```
#include "sqlcli.h"     /* contains headers and constants */
void main ()
{
HENV henv;              /* fill this in with SQLAllocEnv */
HDBC hdbc;              /* fill this in with SQLAllocConnect */
HSTMT hstmt;            /* fill this in with SQLAllocStmt */

SQLAllocEnv(            /* Allocate environment handle; env */
    &henv);

SQLAllocConnect(        /* Allocate connect handle; dbc */
    henv,
    &hdbc);
```

```
SQLConnect(              /* Connect */
   hdbc,
   "OCELOT",SQL_NTS,
   "OCELOT",SQL_NTS,
   "",SQL_NTS);

SQLAllocStmt(           /* Allocate statement handle; stmt */
   hdbc,
   &hstmt);

SQLExecDirect(          /* Do some SQL! */
   hstmt,
   "INSERT INTO Table1 VALUES (1)",SQL_NTS);

SQLFreeStmt(            /* Free the stmt */
   hstmt,
   SQL_DROP);

SQLDisconnect(          /* Disconnect; reverse Connect */
   hdbc);

SQLFreeConnect(         /* Free the dbc; reverse AllocConnect */
   hdbc);

SQLFreeEnv(             /* Free the env; reverse AllocEnv */
   henv);
}
```

The important groups of ODBC calls are:

- The buildup/teardown functions

  Usually you'll see SQLAllocEnv, SQLAllocConnect, SQLConnect, and SQLAllocStmt at program start, then various meat calls will occur, then you'll see SQLFreeStmt, SQLDisconnect, SQLFreeConnect, and SQL-FreeEnv at program end. Lately there's been a trend to use busier function names:

  ```
  SQLAllocHandle(SQL_HANDLE_ENV,...)
  SQLAllocHandle(SQL_HANDLE_DBC,...)
  SQLAllocHandle(SQL_HANDLE_STMT,...)
  SQLAllocHandle(SQL_HANDLE_DESC,...)
  ```

  etc. In nonstandard ODBC, you'll almost always find that, instead of SQL-Connect, the function call used is SQLDriverConnect, which allows for passing more information than merely the data source name, the user-name, and the password.

- The diagnostic functions

  Anything can go wrong, so there's always been an `SQLError` function to return whatever diagnostic information the DBMS might have accumulated. To provide a much deeper level of detail, the latest versions of ODBC and SQL/CLI have two new functions: `SQLGetDiagRec` and `SQLGetDiagField`.

- The desc functions

  Only two desc functions are really necessary: `SQLGetDescField` and `SQLSetDescField`. All the others—`SQLGetDescRec`, `SQLSetDescRec`, `SQLBindCol`, `SQLBindParameter`, `SQLColAttribute`, `SQLDescribeCol`, `SQLDescribeParam`, `SQLNumParams`, `SQLNumResultCols`, and `SQLRowCount`—are just more or less complex combinations of the simple act of "getting a descriptor field" or "setting a descriptor field." For example, if you want to tell the DBMS about the C variables that are to be associated with the result of a SELECT statement, you'd either use `SQLSetDescField` multiple times or `SQLBindCol` once.

- The cursor functions

  A **result set** is what a SELECT returns. The **cursor** is the invisible marker that indicates a position within the result set. You can subdivide the result set into smaller sets (row sets), change the cursor position, or just fetch one or more values at the cursor position into the C variables that got described with a desc function. The principal cursor functions are `SQLFetch`, `SQLFetchScroll`, `SQLSetCursorName`, `SQLGetCursorName`, `SQLSetPos` (ODBC only), and `SQLExtendedFetch` (ODBC only, and obsolete). There's also `SQLGetData` and `SQLPutData`, which merely set values after a fetch is done.

- The catalog functions

  The catalog functions are mere containers for SELECTs that query the database catalog. Because they're containers for SELECTs, these functions return result sets. For example, SQLTables returns a list of tables (both base tables and views) in the database. Other catalog functions are SQLColumns, SQLColumnPrivileges, SQLSpecialColumns, SQL-Procedures, and SQLPrimaryKeys.

- The attribute functions

  The attribute functions either set or get flags and parameters that affect the workings of an entire resource (env or dbc or stmt). Logically enough, there are three pairs of functions: (SQLSetEnvAttr, SQLGet-EnvAttr), (SQLSetConnectAttr, SQLGetConnectAttr), and (SQLSet-StmtAttr, SQLGetStmtAttr). Illogically, there is one more function that gets various unchangeable settings and constants: SQLGetInfo.

- The transaction end function

  SQLEndTran.

Tracing MS Query

As part of our refresher, let's look at how a typical ODBC application communicates with the DBMS. We chose Microsoft Query for an example because it comes preinstalled with many Windows versions. We'll do our peeking with two simple tools: the MS-ODBC Administrator and the MS Notepad editor. If you have an ODBC data source and an MS Windows NT computer, you can follow along with this short exercise.

1. Get your Windows NT machine ready for using ODBC.

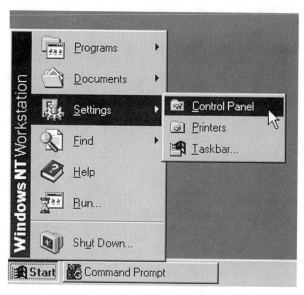

Figure 12–2   *Click Settings/Control panel*

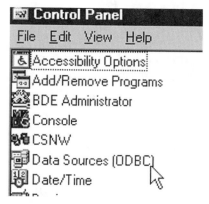

Figure 12–3   *Click Data Sources (ODBC).*

2. Turn ODBC tracing on: Click Settings/Control Panel (see Figure 12-2).

3. Start Microsoft's ODBC Data Source Administrator: Click Data Sources (ODBC) (see Figure 12-3).

4. Click the Tracing tab (see Figure 12-4).

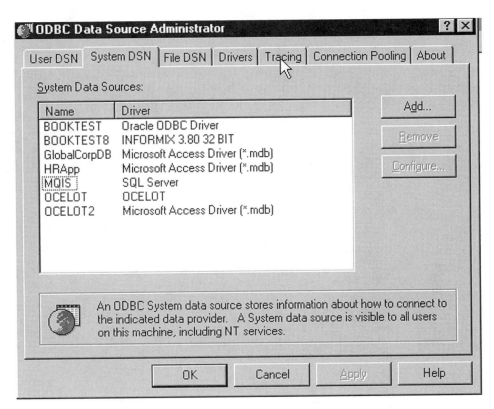

Figure 12–4 *Click the Tracing tab*

5. Click the Start Tracing Now button; it will change to Stop Tracing Now. Click OK (see Figure 12-5). Illogically, as long as this button is set to "Stop Tracing Now," the tracing is *on*. If you're following along, come back here later to turn tracing back off because it slows down ODBC applications tremendously.

6. Now, start Microsoft Query: Click Start/Run and enter the following:
   `C:\WINNT\MSAPPS\MSQUERY\MSQRY32.EXE`

   (The path may be different on your machine; see Figure 12-6.)

7. Click New Query (see Figure 12-7).

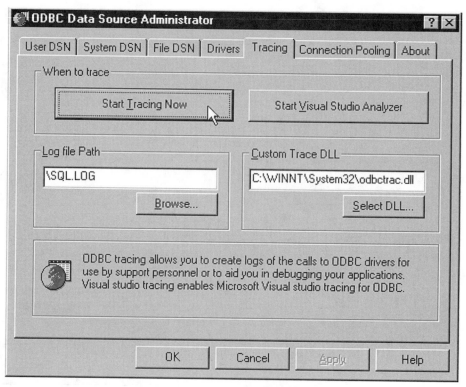

Figure 12–5 *Click the Start Tracing Now button*

Figure 12–6 *Start Microsoft Query*

Figure 12–7   *Click New Query*

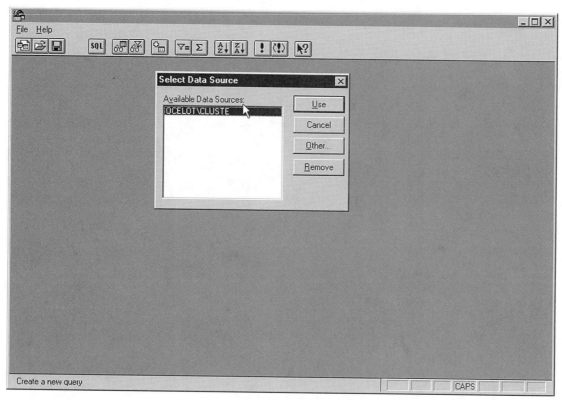

Figure 12–8 *Double-click your data source name*

8. On the Select Data Source dialog box, double-click your choice of data source name (see Figure 12–8).

9. On the Add Tables dialog box, double-click your choice of table, then click Close (see Figure 12–9).

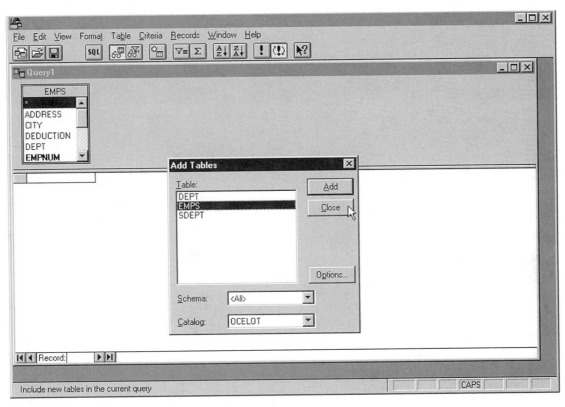

Figure 12–9 *Double-click your table, then click Close*

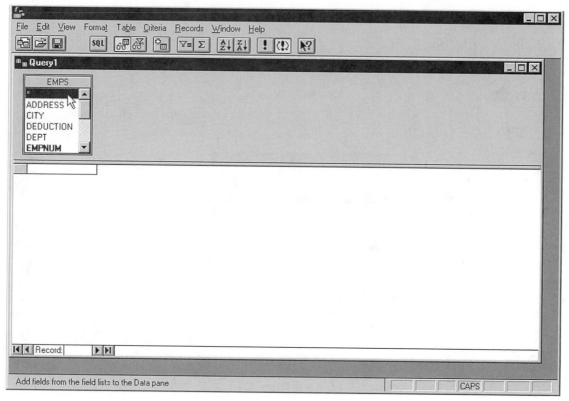

Figure 12-10 *Double-click your column on the Query1 dialog box*

10. On the Query1 dialog box, double-click your choice of column (see Figure 12-10).

11. Click File/Exit (see Figure 12-11).

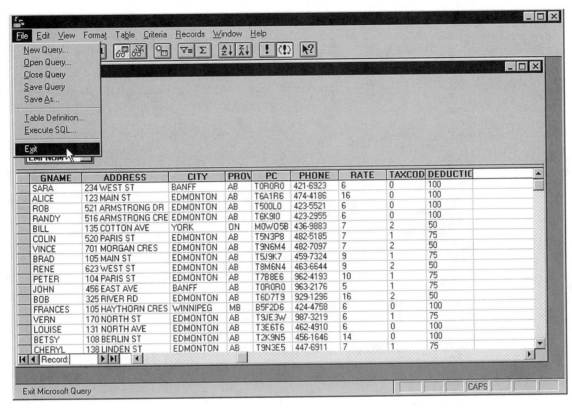

Figure 12–11 *Click File/Exit*

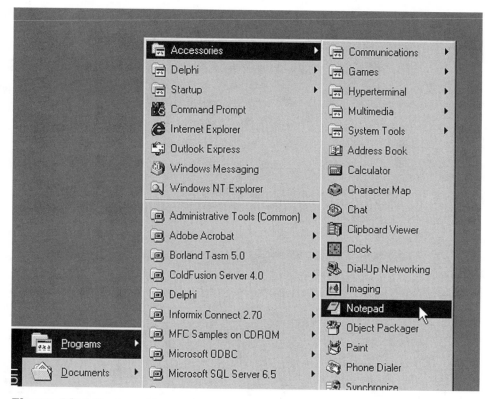

Figure 12–12 *Start Notepad*

12. Now, start Notepad. Click Start/Programs/Accessories/Notepad (see Figure 12-12).

13. Click File/Open, then enter the following:

    C:\SQL.LOG

    (See Figure 12-13.)

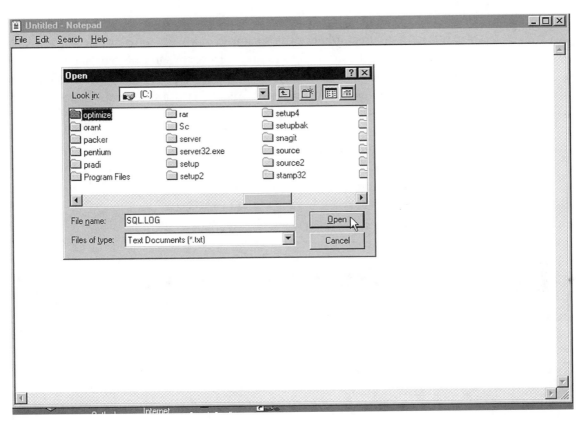

Figure 12–13 *Open SQL.LOG; click File/Open*

Figure 12-14 shows SQL.LOG, the trace file that was on the Tracing dialog box set up at the beginning of this example.

The SQL.LOG file contains an entry for every SQL call that MSQRY32.EXE performed, along with the parameter values and return codes. There's enough on display to allow you to analyze what MS Query did when you used it for your display. For example:

1. MS Query established the connection:

```
SQLAllocEnv         /* allocate env */
SQLAllocConnect     /* allocate dbc */
SQLDriverConnect    /* connect */
...
SQLAllocStmt        /* allocate stmt */
```

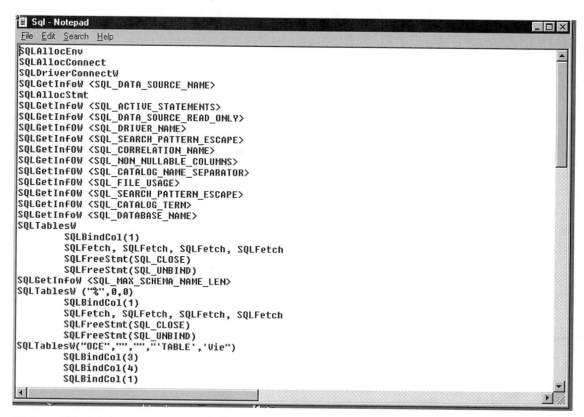

Figure 12–14 *A view of SQL.LOG*

2. MS Query got some information about the connection:

```
SQLGetInfo <SQL_DATA_SOURCE_NAME>
            /* get data source name */
SQLGetInfo <SQL_ACTIVE_STATEMENTS>
            /* how many stmts can be active? */
SQLGetInfo <SQL_DATA_SOURCE_READ_ONLY>
            /* is data source read-only? */
SQLGetInfo <SQL_DRIVER_NAME>
            /* what is the ODBC driver name? */
SQLGetInfo <SQL_SEARCH_PATTERN_ESCAPE>
            /* are % and _ used in SQLTables? */
SQLGetInfo <SQL_CORRELATION_NAME>
            /* what is a correlation called? */
SQLGetInfo <SQL_NON_NULLABLE_COLUMNS>
            /* can columns be NOT NULL? */
SQLGetInfo <SQL_CATALOG_NAME_SEPARATOR>
            /* does "." follow the catalog qualifier? */
SQLGetInfo <SQL_FILE_USAGE>
            /* how many tiers are there? */
SQLGetInfo <SQL_SEARCH_PATTERN_ESCAPE>
            /* what's the LIKE escape character? */
SQLGetInfo <SQL_CATALOG_TERM> >
            /* what is a catalog called? */
SQLGetInfo <SQL_DATABASE_NAME>
            /* what is the database name? */

. . .

SQLGetInfo <SQL_MAX_SCHEMA_NAME_LEN>
            /* how long are schema names? */
```

A series of SQLGetInfo calls is normal at this stage: DBMSs can have different syntaxes and DBMS vendors can use different vocabularies.

3. MS Query got some information about your table and its columns:

```
SQLTables("%",0,0)
            /* what catalogs exist? */
SQLTables("OCE","","","'TABLE','Vie'")
            /* what tables exist? */
SQLGetTypeInfo <SQL_ALL_TYPES>
            /* what data types are supported? */
SQLColumns("OCE","OCELOT","DEPT")
            /* what columns exist? */
SQLSpecialColumns(SQL_BEST_ROWID,"EMPS",SQL_SCOPE_CURROW)
            /* what column is good for the search? */
```

It's normal for an ODBC application to use catalog functions rather than to query the database catalog for this information. The dependence on `SQLSpecialColumns` is especially noteworthy. Without this call, MS Query would not know which of the table's columns to use for unique searches.

4. MS Query selected all columns in all rows:

```
SQLExecDirect(
    "SELECT EMPS.EMPNUM, ... FROM "OCELOT.OCELOT".EMPS EMPS")
```

MS Query requires quirky SQL syntax here; luckily all DBMSs accept double quotes in strange places. This is the only time in the session that an SQL statement actually appears.

5. MS Query got some information about the result set that was returned by the SELECT statement:

```
SQLNumResultCols() /* how many columns in select list? */
loop
   (for each column in select list) {
   SQLDescribeCol()           /* what is column name etc. */
   SQLColAttribute(           /* how wide is column? */
      SQL_COLUMN_DISPLAY_SIZE)
   }
```

6. MS Query fetched each row, transferring data to bound columns:

```
loop
   (for each row till "NO DATA" return or screen is full) {
   loop
      (for each column in select list) {
      SQLBindCol()
      }
   SQLFetch
   }
```

Why is the `SQLBindCol` loop inside the main loop? That's something worth looking at later.

7. Lastly, MS Query performed a teardown by reversing each call that was performed when it connected:

```
SQLFreeStmt          /* reverse SQLAllocStmt */
SQLDisconnect        /* reverse SQLDriverConnect */
SQLFreeConnect       /* reverse SQLAllocConnect */
SQLFreeEnv           /* reverse SQLAllocEnv */
```

Many developers have performed this same exercise with the intent of copying Microsoft's basic methods. The MS Query imitations all go through the same phases: a buildup with resource allocations, a series of SQLGetInfo and catalog-function calls, a point where an actual SQL statement goes down the line, some result processing, and teardown.

SQLPrepare

With ODBC, you can do an SQL statement in one function call:

```
SQLExecDirect("<SQL statement>")
```

or you can split it into two function calls:

```
SQLPrepare("<SQL statement>")

SQLExecute()
```

Which is more efficient? We measured the relative performance of both methods and found that SQLPrepare takes a significant fraction (averaging about 30%) of the total time. If a statement is complex or if the number of rows affected is small, then it helps performance to take the preparation out of the loop, like this:

```
SQLPrepare("<SQL statement>")
loop {
  SQLExecute()
  }
```

Taking an invariant assignment out of a loop is called **hoisting**. We won't waste time showing it's a good idea because that's obvious. What's important is to know when hoisting is *not* worthwhile.

If your DBMS caches SQL statements and reuses the plans, then hoisting is automatic so it's not worthwhile to do it yourself. For example, you would see no gain if you use Oracle.

Hoisting may not be helpful if your intent is to generalize an SQL statement to take advantage of SQLPrepare. For example, suppose you have these three queries:

```
SELECT * FROM Table1 WHERE column1 = 'A'

SELECT * FROM Table1 WHERE column1 = 'B'

SELECT * FROM Table1 WHERE column1 = 'C'
```

To execute the queries, you think that this looks like a clever idea:

```
SQLPrepare(
  "SELECT * FROM Table1 WHERE column1 = ?")
SQLBindParameter() /* to associate the ? with variable x */
  x = 'A'
    SQLExecute()
  x = 'B'
    SQLExecute()
  x = 'C'
    SQLExecute()
```

For the general case, changing a literal to a parameter is good because the DBMS then has no need to reparse the statement multiple times and also because there will be fewer different statements to process. Great . . . but not always!

The danger with this idea is that, although the three SQL statements look similar, the execution plans could be very different if the value A occurs far more frequently than B in the index. If the optimizer knows what the literal is, it also knows whether it's common or uncommon and can modify the execution plan accordingly. If you don't give the optimizer that information, then it has to use a generalized plan that might not be optimal at all.

Statements are not re-prepared when statistics change. Thus, if the loop contains an implied transaction end, the preparation may become invalid—making hoisting definitely not worthwhile. For example, suppose you're updating:

```
SQLPrepare("<UPDATE statement>")
  loop {
    SQLExecute()
    }
```

This sequence is doomed if the DBMS is in auto-commit mode, and if the DBMS invalidates PREPARE statements whenever it commits. Admittedly though, you can get around that difficulty by calling SQLGetInfo(SQL_CURSOR_COMMIT_BEHAVIOR) and SQLGetConnectAttr(SQL_ATTR_AUTOCOMMIT).

Here's a final reason to be cautious of hoisting. In early versions of Microsoft, SQLPrepare causes the creation of a temporary table. Make no mistake, the Boy Scout motto is correct. It's just that "Be prepared" doesn't always mean "Call SQLPrepare." If you're afraid of it, then at least try this: Limit what users can enter (notice that most Internet dialog boxes give only a few options), and depend on the DBMS to reuse plans for queries that are exactly the same.

The Bottom Line: SQLPrepare

If a statement is complex or if the number of rows affected is small, take SQLPrepare out of the loop.

Do generalize an SQL statement to try and take advantage of SQLPrepare unless the query plan depends on a skewed set of data values.

If you must SQLPrepare, limit what users can enter, and depend on the DBMS to reuse plans for queries that are exactly the same.

Fetch Loops

We've already noted that an SQL result set is a set of rows that a SELECT statement (or an equivalent to a SELECT statement, such as a catalog function or a stored procedure that contains a SELECT) returns. A **fetch loop** is a loop that contains calls to a function that takes a row from a result set. For example, suppose a column called column1 contains a number, and you want to display all occurrences of the column. Listing 12–2 shows a common prototype to get this done.

Listing 12–2 *Common prototype for numeric display*

```
SQLRETURN rc;
SQLHSTMT hstmt;
SQLINTEGER numx;
SQLINTEGER numx_indicator;

SQLExecDirect(
    hstmt,
    "SELECT column1 FROM Table1",SQL_NTS);
```

```
for (;;) {
  rc=SQLFetch(hstmt);
  if (rc==SQL_NO_DATA) break;

  SQLGetData(
   hstmt,
   1,
   targettype,         /* insert the correct type here */
   &numx,
   sizeof(numx),
   &numx_indicator);

  if (numx_indicator!=-1) printf("%d.\n",numx);
  }

SQLCloseCursor(
   hstmt);
```

Although the Listing 12–2 prototype works, it could be improved in several places. For example:

- Before the transaction

  Before beginning the transaction, determine when the session starts, and whether numx can contain NULL. Prefetch catalog information and keep the data in application buffers.

- Before the SELECT

  Before selecting, give the DBMS any information that it might be able to use for optimizing the transaction. The calls for this purpose are:

```
SQLSetStmtAttr(
   hstmt,SQL_ATTR_CONCURRENCY,SQL_ATTR_READ_ONLY,...);
SQLSetStmtAttr(
   hstmt,SQL_ATTR_CURSOR_SCROLLABLE,SQL_NONSCROLLABLE,...);
SQLSetStmtAttr(
   hstmt,SQL_ATTR_CURSOR_TYPE,SQL_CURSOR_FORWARD_ONLY,...);
SQLSetStmtAttr(
   hstmt,SQL_ATTR_NOSCAN,SQL_NOSCAN_ON,...);
```

  There is also a call for setting the rowset size:

```
SQLSetStmtAttr(
   hstmt,SQL_ATTR_ROW_ARRAY_SIZE,20,...);
```

  In this context, the **rowset size** is the number of rows that will be fetched at once and is not to be confused with the **result set size**, which is the total number of rows that are selected. Think of it this way:

If a single call to SQLFetch can get 20 rows at once into an array, that's good—because all 20 rows can fit easily in one network packet. Unfortunately, the loop becomes far more complex. If you set the rowset size to 20, you must also (a) redefine numx and numx_indicator as arrays rather than integers, (b) check whether the DBMS returns SQLSTATE 01S02 (which means "I can't support this size so I've changed rowset size to some other value"), and (c) put a second loop, which prints each non-NULL occurrence of numx[n], within the fetch loop. A serious ODBC application *must* use SQL_ATTR_ROW_ARRAY_SIZE.

- Before the loop

  Before beginning the loop, add an error check to ensure that column1 really is an INTEGER and not a SMALLINT or BIGINT. (Passing sizeof (numx) among the SQLGetData arguments has absolutely no effect on anything.) SQLDescribeCol would be appropriate here and would also be useful for testing whether column1 can contain NULL. If column1 can't contain NULL, there's no need for a NULL indicator variable (unless you're going to be doing an outer join or some other query that can evaluate to NULL).

- Before the fetch

  Before you fetch, change the SQLGetData call to SQLBindCol—the use of SQLGetData for a short numeric variable is inappropriate. Use SQLGet-Data only when there is no loop, when the fetch is likely to fail, or when stack space for variables is limited. None of these conditions applies in this prototype. While you're at it, the SQLBindCol call should not only be before the SQLFetch call, you should place it before the loop starts. Frequently, programmers put SQLBindCol somewhere within the fetch loop so that it will be clear what the fetch is doing, but this wastes time. A fetch loop that contains SQLBindCol should end with:

  ```
  SQLFreeStmt(hstmt,SQL_UNBIND);
  ```

- After the loop

  In this particular case, you would expect little advantage from processing the SQLFetch and the C printf statement asynchronously, which is possible by using different threads or via another SQLSetStmtAttr option. (If print speed is a real concern, improve it by fetching everything into an array and then calling printf after closing the cursor.) On the other hand, the asynchronous methods allow the user a chance to cancel, which is often a useful option for fetch loops. Finally, end with SQLEndTran instead of SQLCloseCursor if the DBMS is in manual-commit mode and will thus automatically close cursors when the transaction ends.

The Bottom Line: Fetch Loops

Improve your fetch loops by determining when the session starts and whether you need NULL indicators. Do this before the transaction starts.

Improve your fetch loops by using SQLSetStmtAttr to give the DBMS information that it can use to optimize the transaction for you.

Improve your fetch loops by determining the data type of the columns you're fetching and whether they can contain NULL. Do this before the loop starts.

Use SQLBindCol instead of SQLGetData unless (a) there is no loop, (b) the fetch is likely to fail, or (c) stack space for variables is limited. To save time, put SQLBindCol before the fetch loop starts.

If you invest a lot of your time in a fetch loop, the loop will run much more quickly.

Data-Change Statements

The SQL Standard defines an "SQL-data-change statement" as any of: INSERT, UPDATE, DELETE. If—and only if—a data change involves a large number of rows, you can speed up the ODBC execution of the transaction.

One way to improve data-change performance is to pass several data-change statements at once, to reduce the overhead of network transmissions. Here are three common ways to pass multiple data-change statements:

- If you're using ODBC 3.x, call the function SQLBulkOperations, which allows array passing. This function is not available in standard SQL/CLI, nor in all implementations.

- If you're using standard SQL:1999, enclose multiple statements in a compound statement block, for example:

```
SQLExecDirect(
  hstmt,
  "BEGIN \
    UPDATE Table1 SET column1 = 5; \
    UPDATE Table2 SET column1 = 6; \
  END",SQL_NTS);
```

| **Portability** | Ingres, InterBase, MySQL, and Oracle don't support this feature. |

- Some DBMSs allow INSERTs to contain multiple clauses, as required by the SQL Standard. Take advantage of the feature, like this:

```
SQLExecDirect(
  hstmt,
  "INSERT INTO Table1 VALUES \
    (5, 6, 7), \
    (5, 7, 8), \
    (5, 8, 9)",SQL_NTS);
```

| **Portability** | Ingres, Informix, InterBase, Microsoft, Oracle, and Sybase don't support this feature. |

Another way to improve performance is to set auto-commit mode based on the number of data-change statements you're executing. If you find that most of your transactions contain two or more data-change statements, turn auto-commit mode off with:

```
SQLSetConnectAttr(
  ...,SQL_ATTR_AUTOCOMMIT,SQL_AUTOCOMMIT_OFF,...);
```

If most of your transactions contain only one data-change statement, then auto-commit mode should be on (providing, of course, that there's no reason to believe a ROLLBACK will be necessary). Although auto-commit mode is ugly, it is ODBC's default. Also, short transactions are slightly faster when auto-commit is on, because the client doesn't need to send a separate COMMIT message to the server.

A third way to speed up data changes is to put UPDATE and DELETE statements inside fetch loops, in order to make changes to the row at the "current" cursor position (that is, the last row fetched). The requisite statements here are:

```
UPDATE ... WHERE CURRENT OF <cursor>

DELETE ... WHERE CURRENT OF <cursor>
```

WARNING   Programs that use the WHERE CURRENT OF versions of UPDATE or DELETE (the **positioned UPDATE/DELETE** statements) can have trouble with locks. If you use these statements, you'll also need to concern yourself with transaction isolation modes, cursor sensitivity, and—above all!—timing (see Chapter 15, "Locks"). You don't want to enter a fetch loop that displays rows on the screen and waits for a user to change what's displayed, do you? Well—maybe you do. But in that case, you should use row locators.

After you've executed a data-change statement, you can call SQLRowCount to find out how many rows were affected. Unfortunately, to support SQLRow-Count a DBMS must track and pass more information than is necessary for the performance of the data change itself. Some DBMSs allow you to turn counting off, and you should do so if your program doesn't make use of SQLRowCount.

The Bottom Line: Data-Change Statements

Pass multiple data-change statements at once whenever possible, to reduce the overhead of network transmissions.

Set auto-commit mode based on the number of data-change statements in your transactions. For one data change, auto-commit should be on. For multiple data changes, auto-commit should be off.

Put UPDATE and DELETE statements inside fetch loops and make changes to the row at the current cursor position—but read Chapter 15, "Locks" before you do so.

Turn counting off if your program doesn't make use of SQLRowCount.

Catalog Functions

It's hard to mention catalog functions without bubbling in fury. Their design is contemptible, their effect is pernicious, they are a confusion and a disgrace. That being said, they are also frequently useful and support for catalog functions is far better than support for selections from standard SQL's INFORMATION_SCHEMA tables.

There is one vital datum that you won't find in any INFORMATION_SCHEMA table and therefore can't determine with any standard SQL:1999 function. We refer to the information provided by the ODBC function SQLSpecial-

Columns. Any general program needs to know the optimal set of columns that can be used to identify a row in a table uniquely, and knowing the primary key is not necessarily enough. Of course, one should be able to access a table via primary-key data. The trouble is that there may be faster alternatives, such as the ROWID or some other unique key. When the information from SQLSpecialColumns is available, you can do a data change like this:

1. SELECT a row.
2. Display the row contents on the screen, as part of a dialog box in which the user can change any column data, except the special columns.
3. End the current transaction so that all locks are released.
4. Accept the user's changes.
5. If the user is making a change, SELECT the row again to make sure no other user has made a change, then do:
   ```
   UPDATE (or DELETE) ...
      WHERE <special column> = <original unchanged value>
   ```

The essential element in this plan is that there must be a quick unique identifier, and that's the information SQLSpecialColumns can provide. (See Chapter 15, "Locks," for a more complete example with an analogous technique.)

The Bottom Line: Catalog Functions

Use ODBC's SQLSpecialColumns function to find the optimal set of columns that can be used to identify a row in a table uniquely. Use those columns in search conditions to improve the performance of data-change statements.

Parting Shots

"All the captains voted for themselves first, and for Themistocles second."
—Herodotus, *Histories*

Frequently, the preference is to program for an interface that a language's producer promotes, such as ADO, OLE/DB, or PERL:DBI—but those interfaces may have a lower layer, namely ODBC.

Alternatively, and also frequently, the preference is to program for an interface that a DBMS's producer promotes, such as Oracle OCI or DB Lib—but those interfaces have a higher or alternate layer, namely ODBC.

Because it can't do anything with objects and can't do anything without pointers, ODBC often needs some bridge or mediator to fit the tastes of the modern age. If we were to try to summarize what we think is the general attitude though, it's that ODBC is a solid and near-universal choice—albeit a second choice.

ODBC applications are usually faster than non-ODBC applications, despite attempts by interested parties to show otherwise. We believe that the commandment—Use ODBC—is in itself a good optimization tip. If you accept that at this point, then this chapter has been useful.

13

JDBC

Sun says that JDBC is not an acronym for anything, and www.sun.com says it stands for Java Database Connectivity. Go figure. Anyway, JDBC is the *de facto* standard API for Java programs and **applets**. In this chapter, we won't try to compete with the giant reference books on the subject[1]—remember, we said in Chapter 1, "Facilis Descensus Averni," that we assume you're already familiar with (among other things) programming with an SQL API such as JDBC. Our goal is more specific: to suggest improvements in Java applications written for SQL DBMSs.

In simple terms, a JDBC driver makes it possible to do three things:

- Establish a connection with a data source
- Send queries and data changes to the data source
- Process the results

Listing 13–1 shows a short portion of a JDBC program.

---

1. Such as *JDBC™ API Tutorial and Reference, Second Edition: Universal Data Access For the Java™ 2 Platform*, by Seth White, Maydene Fisher, Rick Cattell, and Mark Hapner. Addison-Wesley, 1999.

Listing 13–1 *A short JDBC program example*

```
Connection con = DriverManager.getConnection(
                "jdbc:odbc:driver",
                "login_name",
                "password");

Statement stmt = con.createStatement();

ResultSet rs = stmt.executeQuery(
                "SELECT column1, column2, column3 FROM Table1");

  while (rs.next()) {
    String s = rs.getString("column1");
    float f = rs.getFloat("column2");
    int i = rs.getInt("column3");
  }

...
```

As Listing 13-1 shows, a typical Java program goes like this: You connect, you query, maybe you update or do something else with the result set. As with ODBC, there's some prepping work at the start to discover what the DBMS can do and what the database contains. (This is necessary because a Java program is general and portable, and capable of ad-hoc decisions. If it weren't, we'd be skipping this chapter entirely in favor of Chapter 11, "Stored Procedures.") In our discussion of JDBC, therefore, we'll focus on performance and portability both, under four main headings: "Connections," "Query Prepping," "Result Sets," and "Data Changes." We'll use JDBC 2.0 for all our examples.

Connections

The traditional and most popular way to connect via JDBC is with the Driver-Manager class, for example:

```
Class.forName("sun.jdbc.odbc.JdbcOdbcDriver");
con = DriverManager.getConnection(
      "jdbc:odbc:ocelot",                    // URL
      "PETER",                               // user
      "SESAME");                             // password
```

In fact, though, there is a lower accessible level. When you call `getConnection`, each registered driver is polled until the first one that responds for the given **Uniform Resource Locator (URL)** is found. This **method** is used in the `Driver` class:

```
con = myDriver.connect(
    "jdbc:odbc:ocelot",
    "UID=PETER;PWD=SESAME");
```

You can bypass `DriverManager`, and call the `Driver` connect method directly. If there are 50 JDBC registered drivers and you want the last one registered, a direct call will be a bit faster.

The newer—and recommended—way to connect via JDBC is with the `DataSource` class, for example:

```
DataSource ds = (DataSource)ctx.lookup("jdbc/ocelot");
Connection con = ds.getConnection("PETER","SESAME");
```

For this to work, the name `"jdbc/ocelot"` must be registered with a **Java Naming and Directory Interface (JNDI)**. Because JNDI naming is probably somebody else's job, and because it doesn't always work, try the `DataSource` method first, and if that throws an exception, then call the `DriverManager` method.

`DataSource` and `DriverManager` both deliver the same thing: a `Connection`. The difference between the two is that the `DataSource` method allows for connection pooling.

Connection Pooling

Assume you have a Java application and a service named DM. DM is always running. Here's what happens with **connection pooling.**[2]

1. The application calls for a connection. DM receives the call. DM gets a `Connection` to the Data Source the usual way (by calling `Driver.`

---

2. Sometimes connection pooling also happens at the middle-tier level (for example, IBM WebSphere implements it)—but middle-tier connection pooling isn't part of JDBC 2.0.

connect), and returns it to the application (see Figure 13–1). But first DM stores a copy of the Connection in its own memory.

2. The application calls disconnect. DM receives the call, and returns an OK to the application. But DM doesn't disconnect from the Data Source (see Figure 13–2).

3. The application calls for a connection again. DM receives this call. DM sees that an extant Connection already is in its memory, so instead of calling Driver.connect, DM returns the existing Connection to the application.

To make it complicated, there's one more wrinkle: the application in the third step can be a *different* application. That is, Application #2 can reuse a Connection after Application #1 has stopped. In other words, DM keeps a "pool" of Connections rather than a mere "cache" of Connections.

The concept of connection pooling brings up two questions:

- Does this mean that a Connection with the data source is immortal? Answer—No. In practice, a Connection is disconnected if it is dormant for a long time.

Figure 13–1   *Application, DM, and data source linked*

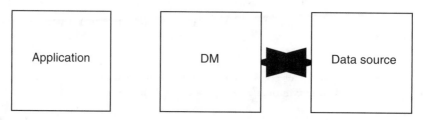

Figure 13–2   *Application and DM connection broken*

- If there's more than one `Connection`, how will DM get the right one? Answer—DM stores the URL and the user strings along with the `Connection`.

Suppose connecting takes three seconds—which is awful but within the range of possibilities. In that case, connecting 100 times takes 300 seconds. But with connection pooling, connecting 100 times takes only 3 seconds, as long as there was no true disconnection.

You could implement connection pooling yourself, by caching `Connections` in some persistent shared place (perhaps an **Enterprise Bean**). Really, though, it's better to let the system handle the administrative details. So your sole job with connection pooling is:

- Allow it to happen by using the right classes.
- If you connect and disconnect and reconnect, use precisely the same parameter values every time.
- If you know that a particular `Connection` will be needed only once, avoid connection pooling.

Pooling is good for Web use, but don't expect `Connection` settings to be preserved.

Connection Settings

A new `Connection` has some fields that are set to default values. These default values are often inappropriate for the sort of work planned, so JDBC provides two `Connection` methods that you can use to change inappropriate settings:

- `setAutoCommit`
  Changes the auto-commit flag.
- `setTransactionIsolation`
  Raises or lowers the transaction isolation level.

Auto-commit

Assume you have a `Connection` called con. Now consider this instruction:

```
con.setAutoCommit(false);
```

In JDBC, the auto-commit flag is `true` by default. There is a simple explanation of what that means, and there is also an arcane explanation. While the simple explanation serves well as a first take, the arcane explanation is truer and contains extra information that you need to know.

- The Simple Rules for Auto-Commit:

  If auto-commit is `true`, COMMIT happens automatically after every SQL statement. If auto-commit is `false`, it doesn't.

- The Arcane Rules for Auto-Commit:

  The arcane explanation is shown as pseudocode in Listing 13-2. In the pseudocode, note that "method completion" means either successful or unsuccessful completion. In theory, this means COMMIT happens just before the return from `executeUpdate`; in practice, some drivers issue an asynchronous COMMIT request and return before the request finishes.

Listing 13-2 *The arcane rules for auto-commit pseudocode*

```
if (auto-commit is true) {
  if (method is executeUpdate) {
    COMMIT happens upon method completion }
  if (method is executeQuery) {
    // NB: "closed" is defined later in this chapter
    COMMIT happens when result set is closed }
  if (method is execute) {
    action varies; depends on SQL statement(s) }
}

if (auto-commit is false) {
  if (schema-change statement e.g. CREATE/ALTER/DROP) {
    COMMIT happens upon statement completion, maybe }
  else {
    nothing happens }
}
```

A default setting of `true` for auto-commit is not SQL Standard-compliant, and some vendors recommend that you set the flag to `false`. Here's their reasoning:

- COMMIT causes transaction end, and with some DBMSs, a transaction end causes prepared statements to become unprepared. For example, this sequence won't work with PostgreSQL:

```
PreparedStatement pstmt = con.prepareStatement(
                          "UPDATE Table1 SET ...");
pstmt.executeUpdate();  // COMMIT happens automatically
pstmt.executeUpdate();  // fails, pstmt no longer prepared
```

Portability   None of the Big Eight cancels prepared statements when you COMMIT.

- COMMIT is expensive, so when you have two or more data-change statements it's always faster to delay the COMMIT until after the final statement finishes.

- Auto-commit is inappropriate for distributed transactions. (Distributed transactions occur when two DBMSs are trying to work in concert.)

On the other hand, if auto-commit is `false`, you must explicitly call the Connection's `commit` method—and that's significant because it causes a message to be sent over the network.

If you want to prevent commits from happening too soon, and yet get the performance advantage of auto-commit, here's how.

- First, read the arcane rules (Listing 13–2) again and notice that the COMMIT happens on method completion. This means you should do multiple data changes with a single method call and a compound SQL statement, like this:

```
Statement stmt = con.createStatement(
                 "BEGIN UPDATE ... UPDATE ... END");
stmt.executeUpdate();
```

- Second, remember that the `setAutoCommit` method can be turned off and on at any time, like this:

```
con.setAutoCommit(false);  // turn auto-commit off
stmt.executeUpdate();      // do statement, delay COMMIT
con.setAutoCommit(true);   // turn auto-commit on
stmt.executeUpdate();      // do statement, do COMMIT
```

The bottom line: People who don't understand the arcane rules should turn auto-commit `off` and use `con.commit()`. Now that you know the rules, though, *you* can control when commits happen without using `con.commit()`.

Isolation level

Again, assume you have a Connection called con. This time, consider these four variations of the same instruction:

```
con.setTransactionIsolation(
    TRANSACTION_READ_UNCOMMITTED);

con.setTransactionIsolation(
    TRANSACTION_READ_COMMITTED);

con.setTransactionIsolation(
    TRANSACTION_REPEATABLE_READ);

con.setTransactionIsolation(
    TRANSACTION_SERIALIZABLE);
```

The appropriate isolation setting for a transaction might be something higher or lower than READ COMMITTED, but there is one definite matter: You have some idea of what your program is going to do, but the DBMS has no idea. So the DBMS's default choice of isolation level is probably a poorer choice than the one you'd make. (The choice of isolation level, and the related matter of read-only transactions—which is controllable with the con.setReadOnly method—is one we consider in Chapter 15, "Locks.")

Connections and DBMS Info

Given a Connection con, you can get an object dbmd with:

```
DatabaseMetaData dbmd = con.getMetaData();
```

The term "database metadata" is misleading because your first need is static information about the DBMS—*not* the database. For example, suppose that you want to create a table with a VARCHAR column—but if the DBMS is Oracle, you want it to be a VARCHAR2 column instead. So you get the dbmd information before you pick the command, like this:

```
String s = dbmd.getDatabaseProductName();        // get DBMS name
  if (strcmp(s,"Oracle") {
  Statement stmt = con.createStatement(
                "CREATE TABLE T1 col1 VARCHAR2(10) ... "); }
```

```
else {
Statement stmt = con.createStatement(
                "CREATE TABLE T1 col1 VARCHAR(10) ... "); }
```

Tip	Since this is static information, you can retrieve `String`s once, when you connect, and keep it in memory until you disconnect. Caching static information, so that you don't have to send more than one query to the DBMS for the same information, is always good.

There are well over 80 dbmd methods to retrieve DBMS information. That's daunting. To save you from worrying about all of them, we ran the most important methods on the Big Eight. The results are shown in Tables 13–1 through 13–5. We believe these DBMS information tables will be useful because they show you what the least common denominators/worst-case scenarios are for the dbmd methods we checked.

To keep the DBMS information tables compact, we abbreviated the headings.

- Table 13–1 contains 26 "get" calls—that is, where the heading shows the call as `CatalogSeparator`, the actual name is `getCatalogSeparator`.

- Table 13–2 contains four "nulls" calls—where the heading shows the call as `AreSortedAtEnd`, the actual name is `nullsAreSortedAtEnd`.

- Table 13–3 contains six "stores" calls—where the heading shows the call as `LowercaseIdentifiers`, the actual name is `storesLowercase-Identifiers`.

- Table 13–4 contains 41 "supports" calls—where the heading shows the call as `AlterTableWithAddColumn`, the actual name is `supportsAlter-TableWithAddColumn`.

- And finally, Table 13–5 contains one "is" call—the actual name of the call is `isCatalogAtStart`, as shown.

In each table, a column is (a) "T" if the DBMS's response to the call is `true`, (b) "F" if the DBMS's response to the call is `false`, and (c) remains blank if the DBMS either returned an empty string or did not respond to the call. For Table 13–1, a "0" in a column means there is either no limit, or the DBMS did not return a known limit for that call.

Table 13-1 *DBMS Information According to DatabaseMetaData Methods; "get" Calls*

Actual Name Starts with "get"

get Call	IBM	Informix	Ingres	InterBase	Microsoft	MySQL	Oracle	Sybase
CatalogSeparator	.						@	.
CatalogTerm		D			d	d	DL	d
DefaultTransactionIsolationLevel	R-C	R-C	S	R-C	R-C	R-C	R-C	R-R
IdentifierQuoteString	"	"	"	"		"	"	"
MaxCatalogNameLength	0	128	0	0	128	0	0	30
MaxCharLiteralLength	4000	0	0	0	524288	0	0	0
MaxColumnNameLength	18	128	32	32	128	64	30	30
MaxColumnsInGroupBy	500	0	300	0	0	0	0	16
MaxColumnsInIndex	16	16	300	0	16	16	0	31
MaxColumnsInOrderBy	500	0	300	0	0	0	0	16
MaxColumnsInSelect	500	0	300	0	4096	0	1000	0
MaxColumnsInTable	500	0	300	0	1024	0	1000	8106
MaxConnections	0	0	0	0	0	0	0	0
MaxCursorNameLength	18	128	64	18	128	64	30	18
MaxIndexLength	255	255	0	0	900	120	0	0
MaxProcedureNameLength	256	128	32	32	134	0	30	30
MaxRowSize	4005	32767	2008	0	8060	0	0	8106
MaxSchemaNameLength	8	32	32	0	128	0	30	30
MaxStatementLength	32765	0	30000	0	524288	8192	0	0
MaxStatements	0	0	1	0	1	0	0	1
MaxTableNameLength	18	128	32	32	128	64	30	30
MaxTablesInSelect	0	0	0	0	32	32	0	0
MaxUserNameLength	128	32	32	128	128	16	30	30
ProcedureTerm	sp	Pr	dp	PR	sp	p	Pr	SP
SchemaTerm	s	O	U		o	o	O	o
SearchStringEscape	\	\	\	\	\	\	\	\

To use the tables, check for the appropriate call when you're constructing a SELECT statement. For example, if this is your SELECT:

```
SELECT column1, SUM(column2), column3
  FROM Table1
  GROUP BY column1, column3
  ORDER BY column1, column3, column2
```

check these three lines in the DBMS information tables:

```
getMaxColumnsInGroupBy          // see Table 13-1
getMaxColumnsInOrderBy          // see Table 13-1
supportsGroupBy                 // see Table 13-4
```

Checking the `getMaxColumnsInGroupBy` and `GetMaxColumnsInOrderBy` calls will reassure you that all DBMSs allow at least 16 columns in GROUP BY and ORDER BY clauses—so you'll know the SELECT doesn't have too many. And checking the `supportsGroupBy` call will tell you that all DBMSs allow GROUP BY—so GROUP BY in the SELECT is always legal. With this information, you can save yourself the bother of writing special code in case the DBMS rejects your syntax. Caveat: Sometimes a DBMS will return incorrect information. For example, here is a method to ask about standard SQL-92 conformance:

```
boolean b = dbmd.supportsANSI92EntryLevelSQL();
```

MySQL will return `true` for this call, but the correct answer is `false` because MySQL doesn't support several SQL-92 Entry Level requirements. Here's another example: Sybase returns `false` for every one of the stores calls shown in Table 13-3. This is obviously incorrect—Sybase must store identifiers in some way!

Notes on Table 13-1:

- `getCatalogTerm` row

    This row is "d" if the response is "database," "DL" if the response is "Database Link," and "D" if the response is "Database." A blank means the DBMS did not respond to the call.

- getDefaultTransactionIsolationLevel row

  The following abbreviations are used for the isolation levels:

  ```
  R=U for READ UNCOMMITTED / IsolationLevel(1)
  R=C for READ COMMITTED   / IsolationLevel(2)
  R=R for REPEATABLE READ  / IsolationLevel(4)
  S for   SERIALIZABLE     / IsolationLevel(8)
  ```

- getMaxColumnsInGroupBy row

  :: For Informix, InterBase, Microsoft, MySQL, and Oracle, our tests showed it was possible to group at least 20 columns.

  :: For Sybase, our tests showed it was possible to group at least 20 columns. This differs from Sybase's response to getMaxColumnsIn-GroupBy, which returns 16.

- getMaxColumnsInOrderBy row

  :: For InterBase and Oracle, our tests showed it was possible to sort up to 254 columns.

  :: For Informix, Microsoft, and MySQL, our tests showed it was possible to sort at least 1,000 columns.

  :: For Sybase, our tests showed it was possible to sort up to 31 columns. This differs from Sybase's response to getMaxColumnsInOrderBy, which returns 16.

- getProcedureTerm row

  This row is "sp" if the response is "stored procedure," "dp" if the response is "database procedure," "PR" if the response is "PROCEDURE," "p" if the response is "procedure," "Pr" if the response is "Procedure," and "SP" if the response is "Stored Procedure."

- getSchemaTerm row

  This row is "s" if the response is "schema", "U" if the response is "User-name," "o" if the response is "owner," and "O" if the response is "Owner." A blank means the DBMS did not respond to the call.

Table 13–2   *DBMS Information According to DatabaseMetaData Methods; "nulls" Calls*
Actual Name Starts with "nulls"

nulls Call	IBM	Informix	Ingres	InterBase	Microsoft	MySQL	Oracle	Sybase
AreSortedAtEnd	F	F	F	F	F	F	F	F
AreSortedAtStart	F	F	F	F	F	T	F	F
AreSortedHigh	T	F	T	T	F	F	F	T
AreSortedLow	F	T	F	F	T	F	T	F

Notes on Table 13-2:

- For InterBase, our tests showed that NULLs sort At End—that is, NULLs come out at the end of a sorted list when you ORDER BY ... ASC as well as when you ORDER BY ... DESC. This differs from InterBase's response to (a) NullsAreSortedAtEnd, which returns false and (b) NullsAreSortedHigh, which returns true.

- For MySQL and Sybase, our tests showed that NULLs sort Low—that is, as if NULLs are less than all other values. In the first case, this differs from MySQL's response to (a) NullsAreSortedLow, which returns false and (b) NullsAreSortedAtStart, which returns true. In the second case, this differs from Sybase's response to (a) NullsAreSortedLow, which returns false and (b) NullsAreSortedHigh, which returns true.

- For Oracle, our tests showed that NULLs sort High—that is, as if NULLs are greater than all other values. This differs from Oracle's response to (a) NullsAreSortedHigh, which returns false and (b) NullsAreSortedLow, which returns true.

Table 13–3 *DBMS Information According to DatabaseMetaData Methods; "stores" Calls*

Actual Name Starts with "stores"

stores Call	IBM	Informix	Ingres	InterBase	Microsoft	MySQL	Oracle	Sybase
LowercaseIdentifiers	F	T	T	F	F	F	F	F
LowercaseQuotedIdentifiers	F	T	T	F	F	F	F	F
MixedCaseIdentifiers	F	F	F	T	T	T	F	F
MixedCaseQuotedIdentifiers	F	F	F	F	T	F	F	F
UppercaseIdentifiers	T	F	T	F	F	F	T	F
UppercaseQuotedIdentifiers	F	F	F	F	F	F	F	F

Table 13–4 *DBMS Information According to DatabaseMetaData Methods; "supports" Calls*

Actual Name Starts with "supports"

supports Call	IBM	Informix	Ingres	InterBase	Microsoft	MySQL	Oracle	Sybase
AlterTableWithAddColumn	T	T	F	T	T	T	T	T
AlterTableWithDropColumn	F	T	F	T	F	T	F	F
ANSI92EntryLevelSQL	T	T	T	T	T	T	T	T
ANSI92FullSQL	F	F	F	F	F	F	F	F
ANSI92IntermediateSQL	F	F	F	F	F	F	F	F
ColumnAliases	T	F	F	T	T	T	T	T
CoreSQLGrammar	T	T	T	T	T	T	T	F
CorrelatedSubqueries	T	F	T	T	T	F	T	T
DataDefinitionAndDataManipulationTransactions	T	F	T	T	T	F	T	F
DataManipulationTransactionsOnly	F	F	F	F	F	F	T	T
ExpressionsInOrderBy	T	F	F	F	T	T	T	T
ExtendedSQLGrammar	T	F	F	T	F	F	F	F
FullOuterJoins	F	F	F	F	F	T	F	F

Feature						
GroupBy	T	T	T	T	T	T
IntegrityEnhancementFacility	T	F	T	T	F	T
LikeEscapeClause	T	T	T	T	T	F
MinimumSQLGrammar	T	T	T	T	T	T
MixedCaseIdentifiers	F	F	T	F	T	T
MixedCaseQuotedIdentifiers	T	T	T	F	T	F
nonNullableColumns	T	T	T	T	T	T
OpenCursorsAcrossCommit	T	F	F	F	T	F
OpenCursorsAcrossRollback	F	F	F	F	T	F
OrderByUnrelated	T	T	T	T	T	T
OuterJoins	T	T	T	T	T	T
PositionedDelete	T	T	T	T	T	T
PositionedUpdate	T	T	T	T	T	T
SelectForUpdate	T	T	T	F	T	T
StoredProcedures	T	T	T	F	T	T
SubqueriesInComparisons	T	T	T	F	T	T
SubqueriesInExists	T	T	T	F	T	T
SubqueriesInIns	T	T	T	F	T	T
SubqueriesInQuantifieds	T	T	T	F	T	T
TableCorrelationNames	T	T	T	T	T	T
TransactionIsolationLevel(0)	F	F	F	F	F	F
TransactionIsolationLevel(1)	T	T	F	T	F	T
TransactionIsolationLevel(2)	T	F	T	T	T	T
TransactionIsolationLevel(4)	T	T	T	F	F	F
TransactionIsolationLevel(8)	T	T	T	T	T	T
Transactions	T	F	T	T	T	T
Union	T	T	T	F	T	T
UnionAll	T	T	T	T	T	T

Table 13–5 *DBMS Information According to DatabaseMetaData Methods; "is" Calls*
Actual Name as Shown

is Call	IBM	Informix	Ingres	InterBase	Microsoft	MySQL	Oracle	Sybase
isCatalogAtStart	F	T	F	T	T	T	F	T

The Bottom Line: Connections

The traditional and most popular way to connect via JDBC is with the `Driver-Manager` class, but there is a lower accessible level: the `Driver` class. A direct call to the `Driver` class is faster if there are many registered drivers and you want one of the last ones registered.

The newer—and recommended—way to connect via JDBC is with the `DataSource` class. `DataSource` and `DriverManager` both deliver the same thing: a `Connection`. The difference between the two is that `DataSource` allows for connection pooling.

If connecting takes 3 seconds, then connecting 100 times takes 300 seconds. With connection pooling, connecting 100 times takes only 3 seconds, as long as there was no true disconnection.

Your sole job with connection pooling is to allow it to happen by using the right classes. If you connect and disconnect and reconnect, use precisely the same parameter values every time.

If you know that a particular `Connection` will be needed only once, avoid connection pooling.

In JDBC, the auto-commit flag is `true` by default.

When auto-commit is `true`, COMMIT happens automatically after every SQL statement. When auto-commit is `false`, you must explicitly call the `Connection`'s `commit` method—and that's significant because it causes a message to be sent over the network.

The Arcane Rules for Auto-Commit are important. Remember them.

COMMIT is expensive, so when you have two or more data-change statements it's always faster to delay the COMMIT until after the final statement finishes.

Auto-commit is inappropriate for distributed transactions.

People who don't understand the Arcane Rules for Auto-Commit should turn auto-commit `off` and use `con.commit()`. Now that you know the rules, though, you can control when COMMIT happens without using `con.commit()`.

Driver Types

JDBC drivers are grouped into four types depending on their neutrality (a vendor-neutral driver can access more than one DBMS brand) and on their use of non-Java code. A driver's type is determined by the following criteria:

Driver Type	Vendor-Neutral	Vendor-Specific	Needs Non-Java DLL	100% Java
Type 1	Yes	–	Yes	–
Type 2	–	Yes	Yes	–
Type 3	Yes	–	–	Yes
Type 4	–	Yes	–	Yes

A Type 1 driver, also called a *JDBC-ODBC bridge*, works with every DBMS. Its calls need to go through a conversion process: JDBC to ODBC to native API code. A famous example of a JDBC-ODBC bridge is Sun.jdbc.odbc.JdbcOdbcDriver.

A Type 2 driver is theoretically somewhat faster than a Type 1 driver because call conversion is more direct: JDBC to native API code. There are no well-known examples of a Type 2 driver.

A Type 3 driver, also called a *net driver*, comes in two parts: (a) a small Java driver that can be downloaded by applets and (b) a middleware package that receives from the driver, translates, and passes on to the server. Sometimes the middleware package uses a Type 1 or Type 2 driver. Famous examples of Type 3 drivers are Merant's SequeLink and IDS Software's IDS Driver.

A Type 4 driver, also called a *two-tier driver*, is locked into a particular DBMS brand, which the driver interfaces to at a low level by emulating what the DBMS's native client library passes in network messages. Famous examples of Type 4 drivers are Ashna's JTurbo and I-net's Sprinta 2000.

Different sources have noted that Type 1 involves a double conversion—so its function overhead must be slow, while Type 4 is written entirely in Java—so it must be slower than native code, while Type 3 is smallest—so its load time must be fast, and on and on. Such factors affect the client alone. Thus, while such factors could affect response time (the time elapsed between the user pressing Enter and the reply appearing on the screen), they do not affect throughput (the number of requests that the server handles per hour).

Since throughput is what counts, it turns out that the driver type alone is not what performance depends on. For example, benchmark tests have found Sun's Type 1 JdbcOdbcDriver to be as fast and as reliable as some nonfree commercial drivers. However, performance *does* strongly depend on the brand name. The best JDBC driver runs up to three times faster than the worst. The reasons that one driver can beat another are (a) caching or pooling so that requests to the target DBMS are reduced and (b) good knowledge of the target DBMS and available commands for it. In other words, SQL performance tuning!

Cache static information, so that you don't have to send more than one query to the DBMS for the same information.

Query Prepping

In this part of the chapter, we will discuss how to "prep" a query—that is, how to pave the way, create the right environment, and optimize the conditions so that the query will run well. We'll follow a query through all its phases: making the statement, getting metadata, setting result set flags, fetching, and using the getXXX methods.

We know this is a lot of trouble for one little SELECT. For many situations you'd be better off following this advice—Just do it! Our painstaking approach is an illustration of all the possible optimizations at each stage, rather than an order that you must actually follow for your own queries. Once you've scanned through our illustration, though, you'll find many occasions to employ a subset of these steps.

Query Statement

We begin our illustration with the step of writing an SQL statement. You can make a SELECT statement with Statement and execute it with executeQuery. Here's an example:

```
Statement stmt1 = con.CreateStatement();

ResultSet rs1 = stmt1.executeQuery(
            "SELECT * FROM Table1");
...

Statement stmt2 = con.CreateStatement();

ResultSet rs2 = stmt2.executeQuery(
            "SELECT * FROM Table2");
```

Stop. Why did we make two stmts? Are they independent?

If stmt2 doesn't have to follow stmt1, then you can set up a second thread and run it in parallel. The idea of "Use two threads" is applicable in practically any case; we'll just mention it once and leave repetitions to your imagination from now on. Note, however, that not all ODBC drivers are reentrant—"Use two threads" is inappropriate if you're using a JDBC-ODBC bridge.

If `stmt2` does have to follow `stmt1`, then you should not make `stmt2` at all. Instead, just reuse `stmt1`, like this:

```
Statement stmt1 = con.CreateStatement();

ResultSet rs1 = stmt1.executeQuery(
                "SELECT * FROM Table1");
...

ResultSet rs2 = stmt1.executeQuery(
                "SELECT * FROM Table2");
```

We're more concerned about reusing objects than a Java programmer normally is for two reasons:

- Garbage collection won't do a complete cleanup because `create-Statement` causes objects to be made outside the program, in the driver and in the DBMS.

- By re-using `stmt1`, we've caused an automatic close of the existing result set. A close *must* happen; otherwise, memory leaks are possible.

Query Syntax

Use consistent, standard, trick-free SQL syntax. You can, of course, use `{escape}` additions for portability. Some drivers try to cache recently used SQL statements, so it's handy if they can find the times that the syntax is duplicated.

getBestRowIdentifier

Several methods in the `DatabaseMetaData` class can be called "catalog functions" because each one has an exact analog among the ODBC catalog functions. The two most interesting methods are `getIndexInfo`, which is equivalent to the ODBC function `SQLStatistics`, and `getBestRowIdentifier`, which is equivalent to ODBC's `SQLSpecialColumns`.

We discussed the importance of `SQLSpecialColumns` in Chapter 12, "ODBC," so we'll just add two remarks about the `getBestRowIdentifier` method here.

- It's possible to over-depend on `getBestRowIdentifier`. The best search will depend not only on the identified column, but also on the desired value. For example, sometimes the optimizer will decide that an index called `Index1` is the best index—but if you search for a very common value, then the optimizer may decide not to use the index. The `getBestRowIdentifier` data doesn't reflect such transient considerations.

- `getBestRowIdentifier` is expensive because all catalog functions are expensive.

The general tips for all catalog functions are:

- Avoid search patterns or blank string arguments.
- Cache the results.
- Make sure you *need* to know the information before using a catalog function.

If you use `getBestRowIdentifier` in order to give the user a choice of columns to use for searching, you will probably have to call `getIndexInfo` and `getColumns` as well. But you can get most of the data using a single call if you know how the DBMS stores catalog metadata.

Remember that the best row identifier is often the DBMS-specific ROWID pseudocolumn. This will not appear in a list created by `getColumns`.

ResultSetMetaData

You should retrieve information about a result set before you get the result set itself. You can do this with a prepared statement. Here's an example:

```
PreparedStatement pstmt = con.preparedStatement(
                    "SELECT * FROM Table1");

ResultSetMetaData rsmd = pstmt.getMetaData();

int i = rsmd.getColumnCount();
```

This example would be a failure if "preparing" and "executing" took the same amount of time. Luckily, most DBMSs will prepare only when you *ask* them to prepare. So this goes quickly.

Once you have an `rsmd` and a column count, you can check each individual column to see whether there should be some change in the strategy. The important methods for this purpose are:

- `getColumnType`

  Retrieves a number indicating the data type. For example, if the column is VARCHAR, the return is 12.

- `getPrecision`

  For character and binary columns, this call retrieves the column size.

- `isNullable`

  Returns `true` if the column can contain NULL.

The decisions you can make with the type, precision, and nullable information include:

- Is this column really necessary during the initial display?

  This criterion is important especially if the column is a BLOB or other large object data type. Remember that even a small BLOB requires extra access time if it's not stored with the rest of the row. Some Web applications will retrieve all the non-BLOBs, then go back and get the BLOBs later if the job is idle or the user clicks for more.

- Is the entire value of the column needed?

  This criterion is important especially if the column is long. If your first display is on an 80-column-wide screen and you see that `column1` is defined as VARCHAR(2000), it's best to retrieve something like:

  ```
  SELECT SUBSTRING(column1 FROM 1 FOR 80)
      FROM Table1
  ```

  rather than:

  ```
  SELECT column1
      FROM Table1
  ```

  If the column is a CHAR but still looks a bit large, a TRIM function is appropriate because DBMSs like Oracle will otherwise return the entire column—including trailing spaces. If you don't want to redo the query but you perceive that lengths are too great, you can limit the returnable size for all character or binary columns with:

  ```
  pstmt.setMaxFieldSize(512);
  ```

  Do this before attaching any parameters to the `pstmt`.

- Is it necessary to test for NULLs?

  The `isNullable` method will tell you whether you have to test for NULLs every time you use a `getXXX` method later, or whether you can skip that step because the column is non-nullable anyway. This is the *only* valid test for nullable columns. Do not depend on information returned by the getColumns catalog function—a column's defined nullability is irrelevant if the query contains an outer join. Besides, any call to a catalog function is going to be more expensive than a call to ResultSetMetaData.

Bottom line: There is still time to abort or revise the query at this stage. All that's happened so far is a prepare. If you decide to continue, keep the rsmd. There are other rsmd methods that are useful for displays.

Dummy Queries

Some DBMSs cannot do a "prepare" alone. They have to go through an "execute" phase as well in order to get result set metadata. That would wreck our plan—we're not ready to look at a result set yet. The traditional work around for this problem is to execute a dummy query. A dummy query is a SELECT statement that you run solely in order to retrieve the ResultSetMetaData information. It is easy to spot because it contains an always-false WHERE clause, for example:

```
SELECT column1, column2
   FROM Table1
   WHERE 0 = 1
```

It might help to replace the literal with an indexed column, like this:

```
SELECT column1, column2
   FROM Table1
   WHERE column1 < <some impossible value>
```

But the best thing you can do is replace dummy queries with real ones. With any of the Big Eight, you can skip the dummy-query phase and prepare the SQL statement that you really intend to execute. (Unfortunately we can't say the same for drivers. We know of one commercial driver that has trouble using a prepared Statement for getting ResultSetMetaData.)

Query Settings

Some settings apply to `stmt` or `pstmt` objects. These settings affect the way that result sets work. In this section, we'll look at three of them: `Scroll Type`, `Concurrency Type`, and `FetchSize`.

Scroll Type

The `Scroll Type` setting has three options:

```
con.createStatement("SELECT * FROM Table1",
                ResultSet.TYPE_FORWARD_ONLY);

con.createStatement("SELECT * FROM Table1",
                ResultSet.TYPE_SCROLL_INSENSITIVE);

con.createStatement("SELECT * FROM Table1",
                ResultSet.TYPE_SCROLL_SENSITIVE);
```

The default scroll type is TYPE_FORWARD_ONLY, and that's definitely the way to leave it if you can tolerate going through the result set from start to end, without skipping or retreating. The other two scroll types are scroll cursors and are both expensive and hard to implement. You will find that scroll cursors are troublesome with some DBMSs.

INSENSITIVE cursors are for high concurrency situations, and their performance is good if the transactions are read-only. What happens behind the scenes is that somebody (probably the JDBC driver) either creates a temporary local table on the server, or fetches the entire result set into a local cache off the server. The effect is that the initial query execution, or possibly the first fetch after the query execution, will be slow. On the other hand, all subsequent fetches will be blazingly fast because it's all coming out of a nearby cache. Don't use an insensitive cursor for a single-row query, because the driver will waste time copying to a cache when it could send directly to you. And don't use an insensitive cursor if the query contains LOBs, because caches lose their value if they overflow the available memory.

SENSITIVE cursors are for low concurrency situations when you want to see whether any other user changes a row while you have it. What happens behind the scenes is that the driver retrieves a list of all the best row identifier values (probably ROWIDs or primary keys), and stores them in cache. When the application asks for a fetch of, for example, Row #14, the driver looks up the value associated with that row—say it's ROWID #123456. Then the driver selects a single row from the server with:

```
... WHERE ROWID = 123456
```

The server returns that row, and the driver passes it on to the application. Thus you can watch a screen change dynamically as other users change the rows you selected. You should not use a sensitive cursor if a call to getBest-RowIdentifier tells you that there is no fast, persistent, unique column lookup possible for the table from which you're selecting.

Concurrency type

The Concurrency Type setting has two options:

```
con.createStatement("SELECT * FROM Table1",
                    ResultSet.CONCUR_READ_ONLY);

con.createStatement("SELECT * FROM Table1",
                    ResultSet.CONCUR_UPDATABLE);
```

The default concurrency type is CONCUR_READ_ONLY. The CONCUR_UPDATABLE concurrency type should be used only if you intend to allow updates of rows that have been fetched, because indicating that a result set is "updatable" will affect the DBMS's locking strategy. Specifically, a DBMS that supports update locks will use them; see Chapter 15, "Locks."

FetchSize

The FetchSize setting has one option:

```
stmt.setFetchSize(n);
```

The overhead for a network message is high, so there's a gain if somebody fetches, say, 25 rows at a time, rather than 1 row at a time. The "somebody" in this case has to be the driver and the DBMS, acting in concert. The way to change the number of rows fetched at once is:

```
boolean b = stmt.setFetchSize(25);   // or rs.setFetchSize(25)
```

There are two fetch sizes: the default `FetchSize` that the DBMS starts off with, and the DBMS's maximum `FetchSize`. If you ask for more than the maximum, then `boolean b` becomes `false`. The default `FetchSize` for each of the Big Eight is one row; the maximum `FetchSize` is 999 rows.

The standard advice is that you should not call `setFetchSize` because the DBMS must have a reason for setting the `FetchSize` default where it is. And that is true. However, at the time that the DBMS is installed, there is no way of knowing how large your rows are. The important factor that affects speed is the number of *bytes* retrieved, not the number of *rows*. So if your result set has very small or very large rows, then you have a reason to change the number of rows per fetch.

A **block fetch** is a fetch that gets multiple rows at once. When using block fetches, keep this in mind: If you fetch 25 rows at a time and some other user changes row #24 while you're working, row #24 is out of date by the time your application sees it. You can use the `refreshRow` method to compensate for this.

The Bottom Line: Query Prepping

You can make a SELECT statement with `Statement` and execute it with `executeQuery`. Using two threads is applicable in practically all cases. But not all ODBC drivers are reentrant—using two threads is inappropriate when you're using a JDBC-ODBC bridge.

If a statement—`stmt2`—has to follow another statement—`stmt1`—then don't make `stmt2` at all. Just reuse `stmt1`.

It's important to reuse objects because (a) garbage collection won't do a complete cleanup and (b) reusing an object causes an automatic close of the existing result set. A close *must* happen, otherwise, memory leaks are possible.

Use consistent, standard, trick-free SQL syntax. Some drivers try to cache recently used SQL statements, so it's handy if they can find the times that the syntax is duplicated.

The general tips for all catalog functions are (a) avoid search patterns or blank string arguments, (b) cache the results, and (c) make sure you need to know the information before using a catalog function.

Remember that the best row identifier is often the DBMS-specific ROWID pseudocolumn. This will not appear in a list created by `getColumns`.

Get information about a result set before you get the result set itself, using `ResultSetMetaData`.

The default scroll type is TYPE_FORWARD_ONLY. Leave the setting there unless you can't tolerate going through the result set from start to end, without skipping or retreating.

Scroll cursors are both expensive and hard to implement. You will find that scroll cursors are troublesome with some DBMSs.

Use insensitive cursors for high concurrency situations. Their performance is especially good for read-only transactions.

Don't use an insensitive cursor for a single-row query.

Don't use an insensitive cursor if the query contains LOBs.

Use sensitive cursors for low concurrency situations when you want to see whether any other user changes a row while you have it.

Don't use a sensitive cursor if a call to `getBestRowIdentifier` tells you that there is no fast, persistent, unique column lookup possible for the table from which you're selecting.

The default concurrency type is CONCUR_READ_ONLY. Leave the setting there unless you intend to allow updates of rows that have been fetched.

Saying that a result set is updatable will affect the DBMS's locking strategy. Specifically, a DBMS that supports update locks will use them.

Fetch multiple rows at once (a block fetch) whenever possible.

If your result set has very small or very large rows, you have a reason to change the number of rows per block fetch.

If you fetch 25 rows at a time and some other user changes row #24 while you're working, row #24 is out of date by the time your application sees it. Use the `refreshRow` method to compensate for this.

Result Sets

That's enough about query prepping. Let's move on. Assume that you have executed a query, and it worked. So now you have a result set. That is, the query returned a bunch of rows and now you can fetch them.

But how many rows do you have, and how should you fetch them, and what will you do when it's over?

How Many Rows?

A common question is—How many rows are in the result set? It's a reasonable question: users care, it affects the scroll bar of a display, and it determines whether you have enough buffer space for an insensitive cursor. Unfortunately, there is no easy way to ask the question. That's a shame, because it's possible the DBMS might have the answer (for proof check out the ODBC function `SQLGetDiagField`, which has an option for returning the query's row count).

Here are three ways to determine the size of the result set:

- If you are going to update the result set, try:

  ```
  int i = executeUpdate();
  ```

  The count returned by `executeUpdate` should be the number of rows that were updated, although (unfortunately) that might also include the number of rows affected by triggers or by foreign keys with ON UPDATE CASCADE clauses.

- If you have a scroll cursor, try scrolling from back to front. The advantage of this method is that you can get the number of rows after your first fetch, like this:

  ```
  ResultSet rs = stmt.executeQuery(
                  "SELECT column1 FROM Table1
                    ORDER BY column1 DESC");
  if (rs.last()) {                // get last row
    int RowCount = rs.getRow(); // get number of last row
    System.out.println(
          "RowCount=" RowCount);
    System.out.println(
          rs.getString(1));
    while (rs.previous()) {
      System.out.println(
            rs.getString(1));  // print in ASC order
      }
    }
  ```

- When all else fails, resort to SELECT COUNT(*). You can do the count inside a subquery in the main search (which guarantees that the count will be correct), or you can execute a separate query to do the count before you process the main query.

getXXX methods

The `getXXX` methods (`getFloat`, `getDate`, etc.) provide the primary way to retrieve data from the database. (The other way is to pass OUT variables to stored procedures but that's more trouble.) For example, after you have executed a query and thus acquired a result set, you could do something like this:

```
boolean b = rs.next();        // fetch the first row
if (b) {
   int c1 = rs.getInt(
         "column1"); }    // get contents for column1
```

Ideally, `column1` should be an SQL INTEGER column. (You can check the column's defined data type by looking at the `rsmd`.) There is a close correspondence between an SQL INTEGER and a Java `int` so there is low **impedance** in such a case. (The impedance analogy is to an electrical circuit that contains two joining wires. If both wires are copper, there is no impedance. When a copper wire meets an aluminum wire, there is impedance.) There doesn't have to be impedance with Java and SQL, because almost all the data types do correspond. You just have to make sure to use the right getXXX method for the SQL data type. Table 13–6 shows the best matches.

The fastest conversion (per byte of data retrieved) is CHAR, then comes INTEGER, then FLOAT and TIMESTAMP . . . with STRUCT and JAVA_OBJECT bringing up the rear. The worst-performing method is `getObject`, which returns a Java Object instead of a specific type.

Impedance

Let's see how impedance can arise with specific methods.

`getString`

The magic word in Table 13–6 is "Unicode"—Java strings have it, SQL CHAR values probably don't (but NCHAR values often do). This means there will be conversions from some 8-bit character set to the Unicode 16-bit representation. This conversion is automatic, and it can be slow. It is, in any case, a potential source of error if a string is represented two different ways depending on whether it's found in an application or in the server code. So everyone will cheer on the day when all DBMS data is in Unicode. But today there are still two major impediments: (a) the size of all CHAR and VARCHAR columns doubles and (b) the DBMS is also accessed by other, non-Java, clients. At the

Table 13–6 *Recommended Matches: Java Methods and SQL/JDBC Data Types*

Java Method	SQL/JDBC Data Type
getByte	TINYINT
getShort	SMALLINT
getInt	INTEGER
getLong	BIGINT
getFloat	REAL
getDouble	FLOAT, DOUBLE
getBigDecimal	DECIMAL, NUMERIC
getBoolean	BIT
getString	CHAR, VARCHAR (presumably Unicode)
getCharacterStream	LONGVARCHAR
getBytes	BINARY, VARBINARY
getDate	DATE
getTime	TIME
getTimestamp	TIMESTAMP
none	INTERVAL
getAsciiStream	LONGVARCHAR
getBinaryStream	LONGVARBINARY
getClob	CLOB
getBlob	BLOB
getArray	ARRAY
getRef	REF
getObject	UDT, STRUCT, JAVA_OBJECT

moment, because the conversion work only slows the driver and not the server, the conversion to Unicode is a noble but non-urgent goal.

`getShort`

Because everybody except Oracle stores a SMALLINT as a 16-bit (short) signed integer, impedance should be nil. But there is a technical hitch: The number –32768 is legal according to Java but not according to ANSI. Similar hitches apply for all the integer data types. Not to worry: Most DBMSs ignore this detail. Only Informix forbids you to store –32768 in a SMALLINT.

getByte

The TINYINT data type is not standard SQL, and there could be a difficulty if it's an unsigned (range 0 to +255) byte rather than a signed (range –128 to +127) byte. Avoid negative TINYINTs.

getDate

Drivers using the JDBC-ODBC bridge are usually slow to convert DATE/TIME/TIMESTAMP columns because of a change in the rather confusing manner with which temporal data types are numbered. The matter is trivial as long as these data types are relatively little used.

getBoolean

Table 13-6 says this is appropriate for the BIT data type, but it's important to know that this means the ODBC BIT type, which is utterly different from the SQL Standard BIT. It has been found that the SQL Standard BOOLEAN data type is troublesome, particularly with PL/SQL stored procedures.

You can save a little bit of time with getXXX methods by following these suggestions.

Close

When you're done with a result set, it must be closed—else other transactions will be blocked. The explicit method call is:

```
rs.close();
```

You can skip rs.close() if the result set is closed automatically. A result set is closed automatically in these cases:

• When COMMIT or ROLLBACK or DISCONNECT happens

- When a new "execute" method call happens on the same Statement object, or a retrieval occurs on the next result set for the same Statement[3]
- In rare cases, with some DBMSs only, when UPDATE ... WHERE CURRENT OF <cursor> or DELETE ... WHERE CURRENT OF <cursor> are executed

  Note: The definition of "automatic COMMIT" depends on the definition of "automatic close" so add these rules to what you need to memorize.

Why would you want to close early?

- Because there are other Statements, and they either need resources or they use the rows in the result set (wasting time with sensitive cursors, etc.).
- Because there are other users, and you're unwilling to block them any longer.

Why would you want *not* to explicitly close?

- Because message passing is reduced if you let closing happen automatically.

We did a few tests on skipping rs.close() when we knew the result set should be closed automatically. Skipping made no significant difference. But we were using a fairly intelligent driver, and we know that other drivers would not be so intelligent.

The Bottom Line: Result Sets

To find out how big a result set is, try:

```
int i = executeUpdate();
```

Or, if you have a scroll cursor, try scrolling from back to front. When all else fails, resort to SELECT COUNT(*).

---

3. Note that you cannot rely on this "auto close" in analogous ODBC situations.

JDBC versus ODBC

There are many similarities between JDBC and ODBC, partly because both follow X/Open standards, and partly because the makers of JDBC were able to learn from the ODBC experience when they started designing. We have observed a few times in this chapter that such-and-such a JDBC method "does the same thing as" such-and-such an ODBC function—right down to use of the same field names or constant values. The differences can usually be attributable to exigencies of the language—for example, ODBC uses pointers a lot whereas JDBC has provisions for objects.

We do see a tendency in JDBC to have several functions where ODBC has only one. For example, one ODBC function for "how NULLs sort" returns four mutually exclusive values. Meanwhile, JDBC requires four functions for "how NULLs sort"; all return `true/false`.

We also see that JDBC is lacking in some functionality that ODBC possesses. There are two noticeable areas:

- In ODBC, there is a thoroughly defined hierarchy:

  `env-> dbc-> stmt-> desc`

  (see Figure 12–1 in Chapter 12, "ODBC").
  In JDBC, there is only:

  `dbc-> stmt`

  (or `Connection` and `Statement` to use the JDBC terms). This was the situation in ODBC 1.0, but the more elaborate structure had to be adopted to accommodate users' needs.

- There are tiny but baffling lacunae in the JDBC metadata functions. For example, we've already mentioned the lack of a row count option for queries. For another example, we note the curious absence of a method named `getSchemaSeparator` to correspond to `getCatalog-Separator`. (ODBC has separate functions for returning the separator characters that one puts between identifiers in fully qualified identifiers such as `Catalog1.Schema1.Table1`.)

Even if you plan to program with JDBC alone, you'll still benefit from a perusal of the ODBC documentation or the standard SQL/CLI specification. It's not necessarily better, but it is put differently, and what's said about ODBC can often be applied to JDBC.

There doesn't have to be impedance with Java and SQL, because almost all the data types do correspond. You just have to make sure to use the right getXXX method for the SQL data type.

The TINYINT data type is not standard SQL, and there could be a difficulty if it's an unsigned byte rather than a signed byte. Avoid negative TINYINTs.

Do getXXX methods in the order that they appear in the result set, and do them only once.

Use getXXX(<integer>) rather than getXXX("<column name>").

Use the wasNull method (which checks for indicators) if—and only if—(a) the getXXX method returns a zero or blank value and (b) the column is nullable.

When you're done with a result set, it must be closed—else other transactions will be blocked. The explicit method call is rs.close().

You can skip rs.close() if the result set is closed automatically.

Close early—that is, close explicitly—when other Statements need resources or the rows in a result set, or when other users shouldn't be blocked any longer.

Close automatically—not explicitly—most of the time, because message passing is reduced if you let closing happen automatically.

Data Changes

The correct way to do an ordinary data change is still the same—Use SQL's INSERT/UPDATE/DELETE statements, or use stored procedures. What are you doing with a cursor for updating in the first place? Oh, well. We will merely touch on the extra features that JDBC provides for executing data changes while traversing result sets.

In the first place, you can try to ensure that result sets are updatable. Your best updatable cursor has the form:

```
SELECT <primary key column>, <other columns>
  FROM <Table>
  WHERE <search condition>
```

That is, the query includes no DISTINCT, GROUP BY, or ORDER BY clauses and contains only one table in the FROM clause—no joining. Note that if you're going to INSERT into the query, the "other columns" should include all columns in the table that are either non-nullable or have no default value.

If your cursor is updatable and you specified that the result set is updatable when you prepped the query, you should be able to use the updateXXX methods. Is there any advantage in doing so? Yes—if you can thereby avoid creating another stmt and parsing it. But do not expect that you are saving a complete parse. In the end, the driver has to construct an UPDATE statement based on the changes that the updateXXX methods caused. One good thing: UpdateRow() will not cause an automatic COMMIT, whereas UPDATE ... WHERE CURRENT OF <cursor> might.

Updating "in batches" is a good idea because—recall our discussion of the subject in Chapter 12, "ODBC"—it reduces network messaging.

Finally, here's a trick that affects data changes with stored procedures. The idea is this: A stored procedure can be called directly with RPC, thus bypassing the DBMS parsing layer. This is especially a feature of Microsoft. However, this call can't use RPC:

```
CALL Sp_proc(12345)
        /* where Sp_proc expects an INTEGER parameter */
```

The problem is that the DBMS would have to translate 12345 from ASCII to binary before calling Sp_proc. Solution: This call *can* use RPC:

```
CALL Sp_proc(?)
```

The Java application would be responsible for setting the parameter (with the setInt method). The trick is to use parameters so that you allow RPC to happen if the DBMS can handle it.

The Bottom Line: Data Changes

The correct way to do an ordinary data change is still the same—Use SQL's INSERT, UPDATE, or DELETE statements, or use stored procedures. Don't bother with cursors.

Updating in batches is a good idea because it reduces network messaging.

A stored procedure can be called directly with RPC, thus bypassing the DBMS parsing layer. The trick is to use parameters so that you allow RPC to happen if the DBMS can handle it.

Parting Shots

If you're using JDBC with applets, define methods with the keyword `synchronized`. That prevents other **synchronized methods** from getting in while an object is being accessed.

You can put Java/JDBC routines in JAR files that the DBMS can read. The SQL procedure declaration would look something like this:

```
CREATE PROCEDURE Sp_proc
   READS SQL DATA
   DYNAMIC RESULT SETS 1
   EXTERNAL NAME <jar:name>
   LANGUAGE JAVA
   PARAMETER STYLE JAVA
```

The assumption here is that the DBMS supports SQL Java (SQLJ) routines, can load JARs, and can invoke a **Java Virtual Machine (JVM)**. Some DBMSs (Informix and Sybase are examples) supply copies of Apache Web Server with their installation CD-ROMS. Oracle takes a different approach and loads its own JVM. With a standard Web server installed, it should be easy for the DBMS to access Java routines as servlets.

14

Data Changes

The term *data change* appears in the SQL Standard document. It means any change to the database that is caused by INSERT, UPDATE, or DELETE statements. We often refer to such changes as *updates* (lowercase), but that's a bit confusing because usually UPDATE (uppercase) refers to the UPDATE statement alone. So we'll use "data change" the way the SQL Standard does: to mean an INSERT, an UPDATE, or a DELETE.

Data-change statements occur less frequently than SELECT statements, but a typical data-change statement is slow. For example, compare these two SQL statements:

```
SELECT column1 FROM Table1
  WHERE column1 = 12345

UPDATE Table1 SET column2 = 10
  WHERE column1 = 12345
```

Both statements must go through the same retrieval steps to find the matching rows, but the UPDATE will be slower, mainly for these reasons:

- The UPDATE must get an exclusive lock instead of a more-permissive shared lock; see Chapter 15, "Locks."

- The UPDATE must check any constraints or triggers.

- The UPDATE must add one, and possibly two, new entries in the log file.

- The UPDATE must shift following rows in the page up or down if the size of the updated row changes. An expanded row might also have to go on a different page.

- The UPDATE must delete and replace any index keys for the changed column.

- If a later COMMIT happens, some writing to disk will occur.

Changing a row always takes at least 3 times longer than retrieving it, and can take 100 times longer in worst-case scenarios. So it's worthwhile to examine the main performance difficulties.

It's impossible to deal with data-change statements in isolation. There are all sorts of effects that we discuss in other chapters, notably Chapter 8, "Tables," Chapter 10, "Constraints," and Chapter 15, "Locks." In this chapter, though, we'll deal only with matters that relate directly to data change: the data-change statements themselves (INSERT, UPDATE, DELETE) and the transaction-end statements (COMMIT, ROLLBACK).

Logs

For some DBMSs, logging is an optional step. Nevertheless it's very rare that database administrators will decide to turn logging off for performance reasons. So it's safe to assume that logging will happen when you do a data change.

When will logging happen? Before data changes become permanent. The reasoning is that, if a database gets smashed, then one can recover from the log. If the data change were written *before* the log entry though, then the last entry in the log would be absent. So the DBMS always logs first.

What goes in the log? A copy of the new data, or a copy of the old data, or both. This point requires emphasis. You might think that the only necessary data in the log is the data-change statement itself—for example, the DBMS could just write this SQL statement into the log file:

```
INSERT INTO Table1 (column1)
  VALUES (1)
```

Well, it could—for instance, Oracle does just that (Oracle calls the SQL-statement log a *journal*). However, Oracle *also* writes a complete "before image" data copy into the log file, along with a complete "before image" index page if a data change also changes an index. And so will most other DBMSs.[1]

Wow, isn't that expensive? Not as much as it appears. In the first place, the writing is sequential and therefore quite fast. In the second place, the log writing can be a parallel operation on a different disk drive from the main file, and the log file can be recycled so there are no allocation problems. In the third place, logging is cheap insurance.

The main thing you should know about logging is that it's one of the reasons your data-change statements are slow. The easiest way to speed them up is to turn logging off for a while. You can ask your DBA to do that in a few situations:

- During a bulk INSERT or "load" because you have a copy of what you're inserting so you can repeat the operation if there's a failure

- For index updates because you can derive an index's keys from the original records if there's a failure

- During operations that copy from one database object to another such as "INSERT ... SELECT" or CREATE INDEX or ALTER statements

The Bottom Line: Logs

Assume logging will happen before data changes become permanent.

Logging is one of the reasons that data-change statements are slow. Speed them up by turning logging off (a) during a bulk INSERT, (b) for index updates/creations, and (c) during operations that copy from one database object to another. Don't turn logging off at any other time.

INSERT

The SQL Standard description of the typical INSERT format is:

```
INSERT INTO <Table> [ ( <column> [,...] ) ]
  <query expression>
```

---

1. Some DBMSs also allow "archive logs" and "audit logs" but the phenomenon is not universal.

IBM Logging

Every data-change statement causes a write to a log, but every DBMS handles the situation in a slightly different manner. As an example, here's how IBM does data-change logging.

With IBM, the logging is of rows or parts of rows:

- INSERT causes a write of the new row's contents (an "after image").
- DELETE causes a write of the old row's contents (a "before image").
- UPDATE causes a write of the changed parts of both old and new rows.

For example, suppose Table1's definition is:

```
CREATE TABLE Table1 (
    column1 CHAR(3),
    column2 CHAR(3))
```

Table1 has one row, containing {'ABC', 'DEF'}. This UPDATE statement:

```
UPDATE Table1 SET column1 = 'AZ'
```

causes this log record to be created:

```
[Row Identifier][bytes #2-3]BEFORE-IMAGE='BC',AFTER-IMAGE='Z '
```

On the other hand, if Table1's definition is:

```
CREATE TABLE Table1 (
    column1 VARCHAR(3),
    column2 CHAR(3))
```

then the same UPDATE statement would affect all bytes as far as the end of the row, and the log record would be larger.

Here are two examples of INSERT:

```
INSERT INTO Table1 (column1)
   VALUES ('The rain in Spain falls in the plain')

INSERT INTO Table1 (column1)
   SELECT column1 FROM Table2
```

If a particular column value appears frequently and is lengthy, then you can save network transmission by making the value the default for the column. For example:

```
CREATE TABLE Table1 (
   column1 VARCHAR(40) DEFAULT 'The rain in Spain',
   ... )

INSERT INTO Table1 DEFAULT VALUES
```

This trick results in some gain if the column value is at least 100 bytes long (GAIN: 6/8).

There is no point in reordering the INSERT columns so that they are in the same order as in the storage page—it doesn't improve performance at all. (And by the way, that order isn't necessarily the same as the defined order, as we discussed in Chapter 7, "Columns.") It does, however, help slightly if the primary key or unique columns appear first in the column list. That is, if this is your table definition:

```
CREATE TABLE Table1 (
   column1 DECIMAL(4,2),
   column2 VARCHAR(40) UNIQUE,
   column3 DATE,
   column4 INTEGER PRIMARY KEY)
```

then performance is slightly better if you do your INSERT like this:

```
INSERT INTO Table1 (column4, column2, column1, column3)
  VALUES (10, 'The Rain', 24.5, DATE '2001-01-01')
GAIN: 2/7
```

WARNING   Don't do this for Sybase on a PRIMARY KEY; it shows a loss. The gain shown is for only seven DBMSs.

When there are many separate INSERT statements to execute, it's helpful if the statements are in order according to the value in some index. This increases the chance that the appropriate index page will be in cache.

Bulk INSERT

It's always good for performance if several insertions are combined. That's because there's a per-statement overhead, including the time needed to look up the table name in a catalog, to check privileges, and to form a network packet. Several ways exist to perform a multiple-row INSERT (usually called a **bulk INSERT** or just a **load**).

The SQL-Standard way to do a bulk INSERT is to repeat the row-expression part of the statement multiple times, as in this example:

```
INSERT INTO Table1
  (column1, column2, column3, column4, column5)
  VALUES (1, 2, 3, 4, 5),
         (2, 3, 4, 5, 6),
         (3, 4, 5, 6, 7)
```

Portability   Only IBM and MySQL support this feature.

This method is rare.

An alternate, but still SQL-Standard way to do a bulk INSERT is with a compound statement:

```
BEGIN
  INSERT INTO Table1 VALUES (1, 2, 3, 4, 5);
```

```
    INSERT INTO Table1 VALUES (2, 3, 4, 5, 6);
    INSERT INTO Table1 VALUES (3, 4, 5, 6, 7);
END
```

Portability	Only IBM, Microsoft, Oracle, and Sybase support this feature outside of a stored procedure.

Compound statements are an excellent idea in many situations, and IBM recommends their use quite strongly. In this particular case, where the same statement is being repeated, they're less than ideal because each repetition must be parsed.

It's also possible to do a bulk INSERT with an ANSI SQL subquery, if the data you want is already in the database:

```
INSERT INTO Table2
  SELECT * FROM Table1 WHERE column1 < 100
```

Portability	MySQL doesn't support subqueries, but the DBMS does support this construct.

The nonstandard way to do a bulk INSERT is to use a special SQL-extension statement that reads data from a file, for example:

```
BULK INSERT ... BATCH SIZE = n INPUT FILE = 'xxx';
   /* Microsoft stuff */
```

This is a common method, but because it's DBMS-specific, a discussion of it is beyond the scope of this book.

The final way to do a bulk INSERT is to load multiple values into an array and pass the entire array as a parameter for a function in an API such as ODBC or JDBC. In effect, you now have to do set management inside an application program, because there is no logical difference between an array of record values and a set of records. The difficulties with this approach are: (a) you need a lot of application memory, and (b) you need a special error-handling routine because a single statement can generate hundreds of errors—one for each row that has a problem. And you must take care to stay within the maximum buffer size for a network, which can be as little as 128KB.

You can prepare for bulk INSERTs by dropping indexes, disabling constraints, and locking the table. Generally such drastic acts only make sense when the number of rows to add is huge, and some validity testing has already been done on the input values. After a huge bulk INSERT, it's a good idea to run the "statistics update" statement for your DBMS so that the optimizer knows about the new situation; sometimes it's necessary to update statistics even during the bulk INSERT, as well as after it.

The Bottom Line: INSERT

If a particular, lengthy, column value appears frequently in INSERT, save network transmission by making the value the default value for that column.

There is no point in reordering INSERT columns so that they are in the same order as in the storage page, though it does help slightly if the primary key or unique columns appear first in the column list.

When you're executing many separate INSERT statements, put the statements in order according to the value in some index.

It's always good for performance if several insertions are combined.

Prepare for bulk INSERTs by dropping indexes, disabling constraints, and locking the table.

After a huge bulk INSERT, run the "statistics update" statement for your DBMS so that the optimizer knows about the new situation.

UPDATE

The SQL Standard description of the typical UPDATE format is:

```
UPDATE <Table> SET
  { <column> = <column expression> [,...] |
    ROW = <row expression> }
  [ WHERE <search condition> ]
```

For example:

```
UPDATE Table1 SET
      column1 = 1,
      column2 = 2,
      column3 = 3
WHERE column1 <> 1
   OR column2 <> 2
   OR column3 <> 3
```

This example updates multiple columns with the same SET clause, which is better than the alternative—using three UPDATE statements would reduce locking but increase logging (GAIN: -8/8 with three UPDATEs instead). A little-known fact about the SET clause is that evaluation *must* be from left to right. Therefore, if any assignment is likely to fail, put that assignment first in the SET clause. For example, if the column3 = 3 assignment in the last UPDATE is likely to fail, change the statement to:

```
UPDATE Table1 SET
       column3 = 3,
       column1 = 1,
       column2 = 2
 WHERE column1 <> 1
    OR column2 <> 2
    OR column3 <> 3
GAIN 6/8
```

With this change, the DBMS will fail immediately and not waste time setting column1 = 1 and column2 = 2.

The UPDATE example also contains a WHERE clause that specifies a precise exclusion of the conditions that are going to be true when the SET clause is done. This is like saying—Make it so unless it's already so. This WHERE clause is redundant, but you might be lucky and find that no rows need to be updated (GAIN: 5/8 if no data change required). By the way, this trick does not work if any of the columns can contain NULL.

Dependent UPDATE

Often two data changes occur in a sequence and are related. For example, you might UPDATE the customer balance then INSERT into a transaction table:

```
BEGIN
  UPDATE Customers
    SET balance = balance + 500
    WHERE cust_id = 12345;
  INSERT INTO Transactions
    VALUES (12345, 500);
END
```

This is improvable. First of all, it would be safer to say that the INSERT should only happen if the UPDATE changed at least one row (the number of changed rows is available to a **host program** at the end of any data-change statement). Second, if it's true that this is a sequence that happens regularly, then the INSERT statement should be in a trigger. (It goes without saying that the whole thing should be in a stored procedure; see Chapter 11, "Stored Procedures.")

When the sequence is two UPDATEs rather than an INSERT and an UPDATE, it sometimes turns out that the best optimizations involve ON UPDATE CASCADE (for a primary/foreign key relationship), or that the columns being updated should be merged into one table.

Batch UPDATE

An UPDATE statement contains a SET clause (the *operation*) and a WHERE clause (the *condition*). Which comes first, the condition or the operation?

You may not remember when batch processing was the norm. It's what used to happen in the days when a single sequential pass of the data was optimal, because of the nature of the devices being employed. The essential loop that identifies a batch-processor goes like this:

```
get next record, do every operation on that record, repeat
```

that is:

```
For each row {
  Do every operation relevant to this row }
```

This contrasts with the normal SQL set orientation, which goes like this:

```
find the records and then do the operations on them
```

that is:

```
For each operation {
  Do every row relevant to this operation }
```

You can change an SQL DBMS into a batch processor by using the CASE operator. For example:

```
/* the set-oriented method */
UPDATE Table1
```

```
    SET column2 = 'X'
    WHERE column1 < 100

UPDATE Table1
  SET column2 = 'Y'
  WHERE column1 >= 100
    OR column1 IS NULL

/* the batch-oriented method */
UPDATE Table1
  SET column2 =
    CASE WHEN column1 < 100 THEN 'X'
         ELSE 'Y'
    END
GAIN: 5/7
```

Portability   InterBase doesn't support CASE. The gain shown is for only seven DBMSs.

The batch-oriented method is reasonable if you are updating 100% of the rows in the table. Generally you should be leery of statements that select everything and then decide what to do based on the selection—such code might just be a transplant from a legacy system. In this example, though, there is an advantage because the WHERE clauses are dispensed with, and because the rows are processed in ROWID order.

The Bottom Line: UPDATE

Update multiple columns with the same UPDATE ... SET clause, rather than with multiple UPDATE statements.

UPDATE ... SET clause evaluation must be from left to right. If any assignment is likely to fail, put it first in the SET clause.

It can be helpful to add a redundant WHERE clause to an UPDATE statement, in cases where it's possible that no rows need to be updated. This won't work if any of the columns can contain NULL.

If you're updating all rows of a table, use batch processing for the UPDATE.

Check out ON UPDATE CASCADE (for a primary/foreign key relationship) if you find you're doing multiple UPDATE statements on related tables in sequence.

Consider whether columns belonging to multiple tables should belong to the same table if they're frequently being updated in sequence.

Put related—and frequently done—UPDATE statements into triggers and/or stored procedures.

DELETE

The SQL Standard description of the typical DELETE format is:

```
DELETE FROM <Table name>
  [ WHERE <search condition> ]
```

The word FROM is optional for Microsoft and Sybase, but once again, there is no reason to leave it out and cause portability trouble. Here's an example:

```
DELETE FROM Table1
  WHERE column1 = 55
```

If all rows in the table are to be deleted, it's a better idea to execute DROP TABLE and then re-create the table, or to use a nonstandard SQL extension row-blaster. For example Informix, Microsoft, and Sybase allow:

```
TRUNCATE TABLE <Table name>
```

And Ingres allows:

```
MODIFY <Table name> TO TRUNCATED
```

Such statements, however, do not allow for logging or for DELETE triggers. But TRUNCATE has advantages—it won't cause dropping of related constraints, indexes, or optimizer statistics. Because you usually won't want these objects to be dropped in addition to the table, TRUNCATE involves less maintenance at rebuild time.

The Bottom Line: DELETE

If all rows in the table are to be deleted, it's a better idea to execute DROP TABLE and then re-create the table or to use TRUNCATE.

TRUNCATE involves less maintenance.

Ugly Updates

Microsoft and Sybase have trouble when a data-change statement causes row movement (what they call an *out-of-place update*). All DBMSs have trouble when a data-change statement causes temporary violation of UNIQUE constraints. Ugly updates won't cause errors, but they are markedly slower than "regular" updates. For example, the Big Eight take about 50% longer (on average) to do an **out-of-place update** than a regular data-change statement.

The marks of an ugly update vary depending on DBMS, and even on DBMS version. We have gathered together a list based on vendor recommendations. Because the list is a composite, not all items on it will apply to any single DBMS. Take it as a weak set of guidelines.[2]

- A data change should affect only one row if a UNIQUE-indexed column is changed. A well-known problem with UNIQUE-indexed columns can be seen in this statement:

```
UPDATE Table1
  SET unique_column = unique_column + 1
```

If the current values in unique_column are {1, 2} and the DBMS updates only one row at a time, then after the first row is changed, the values in unique_column will be {2, 2}—a violation of the UNIQUE constraint. To avoid this situation, some DBMSs will do the UPDATE in two separate steps: First the DBMS will DELETE all the old values, then it will INSERT all the new values. That's a solid solution but rather slow. And it's unnecessary if the UPDATE statement contains a clause that makes it clear there's only one row to change, as in this example:

```
UPDATE Table1
  SET unique_column = unique_column + 1
  WHERE unique_column = 55
```

Microsoft and Sybase call this the "deferred update" and also apply it for this situation:

```
INSERT INTO Table1
  SELECT * FROM Table1
```

---

2. These guidelines do not apply for InterBase, because InterBase stores a record of the difference (a "delta" record) instead of just replacing the original data.

- A data change should not cause changes to any variable-length columns. Even if the new value is shorter or the same length as the old value, the DBMS will adopt a pessimistic strategy on the assumption that a migration could occur. For example, Microsoft and Sybase will treat the change as an out-of-place update. However, if the total row size ends up shorter after the data change, the effects are less bad.

- There should be no INSERT/UPDATE/DELETE trigger at all, or at least there should be no trigger that affects the same row that's being changed. The problem is that data-change triggers need "before" and "after" copies of the data, and the DBMS has to produce extra information in the log file so that the "before" and "after" copies contain static information.

- The changed column should not be in a primary key. That's especially so if the primary key is the cluster key for a clustered index.

- There should be no replication.

- There should be only one table in the data-change statement. Watch out for views containing subqueries that refer to other tables.

- When several columns are changed, they should be contiguous or nearly contiguous. Remember that columns are not always in the same order that you specify in the CREATE TABLE definition, because some DBMSs shift variable-length columns to the end of the row.

- The WHERE clause of an UPDATE statement should not contain a reference to a column that's changed in the SET clause. That is, avoid statements like:

```
UPDATE Table1
  SET indexed_column = indexed_column + 1
  WHERE indexed_column >= 0
```

Such statements can confuse a DBMS that retrieves and processes rows in one pass, instead of getting the entire set of matching rows before processing the first one. Consider what would happen with this example if all rows contain the value 0 in indexed_column.

- The SET clause of an UPDATE statement should not change columns that have just been used in a SELECT statement. SELECT statements are pooled in a global area (for example, in Oracle's SGA) so that repetitions of the same SELECT can bypass the optimizer—the DBMS just passes back the same result set. The updating of critical columns invalidates this plan.

In closing, let's look at a "tip" we've seen that is a really bad idea. Consider this SQL statement:

```
UPDATE Table1
  SET column1 = column1
  WHERE column2 = 5
```

The trick in this statement is that you can get a count of the rows WHERE column2 = 5 because data-change statements always return a count of the number of rows affected. But it's smarter—and quicker—to use good old COUNT(*).

The Bottom Line: Ugly Updates

Put related—and frequently done—data-change statements into triggers and/or stored procedures.

A data change should affect only one row if a UNIQUE-indexed column is changed.

A data change should not cause changes to any variable-length columns.

A data change should not affect a primary key.

When you're doing a data change, there should be no INSERT/UPDATE/ DELETE trigger at all, or at least no trigger should affect the same row that's being updated.

There should be no replication.

Only one table should be referenced in a data-change statement.

When several columns are updated, they should be contiguous or nearly contiguous.

The WHERE clause of an UPDATE statement should not contain a reference to a column that's changed in the SET clause.

An UPDATE … SET clause should not change columns that have just been used in a SELECT statement.

FETCH and Data Changes

It's common practice to fetch a row, then UPDATE it with an UPDATE … WHERE CURRENT OF <cursor> statement, or to fetch a row, then DELETE it with a DELETE … WHERE CURRENT OF <cursor> statement. Such techniques are unfriendly in multiuser environments. If it's predictable that a data change will happen after a fetch, then:

- You can incorporate the prediction in the WHERE clause so that the selection and data change take place together.

- You can incorporate the prediction in a trigger so that the data change becomes situationally dependent.

In short, you don't want to follow this procedure:

```
SELECT ...
OPEN <cursor>
FETCH ...
    IF <search condition> THEN UPDATE ...
```

Instead, you want to just do this:

```
UPDATE ... WHERE <search condition>
```

To avoid the WHERE CURRENT OF clause and cursor trouble, use a ROWID or serial (auto_increment) column.

The Bottom Line: FETCH and Data Changes

Don't SELECT/fetch/test/<data change>. Do UPDATE...WHERE <condition>/ test and DELETE...WHERE <condition>/test.

To avoid WHERE CURRENT OF and cursor trouble, use a ROWID or serial column.

COMMIT and ROLLBACK

It should be true that a COMMIT will actually guarantee that data is written to the disk and flushed. That is, it should be safe to pull the power plug as soon as COMMIT is done. Unfortunately, any DBMS that makes that guarantee must fight the operating system, because the operating system prefers to do lazy writes and keep its caches until a physical write is convenient. Therefore COMMIT is always going to be slow. This is true even if the DBMS doesn't wait until the database is updated, because at the very least it must wait until the log file is updated.

We've mentioned before that all DBMSs have a nonstandard flag called the *auto-commit flag*. If the flag is on, then COMMIT happens automatically after every data-change statement has been executed. If the auto-commit flag is off, then you must issue an explicit COMMIT yourself. Here are the usual rules:

- If there is only one data-change statement in the transaction, then auto-commit should be on.
- If there are multiple data-change statements in the transaction, then auto-commit should be off.
- The auto-commit flag is on by default if you are using ODBC or JDBC or most other APIs.

Transactions can be difficult, though, because of the following odd behavior by DBMSs:

- IBM, Informix, and Ingres act correctly whether the auto-commit flag is on or off.
- InterBase and Oracle won't allow you to ROLLBACK **Data Definition Language (DDL)** statements (e.g., CREATE TABLE) even if the auto-commit flag is off. But they do allow you to ROLLBACK **Data Manipulation Language (DML)** statements (e.g., INSERT) if the auto-commit flag is off.
- Even if the auto-commit flag is off, Microsoft and Sybase will do automatic COMMITs unless you issue an explicit BEGIN TRANSACTION statement. Generally, you can't ROLLBACK DDL statements with these DBMSs, but you can ROLLBACK DML statements.
- If your DBMS is MySQL, auto-commit is always on and ROLLBACK is not possible.

The net effect is that it's really rather difficult to use transactions. The idea is to reduce the number of network messages because a COMMIT message doesn't have to be sent. But you should make what efforts you can to delay COMMIT if (a) auto-commit would compromise data integrity, or (b) you have several statements that will probably change the same pages in the same database files.

When performing a transaction, the DBMS can make one of two possible assumptions: that COMMIT is likely to happen, or that ROLLBACK is likely to happen. If COMMIT is likely, then the DBMS's best strategy is this:

```
When a data change happens {
  Put a copy of the original data page in the log file.
  Change the data page immediately. }
When a COMMIT happens {
  Just flush the log file. }
When a ROLLBACK happens {
  Read the original from the log file.
  Copy it to the data page. }
```

If ROLLBACK is likely, then this is the DBMS's best strategy:

```
When a data change happens {
  Put a copy of the changed data page in the log file. }
When a COMMIT happens {
  Read the change from the log file.
  Copy it to the data page.
  Flush. }
When a ROLLBACK happens {
  Mark the log entry as invalid.
  Do nothing else. The original data is untouched. }
```

Most DBMSs assume that COMMIT is likely. That's okay, but it has the unfortunate consequence that you can't play "what-if" games in your transactions. Start with the belief that your transaction will go through, because if you have to abort it, a ROLLBACK takes longer than a COMMIT. Remember also that logging and COMMIT processing happen in separate threads so you won't see this effect by simply timing your transaction. But the effect is there and will affect throughput.

Portability   Ingres, InterBase, Oracle, and Sybase assume COMMIT is likely. IBM, Informix, and Microsoft assume ROLLBACK is likely. MySQL doesn't support transactions.

Usually, the actual event order is that a data-change statement changes an in-memory copy of a page and creates an in-memory log record. COMMIT ensures that a separate thread (the log writer) has flushed the log records *only*. Flushing of the changed data pages can happen later.

Tip	If ROLLBACK is expensive, then start a transaction with the operation that's most likely to fail. For example, in a library circulation transaction, scan the patron's card before scanning the material the patron wishes to borrow (GAIN: 7/7).

The Bottom Line: COMMIT and ROLLBACK

COMMIT is always going to be slow.

Watch out for operating system caches. COMMIT hasn't really happened until these buffers are written to disk and flushed.

If only one data-change statement is in the transaction, then auto-commit should be on.

If multiple data-change statements are in the transaction, then auto-commit should be off.

Make an effort to delay COMMIT if (a) auto-commit would compromise data integrity, or (b) you have several statements that will probably change the same pages in the same database files.

Start with the belief that your transaction will go through—that is, write your transaction based on the assumption that COMMIT will be successful, not that ROLLBACK will be necessary.

If ROLLBACK is expensive, start a transaction with the operation that's most likely to fail.

Parting Shots

From a performance point of view, the perfect transaction is discrete, is short, is nondistributed, changes only one data page, changes a page only once, and avoids reading what it's just written.

15

Locks

Here's a locking analogy to consider.

Think of an office with men's and women's washrooms. Doubtless a man could actually lock the men's washroom when he goes in, but that would be inefficient for three reasons: (1) men who only want to comb their hair are excluded whether or not their purpose would conflict with another occupant's; (2) other men can't tell from a distance whether the door is locked; (3) nobody can open the door for maintenance or emergencies. To avoid these problems, it's smarter to use a system of signs. For example, a man scrawls "occupied" on the wall by the bathroom door or, better yet, he flies a flag above his cubicle so that everyone knows where he's going. Of course, there are different flags for urinals (which can be shared) and for cubicles (of which there's only one). Women have flags too, but because they use a different washroom they can ignore the men's flags. The system works if the men check the flags before going to the washroom, lower their own flags as soon as they get out, time their trips for low traffic periods, and avoid declaring emergencies. The measure of the system's efficiency isn't how quickly any given man can go—that's merely response time. What counts is how much everyone can accomplish in a period—that's throughput.

DBMSs work the same way. The usual term for this process is *locking*, though, as our analogy shows, it's really a system of signing and flagging. Let's get some other obvious terminology out of the way.

- A data change is an INSERT, UPDATE, or DELETE statement.

- A transaction-end is a COMMIT or ROLLBACK statement.

- A **transaction** is a series of SQL statements. It begins with the first SQL statement since the last transaction-end and finishes with a transaction-end statement.

- A **read-only transaction** is a transaction that doesn't do a data change.

- When two transactions have overlapping start or end times, they are **concurrent transactions**. To prevent concurrent transactions from interfering with each other, the DBMS arranges a **lock**.

Your DBMS is responsible for arranging locks, but you control them indirectly. You can enforce your control using statements like SET TRANSACTION and the non-standard SQL extension LOCK TABLE, as well as with a more subtle mechanism: arranging the statements of your transactions correctly. The problem all programmers face here is that if you know only a little about locks, it's very easy to write very bad code indeed. So you must know a lot. In this chapter, we'll give you the information you need to enforce your control of locking efficiently and effectively. We'll look at what a lock is, describe lock modes, talk about why granularity matters, and explain what the various transaction isolation levels do.

What Is a Lock?

Physically, a lock is one of three things: a latch, a mark on the wall, or a RAM record.

Latches

A **latch** is a low-level on-off mechanism that ensures two processes or threads can't access the same object at the same time. You can make latches with, for example, the MS Windows NT API CreateMutex or CreateSemaphore functions. Consider the following situation (we'll call it Situation #1).

- Transaction #1 reads the first byte of a row in shared memory.

- Transaction #2 interrupts and clears the row.

- Transaction #1 continues to read, and probably crashes—unacceptable!

To avoid the crash, Situation #1 must change. Here's what should happen.

- Transaction #1 gets a latch associated with the row it's going to read.

- Transaction #1 reads the first byte of the row in shared memory.

- Transaction #2 interrupts and tries to get the same latch.

- Transaction #2 fails to acquire the latch so it goes back to sleep.

- Transaction #1 continues to read, and does not crash.

- Transaction #1 releases the latch.

- Transaction #2 interrupts again, gets the latch, and clears the row.

- Transaction #2 releases the latch.

More concisely, the second situation uses mutexes or semaphores or Enter-CriticalSection calls so that, when one thread starts to read a row, other threads are prevented from interrupting the read and changing the end of the row. MySQL uses a single statement latch for all processes, which means that two SQL statements cannot execute at the same time. The rest of the Big Eight are less extreme; they latch only while reading and writing bits of shared memory.

A latch must be on for every shared bit of memory and must go off as soon as the memory has been read/written. Generally a transaction holds a maximum of one latch at any time, and that time is less than one millisecond. A second transaction that tries to get the same latch is blocked, so it must either spin (i.e., retry after an interval), or it must be enqueued (i.e., get in line). The words "blocked," "spin," and "enqueued" are forgettable jargon, but "latch" is a vital word because all multi-thread or multi-process DBMSs use latches.

Marks on the wall

A **mark on the wall** (properly known as an **ITL slot**) is used occasionally, primarily by Oracle, to mark a row in a page of a data file. By putting a mark right beside the row accessed by a transaction, the DBMS ensures that no other transaction has to spend much time checking whether the row is locked. This mechanism only works when the number of locks in a page is small enough to fit in the page, so marks on the wall are appropriate mostly for exclusive locks (see "Lock Modes" later in this chapter).

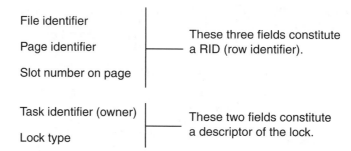

Figure 15–1   *A Microsoft lock record*

RAM records

A **RAM record** (or **lock record**) is the usual mechanism for locks of rows, pages, or tables. The RAM record is a permanent memory area that contains data describing what's locked, and how. For example, Microsoft's 32-byte lock records contain the information shown in Figure 15–1.

Keeping lock records in memory can cause high overhead. For example, if lock records are in order by time of creation rather than in order by RID or indexed by RID, they're quite a jumble. When the DBMS wants to lock a row, it must first scan all the lock records to see whether another transaction already has a lock on that row. So if Transaction #1 has done a scan and locked all of a table's rows (assume there are 50,000 rows), and then Transaction #2 does a scan of the same table, Transaction #2 must, on average, check 50,000/2 locks for each page for a total of 50,000 * (50,000/2) = 1,250,000,000 checks. To prevent such unacceptable situations, a DBMS will reduce lock longevity and lock count through practices like escalation. We'll discuss escalation later in this chapter.

When the DBMS encounters a lock that it can't pass, it has two choices: it can return an error to the user (NO WAIT), or it can try spinning and enqueuing (WAIT). Oracle lets you choose whether you want NO WAIT or WAIT. Other DBMSs insist on WAIT, but they will time out if a specific period expires (say, one minute). Generally the DBMS vendors think it's better to WAIT, because users who receive an error message will probably just try again from the beginning of the transaction.

Lock Modes

Lock mode (or **lock type**) is the term for the type of lock a DBMS has arranged for a transaction. When DBMS makers pretend to offer a bizarre plethora of lock modes, we must force the truth from them: there are only three lock modes, and usually two are enough. The rest are fine distinctions and nuances, and we won't discuss them here. The three lock modes are shared, update, and exclusive.

A lock's mode determines (a) what other locks can coexist with this lock and (b) whether other transactions have read and/or write permission when this lock exists. (For the record, a latch is an exclusive lock on anything. In this section, though, we're discussing only the non-latch locks—those used for locking rows, pages, or tables—and we'll use the generic word "object" to mean a row, a page, or a table.)

The coexistence rules for locks are simple.

- A **shared lock** may coexist with any number of other shared locks, or with one update lock on the same object.

- An **update lock** may coexist with any number of shared locks, but not with another update lock nor with an exclusive lock on the same object.

- An **exclusive lock** on an object may not coexist with any other lock on that object.

Table 15–1 shows these rules graphically.

The lock rules for read and/or write permission are not so simple. It's often said that you need a shared or update lock to read, and you need an exclusive lock to write, but that's not always true. In this context, "read" means either "access" or "add to result set," while "write" means "data change"—it doesn't imply "physical write to disk," though that can certainly happen. In simple terms, though, these are the rules.

Table 15–1 *Lock Modes and Coexistence*

Locks on One Object					Comment
Shared	Shared	Shared	Shared	Shared	*n* shared locks may coexist with one another
Shared	Shared	Update	Shared	Shared	*n* shared locks may coexist with one update lock
Exclusive					one exclusive lock may not coexist with any other lock

- Shared locks are for reading. At most levels you can't read an object unless you have a shared lock on it.

- Update locks are for reading when updating is planned. They're not strictly necessary, but are used by most DBMSs. Despite the name, if you have an update lock on an object you can *not* write the object. Update locks are like shared locks for permissions, but like exclusive locks for coexistence.

- Exclusive locks are for writing. If you have an exclusive lock on an object, you can write that object. Because of this, some people call exclusive locks "intent-to-update" locks, a term you should avoid, because there are other locks with similar names. You need an exclusive lock to write, and an exclusive lock will prevent other transactions from acquiring shared locks in order to read. Exclusive locks are thus the barriers to concurrency.

Usually a transaction reads an object before it tries to write the object, so an exclusive lock is normally an upgrade from a shared or update lock. For example, assume a transaction reads a table and gets a shared lock on Row #1. Later on, the transaction does a data change, so it changes the shared lock on Row #1 to an exclusive lock on Row #1. We'll look at how locks affect read/write permissions in greater detail later in this chapter.

Versioning

The description of lock modes applies to all of the Big Eight except InterBase and Oracle. These DBMSs do use exclusive locks, and they do use shared locks for tables, but they have a variation: sometimes they don't use shared locks for rows. Instead, they use **versioning,** also known as **Multi Version Concurrency Control (MVCC).** Here's how Oracle handles MVCC.

- The DBMS keeps a log of data changes. A changed page has two versions: the original is in the log file, and the new version is in the main file.

- The DBMS also keeps a global big-integer serial number called the **System Change Number (SCN).** When a new transaction starts, Oracle increments the SCN and assigns the incremented integer as the SCN for that transaction.

- When a page is written, Oracle stores the transaction's SCN in the page, and the transaction's SCN becomes the SCN for that page.

Given this description, consider the following scenario.

- Page #1 has SCN = 500.
- Transaction #1 starts. It gets SCN = 1000.
- Transaction #2 starts. It gets SCN = 1001.
- Transaction #2 reads Page #1 (SCN = 500).
- Transaction #2 writes the page. Thus Page #1 gets SCN = 1001 (the same as Transaction #2). Now there are two versions of the page, as shown in Figure 15–2. The new version, with SCN = 1001, is in the main file, while the old version, with SCN = 500, is in the log file.
- Transaction #1 reads Page #1.
- Transaction #1 compares its own SCN (1000) to the page's SCN (1001). Because the transaction's SCN is less than the page's SCN, Transaction #1 knows it must search the log file for the original copy of the page (in Oracle-speak, this log is called the ROLLBACK SEGMENT or "undo tablespace"). Why? Because the higher SCN for the page means that another transaction has performed an uncommitted data change and it isn't safe for Transaction #1 to base its work on such possibly transient data.
- Transaction #1 reads the Page #1 copy in the log file, and continues.

What's significant about this scenario is that Transaction #2's change doesn't block Transaction #1's read, because in the end Transaction #1 reads the original, *prechange* row. Thanks to this method, Transaction #2 doesn't have to worry whether Transaction #1 might read the page, and so there is no need for a shared lock: blocking is impossible!

Versioning works if there is a mechanism to keep previous versions available (such as a log), and if there is only one transaction that does the writing while all other transactions are readers. Versioning fails if two transactions are writers (because one of them must be writing an obsolete page), so exclusive locks are still needed. Still, either you can hope that Transaction #2 will end with ROLLBACK, or you can check whether Transaction #2 really affected the row that Transaction #1 wants.

Versioning bogs down if Transaction #1 lasts for hours, because as time goes on there are more changed pages, and every changed page causes multiple reads of the main file and the log file.

Bottom line: Versioning's great when there's only one data-change transaction and zero long-lasting transactions.

You'll have noted that using versioning instead of locking implies a fair amount of difference in the way DBMSs handle concurrent transactions. Because this chapter is specifically about locking—that is, non-versioning DBMSs—we'll ignore these differences during our discussion and summarize the InterBase/Oracle versioning exceptions in another sidebar.

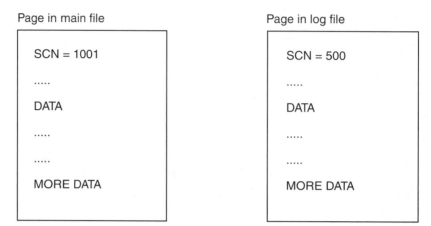

Figure 15–2   *Two versions of the same page under MVCC*

Granularity

The **granularity** of a lock refers to the size of the locked area. If you lock a row, the granularity is small. If you lock a table, the granularity is large. Both have advantages and disadvantages.

- When you lock a row, the chances are that you won't block other transactions; thus concurrency is high. On the other hand, there are many locks, so overhead is greater.

- When you lock a table, the chances are that you will block other transactions; thus concurrency is low. On the other hand, there are only a few locks, so overhead is smaller.

Consider the chart shown in Figure 15–3. It shows that, as lock granularity moves from the database level to the column level, overhead increases. (Overhead goes up because there are more locks to manage as you move from large to small granularity; i.e., there are more columns than tables, so column locks take extra work.) It also shows that concurrency increases as granularity gets smaller. Where do you want to be on Figure 15–3's line? Well, we made another chart to show what each DBMS actually allows; see Table 15-2.

Notes on Table 15-2:

- Some versions of IBM support page locks.

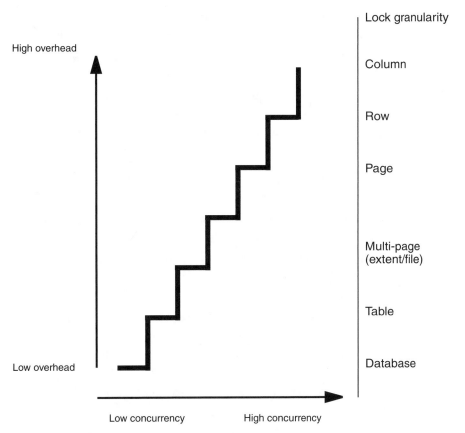

Figure 15-3 *Concurrency versus overhead*

Table 15-2 *DBMS Granularity Support*

	Database Lock	Extent Lock	Table Lock	Page Lock	Row Lock	Column Lock
IBM	Yes	Yes	Yes	No	Yes	No
Informix	Yes	Yes	Yes	Yes	Yes	No
Ingres	Yes	Yes	Yes	Yes	Yes	No
InterBase	Yes	Yes	Yes	Yes	Yes	No
Microsoft	Yes	Yes	Yes	Yes	Yes	Yes
MySQL	Yes	Yes	Yes	No	No	No
Oracle	Yes	Yes	Yes	Yes	Yes	No
Sybase	Yes	Yes	Yes	Yes	Yes	No

- Microsoft and Sybase support simplistic row-level locking only for inserts. Extent locks occur only when table size increases.
- MySQL supports page locking only for **Berkeley DB (BDB)** tables.

One way to encourage row-level locking is to ensure that there are few rows in a page. You can do this by shrinking the page size or by declaring that some of the page should be left blank at first with the DBMS's PCTFREE/FILL-FACTOR setting.

Escalation

Escalation is the act of consolidating several real or potential small-grain locks into a single big-grain lock. Concurrency gets worse, but overhead gets better.
DBMSs will escalate page locks to table locks if:

- There is a full table scan
- A large number of page locks exists. (For example, for Microsoft the figure is either 200 or half the pages in the table; the "large number" is called the lock escalation threshold and is often a value that DBAs can reset.)

DBMSs also support explicit locking of tables, either with one of these non-standard SQL extension-statements:

```
LOCK [ SHARED | EXCLUSIVE ] TABLE <Table name>

LOCK TABLE <Table name> IN [ SHARE | EXCLUSIVE ] MODE

LOCK TABLES <Table name> [ READ | WRITE ]
```

or a similar SQL extension, like Ingres's SET LOCKMODE, InterBase's RESERVED clause in the SET TRANSACTION statement, Microsoft's (hint) in the DML statements, and Sybase's LOCK {DATAROWS | DATAPAGES | ALLPAGES} clauses in the CREATE TABLE and ALTER TABLE statements. To keep it simple, we'll call all these options "the LOCK statement" throughout this book.

The LOCK statement exists because programmers may be able to predict escalation better than the DBMS can. For example, suppose a transaction starts with an SQL statement that reads 100 rows and ends with a statement that reads 10,000 rows. In that case, it makes sense to issue a LOCK statement right at the beginning of the transaction so that the DBMS doesn't waste time making page locks that it will then have to escalate. For another example, suppose that during the night there are very few transactions. In that case, it also makes sense to issue a LOCK statement, because the overhead will go down without affecting concurrency (because there's no concurrency to affect). As a general rule, if there are no concurrent transactions, then throughput is not a problem, so you might as well concentrate on response time. It does *not* make sense to use a LOCK statement on a regular basis, though, because overhead is cheap until there are many thousands of lock records in memory.

Of course, the first thing to do is tune your query to reduce concurrency problems. Explicit LOCK escalation is what you do if you can't tune further.

Intent Locks

If `Table1` contains Page #1, and there's already a shared lock on Page #1, then the Law of Contagion says another transaction can't get an exclusive lock on `Table1`.[1] Implicitly, any small-grain lock implies a shared big-grain lock.

Most DBMSs turn this principle into an explicit rule: if there is one or more locks on pages belonging to a table, then there will also be a lock on the table itself, as a separate lock record. The usual name of the big-grain lock is **intent lock**. Thus, a small-grain lock implies a corresponding intent lock on all coarser granularity levels.

You have no control over intent locks; we only mention them by way of reassurance. If you try to lock a table, the DBMS won't have to search umpteen dozen page locks looking for conflict; it only needs to look for an intent lock on the table. Intent locks are thus a way to lessen overhead, and it's up to the DBMS to decide whether to deploy them. Some DBMSs make intent locks for indexed searches only.

Table 15–3 summarizes the level of support the Big Eight provide for locks and lock modes.

The Bottom Line: Locks

A shared lock on an object may coexist with any number of other shared locks, or with one update lock. Shared locks are for reading.

---

1. The Law of Contagion is a principle of magic. See Sir James George Frazer, *The Golden Bough: A Study in Magic and Religion*, chapter 3, "Sympathetic Magic."

Table 15–3   *DBMSs, Lock Modes, and Granularity: A Summary*

	Shared Lock	Update Lock	Exclusive Lock	Intent Lock	Default Granularity
IBM	Yes	Yes	Yes	Yes	Row
Informix	Yes	Yes	Yes	Yes	Page
Ingres	Yes	Yes	Yes	Yes	Row or page
InterBase	Yes	Yes	Yes	Yes	Row
Microsoft	Yes	Yes	Yes	Yes	Row
MySQL	Yes	Yes	Yes	Yes	Table
Oracle	Yes	No	Yes	No	Row
Sybase	Yes	Yes	Yes	Yes	Row

An update lock on an object may coexist with any number of shared locks, but not with another update lock nor with an exclusive lock. Update locks are for reading when updating is planned.

An exclusive lock may not coexist with any other lock on the same object. Exclusive locks are for writing. Usually a transaction reads an object before it tries to write it, so an exclusive lock is normally an upgrade from a shared or update lock.

Exclusive locks are the barriers to concurrency.

Implicitly, any small-grain lock implies a shared big-grain lock. DBMSs make explicit locks, called intent locks, to reflect this. Thus, if a page of a table is locked, there will also be an intent lock on the table. You have no control over intent locks.

The granularity of a lock refers to the size of the locked area. If you lock a row, the granularity is small. If you lock a table, the granularity is large.

When you lock a row, the chances are that you won't block other transactions, thus concurrency is high. On the other hand, there are many locks, so overhead is greater.

When you lock a table, the chances are that you will block other transactions, thus concurrency is low. On the other hand, there are only a few locks, so overhead is smaller.

One way to encourage row-level locking is to ensure that there are few rows in a page. You can do this by shrinking the page size or by declaring that some of the page should be left blank at first.

Escalation is the act of consolidating several small-grain locks into a single big-grain lock. Concurrency gets worse, but overhead gets better.

Use the SQL-extension LOCK statement to force big-grain locks in situations where you can predict escalation.

If there are no concurrent transactions, then throughput is not a problem, so you might as well concentrate on response time.

Isolation Levels

All DBMSs except for IBM support the SQL SET TRANSACTION statement, though they may have differing optional clauses. The essential syntax, though, always looks like this:

```
SET TRANSACTION
  [ ISOLATION LEVEL
       { READ UNCOMMITTED
       | READ COMMITTED
       | REPEATABLE READ
       | SERIALIZABLE } ]
  [ READ ONLY ]
```

If you're using ODBC, you can set the isolation level permanently using this function call, which works with all of the Big Eight:

```
SQLSetConnectAttr(...SQL_ATTR_TXN_ISOLATION,...)
```

With JDBC, this is the call:

```
Connection.setTransactionIsolation(...)
```

The SQL Standard states that the **isolation level** of a transaction determines the type of concurrency problem that will be tolerated for the transaction. In order from lowest level of isolation to highest, the options are READ UNCOMMITTED, READ COMMITTED, REPEATABLE READ, and SERIALIZABLE. The Standard does not specify how a DBMS should enforce these rules; that decision is left up to the vendor. We've already noted that most DBMSs use locking to resolve concurrency problems; in this chapter, therefore, we discuss the isolation levels only in terms of locking.

READ UNCOMMITTED is the lowest level of transaction isolation; it also gives you the highest concurrency level. No locks are issued and no locks are checked during the transaction. READ UNCOMMITTED tells the DBMS you want it to allow reading of rows that have been written—but not committed—by other transactions, and always implies a READ ONLY transaction, that is, no data changes allowed.

The next level of transaction isolation, **READ COMMITTED,** still allows for a fairly high concurrency level. Shared locks are mandatory but can be released before the transaction ends. READ COMMITTED tells the DBMS you want it to allow reading of rows that have been written by other transactions only after they have been committed.

REPEATABLE READ is the next level; concurrency drops sharply. Shared locks are mandatory and will not be released until the transaction ends. REPEATABLE READ tells the DBMS it must not allow a situation where one transaction gets two sets of data from two reads of the same set of rows because a second transaction changed that set of rows between the two reads.

SERIALIZABLE is the final and highest level of transaction isolation and thus gives you the lowest concurrency level. The DBMS may lock whole tables, not just rows (or paths to objects rather than just the objects) during the course of a transaction. SERIALIZABLE tells the DBMS you want it to execute concurrent transactions in a manner that produces the same effect as a serial execution of those transactions.

Of course, supporting the SQL statement syntax and *doing* something with the statement are different things! The SQL Standard allows a DBMS to auto-upgrade isolation levels. For example, if you specify an isolation level of REPEATABLE READ, you'll probably actually get SERIALIZABLE. Furthermore, any DBMS can ignore the READ ONLY clause, because it's just an optimizer hint. The main point, however, is that you can change the transaction isolation level. When you do, certain effects happen, and those effects are the same no matter which DBMS you use.

That may sound surprising, because we all know that the SQL Standard doesn't say *how* SET TRANSACTION should work—it only specifies what the effect of the statement must be. So you may think of the sameness of DBMSs as a lucky coincidence. We think it's conformist: faced with many alternatives, all implementors decided to support transaction isolation by turning locks on or off at appropriate moments in the transaction. Table 15–4 shows the SQL Standard requirements, and the level of support the Big Eight have for the various transaction isolation levels.

Table 15–4 *ANSI/DBMS Isolation Level Support*

	READ ONLY	R-U	R-C	R-R	S	Default Isolation Level
ANSI SQL	Yes	Yes	Yes	Yes	Yes	S
IBM	Yes	Yes	Yes	Yes	Yes	R-C
Informix	Yes	Yes	Yes	No	Yes	R-C
Ingres	Yes	No	Yes	Yes	Yes	S
InterBase	No	No	Yes	Yes	Yes	R-C
Microsoft	Yes	Yes	Yes	Yes	Yes	R-C
MySQL	No	No	Yes	No	No	R-C
Oracle	Yes	No	Yes	No	Yes	R-C
Sybase	No	Yes	Yes	Yes	Yes	R-R

Notes on Table 15–4:

- The following abbreviations are used for the various isolation levels:
  R-U for READ UNCOMMITTED
  R-C for READ COMMITTED
  R-R for REPEATABLE READ
  S for SERIALIZABLE
- Default Isolation Level column
  This column shows the isolation level the DBMS will provide if you
  don't specify one. Note that the default is important because the DBMS
  optimizer assumes that the default will be true when an SQL statement
  is executed. It doesn't know the actual isolation level in advance.

We mentioned earlier that the lock rules for read and/or write permission
are not simple. This is because the isolation level chosen also affects read-write
permissions. Now that we've looked at the transaction isolation levels, we can
go into this in greater detail. First, recall that "read" means either "access" or
"add to result set," while "write" means "data change"—it doesn't imply "physical write to disk," though that can certainly happen. Table 15–5 shows the lock
rules for read/write permission on READ UNCOMMITTED transactions, Table 15–6 shows the rules for READ COMMITTED transactions, Table 15–7
shows the rules for REPEATABLE READ transactions, and Table 15–8 shows the
rules for SERIALIZABLE transactions.

Table 15–5 *Lock Modes and Read/Write Permissions for READ UNCOMMIT-TED Transactions*

	Shared Lock	Update Lock	Exclusive Lock
When acquired	Never	Never	Never
When released	N/A	N/A	N/A

Table 15–6 *Lock Modes and Read/Write Permissions for READ COMMITTED Transactions*

	Shared Lock	Update Lock	Exclusive Lock
When acquired	Before read	Before read	Before update
When released	After read	After read	Transaction end

Table 15–7 *Lock Modes and Read/Write Permissions for REPEATABLE READ Transactions*

	Shared Lock	Update Lock	Exclusive Lock
When acquired	Before read	Before read	Before update
When released	Transaction end	Transaction end	Transaction end

Table 15–8 *Lock Modes and Read/Write Permissions for SERIALIZABLE Transactions*

	Shared Lock	Update Lock	Exclusive Lock
When acquired	Before read	Before read	Before update
When released	Transaction end	Transaction end	Transaction end

Notes on Tables 15-5 through 15-8:

- Except in the READ UNCOMMITTED level, you must have a shared lock before reading.

- The locks acquired for the SERIALIZABLE level are more extensive than the locks for the REPEATABLE READ level. For example, Microsoft locks a range of index keys as well as the rows to which they point.

Concurrency Problems and Isolation Levels

Recall that transactions are concurrent when they have overlapping start or end times. There are four general problems that can arise from concurrent transactions. In order of seriousness, they are: the Lost Update, the Dirty Read, the Non-repeatable Read, and the Phantom. Here are examples of each, using timeline points (the lower the event in the chart, the later in time the event takes place).

Lost Update

Transaction #1	Transaction #2
...	Read Row #1
Read Row #1	...
Data change Row #1	...
...	Data change Row #1
COMMIT	...
...	COMMIT

The **Lost Update** problem occurs when two transactions read and make a change to the same row. When the first transaction COMMITs, its change is lost because the second transaction's change supersedes it. The result is as if Transaction #1's change never happened. You can avoid Lost Update by using an isolation level of READ UNCOMMITTED or higher.

Dirty read

Transaction #1	Transaction #2
Read Row #1	...
Data change Row #1	...
...	Read Row #1
ROLLBACK	...
...	COMMIT

The **Dirty Read** problem occurs when a transaction reads a row that has been changed but not committed by another transaction. The result is that Transaction #2's work is based on a change that never really happened. You can avoid Dirty Read by using an isolation level of READ COMMITTED or higher.

Non-repeatable read

```
Transaction #1              Transaction #2
...                         Read Row #1
Read Row #1                 ...
...                         Data change Row #1
Read Row #1                 ...
...                         COMMIT
COMMIT                      ...
```

The **Non-repeatable Read** problem occurs when a transaction reads a set of rows twice, once before and once after another transaction does a data change that affects those rows. The result is that Transaction #1 gets conflicting data from its reads. You can avoid Non-repeatable Read by using an isolation level of REPEATABLE READ or higher.

Phantom

```
Transaction #1              Transaction #2
Read set of Rows            ...
...                         data change same set of Rows
Re-read set of Rows         ...
```

The **Phantom** problem occurs when a transaction reads multiple rows twice, once before and once after another transaction does a data change that affects the search condition in the first transaction's reads. The result is that Transaction #1 gets a different (larger) result set back from its second read. We call this the "now-you-don't-see-it-now-you-do" phenomenon. You can avoid the Phantom only by using an isolation level of SERIALIZABLE.

A Phantom can affect transactions that contain at least two search conditions that overlap or depend on one another, as the following example shows.

- Transaction #1 asks for all rows with a column1 value equal to 15. Assume the result set returned has 12 rows.
- Then Transaction #2 inserts three new rows where column1 has a value of 15.
- Then Transaction #1 repeats its read. The result is that Transaction #1 gets 15 rows the second time around. The three extra rows are the phantoms.

Table 15-9 recaps the concurrency problems tolerated under each isolation level.

Table 15–9 *Concurrency Problems Tolerated under Each Isolation Level*

Isolation Level	Lost Update	Dirty Read	Non-repeatable Read	Phantom
READ UNCOMMITTED	No	Yes	Yes	Yes
READ COMMITTED	No	No	Yes	Yes
REPEATABLE READ	No	No	No	Yes
SERIALIZABLE	No	No	No	No

READ UNCOMMITTED Transactions

As Table 15–9 shows, sometimes a READ UNCOMMITTED transaction can return data that came from a Dirty Read; this sounds upsetting. But do you use an Internet search engine? If so, you tolerate result sets where at least 1% of the results either have nothing to do with your query or refer to nonexistent pages. But at least you didn't have to wait long. Besides, if the other transactions are deferring writes, the chances of Dirty Read are negligible.

READ UNCOMMITTED transactions must be READ ONLY, so that a Lost Update won't happen. And that's all! If your DBMS supports READ UNCOMMITTED, then

```
SET TRANSACTION ISOLATION LEVEL READ UNCOMMITTED READ ONLY
```

is the same as saying, "Don't bother checking any locks, I'd ignore them anyway. And don't bother setting any locks, I won't be changing anything that will affect somebody else. And, oh yeah, turn off that versioning stuff too."

During the rare times when all transactions are READ UNCOMMITTED, all locks are off and throughput is at its peak. As an example, we ran a test with one of the Big Eight DBMS's, consisting of 10,000 SELECT statements, each looking for a random key value in an index. The first time we ran the test, we set all transactions to READ UNCOMMITTED using an ODBC function. Then we ran it again, leaving the transactions at the InterBase default of READ COMMITTED. The READ UNCOMMITTED test was 200% faster than the READ COMMITTED test. To be fair, we then tried the READ COMMITTED test once again using a LOCK TABLE ... SHARED statement, but it was still slower.

READ UNCOMMITTED is a good isolation level to specify for (a) transactions that are slow and (b) transactions that are likely to have small errors or errors that will cancel one another out. Typical READ UNCOMMITTED situations are letting patrons look up a book in a library catalog or letting Internet browsers see an occasionally changing list of the Top Ten song hits.

READ COMMITTED Transactions

For READ COMMITTED transactions, just ask yourself: Is a Non-repeatable Read tolerable? Sometimes this is a no-brainer. If your transaction will never try to repeat a read, then of course Non-repeatable Reads are tolerable. So what kind of transaction never tries to repeat a read? Here's an example.

```
(transaction start)
SELECT * FROM Table1 WHERE column1 = 15;

for (;;) {
  ...
  FETCH NEXT ...
  if (NOT_FOUND) break;
  ...
  }

(transaction end)
```

For READ COMMITTED transactions, assume row locks, no versioning, and no updating. We can guarantee that, for every row that the FETCH NEXT in this example fetches, the row still exists and contains a column1 value equal to 15. No other transaction can interrupt and change those facts, because during the SELECT a shared lock is set by the DBMS. So it is safe to use READ COMMITTED here.

Things would be different if a scroll cursor was used and the fetch wasn't always FETCH NEXT. In such cases, there is no guarantee that a row will be the same the second time it's fetched. Why? Because once you finish with Row #1 and ask for the next row, the DBMS releases the shared lock on Row #1. Clearly that's good—the sooner a lock goes away, the more concurrency there is. It has to be said, though, that when there's only one SQL statement in the transaction, we couldn't find cases where READ COMMITTED yields any more throughput than REPEATABLE READ. Gains appear only when result sets are large and several SQL statements are in the transaction.

READ COMMITTED is a good isolation level to specify for transactions that contain only one SQL statement. Typical READ COMMITTED situations are changing a name or adding a club member.

REPEATABLE READ Transactions

In earlier days REPEATABLE READ was the highest possible isolation level. For some DBMSs, it still is. REPEATABLE READ won't let through Lost Updates, Dirty Reads, or Non-repeatable Reads; it allows only Phantoms, which are rare.

With regard to locking, the philosophy of REPEATABLE READ transactions is to keep locks until the transaction ends. In this respect they differ from READ COMMITTED transactions, which free locks after finishing with a row. In general, it's a bad idea to access the same row twice in a READ COMMITTED transaction, because you're (a) getting a lock, then (b) freeing the lock, and then (c) getting the same lock again.

When two SQL statements in the same transaction have overlapping WHERE search conditions, or no WHERE clauses at all, there is a danger of a Phantom appearing. For example, consider these two SQL statements:

```
SELECT * FROM Table1
   WHERE column1 = 5

UPDATE Table1                    /* there might be a Phantom here */
   SET column1 = 5
   WHERE column1 = 6
```

Even programmers who understand nothing of Phantoms can obey this rule of thumb: Don't write overlapping transactions. In the previous example, we should have done the UPDATE first.

If your WHERE clause is always for a single row on a unique key, and fetch succeeds, Phantoms can't happen with the REPEATABLE READ isolation level.

If you need the security of REPEATABLE READ, but you would still like locks to get an early release, here are some tricks to force the DBMS to do what you want.

```
Example #1:
(transaction start)
SELECT * FROM Table1

SAVEPOINT savepoint1

SELECT * FROM Table2

ROLLBACK TO SAVEPOINT savepoint1
(transaction end)
```

In Example #1, the ROLLBACK TO SAVEPOINT statement will eliminate the locks on Table2 only (assuming the DBMS supports this SQL:1999 instruction). ROLLBACK TO SAVEPOINT is also useful if a lock attempt fails and you want to try a different tack.

```
Example #2:
SELECT * FROM Table1;

for (n=0; n<#-of-rows; ++n) {
  FETCH ... INTO :x[n];
  if (NOT_FOUND) break;
}

ROLLBACK;

for (n=0; n<#-of-rows; ++n) {
  printf("x[n]=%d\n",x[n]);
}
```

In Example #2, the ROLLBACK statement comes before the display. If we'd used a scalar variable for the fetch instead, we would also have had to call printf() from within the fetch loop, thus delaying the transaction end. If you can make big arrays, you can end transactions early. By the way, we don't bother to close the cursor. ROLLBACK handles that.

REPEATABLE READ is a good isolation level to specify for transactions that contain multiple SQL statements involving data changes. Typical REPEATABLE READ situations are transferring money from one bank account to another or producing a customer invoice.

SERIALIZABLE Transactions

SERIALIZABLE is the default isolation level specified by the SQL Standard and is supported by all the Big Eight except MySQL. But all of the Big Eight except Ingres recommend either READ COMMITTED or REPEATABLE READ for the default. That tells us that nobody else has found a practical way to implement SERIALIZABLE and look good at the same time. You must avoid the SERIALIZABLE level unless it's utterly necessary but, alas, it sometimes *is*.

For example, suppose you're coding an application for a bank and want to retrieve and display all bank account balances, followed by a total. The total shown must really equal what you'd get by adding up all the individual account lines, so Phantoms are intolerable. This means you can't use REPEATABLE

READ for your transaction. Before DBMSs supported SERIALIZABLE, there was still a way to ensure serialization, namely with a non-standard SQL-extension LOCK statement such as

```
LOCK TABLE Accounts IN SHARE MODE
```

(or whatever the LOCK statement is for your DBMS). In fact, some DBMSs will internally support SERIALIZABLE through the simple device of huge-grain locks, while others try to be more sophisticated. Here is a sampling of what DBMSs do to support this isolation level.

- Microsoft keeps locks on a range of index keys, thus blocking transactions that use overlapping WHERE clause search conditions. Unlike ordinary index page locks, these range locks are not released until the transaction ends.
- MySQL allows LOCK TABLES ... UNLOCK TABLES to span statements (statements in MySQL constitute transactions unless you install an optional package).

SERIALIZABLE is a good isolation level to specify for transactions that contain quickly executed SQL statements that affect only a few rows at a time. Typical SERIALIZABLE situations are master/detail, member/aggregate, or account-balance/total-balance reports.

Bog-standard MySQL won't support SERIALIZABLE transactions (recall that our policy is to ignore non-default installation options; see Chapter 1, "Facilis Descensus Averni"). The usual solution involves MySQL's non-standard SQL-extension LOCK TABLES statement, but here's another example involving the dread "bank transfer." This transaction should be serializable, and it involves two updates on the same table.

```
(transaction start)
UPDATE Customer1
   SET balance = balance - 5
   WHERE custid = 1

UPDATE Customer1
   SET balance = balance + 5
   WHERE custid = 2
(transaction end)
```

If you're using MySQL, you could cause this transaction to be SERIALIZ-ABLE by using a single UPDATE statement with CASE, like this:

```
UPDATE Customer1
    SET balance =
        CASE WHEN custid = 1 THEN balance - 5
             WHEN custid = 2 THEN balance + 5
        END
    WHERE custid IN (1, 2)
```

This works because (a) MySQL doesn't have atomic transactions, and (b) MySQL *does* have atomic statements, therefore (c) transactions must be statements. It's not smart, because MySQL handles ORs badly,[2] but might do in a pinch.

READ ONLY or FOR UPDATE

You can specify that a transaction will be READ ONLY, or its opposite, FOR UPDATE, using the SET TRANSACTION statement, the ODBC SQLSetConnectAttr function call, the JDBC isReadOnly method, or the embedded SQL DECLARE CURSOR . . . FOR UPDATE clause. (If you don't specify the option you want, the DBMS probably assumes FOR UPDATE rather than READ ONLY.) It's important to make this specification, as the value affects locking strategy drastically.

FOR UPDATE transactions cause update locks. Recall that update locks are less concurrent than shared locks because they won't coexist with other update locks on the same object. So why are they there? Well, follow this scenario with our old pals Transaction #1 and Transaction #2.

- Transaction #1 gets a shared lock.

- Transaction #2 gets a shared lock on the same object.

- Transaction #1 tries to upgrade to an exclusive lock, but it must wait (because of Transaction #2's lock).

- Transaction #2 tries to upgrade to an exclusive lock, but it must wait too (because of Transaction #1's lock).

- Deadlock!

---

2. Recall that DBMSs will process an IN list as a series of ORs.

A **deadlock** is a condition that arises when two or more transactions are waiting for one another to release locks. Now consider the same scenario using update locks rather than shared locks.

- Transaction #1 gets an update lock.
- Transaction #2 tries to get an update lock on the same object, but it must wait (because of Transaction #1's lock).
- Transaction #1 upgrades to an exclusive lock.
- Transaction #1 continues until end of transaction, when it releases all locks.
- Transaction #2 tries again; gets the update lock it needs.
- Transaction #2 upgrades to an exclusive lock.
- No deadlock!

FOR UPDATE transactions have fewer deadlocks.
Now here's the bad news about update locks.

- Update locks aren't released as quickly as shared locks when transactions are READ COMMITTED.
- Update locks force more waiting because, by definition, they are exclusive when transactions are READ COMMITTED, REPEATABLE READ, or SERIALIZABLE.

Unfortunately, you always get more update locks than you need. Consider these two examples.

```
Example #1:
UPDATE Table1
  SET unindexed_column = 1
  WHERE indexed_column = 2
```

In Example #1, the search is via the index on `indexed_column`. But because the index won't be updated, update locks are made on the index pages unnecessarily.

```
Example #2:
UPDATE Table1
  SET unindexed_column = 1
  WHERE unindexed_column = 2
```

In Example #2, the search is via a table scan. But many rows won't match the search condition, so update locks are made on table pages unnecessarily.

Our conclusion is that READ ONLY transactions help concurrency more than you might at first expect. READ ONLY is particularly "lock friendly" when combined with versioning or with the READ COMMITTED isolation level.

Deadlocks

We've just seen that update locks are useful for deadlock avoidance. Because deadlock avoidance is something everybody wants, here are some tips to gain that end.

- If your DBMS supports only shared and exclusive locks (not update locks), then the most common deadlocks occur when a shared lock is upgraded to an exclusive lock. Avoid this by making locks exclusive at the start, with dummy UPDATE statements containing non-updating clauses like SET column1 = column1.

- Similarly, deadlocks occur if the DBMS tries to escalate. When eventual escalation is a certainty, accelerate it to the start of the transaction with a dummy UPDATE or a LOCK statement.

- Don't change index columns or, conversely, don't index changeable columns. If all accesses are via an index but all changes are of unindexed columns, then a single UPDATE statement can never ask for more than one exclusive lock (for the table's row or page).

Deadlocks are rare if all transactions access objects in a fixed order. For example, the following situation is bad.

- Transaction #1 exclusive locks Table1.
- Transaction #2 exclusive locks Table2.
- Transaction #1 tries to get a lock on Table2, and must wait.
- Transaction #2 tries to get a lock on Table1, and must also wait.
- Deadlock!

Here's another example, this time of a good situation.

- Transaction #1 exclusive locks `Table1`.
- Transaction #2 tries to get an exclusive lock on `Table1`, and must wait.
- Transaction #1 gets an exclusive lock on `Table2`.
- Transaction #1 is unblocked, so it proceeds to end of transaction and releases all locks.
- Transaction #2 tries again and gets an exclusive lock on `Table1`.
- Transaction #2 gets an exclusive lock on `Table2`.
- Transaction #2 is unblocked, so it proceeds to end of transaction and releases all locks.

The only difference between the "bad" example and the "good" example is that, in the good example, Transaction #1 and Transaction #2 both asked for locks in the same order: first on `Table1`, then on `Table2`. You can ensure such situations happen by always following this policy: when all else is equal, master tables before detail tables, DELETE before INSERT, and UPDATE ... WHERE x = 1 before UPDATE ... WHERE x = 2.

Avoid exclusive index-page locks by including the index column in your data-change statement. For example, instead of executing Statement #1, use Statement #2:

```
Statement #1:
UPDATE Table1
   SET indexed_column = 5
   WHERE column1 = 77

Statement #2:
UPDATE Table1
   SET indexed_column = 5
   WHERE column1 = 77
     AND indexed_column <> 5
```

Now here is a different kind of tip: split transactions up however you can. For example, instead of writing a single transaction to get a ROWID and UPDATE it, code a read transaction to get the ROWID and then code a write transaction to do the data change for that ROWID. Or instead of writing a single transaction to change two columns of a table or to change many rows of a table, code separate passes to change first `column1` and then `column2`, or code separate passes to change only the first 20 rows and then the next 20 rows and so on. Splitting transactions is a fearsome tool for avoiding deadlocks, although at the cost of both throughput and response time.

Finally, because you can't be sure that you'll always be able to avoid deadlocks, make sure your application includes code that will handle a "deadlock" error return from the DBMS.

The Bottom Line: Isolation Levels

The isolation level of a transaction determines the type of concurrency problem that will be tolerated for the transaction. The sooner a lock is released, the better.

You can set a transaction's isolation level with the SQL SET TRANSACTION statement, with the ODBC function call `SQLSetConnectAttr(...SQL_ATTR_TXN_ISOLATION,...)`, or with the JDBC method `setTransactionIsolation(...)`.

READ UNCOMMITTED gives you the lowest isolation and the highest concurrency level. No locks are issued or checked during the transaction; the DBMS will allow reading of rows that have been written but not committed by other transactions. No data changes are allowed at this level.

READ COMMITTED gives you medium isolation and a fairly high concurrency level. Shared locks are mandatory but can be released before the transaction ends; the DBMS will allow reading of rows that have been written by other transactions only after they have been committed.

REPEATABLE READ gives you fairly high isolation, but concurrency drops sharply. Shared locks are mandatory and will not be released until the transaction ends; the DBMS will not allow a situation where one transaction gets two sets of data from two reads of the same set of rows because a second transaction has changed that set of rows between the two reads.

SERIALIZABLE gives you the highest isolation and the lowest concurrency level. The DBMS might lock whole tables, not just rows, during a transaction. In effect, the DBMS will execute concurrent transactions in a manner that produces the same effect as a serial execution of those transactions.

Transactions are concurrent when they have overlapping start or end times. There are four general problems that can arise from concurrent transactions: the Lost Update, the Dirty Read, the Non-repeatable Read, and the Phantom.

To avoid Lost Updates, set your transaction isolation level to READ UNCOMMITTED or higher. READ UNCOMMITTED is a good isolation level to specify for (a) transactions that are slow and (b) transactions that are likely to have small errors, or errors that will cancel one another out.

To avoid Dirty Reads, set your transaction isolation level to READ COMMITTED or higher. For READ COMMITTED transactions, assume row locks, no versioning, and no updating. READ COMMITTED is a good isolation level to specify for transactions that contain only one SQL statement.

To avoid Non-repeatable Reads, set your transaction isolation level to REPEATABLE READ or higher. REPEATABLE READ is a good isolation level to specify for transactions that contain multiple SQL statements involving data changes.

Use savepoints to force REPEATABLE READ transactions to release locks early.

To avoid Phantoms, set your transaction isolation level to SERIALIZABLE. SERIALIZABLE is a good isolation level to specify for transactions that contain quickly executed SQL statements that affect only a few rows at a time.

If your WHERE search condition is always for a single row on a unique key, and fetch succeeds, Phantoms can't happen with REPEATABLE READ.

If you can make big arrays, you can end transactions (and release locks) early.

You can specify that a transaction will be READ ONLY, or its opposite, FOR UPDATE, using the SET TRANSACTION statement, the ODBC function call `SQLSetConnectAttr`, the JDBC method `isReadOnly`, or the embedded SQL DECLARE CURSOR . . . FOR UPDATE clause. It's important to be explicit about this, as the specification affects locking strategy drastically.

READ ONLY transactions help concurrency. READ ONLY is particularly lock friendly when combined with versioning or with the READ UNCOMMITTED isolation level.

FOR UPDATE transactions cause update locks and thus have fewer deadlocks.

Update locks aren't released as quickly as shared locks when transactions are READ COMMITTED.

Update locks force more waiting because they are exclusive when transactions are READ COMMITTED, REPEATABLE READ, or SERIALIZABLE.

If your DBMS doesn't support update locks, force exclusive locks at the start of your transactions with dummy UPDATE statements or use your DBMS's LOCK statement.

Don't change indexed columns.

Don't index frequently changed columns.

Deadlocks are rare if all transactions access objects in a fixed order. Follow this policy: when all else is equal, master tables before detail tables, DELETE before INSERT, and UPDATE . . . WHERE x = 1 before UPDATE . . . WHERE x = 2.

Avoid exclusive index-page locks by including the index column in the data-change statement.

Splitting transactions is a fearsome tool for avoiding deadlocks, but costs both throughput and response time.

Index Locks

You can lock B-tree index pages the same way that you lock table pages, but beware: index pages are "*shiftier*" (because data-change statements cause shifting and splitting), "*big-grainier*" (because typical index pages hold many small keys), and "*bottleneckier*" (because all index searches begin with the same page at the top node). Some special tweaks are therefore necessary. We'll tell you about them, with the warning that these considerations do not apply in all cases.

1. The DBMS will release index locks early. During a SELECT via an index, shared locks are set for the index and for the table pages that the matching index keys point to. In READ COMMITTED transactions, the index locks disappear after the SELECT is executed instead of after the fetch, as the following example shows.

```
SELECT ...
    /* index locks released here */

FETCH ...
    /* table locks released here */
```

2. The DBMS will split upper-level index pages before they're full. Suppose the current index has a nearly full top node pointing to a nearly empty leaf node. In this situation, the DBMS cannot travel all the way down, split a leaf node, then travel all the way back splitting upper nodes as it goes—that would cause deadlocks. So the DBMS can, and will, split top nodes "in anticipation," even when such action is unnecessary.

3. The DBMS will make an effort to prevent keys from shifting during a transaction. For example, Microsoft and Oracle will only mark a deleted key as "deleted" rather than actually removing the key and shifting all following keys backward. As another example, Sybase will add a pointer to an overflow page rather than actually inserting a new key and shifting all following keys forward.

4. The DBMS will use marks on the wall to stop concurrent transactions from passing through the same place. Consider the situation shown in

Table 15–10   *Marks on the Wall in an Index*

Index Leaf Page	
BELGRADE	
LJUBLJANA	Transaction #1 puts a mark on the wall here.
SARAJEVO	
SKOPJE	Transaction #1 puts a mark on the wall here.
ZAGREB	

Table 15-10, where Transaction #1 has placed a mark on the wall for two index keys.

Now, if Transaction #2 does this SELECT:

```
SELECT * FROM Table1
    WHERE column1 BETWEEN 'BELGRADE' AND 'SARAJEVO'
```

it will encounter Transaction #1's mark on LJUBLJANA and wait for it to be removed. Meanwhile, if Transaction #1 actually deletes LJUBLJANA, the mark disappears, which is another reason that index keys can't be physically deleted during a transaction. This "key range locking" is an effective way to lock index keys instead of index pages. The flaw is the horrific amount of time that it takes. Key range locks occur only in transactions with isolation level SERIALIZABLE.

5. The DBMS will treat a lock for a strong-clustered table as if it's an index lock, not a table lock. That has to happen because a clustered table is organized as a B-tree. This constitutes a warning that the locking rules change when the table is clustered.

As for bitmap indexes, they don't present special locking problems. Updating bitmap indexes is slow because each row is indexed in multiple pages; however, the bitmap is in ROWID order so the B-tree's difficulties (shifts, big-grain locks, and bottlenecks) won't come up. That's not the case with SERIALIZABLE transactions, which are simply incompatible with bitmap indexes.

The Bottom Line: Index Locks

Index locks favor READ COMMITTED transactions.

Changes to index keys cause unexpected splits and blocks.

Putting one index on a table doesn't merely double the locking: effects are geometric.

Hot Spots

"Nobody goes there anymore because it's too crowded."
—Yogi Berra

When we say Moose Jaw is the hot spot to be this year, we're talking not about weather but about popularity. Similarly, a hot spot isn't exactly where the disk drive head is burning from friction. Rather, it's an object that many processes are trying to get at the same time.

Not all hot spots are hellish. If every transaction is READ UNCOMMITTED, or if traffic is light, then it's wonderful to find that a page is still in the cache, left over from the last user's access. The hot spots we're talking about here, though, are the malignant kind: hot spots that cause exclusive locks and block other processes.

INSERT statements cause hot spots because the DBMS tries to put all new rows at the end of the table file-section (unless it's a clustered table). Because the table file has only one end, INSERT statements always try to get locks for the last page in the file. The DBMS can help here; for example, Microsoft can use row locks rather than page locks for INSERTs. Another palliative is to use clustered indexes (recall from Chapter 9, "Indexes," that, with clustered indexes, newly inserted rows can be anywhere in the file because they're put in order by the cluster key).

Index splits cause hot spots too, because DBMSs try to put new index pages together in the index file. The DBA can avoid such hot spots by setting some parameters to make the DBMS look first at "the end of the extent" rather than "the end of the file," although that technique wastes space.

Globals also cause hot spots. Typical examples are reporting applications that change a single row containing a "date of last report" field or bank withdrawals that immediately update the general ledger. Another example of a global is an interest rate: if interest rates change only once a day, can you read them in once to a program variable instead of looking them up in a table?

Another cause of hot spots is using sequences, or monotonics. If you use sequencing—that is, if you use SERIAL data types or IDENTITY columns, or auto-incrementing objects—here is a question for you: Given that the number following 12345678 is 12345679, what is the probability that two keys containing those values will end up on the same index page? If you answered nearly 100%, you're right! There are three easy fixes for sequence hot spots.

- Store the digits of the sequence in reverse; that is, store the numbers as 87654321 and 97654321. Because the difference is now at the *start* rather than at the *end* of the key, the keys won't sort near each other. Oracle supports this idea explicitly with its "reverse indexing" option. Of course, it's not such a good idea if you often ORDER BY sequence_ column when you SELECT.

- Use a unique-key generator rather than a true sequence. For example, a stored procedure can form a Microsoft **Global Unique Identifier (GUID)** using the network connection information Node ID, the date, and the time of day to a high precision.

- Add the sequence number to some nearly unique value derived from the row itself, such as a surname. If someone objects that sequence numbers are useful because they can easily tell how many rows there are by looking at MAX(sequence_column), we counter that rows can be deleted, transactions can be rolled back after a sequence number is generated, and UNION can cause an increment, and all these things muck up the nice monotonic sequence. And what's more, global sequence numbers are a cause of locking trouble in themselves, because the DBMS has to put a latch on the number while incrementing and retrieving it.

The Bottom Line: Hot Spots

Wherever order exists, if it doesn't correspond to some user need, add a pinch of chaos.

Optimistic Locking

Optimistic locking is locking at COMMIT time rather than locking during the course of a transaction. With optimistic locking, conflicts don't cause waits, they cause rejections. This is indeed optimistic, because you must pray that trouble will be rare. Let's look at how you can handle a common database application requirement with optimistic locking.

The requirement is that you must display an on-screen form giving existing database information, like an address and phone number. A user will edit the

Oracle Locking

To avoid misleading you, we once again stress that a versioning DBMS like Oracle doesn't handle concurrency in the manner we've been describing throughout this chapter. Here is a summary of the major differences in method.

SHARED and UPDATE LOCKS: Oracle won't need them. You can explicitly ask for shared locks with Oracle's non-standard SQL-extension LOCK TABLE statement, but typical transactions get only exclusive locks. These locks are done with marks on the wall, not with RAM records.

ESCALATION: Oracle won't do it. All automatic exclusive locks have row-level granularity.

SET TRANSACTION ISOLATION LEVEL READ UNCOMMITTED: Oracle won't actually support READ UNCOMMITTED. Instead, it upgrades to a higher level.

SET TRANSACTION ISOLATION LEVEL READ COMMITTED: Oracle supports READ COMMITTED by exclusive-locking writes and by using the log to read data rows "as at start of SQL statement."

SET TRANSACTION ISOLATION LEVEL REPEATABLE READ: Oracle won't actually support REPEATABLE READ. Instead, it upgrades to SERIALIZABLE.

SET TRANSACTION ISOLATION LEVEL SERIALIZABLE: Oracle supports SERIALIZABLE by exclusive-locking writes and by using the log to read data rows "as at start of transaction."

SET TRANSACTION READ ONLY: Oracle supports READ ONLY transactions by using the log to read data rows "as at start of transaction"—which in effect means that a READ ONLY transaction will effectively be at "repeatable read" isolation level.

information on the form, and you must write the edited information back to the database. Nothing remarkable about that . . . except that the user can take forever to fill in the form. Be realistic—you can't lock for the whole time this may take.

To handle this situation, your address records need to contain two fields in addition to the address information itself: a unique row identifier and a unique serialized transaction identifier. Let's use a GUID for the unique row identifier and a timestamp for the unique serialized transaction identifier. (In this case, the timestamp has nothing to do with date plus time, it's just a number that shows us the order of transactions. With Microsoft this is the TIMESTAMP field that goes in each row automatically, with Oracle you can generate a timestamp with a SEQUENCE object, and with other DBMSs you can do your own generation with a stored procedure or use a "serial" data type as shown in Table 7–10 in Chapter 7, "Columns.") A transaction with a higher serial number is "younger" than another transaction.

Here's how the system works. Whenever you INSERT or UPDATE, you also set the timestamp field to equal the transaction's current timestamp, and whenever you SELECT, you select the unique identifier and the timestamp *only*. In both cases, you then examine the timestamp to see if a younger transaction has changed the row. If that has happened, you ROLLBACK the transaction and ask the user to try again.

Let's try it out. Assume you have a table called Addresses, with these columns: guid_column, timestamp_column, address, phone. The Addresses table is already populated with the rows shown in Table 15–11.

The first thing to do is get a timestamp for yourself. For the sake of simplicity, assume that the current timestamp value is in a one-row table of timestamps and that you must increment it yourself (although in a real situation you'll certainly want to use the DBMS's utility to do this). These four SQL statements accomplish this task:

```
(Addresses_transaction start)

SET TRANSACTION ISOLATION LEVEL SERIALIZABLE

SELECT timestamp_counter
  INTO :transaction_timestamp
  FROM Timestamp_table

UPDATE Timestamp_table
  SET timestamp_counter = timestamp_counter + 1

COMMIT
```

The next step is to execute a SELECT to get the original address information for a row, using the GUID field. (You could use a non-unique field, but then

Table 15–11 *Addresses Table*

guid_column	timestamp_column	address	phone
gui-apr-001	00005000	1 First Avenue	470-1111
gui-apr-062	00005000	2 Second Avenue	470-2222
gui-mar-517	00005000	3 Third Avenue	470-3333
gui-mar-118	00005000	4 Fourth Avenue	470-4444
gui-jan-176	00005000	5 Fifth Avenue	470-5555

you'd have to select into arrays, which would merely complicate the example.) The transaction needs three SQL statements and looks like this:

```
SET TRANSACTION ISOLATION LEVEL READ UNCOMMITTED

SELECT guid_column,
       timestamp_column,
       address,
       phone
  INTO :address_guid,
       :address_timestamp,
       :address_address,
       :address_phone
  FROM Addresses
  WHERE guid_column = 'gui-mar-517'

COMMIT
```

Notice the COMMIT statement. You haven't finished yet, but you have told the DBMS the transaction is over.

The third step is to put up a screen form, a Web form, or something similar for the user to edit:

```
MessageBox(address_address, address_phone, MB_OK);
```

When the user has finished editing the form, there will be new information in the address_address and address_phone variables. Again, in a real situation, you would now validate that the data has changed, looks like a valid address and phone number, and so on. But let's skip to the fun part. Here's the transaction and subsequent code that actually does the UPDATE:

```
SET TRANSACTION ISOLATION LEVEL READ COMMITTED

UPDATE Addresses
  SET timestamp_column = :transaction_timestamp,
      address = :address_address,
      phone = :address_phone
  WHERE guid_column = 'gui-mar-517'
    AND timestamp_column = :address_timestamp
```

```
{ Call SQLRowCount to get update_count = # of rows
  updated by UPDATE statement }

COMMIT

IF update_count==0 THEN BEGIN
  MessageBox("Row was updated while you were editing.\
           Please re-try.");
  GOTO (Addresses_transaction start);
  END
```

Notice the UPDATE statement in this transaction. The clause AND `time-stamp_column = :address_timestamp` is subtle. If `timestamp_column` doesn't have the same value as it had when the row was read the first time, then the row won't be found and the number of rows updated will equal zero. The count of the updated rows is always returned automatically, and the transaction cleverly uses the automatic count so that one SQL statement both updates *and* tests for change. Because `update_count` will equal zero only if an interruption occurred, the user is then asked to do the whole thing again. Admittedly, if retries happen frequently or after the user has done lots of work, the user will be mad. But we're being optimistic, remember?

Now consider what happens if another user accesses the same row and edits the screen form at the same time. When User #2 tries to UPDATE the row, a rejection will occur because the first user has already updated and the `time-stamp_column` therefore has the earlier transaction timestamp value.

Often the functionality of optimistic locking is hidden in the driver or in a program that generates SQL statements, so you may not have seen optimistic locking frequently, even though it's very common. One potential flaw of optimistic locking is that, if you don't define a unique field or primary key, then an SQL generator will use a WHERE clause that contains every value in the row; so make sure there's a single unique field that nobody can change.

The Bottom Line: Optimistic Locking

If everyone uses the same program, then Lost Update can't happen. Our optimistic locking example is an illustration of READ COMMITTED in a transaction that can take a very long time.

The Scan Trick

Here's another task that could take too long.

- Display 25 rows on the screen.
- If the user clicks the scroll bar downwards, display the next 25 rows.

This task can be accomplished with optimistic locking and fetching into an array, but there's a better way.

Assume you have a table with an indexed primary or unique key. Assume further that the DBMS optimizes the MAX and MIN functions, and supports some version of the non-standard SQL-extension SET ROWCOUNT command (each of the Big Eight do). Here's the transaction to use:

```
SET TRANSACTION ISOLATION LEVEL READ COMMITTED

SQLSetStmtAttr(
    ...SQL_ATTR_MAX_ROWS,25...)          /* SET ROWCOUNT equivalent */

SELECT * FROM Table1
    WHERE unique_field > MAX(:last_unique_field)

for (n=1; n<=25; ++n)
  FETCH ...
  }

ROLLBACK

NB: last_unique_field = value of last unique_field in the last fetch
in the loop
```

This is another example of a READ COMMITTED transaction. The second time this is run, the value of `last_unique_field` will be the same as it was for the twenty-fifth row the previous time the transaction was run, so it's possible to go forward indefinitely. It's trivial to conceive of going both forward and backward, detecting end, and so on. The only essential matter is that, because the transaction ends after each screenful, Non-repeatable Reads and Phantoms are inevitable in such scroll cursor emulations. This scan trick works even if you're updating, but you should avoid changing the unique key. (Note that this functionality may be provided automatically by a higher-level interface; see our discussion of cursor rowsets in Chapter 12, "ODBC." Cursor rowsets act similarly, but may lock too much.)

Parting Shots

Our mantras in this chapter have been "Keep transactions short" and "Avoid conflict." Here are some ways to attain such ends.

Put calculations and validity tests before the transaction starts. That's an argument for doing some validation on the client.

End transactions. In many situations, saying CLOSE CURSOR isn't enough; for example, in read-only situations you can't depend on auto-commit. You should explicitly COMMIT or ROLLBACK, with whatever tool you're using.

Partition data so that volatile fields are in one place and changeless fields are in another. It's sufficient to follow the usual normalization rules.

Partition applications so that unlike operations are separated. For example, the employee reporting program has no need to access customer address data.

Replicate so that reporting transactions don't interfere with updating transactions.

Carry over information from one transaction to the next. For example, a typical library application gets the patron's ID once, then processes each book withdrawal as a separate transaction. There's no need to reread the patron record each time.

Assume the DBMS will initially give higher scheduling priority to the transaction with the lowest isolation level.

16

Clients and Servers

The simplest client/server system has a client and a server, as Figure 16-1 illustrates. Commonly, though, a system involves more than one client and includes middleware between the client and the server, as Figure 16-2 shows. We could draw several more architecture diagrams showing more clients, more middleware, and more servers. We could add hardware pictures if each component is on a separate machine. We could put in more components that are technically outside the system, such as an Apache Web Server. But Figures 16-1 and 16-2 are reasonably truthful depictions of reality. The fact is, as Robert Orfali and Dan Harkey have observed, "Over 80% of the existing client/server installations are single server and have less than 50 clients."[1]

In this chapter, we'll discuss client/server architecture. Specifically, we'll look at what the components (client, connection, middleware, server) do, and what good it is to know what they do. The bitter truth is that programmers can't do much to change the architecture. But it is useful to have a general idea of what's going on, so you can avoid blunders.

---

1. *Client/server programming with Java and CORBA,* Wiley Computer Press.

Figure 16–1   *A simple client/server system*

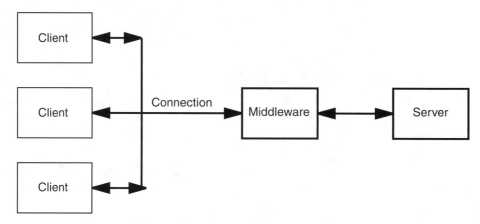

Figure 16–2   *A client/server system with middleware*

Middleware

"The usefulness, or utility, of a network equals the square of the number of users."

—Metcalfe's Law

Let's begin in the middle.

The fact is that pure client/server is rare; it's just a simple way to talk about the subject. We usually ignore the fact that there might be something between the client and the server. This something has various purposes and goes by various names, like "Distributed Application Services," "Transaction Monitors," "Middleware," and "Middle Tier." Whatever it's called, middleware usually becomes necessary when there's more than one transaction per second. Middleware's functions are as follows:

- To take the communications job out of the server's hands. Setting up connections, receiving messages, monitoring for timeout or network error, logging what's going in or out—all of these functions *could* be done by the server, but throughput should get better if the server can concentrate on database management.

- To make basic error tests, such as whether the client is fetching when there's no result set available. We say "basic" error checks because we don't expect the middleware to understand SQL. The middleware package only knows that "execute SQL SELECT statement" and "fetch" are different message types. Therefore the middleware won't need to parse any SQL statements to determine whether an ordering error exists.

- To enforce business rules. If the client is requesting something at the wrong time from the wrong place, the middleware can catch that error.

- To customize the query. This is not easy, and it is a feature of more expensive middleware. The software must be able to parse the SQL statement in order to determine whether the syntax is correct for the specific server and, if not, fix it.

- To keep a pool of duplicate queries. This isn't easy either. If User SAM executes a SELECT * FROM Table1 statement and later User SUZIE also executes SELECT * FROM Table1, then it might seem like the middleware can reuse SAM's connection to answer SUZIE's question. In fact, though, that's impossible unless the middleware knows that SAM and SUZIE are working with the same schema and similar privileges, *and* that SAM didn't change Table1.

It's good to write SQL statements that won't confuse the middleware. Here are some tips.

- Avoid unnecessary syntax shortcuts. Often these work with only one brand of DBMS.

- Use the same spacing and comments every time you repeat a statement.

- Always add schema qualifiers to table names.

You might find yourself programming your own piece of middleware. When you do, remember to keep the tiers separate. The conventional separation logic is as follows:

- If a task is related to keyboards or screens, then the client handles it.

- If a task is related to databases, then the server handles it.

- If a task is related to message massages, then the middleware handles it.

Notice that the middle tier doesn't do much on the way *back;* that is, server-to-client isn't much affected by the middle.

The Bottom Line: Middleware

Middleware's functions are (a) to take the communications job out of the server's hands, (b) to make basic error tests, (c) to enforce business rules, (d) to customize the query, and (e) to keep a pool of duplicate queries.

Write SQL statements that won't confuse the middleware. Avoid unnecessary syntax shortcuts, use the same spacing and comments every time you repeat a statement, and add schema qualifiers to table names.

If a task is related to keyboards or screens, then the client handles it.

If a task is related to databases, then the server handles it.

If a task is related to message massages, then the middleware handles it.

Server Processes and Threads

"The number of transistors on a microprocessor doubles approximately every 18 months."

—Moore's Law

It is facile to think of a server as a machine with a DBMS program running on it. Technically, that statement is true, but we really must stretch the definition of "a machine" and the definition of "a program" before it becomes true.

All large DBMSs are oligolithic (from the Greek for "a few stones"). At any moment there are several processes or threads running simultaneously. (In this chapter, we'll say "process/thread" to mean both processes and threads.) There is a difference between a process and a thread.

- Processes have their own memory.
- Threads share the same address space.

The result is that a process tends to be large (a few megabytes) while a thread is smaller (a few hundred kilobytes). On the other hand, processes tend to be safer because they are less able to interfere with one another. Different DBMS vendors have different preferences. For example IBM, Informix, and Oracle favor processes, while Microsoft and Sybase favor threads (or even fibers, which are very thin threads on MS Windows NT systems).

The larger DBMSs can run most or all of the following types of processes or threads.

System Processes/Threads

- The COMMIT writer watches for database pages marked as new or updated, organizes them, and issues disk-write calls for them.
- The log writer ensures that log records are definitely put on disk.
- The monitor watches for stuck jobs, new connections, and idleness.
- The scheduler decides which job gets to run next. (Sometimes this is a middleware job, but a DBMS like Microsoft comes with its own "thread pooler" option.)
- The over-nighter handles background jobs that require passes through many rows, for the sake of backup, replication, recovery, redistribution, index creation, loads, and reorganization.

Per-Client Processes/Threads

The temporary threads come into existence during execution of a single SQL statement. The threads run in parallel. Each thread works on a completely separate area of memory and disk. (If it were otherwise then threads would have to constantly synchronize with each other and there would be no point in assigning parallel threads.) Teradata's list of possible threads, which is larger than most DBMSs mention, is as follows:

- Table Scan: Each thread gets a separate table file or chunk.
- Index Scan: Each thread gets a separate index section.
- Index Read: Each thread gets a separate index entry.
- INSERT: Each thread gets a separate inserted row or page.
- DELETE: Each thread gets a separate deleted row or page.
- UPDATE: Each thread gets a separate updated row or page.
- Sort: Each thread gets a separate group of result-set rows (prior to merging).
- Join: Each thread joins a different pair of tables.
- Catalog Access: Each thread gets a look at the system catalog.

- Statistics: Each thread updates statistics while doing data I/O.

- Pipeline: One thread maintains a common area so that job A can feed to job B one row at a time. For example, data from a "scan" thread goes directly to a "join" thread.

- Parse: Each thread handles a separate statement portion, for example, a subquery.

Multi-thread architecture involves tremendously important considerations.

1. There can be no parallel threading if there is no separateness. That means it's important to partition your data and follow normalization rules; see Chapter 8, "Tables."

2. There can be no huge benefit from parallel threading if there is only one CPU. That is why you should be skeptical of benchmarks that compare, say, MySQL with Oracle. The benchmarks probably come from a single-processor computer, which makes MySQL look good because it has fewer threads. Oracle starts to look better when there are several CPUs so that each thread is truly processed in parallel.

3. There is no way to predict "response time" based on the number of rows or the number of steps in the statement process. For example, you cannot say that transaction A (which INSERTs two rows and then does a ROLLBACK) is much faster than transaction B (which INSERTs four rows and then does a COMMIT). Because transaction B can take advantage of "the Commit Writer" parallel thread as well as the "INSERT" parallel thread, it can be done nearly as quickly, in theory.

Remember that there are two ways to measure performance: response time (the time between arrival and departure of a particular statement) and

Benchmarks

We should explain that all timing tests for this book were done with a single-CPU computer, so comparisons between DBMSs would be misleading. The results wouldn't give full points to the DBMS with the best threading mechanisms.

throughput (the number of statements that the system can handle in a unit of time). Multi-threading is less helpful for throughput than for response time. This becomes obvious if the system is near saturation. For example, suppose one user does an INSERT. Because different parts of the statement are parallelized, the INSERT will be done more quickly, and response time improves. But now suppose that *two* users do a similar INSERT simultaneously. The statements will block one another with locking, will both try to get time-slices on the same CPU with their multifarious threads, and will both have to queue for the system processes like the Scheduler or the Commit Writer, thus throughput does not improve.

Bottom line: Organize so that multi-threading is possible, but don't hope it will make things better on an overloaded system. The most important thing is to minimize synchronization. That entails separating parts of statements or parts of databases, so that different threads don't need to access the same thing or to communicate with one another. And if your DBMS is a process-per-client rather than a thread-per-client system, it behooves you to disconnect when you're done so the server won't waste space on you.

Separateness and Parallelism

We said earlier that there can be no parallel threading if there is no separateness. Separateness usually means partitioning. A partition is a part of a database that consists of its own data and indexes (and often, its own configuration files and transaction logs). Tables can be located in one or more database partitions—that is, a partitioned table can have some of its rows stored in one partition and other rows stored in other partitions.

Because data is divided across partitions, you can use the power of multiple processors to execute SQL statements. The DBMS will automatically decompose SELECT and data-change statements into subrequests, and execute the subrequests in parallel among the applicable partitions. The fact that a table is split across multiple partitions is transparent to users issuing SQL statements.

Executing the components of a task (e.g., a SELECT statement) in parallel can enhance performance dramatically. The main types of parallelism are I/O and Query.

- I/O parallelism refers to the process of writing to, or reading from, two or more I/O devices simultaneously and can result in significant improvement in throughput.

- Query parallelism refers to the simultaneous processing of parts of a single SQL statement. In general, the DBMS subdivides what is usually considered a single database operation (e.g., creating an index or resolving a SELECT) into multiple parts, many or all of which can be run in parallel (a) within a single partition or (b) across multiple partitions on either one machine or on multiple machines. The result set is thus returned more quickly than if the query were run in serial fashion.

For an example of how to ensure you're getting the most out of your DBMS's parallelism abilities, consider how it's done with IBM.

- One type of parallel environment supported by IBM allows multiple processors to share access to a database so that SQL statements can be divided among the processors. You can specify the degree of parallelism to implement when compiling your application by using IBM's non-standard CURRENT DEGREE niladic function, or the DEGREE bind option. (Degree means the number of concurrently executing parts of an SQL statement you want to allow.) Each degree of parallelism adds to the system memory and CPU overhead.

- IBM provides three configuration parameters that you can use to control and manage parallelism. The first is the intra_parallel parameter; it enables or disables instance parallelism support. The second is the max_querydegree parameter; it sets an upper limit for the degree of parallelism that can be used for any query and overrides the CURRENT DEGREE function and/or the DEGREE bind option values. The third configuration parameter is the dft_degree parameter; it sets the default value for CURRENT DEGREE and the DEGREE bind option. If you run a query with DEGREE = ANY, IBM's optimizer chooses the degree of parallelism based on a number of factors, including the number of processors and the characteristics of the query. The actual degree used at runtime may be lower than the number of processors, depending on these factors.

The Bottom Line: Server Processes and Threads

Processes have their own memory. A process tends to be large (a few megabytes).

Threads share the same address space. A thread tends to be small (a few hundred kilobytes).

Processes tend to be safer than threads, because they are less able to interfere with one another.

There can be no parallel threading if there is no separateness. That means it's important to partition your data and follow normalization rules.

There can be no huge benefit from parallel threading if there is only one CPU.

There is no way to predict response time based on the number of rows or the number of steps in the statement process.

There are two ways to measure performance: response time (the time between arrival and departure of a particular statement) and throughput (the number of statements that the system can do in a unit of time).

Multi-threading is less helpful for throughput than for response time. Organize your work so that multi-threading is possible, but don't hope it will make things better on an overloaded system.

The most important thing is to minimize synchronization. Separate parts of statements or parts of databases, so that different threads don't need to access the same thing or communicate with each other.

If your DBMS is a process-per-client rather than a thread-per-client system, disconnect when you're done so the server won't waste space on you.

What Should the Client Do?

"The processing power of computer hardware grows exponentially with the price."
—Grosch's Law

A client is a terrible thing to waste. There are so many things that a 1GHz computer can do besides accepting user input or formatting pretty screens. Unfortunately the logic is made of iron.

- Thesis: Clients can process data in parallel with the server.
- Antithesis: But in order to get the data, they must ask for more than the user actually needs.
- Synthesis: Therefore the time saved in computing is wasted on communicating.

For example, suppose you decide to implement the DISTINCT operation on the client. That is, instead of sending Query #1 to the server, you send Query #2.

```
Query #1:
SELECT DISTINCT column1, column2
  FROM Table1
  ORDER BY column2

Query #2:
SELECT column1, column2
  FROM Table1
  ORDER BY column2
```

Then, for each row that gets fetched, you compare the row with all the rows already fetched, and if the new row is equal, you discard it. This has an advantage: the server doesn't have to sort by `column1` to find the duplicates. Unfortunately, even if only 10% of the rows are duplicates, this scheme turns out to be slower than passing SELECT DISTINCT to the server (GAIN: –7/8 if 10% or more duplicates).

That's not to say that you can't do any result-set processing on the client. There are all sorts of things you can do with result sets: capitalize, count, duplicate, group, sort, store, and so on. What you shouldn't do is filter.

Client Model

For a model, consider what Microsoft Access, a popular front end, does.

First, Access accepts user input. The front end is smart enough to understand SQL-like queries, so it knows quickly whether a table can be accessed from a local (i.e., on the client machine) database, or whether the query must be passed on to the server. Access also knows how to reformat the query so that the server will understand it. For example, the query

```
SELECT Date() FROM [Table1]      -- Access syntax
```

will be transformed to

```
SELECT Getdate() FROM Table1     -- SQL Server syntax
```

In any case, anything passed to the server will be canonical; that is, it will be shorn of any stylistic or personal quirks that cause SQL statements to look different when they're logically the same.

At this point, Access offers a choice of query methods. The obvious one is the **Pass Through Query (PTQ).** With PTQs, the plan is to SELECT and fetch all the rows immediately, then close the cursor on the server side. The client can then take all the time in the world to play with the fetched results, because the server isn't tied up. On the downside, a PTQ result set must be read-only, because the transaction's over as far as the server is concerned.

The trickier query method is the locally processed query. With locally processed queries, the plan is to SELECT and then fetch all the row identifiers (primary keys or RIDs), but not the actual data. This can save space compared to a PTQ, because a list of row identifiers is almost certain to be smaller than a list of the row contents themselves. Whenever fetches are necessary—for example, because the user scrolls the screen display—a new SELECT statement is sent to the server.

```
.SELECT * FROM Table1
   WHERE <row identifier = x>
      OR <row identifier = y>
```

Because the row identifiers are known, data changes are possible, too.

```
UPDATE Table1 SET column1 ...
   WHERE <row identifier = x>
```

However, some care must be employed in case another user is updating the same rows. This becomes a matter for locking; see Chapter 15, "Locks." The important thing here is that Access is able to decide when a transaction can be terminated on the server side. Usually it can terminate the transaction very quickly without tying up fetched rows, as an unsophisticated front end would do.

Sometimes this sophistication goes too far. For example, suppose you use a function in your query that Access understands, but the server doesn't. In that case, Access will bring in all the rows so that it can process them locally. Moral: Never use a non-standard scalar function!

Finally, Access will handle all on-screen formatting of the result set: the scroll bars, the pictures, the beeps, the image transformations for BLOB images, and all the other details that go into a GUI application. Once again, this activity takes place after Access has signalled the server that it is finished with the query.

This has been an idealized picture of what a front-end program running on a client should do. The logic is not that you should go out and buy Access

(Microsoft doesn't pay us for testimonials), but that you should study how Access works and emulate its activities as a good client.

The Bottom Line: Client Tips

Seventeen ways to make your application a better client (with apologies to Paul Simon):

There are all sorts of things you can do with result sets on the client: capitalize, count, duplicate, group, sort, store, and so on. What you shouldn't do is filter.

Clients should transform input and transform output, but not try to take over basic server functions.

The best clients will close result sets early so that the server can release locks. The most realistic objective is not to shove tasks from the server to the client, but to make the client smart enough that it can figure out the quickest way to deal with the server.

Use client threads. Of course any client can fork (i.e., start a separate thread) and do low-priority INSERTs on the other thread. And any client can save up its UPDATEs and let a timer send the requests later on the same thread. The trouble is (because it's not the server doing the accumulations), a connection failure can lose the transaction permanently.

Canonize SQL statements. At least remove trail spaces or multiple spaces (provided they're not inside quotes!), and change capitalization to a consistent scheme. (Do this only if middleware is absent. Generally, formatting statements for the server is a job for the middle tier.)

Use compound statements. By packing several SQL statements into one message, you reduce the network traffic.

Fetch several rows at once. The usual recommendation is that database rows should be short; they are therefore probably shorter than the packet size, or the most efficient size for network transfer. To fetch several rows at once you must persuade the DBMS to increase the rowset size, and you must use a special variant of fetch. These possibilities are available in both ODBC and JDBC.

Use stored queries. This is important enough that there's a chapter on the subject; see Chapter 11, "Stored Procedures."

Set a limit to the number of rows you want to retrieve. There are several ways to set limits. In ODBC you use an SQLSetStmtAttr function, in JDBC you use setFetchSize, in SQL statements you can use a non-standard SQL-extension like Microsoft's SELECT TOP or Informix's SELECT FIRST (see Chapter 6, "Subqueries").

Reject any user queries that begin with SELECT * or at least use the DBMS's catalog/metadata to discover whether "*" implies that BLOBs will be fetched. If so, eliminate them.

Choose servers. For example, you can tell what the probable home branch is from the IP or the client-ID. Then you know which server to prefer.

Retrieve timestamps when you fetch. A timestamp will tell you when the row was inserted or last updated. If your query is read-only, and you retrieved the timestamp and all columns except the BLOB column, and the timestamp is from long ago, you can fetch the BLOB from a replicated server instead of going back to the original one.

Cache information in the client memory. This is particularly good for metadata information, because catalog functions are quite time consuming. It's not perfect, because metadata information is slightly volatile, but you're safe if some other user deletes a table; you'll just get an error message when you try to use it.

Run an error test on a non-urgent server. If there's a location where you can store a duplication of the catalog information (without the data), then put an alternate server at that location so you can parse statements on it. Again, if the duplicated catalog becomes out of date, you're only risking an error message.

Keep statistics. If there are several queries that are similar but not quite the same, there is a candidate for parameterization or reuse.

Trim. Most DBMSs are going to truncate the spaces in a VARCHAR anyway, so don't bother sending them.

Metamorphose. There are standard ways to retrieve information about the DBMS, including its product identification and version number. Adjust the syntax of your statement to match what that DBMS does best.

Parting Shots

> "Work expands to fill the time available."
> —Parkinson's Law

At the moment, most people would agree that the server is the place to concentrate efforts. We've tried our best to say so ourselves: even in this chapter, we felt it was necessary to devote some space toward a fuller understanding of what a server is.

If there are many client computers, and they're far away, and they're all a little different, then it's too much trouble to deploy and code for all the computers. So quite apart from performance considerations, there are reasons that large organizations avoid writing custom code solutions for client computers. In other words, administrative reasons have made client-specific coding less popular than it would be if performance were the trump goal. In such situations, consider applying our client tips to your middleware code instead.

There are many things that you can and should do with a client, provided you keep within its proper gamut: preparing queries and massaging results. There are many things an intelligent front end can do to make a server's job easier—not by sharing the load, but by reducing it.

Bottom line: client good, network good, middleware good, server good. All client/server good—even if Oracle Corporation's CEO did once say that "client/server was a tremendous mistake."

17

Cost-Based Optimizers

Supposedly, a **rule-based optimizer (RBO)** differs from a **cost-based optimizer (CBO).** Consider this SQL statement:

```
SELECT * FROM Table1
  WHERE column2 = 55
```

Assume that `column2` is an indexed, non-unique column. A rule-based optimizer will find `column2` in the system catalog and discover that it is indexed, but not uniquely indexed. The RBO then combines this data with the information that the query uses the equals operator. A common assumption in the field of optimization is that "`= <literal>`" search conditions will retrieve 5% of all rows. (In contrast, the assumption for greater-than conditions is that they will retrieve 25% of all rows.) That is a narrow search, and usually it's faster to perform a narrow search with a B-tree rather than scan all rows in the table. Therefore the rule-based optimizer makes a plan: find matching rows using the index on `column2`.

Notice that the rule-based optimizer is using a *non-volatile datum* (the existence of an index) and a *fixed assumption* (that equals searches are narrow).

A cost-based optimizer can go further. Suppose the system catalog contains three additional pieces of information: (1) that there are 100 rows in `Table1`,

(2) that there are two pages in Table1, and (3) that the value 55 appears 60 times in the index for column2. Those facts change everything. The equals operation will match on 60% of the rows, so it's not a narrow search. And the whole table can be scanned using two page reads, whereas an index lookup would take three page reads (one to lookup in the index, two more to fetch the data later). Therefore the cost-based optimizer makes a different plan: find matching rows using a table scan.

Notice that the cost-based optimizer is using *volatile data* (the row and column values that have been inserted) and an *override* (that the contents are more important than the fixed assumptions).

In other words, a cost-based optimizer is a rule-based optimizer that has additional, volatile information available to it so that it can override the fixed assumptions that would otherwise govern its decisions. The terminology causes an impression that one optimizer type is based on rules while the other is based on cost. That's unfortunate because both optimizer types use rules and both optimizer types have the goal of calculating cost. The reality is that cost-based is an extension of rule-based, and a better term would have been something like "rule-based++."

Most vendors claim that their DBMSs have cost-based optimizers, as you can see from Table 17–1. The claims don't mean much by themselves. What's important is whether the optimizer estimates cost correctly and how it acts on the estimate. In this chapter, we'll look at the actions DBMSs take to fulfill their claims.

Table 17–1   *Cost-Based Optimizers*

	Claims to be CBO	"Explains" the Access Plan	"Updates" Statistics for the Optimizer
IBM	Yes	EXPLAIN	RUNSTATS
Informix	Yes	SET EXPLAIN	UPDATE STATISTICS
Ingres	Yes	EXECUTE QEP	optimizedb utility
InterBase	Yes	SELECT ... PLAN	SET STATISTICS
Microsoft	Yes	EXPLAIN	UPDATE STATISTICS
MySQL	No	EXPLAIN	ANALYZE TABLE
Oracle	Yes	EXPLAIN PLAN FOR	ANALYZE
Sybase	Yes	SET SHOWPLAN ON	UPDATE STATISTICS

Notes on Table 17–1:

- Claims to be CBO column

  This column is "Yes" if the DBMS's documentation makes the claim that it operates with a cost-based optimizer.

- "Explains" the Access Plan column

  This column shows the non-standard statement provided by the DBMS so that you can examine the **access plan** the optimizer will use to resolve an SQL statement. For example, if you want to know how Oracle will resolve a specific SELECT statement, just execute an EXPLAIN PLAN FOR statement for the SELECT.

- "Updates" Statistics for the Optimizer column

  This column shows the non-standard statement or utility the DBMS provides so that you can update volatile information, or statistics, for the optimizer. For example, if your DBMS is MySQL and you've just added many rows to a table and want the optimizer to know about them, just execute an ANALYZE TABLE statement for the table.

Cost

A statement's cost is the amount of resources consumed at execution time. That's impossible to calculate exactly and for all time, but we can make a stab at it.

- One *CPU unit* is the amount of time needed to execute one operation.
- One *I/O unit* is the amount of time needed to read or write one page.
- One *Com unit* is the amount of time needed to send one network message.

Oracle Has Two Optimizers

In Oracle and only in Oracle, one must distinguish the capitalized terms Rule-Based Optimizer and Cost-Based Optimizer, because Oracle uses those terms to refer to separate tools. The Oracle Cost-Based Optimizer is an enhanced alternative to the Rule-Based Optimizer, which is no longer being maintained.

The relative unit weights vary with time, but here's an approximation, based on Oracle's CBO weights for disk accesses versus cached accesses.

- One I/O unit equals 1000 CPU units.
- One Com unit equals 1.5 I/O units.

When a DBMS estimates cost for one statement, it lacks full information about what statements will occur before and after at execution time. Therefore, it can only guess what will be in cache, whether processors will be available, how much locking will be going on, and so forth; all of these items depend on activity, and the optimizer doesn't base cost estimates on activity. It bases them, as we've seen, on rules and database contents. (That's why DBAs have to monitor activity all the time.)

When executing SQL statements, then, the decisions made by the DBMS are strongly influenced by the optimizer's picture of the database contents. This picture, or data model, is used to estimate the costs of the various access plans that could be used to resolve a specific SQL statement. A key element in the data model is a set of statistics about the data, stored in the system catalog. A change in the data statistics can result in a change in the access plan selected as the most efficient method of getting the data you need.

Optimizer Terminology

Here are some common terms you'll come across when you're examining your DBMS's optimizer documentation.

Access plan: the plan used by the optimizer to resolve an SQL statement.

Cardinality: the number of rows in an object (table or result set). For a table, this is decided by INSERT statements.

Cost: the amount of resources consumed during the execution of an SQL statement (that is, the total execution time required to resolve the statement).

Degree: the number of attributes. This is decided by the CREATE statement for the object.

Heuristic: an educated guess. Well, everything is an educated guess, but quality optimizers have more information available.

Statistics and Histograms

We've noted that cost-based optimizers need volatile data in the system catalog. That data is called **statistics** (no, we don't know why it's called statistics). The DBMS has utilities and/or non-standard SQL statements for keeping statistics up to date, but they're slow—updating statistics for a table can take as long as creating an index for the table. Therefore, the updating is never automatically performed by the DBMS. Someone (usually the DBA) has to issue an "update statistics" instruction when it becomes clear that statistics are out of date. Careful administrators believe that statistics updating should happen after about 10% of the rows have been changed due to INSERT, UPDATE, or DELETE statements, or after any CREATE INDEX statement, and they will schedule automatic "update statistics" jobs accordingly.

The DBMSs that sport cost-based optimizers keep most or all of the following statistics:

- The number of data pages.

- The number of index pages.

- The number of index levels.

- The number of leaf pages in each index.

- The number of distinct values in the first column of a compound index. There is also a statistic for the number of distinct values in the first two columns of a compound index, the number of distinct values in the first three columns of a compound index, and so on.

- The number of pages that are not empty.

- The number of rows that have been moved from their original page to other (overflow) pages.

- The degree of clustering of an index, that is, the extent to which the physical sequence of rows in a table actually follows the order of an index.

- The number of rows in a table.

- The number of columns in a table.

- The average length of a column's data.

- The number of NULLs in a column.

- The percentage of distinct values in a column. This is called "selectivity" and usually is available for indexed columns only.

- The number of occurrences of frequently used column values.

- The second-smallest and second-largest values for a column. Experience shows that MIN and MAX values are often far outside the regular distribution, hence the choice of second-smallest and second-largest to distinguish a column's normal range of values.

All these statistics are easy to calculate and take very little storage space in the system catalog. So what's tough? Histograms.

A **histogram** is detailed information on the distribution of values over a column. For example, suppose you have the following table:

```
CREATE TABLE Table1 (
    column1 VARCHAR(15),
    column2 INTEGER)
```

Both columns of Table1 are indexed. A subset of the values contained in Table1.column1 is shown in Table 17–2.

The classic histogram is an ordered list of values with the number of times each value occurs. Table 17–3 shows the histogram for Table1.column1.

It's possible to get a classic histogram with this type of query:

```
SELECT column1, COUNT(*)
    FROM Table1
    GROUP BY column1
```

But the result is large and one objective is to store all statistics in RAM. So the DBMS uses a compression method instead. One compression method stores singletons (values with only one occurrence) separately, or not at all. Another compression method takes samples of every nth row. This is easy if there's an index; the DBMS just reads the top level of the B-tree.

Once the histogram is in place, if someone executes this SQL statement:

```
SELECT * FROM Table1
    WHERE column1 = 'Turkmenistan'
```

the DBMS can do a quick in-RAM binary search of the histogram for column1 during the optimization phase and find out how selective the search condition

Table 17–2   *Table1's Data*

column1
Uzbekistan
Tajikistan
Afghanistan
Pakistan
Baluchistan
Turkmenistan
Kirghizstan
Khalistan
Pushtunistan
Waziristan
Afghanistan
Turkmenistan
Uzbekistan
Afghanistan
Khalistan
Afghanistan

Table 17–3   *Histogram for* `Table1.column1`

column1 Value	Number of Occurrences
Afghanistan	4
Baluchistan	1
Khalistan	2
Kirghizstan	1
Pakistan	1
Pushtunistan	1
Tajikistan	1
Turkmenistan	2
Uzbekistan	2
Waziristan	1

is. Usually this is more than enough information to form an access plan. Typically there will be histograms for all the important columns (which are often the same as the indexed columns). For other columns, the optimizer will depend on the easier-to-get statistics.

Once the optimizer has looked up the statistics, it can plug them into formulas. There is one formula for each ANDed or ORed search condition in a WHERE clause. First the optimizer uses a formula to calculate the cost of each step. Then the optimizer uses a formula to calculate the output from each step, so that if there are two steps, the optimizer will know what the input size and order are for the second step. As an example, consider this query:

```
SELECT * FROM Table1
  WHERE column1 = 'Waziristan'
    AND column2 = 55
```

Assume that `Table1` contains 100 rows and the value 55 appears 60 times in the index for `column2`. With the statistics available to it, the optimizer can determine that column1 is indexed and can also determine (from the column1 histogram) that approximately one row will be returned. It can also determine that column2 is indexed and that column2's histogram says that the value 55 occurs about 60 times. Thus the optimizer has a choice of three different access plans:

- Plan #1

  Lookup column1 in its index.

  Lookup column2 in its index.

  Merge results of the lookups.

- Plan #2

  Lookup column1 in its index.

  For each result, read column2 in the table and filter out if the value isn't 55.

- Plan #3

  Lookup column2 in its index.

  For each result, read column1 in the table and filter out if the value isn't Waziristan.

Clearly, Plan #2 has the smallest cost, so the optimizer throws the other plans away. They will not be available at execution time.

This is a trivial example. It should be emphasized that the DBMS's biggest advantage from a cost-based optimizer becomes evident only when an SQL statement uses a join. Because there are possible plans for each join step, and because the number of possible plans can rise exponentially (for example, a four-way join has 4! [four factorial] plans to choose from), a WHERE clause with a multi-way join and a few semi-joins (subqueries) is too hard for a human. Your job is to optimize everything else, ensure the DBMS has what it needs, and let the optimizer do its job.

Analyzing Statistics

Analyzing the DBMS statistics can tell you when reorganization is necessary. Here are some things to look for.

- Degree of clustering. In general, only one of the indexes in a table can have a high degree of clustering. If your DBMS collects cluster ratio statistics, check them occasionally. A low cluster ratio leads to more I/O, since after the first access of each data page, it is less likely that the page is still in the buffer pool the next time it is accessed. (The cluster ratio shows the percentage of data rows that are in the same page order as the index keys.)

- Row overflow. This number shows how many rows are no longer present on their original page because of an expanding or shrinking update. In such cases, a pointer is kept at the row's original location. This can hurt performance, because the DBMS must follow the pointer to find the row's contents. Processing time is increased; more I/Os may be needed to get the data. As the number of overflow rows increases, the potential benefit of reorganizing your table also increases.

- Empty versus total pages. Compare the figure for the number of pages with rows to the total number of pages that a table contains. Empty pages occur when entire ranges of rows are deleted. Empty pages will still be read for a table scan. As the number of empty pages grows higher, so does the need for a table reorganization.

- Number of index leaf pages. This number predicts how many index page I/Os are needed for a complete scan of the index. Recall that random data changes can cause leaf page splits, which increase the size of an index beyond the minimum amount of space required. Rebuild your indexes to solve this problem. Don't forget to use PCTFREE/FILLFACTOR so that your DBMS will leave room in the rebuilt index for future data changes.

Ideally, you should rebind application programs after running statistics, because the optimizer may choose a different access plan for your queries, given the new statistics.

Multi-Column Statistics

Histograms are for columns, not combinations of columns. Even if you have a multi-column compound index, the DBMS will prefer to calculate full histograms for the first column only.

EXPLAIN

The non-standard EXPLAIN statement (see Table 17–1) is the vital way to find out what the optimizer has done. We haven't mentioned it up to now because this book's primary goal has been to show what *you* can do before the fact. But EXPLAIN is the way to measure whether your estimates correspond to DBMS reality. In many shops, it's customary to get an EXPLAIN for every SQL statement before submitting it for execution. That is quite reasonable. What's perhaps less reasonable is the custom of trying out every transformation one can think of and submitting them all for explanation. That is mere floundering. Understanding principles—in other words, estimating what's best *before* the fact—is more reliable and less time consuming. So don't flounder—read this book!

Here is an example of a typical EXPLAIN output, from Informix:

```
SET EXPLAIN ON
QUERY:
SELECT column1, column2 FROM Table1;
Estimated cost: 3
Estimated # of rows returned: 50
1) Owner1.Table1 : SEQUENTIAL SCAN
```

With most DBMSs, the EXPLAIN result goes to a table or file so you can select the information you need. In many cases, the EXPLAIN statement's output is much harder to follow than the short example we show here, which is why graphic tools like IBM's Visual EXPLAIN are useful.

Hints

Most DBMSs provide some non-standard way to override the optimizer if you judge that its estimates or formulas are wrong. Commonly the mechanism is a *hint*, which often looks like a comment or parenthetical clause in the SQL statement but in fact is a direction to the optimizer. Here's an example from Oracle:

```
SELECT /*+ INDEX(Table1 Index1) */
       column1, column2
   FROM Table1
   WHERE column1 >55
```

And here's one from Sybase:

```
SELECT column1, column2
  FROM Table1 (INDEX Index1 PREFETCH 16)
  WHERE column1 > 55
```

Hints are important enough to warrant mention, but there is no such thing as a portable hint; every DBMS (except IBM) has its own optimizer-specific hint set. We'll therefore limit ourselves to listing the most common hints, without getting into syntax.

- The predicate that follows is probably `true`.
- Stop trying to optimize if time-to-estimate is greater than time-to-execute.
- Use rule-based optimizer instead of cost-based optimizer.
- Prefer index X on table Y.

DBA note: Administrators can influence some DBMS's plans more generally with a manual override of the statistics, for example, by declaring that the selectivity of an index is 80% rather than 40%.

Parting Shots

After getting through the earlier chapters of this book, you're aware to a more or less painful degree that many optimizations are your responsibility. This last chapter has been a bit of good news: you have an ally. Until a few years ago, many DBMS optimizers were weak because they took only static information into account. Nowadays, optimizers are more useful because they also take dynamic data-related information into account. Perhaps soon the next phase will come, and optimizers will take user activity into account as well. Certainly, no optimizer can guarantee that the access plan it chooses will be perfect every time, but there's such a thing as progress.

We salute the DBMSs that we have been discussing for so long.

Appendix **A**

Further Reading

Bowman, Judith. *Practical SQL: The Sequel*. Boston: Addison-Wesley, 2000.

Celko, Joe. *SQL for Smarties: Advanced SQL Programming*. San Francisco: Morgan Kaufmann Publishers, 2000.

Delaney, Kalen. *Inside Microsoft SQL Server 2000*. Redmond, WA: Microsoft Press, 2000.

Dewdney, A. K. "On the spaghetti computer and other analog gadgets for problem solving." S*cientific American* 19 (June 1984).

DuBois, Paul. *MySQL*. Indianapolis: New Riders Publishing, 1999.

Flannery, Ron. *Informix Handbook*. Upper Saddle River, NJ: Prentice Hall PTR, 2000.

Gulutzan, Peter, and Trudy Pelzer. *SQL-99 Complete, Really*. Lawrence, KS: R&D Books, 1999.

International Organization for Standardization. *Database Language SQL*. ISO/IEC 9075-1:1999 (SQL/Framework).

International Organization for Standardization. *Database Language SQL*. ISO/IEC 9075-2:1999 (SQL/Foundation).

International Organization for Standardization. *Database Language SQL*. ISO/IEC 9075-3:1999 (SQL/CLI).

International Organization for Standardization. *Database Language SQL*. ISO/IEC 9075-4:1999 (SQL/PSM).

Kline, Kevin, Lee Gould, and Andrew Zanevsky. *Transact-SQL Programming*. Sebastopol: O'Reilly & Associates, 1999.

Kyte, Thomas. *Expert One on One: Oracle*. Chicago: Wrox Press, 2001.

Loney, Kevin, and George Koch. *Oracle8i: The Complete Reference*. Berkeley: Osborne McGraw-Hill, 2000.

Mullins, Craig. *DB2 Developer's Guide*. Indianapolis: SAMS Publishing, 2000.

North, Ken. *Database Magic with Ken North*. Upper Saddle River, NJ: Prentice Hall PTR, 1998.

Orfali, Robert, and Dan Harkey. *Client/server programming with Java and CORBA*. New York: Wiley Computer Press, 1997.

White, Seth, Maydene Fisher, Rick Cattell, Graham Hamilton, and Mark Hapner. *JDBC API Tutorial and Reference,* 2d ed. Boston: Addison-Wesley, 1999.

Yevich, Richard, and Susan Lawson. *DB2 High Performance Design and Tuning*. Upper Saddle River, NJ: Prentice Hall PTR, 2000.

Appendix B

Glossary

This glossary contains only terms that specifically are used for SQL optimization. For terms that apply to the subject of SQL in general, consult the 1,000-term glossary on our Web site, ourworld.compuserve.com/homepages/OCELOTSQL/glossary.htm.

Before the definition there may be a "Used by" note. For example, "Used by: Microsoft, Sybase" indicates that Microsoft and Sybase authorities prefer the term and/or definition. The words "Used by: this book only" indicate a temporary and non-standard term that exists only for this book's purposes.

When a word has multiple meanings, the first definition is marked "[1]" and subsequent definitions are marked with incremented numbers. "*See*" and "*see also*" refer to other terms in this glossary.

Numbers/Symbols

_rowid—*see* row identifier
    Used by: MySQL

1NF   First normal form table, a table that contains only scalar values.

2NF   Second normal form table, a 1NF table that contains only columns that are dependent upon the entire primary key.

3NF   Third normal form table, a 2NF table whose non-key columns are also mutually independent; that is, each column can be updated independently of all the rest.

A

access plan   The plan used by the optimizer to resolve an SQL statement.

ADO   ActiveX Data Objects, an API that enables Windows applications to access a database.

aggregate function—*see* set function

API   Application Programming Interface, the method by which a programmer writing an application program can make requests of the operating system or another application.

applet   A Java program that can be downloaded and executed by a browser.

B

B-tree   A structure for storing index keys; an ordered, hierarchical, paged assortment of index keys. Some people say the "B" stands for "Balanced."

back compression   Making index keys shorter by throwing bytes away from the back. *See also* compression, front compression.

balanced tree—*see* B-tree

BDB   Berkeley DB, an embedded database system that is bundled with MySQL.

big-endian   A binary data transmission/storage format in which the most significant bit (or byte) comes first.

binary sort   A sort of the codes that are used to store the characters.

bitmap   Multiple lines of bits.

bitmap index   An index containing one or more bitmaps. *See also* bitmap.

bit vector   A line of bits.

block—*see also* page
Used by: Oracle
[1] Oracle-speak for the smallest I/O unit in a database. All other DBMSs use the word *page*.
[2] When Job #1 has an exclusive lock on `Table1` and Job #2 tries to access `Table1`, Job #2 must wait—it is blocked.

block fetch   A fetch that gets multiple rows at once.

blocking unit—*see* page

BNF   Backus-Naur Form, a notation used to describe the syntax of programming languages.

bookmark—*see also* row locator
Used by: Microsoft
A pointer in an index key. If the data is in a clustered index, the bookmark is a clustered index key. If the data is not in a clustered index, the bookmark is an RID.

buffer—*see* buffer pool

buffer pool   A fixed-size allocation of memory, used to store an in-memory copy of a bunch of pages.

bulk INSERT   A multiple-row INSERT submitted to the DBMS as a single unit for processing all at once.

bytecode   An intermediate form of code in which executable Java programs are represented. Bytecode is higher level than machine code, but lower level than source code.

C

cartesian explosion   The effect on the size of a cartesian join's product as the joined tables grow in size. During a join, the DBMS creates a temporary table to hold the join result. The temporary table's size is the product of the sizes of the two original tables, which means the processing time goes up geometrically if `Table1` and `Table2` get bigger.

cartesian join   The set of all ordered pairs {a, b} where a is a member of set A and b is a member of set B. In database terms, a cartesian product joins all rows in `Table1` with all rows in `Table2`. Thus if `Table1` has the values {T_a1, T_b1} and `Table2` has the values {T_a2, T_b2} then the cartesian product is {(T_a1, T_a2) (T_a1, T_b2) (T_b1, T_a2) (T_b1, T_b2)}. Cartesian products are useful for explanation, but when we see an operation which "goes cartesian," we usually criticize the optimizer. Also known as a cross join.

cartesian product—*see* cartesian join

case insensitive   A sort order that considers `'SMITH'` and `'Smith'` to be equal.

case sensitive   A sort order that considers 'SMITH' and 'Smith' to be two different strings.

CBO   Cost-based optimizer, an optimizer that uses volatile data (e.g., the row and column values that have been inserted) and an override (e.g., that the database contents are more important than the fixed optimizing assumptions) to determine the optimal query resolution plan. A cost-based optimizer is a type of rule-based optimizer that has additional volatile information available to it so that it can override a fixed assumption.

CGI   Common Gateway Interface, a standard way for a Web server to pass a Web user's request to an application program and to receive data back to forward to the user.

cluster   Used by: Microsoft, Sybase
A structure for storing data in a specific order; that is, an index that has data pages at the leaf layer. The main idea behind clusters is that all rows should be kept in order permanently according to some column value, such as the primary key.

clustered index   An index that the DBMS uses to determine the order of data rows, according to values in one or more columns, called the cluster key. With a strong-clustered index, the data pages are the index's leaves and are thus always in order. With a weak-clustered index, data pages are separate from index leaf pages and the rows need not be 100% in order. The terms *weak clustered index* and *strong-clustered index* are not common usage; they appear only in this book.

clustered key or clustered index key   The column chosen to be the index key for a clustered index.

collating sequence—*see* collation

collation   A set of rules that determines the result when character strings are compared.

composite index—*see* compound index

composite table   A table that contains column values derived from two or more other tables.

compound index   An index whose keys contain values derived from more than one data column.

compression   Making index keys shorter by throwing bytes away from the front or from the back. *See also* back compression, front compression.

concurrency   The ability of multiple transactions to share the same database simultaneously.

concurrent transactions   Two transactions that have overlapping start or end times. To prevent concurrent transactions from interfering with each other, the DBMS may arrange a lock.

connection pooling   A facility that allows connections to a data source to be stored and reused. A Java term.

constant propagation   Substituting a constant value for an expression.

control interval—*see* page

cost   The total execution time required for an SQL statement.

cost-based optimizer—*see* CBO

covering index   An index that contains every column in the select list of a query.

cursor   A marker that indicates the current position within a result set.

D

data block—*see* block, page

data change statement   An SQL statement that changes data; INSERT, UPDATE, or DELETE.

data source   A repository for storing data. An ODBC/JDBC term.

DBA   Database Administrator, the individual who directs or performs all activities related to maintaining a successful database environment.

dbc   Database connection, an ODBC resource.

DBMS   Database Management System, a program that lets one or more computer users create and access the data in a database.

dbspace—*see* tablespace
Used by: Informix

DDL   Data Definition Language, SQL statements that define or destroy data objects, like CREATE TABLE, ALTER TABLE, and DROP TABLE.

deadlock   A condition that arises when two or more transactions are waiting for one another to release locks.

denormalize   Break the normalization rules deliberately, in an attempt to gain speed or save space.

denormalization—*see* denormalize

denormalizing—*see* denormalize

dense index—*see* unique index

density (of an index or table)   The reciprocal of the count of the number of distinct keys. For example, suppose you have these key values: {A,C,C,D,D}. The number of distinct keys, that is, the number that a SELECT DISTINCT ... statement would return, is three: {A,C,D}. Now recall from your arithmetic classes that reciprocal = 1/N—that is, the reciprocal of a number N is the number that would yield one when multiplied by N. The reciprocal of 3 is 1/3; therefore, the density for our example is 1/3. It's possible to get a preliminary guess of the number of rows that column1 = <literal> will return by multiplying the table's cardinality by the density of the index.

WARNING: The following definitions of density from vendor manuals or other texts are imprecise or confusing: "the average number of rows which are duplicates" (Sybase); "density is inversely proportional to index sensitivity" (various).

dependence   A concept used in normalization. If the value of column1 uniquely determines the value of column2, then column2 is functionally dependent on column1. If the value of column1 limits the possible values in column2 to a specific set, then column2 is set dependent on column1.

desc   Descriptor for SQL statement parameters, an ODBC resource.

deterministic (function)   A function that always generates the same outputs, given the same inputs.

dictionary sort   A sort that results in a list that is very close to what one expects to see in an English dictionary.

dictionary sort with tie-breaking   A dictionary sort with multiple passes to sort accented characters differently from unaccented characters and uppercase letters differently from lowercase letters.

Dirty Read   A problem arising with concurrent transactions. The Dirty Read problem occurs when a transaction reads a row that has been changed but not committed by another transaction. The result is that Transaction #2's work is based on a change that never really happened. You can avoid Dirty Read by using an isolation level of READ COMMITTED or higher.

DML   Data Manipulation Language, SQL statements that manipulate data, like INSERT, UPDATE, and DELETE.

driven table—*see* inner table

driver   The table that the DBMS examines first when evaluating a join or subquery expression.

driving table—*see* outer table

DSS   Decision Support System, a computer application that provides support for business decision making.

E

elevator seeking   Travelling through a disk's physical locations in the manner of an elevator, instead of jumping backward or forward for each request, an operating system term.

Enterprise Bean   A server component written in Java.

env   Environment, an ODBC resource.

equijoin   A join using the equals operator in the join expression.

escalation   The act of consolidating several real or potential small-grain locks into a single big-grain lock. Concurrency gets worse, but overhead gets better.

exclusive (lock mode)   A lock that may not coexist with any other lock on the same object.

expanding update   A data-change statement that increases the size of a row.

extent—*see also* read group
    A group of pages that are allocated together, as part of the initial creation of an object or when an existing extent becomes full.

F

fetch loop   A loop that contains calls to a function that takes a row from a result set.

file   A group of contiguous extents.

FILLFACTOR   Used by: Informix, Ingres, Microsoft, Sybase
    Percent (of a page) to fill. *See also* PCTFREE.

filter—*see* restrict

first normal form—*see* 1NF

flatten (a query)   A plan to process a subquery: make everything one level, that is, transform the query to a join, then process as a join.

flattened (query)—*see* flatten

FPU   Floating Point Unit, a microprocessor that manipulates numbers faster than the basic microprocessor used by a computer.

fragment—*see* partition
Used by: Informix
What Informix users call a partition.

fragmentation
[1] Used by: everyone except Informix. The tendency for row[x] to be not immediately followed by row[x+1] because of blank spots or disordering.
[2] Used by: Informix. What Informix users call partitioning.

freelist   Used by: Oracle
A list of pages that have free space in them.

front compression   Making index keys shorter by throwing bytes away from the front. *See also* compression, back compression.

functionally dependent   A concept used in normalization. If the value of column1 uniquely determines the value of column2, then column2 is functionally dependent on column1.

G

granularity (of a lock)   The size of the locked area—database, file, table, page, row, or column.

GUID   Used by: Microsoft
Global Unique Identifier, the Microsoft unique-key generator.

H

hash   A number (often a 32-bit integer) that is derived from column values using a lossy compression algorithm. DBMSs occasionally use hashing to speed up access, but indexes are a more common mechanism.

hash join   A method for producing a joined table. Given two input tables Table1 and Table2, processing is as follows:
(a) For each row in Table1, produce a hash. Assign the hash to a hash bucket.

(b) For each row in `Table2`, produce a hash. Check if the hash is already in the hash bucket. If it is: there's a join. If it is not: there's no join.

heap   A structure for storing data in an unstructured manner. When you add something to a heap, it goes wherever there is free space, which probably means at the end. Existing data is not moved to make free space available for new data.

heap-organized table—*see* heap

histogram   Detailed information on the distribution of values over a column; information stored for the sake of the optimizer.

hoisting   Taking an invariant assignment out of a loop.

host program   A computer program, written in a non-SQL language, containing calls to an SQL API or containing embedded SQL statements.

hot spot   A page in either the index or data file that every job wants to access at the same time.

I

impedance   A lack of correspondence between two data types, one of which is being assigned to the other.

index-organized table—*see* cluster
   Used by: Oracle

inner table   The table in the inner loop of a nested-loop join. When you write an SQL statement with an inner join, the inner table is determined by the DBMS based on its join strategy for that statement. When you write an outer join, though, the order of the join determines the inner table: for the join expression `Table1 LEFT JOIN Table2` the inner table must be `Table2` and for `Table1 RIGHT JOIN Table2` the inner table must be `Table1`.

in-place update—*see also* out-of-place update
   Used by: Microsoft, Sybase
   A data change that does not cause a row to move.

intent lock   A lock of a larger object related to a locked small object. Implicitly, any small-grain lock implies a shared big-grain lock. If there is one or more locks on pages belonging to a table, then there will also be a lock on the table itself, as a separate lock record.

in-to-out   A plan to process a subquery; for each row in the inner query, lookup in the outer query.

isolation level (of a transaction)   In standard SQL, a setting that determines the type of concurrency problem that will be tolerated for a transaction. In order from lowest level of isolation to highest, the options are: READ UN-COMMITTED, READ COMMITTED, REPEATABLE READ, and SERIALIZABLE.

ITL slot—*see* mark on the wall

J

JDBC   Java Database Connectivity, an API for SQL programs.

JNDI   Java Naming and Directory Interface, an API that provides naming and directory services for Java programs.

join   The relational operator that allows data from multiple tables to be combined. A join matches rows of multiple tables based on columns with common values.

join expression   The WHERE clause search condition that tells the DBMS over which columns it is to join two tables.

join index   An index that contains keys from more than one table, interspersed, to aid with join expressions.

JVM   Java Virtual Machine, a platform-independent programming language that converts Java bytecode into machine language and executes the result.

L

latch   A low-level on-off mechanism that ensures two processes or threads can't access the same object at the same time. *See also* lock.

leaf (page of an index)   A page at the bottom level of a B-tree (the page at the top level is the root). Typically a leaf page contains pointers to the data pages (if it's a non-clustered index) or to the data itself (if it's a clustered index).

little-endian   A binary data transmission/storage format in which the least significant bit (or byte) comes first.

load—*see* bulk INSERT

LOB   Large object, for example, a BLOB (binary large object) or a CLOB (character large object).

lock   A method the DBMS uses to prevent concurrent transactions from interfering with one another. Physically, a lock is one of three things: a latch, a mark on the wall, or a RAM record.

locking level—see granularity

lock mode   The type of lock a DBMS has arranged for a transaction. Options are exclusive, shared, or update.

lock record—*see* RAM record

lock type—*see* lock mode

Lost Update   A problem arising with concurrent transactions. The Lost Update problem occurs when two transactions read and make a change to the same row. When the first transaction COMMITs, its change is lost because the second transaction's change supersedes it. The result is as if Transaction #1's change never happened. You can avoid Lost Update by using an isolation level of READ UNCOMMITTED or higher.

LRU   Least-Recently-Used, an algorithm that replaces the page that hasn't been accessed for the longest time

M

mark on the wall   An ITL slot or mark put against a row by the DBMS. By putting a mark right beside the row accessed by a transaction, the DBMS ensures that no other transaction has to spend much time checking whether the row is locked. *See also* lock.

materialization   Temporarily writing rows; usually this means physically copying data from the DBMS server to the client. To evaluate some expressions, the DBMS will create a temporary table, put the rows from the original table(s) into the temporary table, and select from the temporary copy; this is known as materialization.

materialize—*see* materialization

materialized view   A view whose rows take up space. When you select from a view, the DBMS can elect to do one of two things: (a) it can get the rows from the original table, convert any derived columns, and pass the results to the application or (b) it can create a temporary table and put the rows from the original table(s) into the temporary table, then select from the temporary copy. The latter case results in a materialized view. Materialization is often necessary when there is no one-to-one correspondence between the original table's rows and the view's rows (because there is a grouping) or when many tables are affected and concurrency would be harmed (because there is a join).

merge join—*see* sort-merge join

merge scan—*see* sort-merge join

method   A procedure associated with a Java class or interface.

migrated row   A row at the end of the table due to an expanding update overflow.

migration   The process of finding a home for an expanding update. When a page overflows due to a data change that increases the length of a variable-length column, a row must be shifted to another page. In practice, a pointer to the overflow page is left in the place of the original row. *See also* shift.

multi-column index—*see* compound index

MVCC   Multi Version Concurrency Control, a mechanism that sometimes doesn't use shared locks for rows. *See also* versioning.

N

NaN   Not a Number. In the IEEE definition for floating-point numeric representation, a NaN is a number that cannot be represented (such as the result after a division by zero) and is thus assigned a special code.

nested-loop join   A method for producing a joined table. Given two input tables `Table1` and `Table2`, processing is as follows:
```
for (each row of Table1) {
  for (each row of Table2) {
    compare and produce joined (Table1, Table2) row
  }
}
```
Notice the for loop nested within a for loop.

niladic function   A function that has no arguments, for example, SQL's CURRENT_DATE and CURRENT_USER.

non-clustered index   An index with a structure completely separate from the data rows it indexes; normally a B-tree. The lowest rows of a non-clustered index contain the index key values, with each key value pointing to the data rows that contain that key. The data rows are not stored in an order based on the index key, but rather in a heap.

non-deterministic (function)   A function that may generate different outputs each time it is run, even if the inputs are always the same.

Non-repeatable Read   A problem arising with concurrent transactions. The Non-repeatable Read problem occurs when a transaction reads a row twice, once before and once after another transaction does a data change. The result is that Transaction #1 gets conflicting data from its reads. You can avoid Non-repeatable Read by using an isolation level of REPEATABLE READ or higher.

normalization   The process of designing a database so that its tables follow the rules specified by relational theory. In practice, this usually means that all database tables are in third normal form. *See also* 1NF, 2NF, 3NF.

normalize   To rearrange columns within tables or move columns from one table to another, as part of the database design process, according to rules based on relational theory. In a normalized table, one set of columns is the primary key (which uniquely identifies a row of the table) and all other columns are functionally dependent upon the entire primary key. *See also* 1NF, 2NF, 3NF.

normalizing—*see* normalization, normalize

NTFS   NT File System, the file system that the Microsoft Windows NT operating system uses for storing and retrieving files.

O

ODBC   Open Database Connectivity, an API for SQL programs.

OLTP   Online Transaction Processing, a type of computer processing in which the system responds immediately to user requests.

optimistic locking   Locking that assumes conflict is unlikely. Generally, this means avoiding locks and checking for conflict between two transactions only after data changes have been made.

outer table   The table in the outer loop of a nested-loop join. When you write an SQL statement with an inner join, the outer table is determined by the DBMS based on its join strategy for that statement. When you write an outer join, though, the order of the join determines the outer table: for the join expression `Table1 LEFT JOIN Table2` the outer table must be `Table1` and for `Table1 RIGHT JOIN Table2` the outer table must be `Table2`.

out-of-place update   Used by: Microsoft, Sybase
A data change that causes a row to move.

out-to-in   A plan to process a subquery; for each row in the outer query, lookup in the inner query.

P

packed decimal   A number representation where each number is expressed as a sequence of decimal digits and then each decimal digit is encoded as a four-bit binary number (or nibble). In some cases, the rightmost nibble contains the sign (positive or negative).

page   A fixed-size hopper that stores rows of data or index keys; a minimal unit for disk I/O. Depending on the DBMS, a page is also called a data block, a block, a blocking unit, a control interval, or a row group.

page read   A transfer from disk to memory.

partition   Used by: everyone except Informix
A group of contiguous extents. Often a partition is a file, but it doesn't have to be.
Informix calls this a fragment.

partitioning   Used by: everyone except Informix
The process of splitting a database object (usually a tablespace, table, or index) into two or more physical locations, or partitions, that is, a splitting of a logical group of pages (for example, the pages of a table) into chains or files which are physically removed from each other, perhaps on separate disks. Informix calls this fragmentation.

PCTFREE   Used by: IBM, Oracle
Percent (of a page) to leave free. *See also* FILLFACTOR.

pessimistic locking   Locking that assumes conflict is likely. Generally, this means locking an entire object at the beginning of a transaction and not releasing the lock until transaction end.

Phantom   A problem arising with concurrent transactions. The Phantom problem occurs when a transaction reads multiple rows twice; once before and once after another transaction does a data change that affects the search condition in the first transaction's reads. The result is that Transaction #1 gets a different (larger) result set back from its second read. You can avoid Phantoms by using an isolation level of SERIALIZABLE.

PL/SQL   Used by: Oracle
Procedure Language extensions to SQL, Oracle term for stored procedures.

positioned delete   A DELETE statement that allows you to delete the row at the current cursor position. Syntax: DELETE … WHERE CURRENT OF <cursor>.

positioned update   An UPDATE statement that allows you to update the row at the current cursor position. Syntax: UPDATE … WHERE CURRENT OF <cursor>.

precompiler   A utility you use to "compile" SQL code before you compile the host program, that is, a utility that converts SQL statements in a host program to statements that a compiler can understand. A remnant of embedded-SQL days; there is no such thing as an SQL compiler.

prepared statement   An SQL statement that has been parsed and planned, for example, with ODBC's SQLPrepare function.

project   A relational-theory term. Decide which columns will be operated on (using a select list). The project operation picks the columns that will be in the result set by evaluating an SQL statement's select list.

pseudocolumn   A virtual column, as opposed to a real, physical column. Pseudocolumns take up no space in the row.

PSM   Persistent Stored Modules, SQL Standard term for stored procedures.

PTQ   Used by: Microsoft
Pass Through Query, a Microsoft Access query option.

Q

query   A SELECT statement.

R

RAM record   Used by: this book only. The usual mechanism for locks of rows, pages, or tables, a RAM record is a permanent memory area containing data that describes which objects are locked as well as how the objects are locked (e.g., shared, exclusive, update, etc.).

RBO   Rule-based optimizer, an optimizer that arranges execution plans using fixed data and assumptions, such as statement syntax and existence of indexes.

R-C   Used by: this book only
Non-standard abbreviation for the READ COMMITTED transaction isolation level.

read—*see* page read

READ COMMITTED   A transaction isolation level that ensures mandatory shared locks but allows them to be released before the transaction ends. READ COMMITTED tells the DBMS you want it to allow reading of rows that have been written by other transactions only after they have been committed.

read group   A group of contiguous pages that are read together.

read-only transaction   A transaction that doesn't do a data change.

READ UNCOMMITTED   A transaction isolation level that ensures no locks are issued and no locks are checked during the transaction. READ UN-COMMITTED tells the DBMS you want it to allow reading of rows that have been written but not committed by other transactions.

REPEATABLE READ   A transaction isolation level that ensures mandatory shared locks, which will not be released until the transaction ends. RE-PEATABLE READ tells the DBMS it must not allow a situation where one transaction gets two sets of data from two reads of the same row because a second transaction changed that row between the two reads.

response time   The time a statement takes to execute.

restrict   Decide which rows will be operated on (using a predicate); a relational-theory term. The restrict operation picks the rows that will be in the result set by evaluating an SQL statement's search condition. Also known as *filter*.

restrictive expression   An expression which causes a restrict, that is, the part of an SQL statement's search condition that tells the DBMS which rows belong in the result set.

result set   What a SELECT statement (or an equivalent to a SELECT, such as a catalog function or a stored procedure that contains a SELECT) returns.

result set size   The number of rows in a result set, that is, the numbers of rows selected.

RID—*see* row identifier
Used by: IBM, Microsoft, Sybase

RLE   Used by: InterBase
Run-Length Encoding, a compression method that converts consecutive identical characters into a code consisting of the character and the num-

ber marking the length of the run. For example, if a string is 'AAAAA' then the storage is (5)(A).

root (node of an index)   A B-tree index is hierarchical, with a top page (where searching starts) containing keys that point to a mid page, which contains keys that point to a leaf page. The top page is known as the root, as if the tree is upside down with the leaves at the bottom and the root at the top.

row group—*see* page

ROWID—*see* row identifier
Used by: Informix, Oracle

row identifier   An identifier that uniquely describes a row of a table or index to the DBMS; generally a physical address. *See also* row locator.

row locator   The pointer from an index key to a data row. *See also* row identifier.

rowset size   The number of rows of a result set that can be fetched at once.

RPC   Remote Procedure Call, a protocol that enables two computers on a network to request and send services to one another without having to understand network details.

R-R   Used by: this book only
Non-standard abbreviation for the REPEATABLE READ transaction isolation level.

R-U   Used by: this book only
Non-standard abbreviation for the READ UNCOMMITTED transaction isolation level.

rule-based optimizer—*see* RBO

S

S   Used by: this book only
Non-standard abbreviation for the SERIALIZABLE transaction isolation level.

SCN   Used by: Oracle
System Change Number, a number, internal to Oracle, that is incremented over time as data changes are written to the log.

search condition   A predicate, or combination of predicates, that returns true/false/unknown; generally found in an SQL WHERE clause.

second normal form—*see* 2NF

selectivity (of an index) The number of distinct values divided by the total number of values. For example, if the values are {A,A,B,B} then the number of distinct values, that is, the number that a SELECT DISTINCT . . . statement would return, is two, while the total number of values is four. So selectivity is 2/4 in this case. Selectivity is usually expressed as a percentage ("selectivity is 50%"), but some express it as a ratio ("selectivity is 0.5") instead.

WARNING: The following definitions of selectivity from vendor manuals or other texts are imprecise or confusing: "the number of rows in the table divided by the number of distinct values" (Oracle); "the ratio of duplicate key values in an index" (Sybase).

WARNING: The phrase "high selectivity" means either "a large selectivity number" or "a small selectivity number" depending on who is saying it.

select list Everything between the keyword SELECT and the keyword FROM in a SELECT statement.

sequencing Forcing rows to be close together by using SERIAL data types or IDENTITY columns or auto-incrementing objects.

SERIALIZABLE A transaction isolation level that ensures the DBMS will lock paths to objects, not just objects, during the course of a transaction. SERIALIZABLE tells the DBMS you want it to execute concurrent transactions in a manner that produces the same effect as a serial execution of those transactions.

serialized transaction A transaction during which other users are prevented from making data changes.

set dependent A concept used in normalization. If the value of column1 limits the possible values in column2 to a specific set, then column2 is set dependent on column1.

set function A function that takes a collection of values and returns a single value as a result. The SQL Standard set functions are AVG, COUNT, MAX, MIN, and SUM.

set operator An operator that merges two or more sets. The SQL Standard set operators are EXCEPT, INTERSECT, and UNION.

shared (lock mode) A lock that may coexist with any number of other shared locks, or with one update lock, on the same object.

shift   Movement of rows caused by a change in the row size. When the length of a row is changed due to an UPDATE or DELETE operation, that row and all subsequent rows on the page may have to be moved or shifted. *See also* migration.

shrinking update   A data-change statement that decreases the size of a row.

skew   An observation about the distribution of values in a set. If value1, value2, and value3 each occur five times, there is no skew: the values are evenly distributed. On the other hand, if value1 occurs five times and value2 occurs ten times and value3 occurs 100 times, there is skew: the values are unevenly distributed.

sort key   Used by: this book only
A string with a series of one-byte numbers that represents the relative ordering of characters.

sort-merge join   A method for producing a joined table. Given two input tables Table1 and Table2, processing is as follows:
(a) Sort Table1 rows according to join-column values.
(b) Sort Table2 rows according to join-column values.
(c) Merge the two sorted lists, eliminating rows where no duplicates exist.

SPL   Used by: Informix
Stored Procedure Language, Informix term for stored procedures.

splitting (an index)   A process whereby the DBMS makes a newly inserted or updated key fit into the index when the key won't fit in the current page. To make the key fit, the DBMS splits the page: it takes some keys out of the current page and puts them in a new page.

statistics   Volatile data about the database, stored in the system catalog so that the optimizer has access to it.

stmt   Statement container, an ODBC resource.

strong-clustered index—*see* clustered index
Used by: this book only

subquery   A SELECT within another SQL statement, usually within another SELECT.

subselect—*see* subquery

synchronized (method)   An attribute of a Java method that provides concurrency control among multiple threads sharing an object.

syntax   Used by: this book only
A choice of words and their arrangement in an SQL statement.

T

table scan   A search of an entire table, row by row.

tablespace   A file or group of files that contain data.

third normal form—*see* 3NF

throughput   The number of operations the DBMS can do in a time unit.

tid—*see* row identifier
Used by: Ingres

transaction   A series of SQL statements that constitute an atomic unit of work: either all are committed as a unit or they are all rolled back as a unit. A transaction begins with the first statement since the last transaction end and finishes with a transaction end (either COMMIT or ROLL-BACK) statement.

transform   The process of rewriting an SQL statement to produce the same result, but with different syntax. When two SQL statements have different syntax but will predictably and regularly produce the same outputs, they are known as transforms of one another.

transitively dependent   A concept used in normalization. If `column2` is dependent on `column1` and `column3` is dependent on `column2`, then it is also true that `column3` is dependent on `column1`; the Law of Transitivity applies to dependence too.

U

UDT   User-defined data type, a data type defined by a user using the SQL CREATE TYPE statement.

Unicode   A character encoding. Used in Java and sometimes used by DBMSs to support the SQL NCHAR/NCHAR VARYING data type.

unique index   An index with perfect selectivity, that is, an index with no duplicate values allowed. Standard SQL allows multiple NULLs in a unique index, since a NULL is not considered to be equal to any other value, including another NULL. Many DBMSs, however, accept only one NULL in a unique index. Some DBMSs won't allow even a single NULL.

uniquifier   Used by: Microsoft

A 4-byte value added to a clustered index key to make it unique

update (lock mode)   A lock that may coexist with any number of shared locks, but not with another update lock nor with an exclusive lock on the same object.

URL   Uniform Resource Locator, the electronic address for an Internet site.

V

vector   A one-dimensional array.

versioning   A mechanism that sometimes doesn't use shared locks for rows. Versioning is also known as Multi Version Concurrency Control (MVCC).

W

weak-clustered index—*see* clustered index

Used by: this book only

Index

Also from Addison-Wesley

SQL Queries for Mere Mortals
A Hands-On Guide to Data Manipulation in SQL
By Michael J. Hernandez and John L. Viescas

SQL Queries for Mere Mortals will help new users learn the foundations of SQL queries, and will prove an essential reference guide for intermediate and advanced users.

0-201-43336-2 • Paperback • 528 pages • © 2000

Database Design for Mere Mortals
A Hands-On Guide to Relational Database Design
By Michael J. Hernandez

Database Design for Mere Mortals will provide any developer with a common-sense design methodology for developing databases that work.

0-201-69471-9 • Paperback • 480 pages • © 1997

The Practical SQL Handbook, Fourth Edition
Using SQL Variants
By Judith S. Bowman, Sandra L. Emerson, and Marcy Darnovsky

This latest edition of the best-selling implementation guide to the Structured Query Language teaches SQL fundamentals while providing practical solutions for critical business applications.

0-201-70309-2 • Paperback • 512 pages with CD-ROM • © 2001

Practical SQL
The Sequel
By Judith S. Bowman

For those who are working with SQL systems—or preparing to do so—this book offers information organized by use rather than by feature. Readers can turn to specific business problems and learn how to solve them with the appropriate SQL features.

0-201-61638-6 • Paperback • 352 pages with CD-ROM • © 2001

informIT

YOUR GUIDE TO IT REFERENCE

Articles

Keep your edge with thousands of free articles, in-depth features, interviews, and IT reference recommendations – all written by experts you know and trust.

Online Books

Answers in an instant from **InformIT Online Book's** 600+ fully searchable on line books. For a limited time, you can get your first 14 days **free**.

Safari
POWERED [
TECH BOOKS ONLI

Catalog

Review online sample chapters, author biographies and customer rankings and choose exactly the right book from a selection of over 5,000 titles.